Baltimore

JENNIFER WALKER

Contents

Discover Baltimore....... **18**
Planning Your Trip............. 20
The Two-Day Best of Baltimore... 24
Crab Feasts 25
Top 10 for Kids............... 27

Sights..................... **29**

Restaurants.............. **67**

Nightlife **121**

Arts and Culture........**143**

Sports and Activities **163**

Shops **190**

Hotels................... **222**

Excursions **240**

Background **273**

Essentials.............. **302**

Resources................ **319**

Index.................... **324**

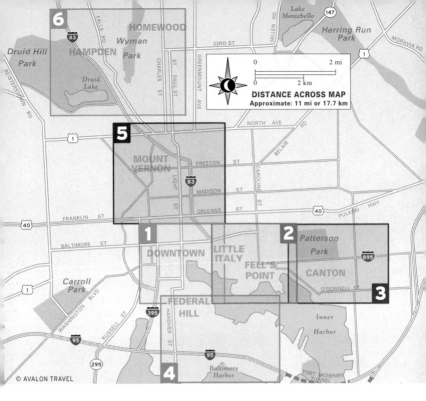

Maps

MAP 1: **Downtown and Inner Harbor** 4-5

MAP 2: **Little Italy, Harbor East, and Fell's Point** 6-7

MAP 3: **Canton** 8-9

MAP 4: **Federal Hill** 10-11

MAP 5: **Mount Vernon and Station North** 12-13

MAP 6: **Hampden and Homewood** 14-15

MAP 7: **Greater Baltimore** 16-17

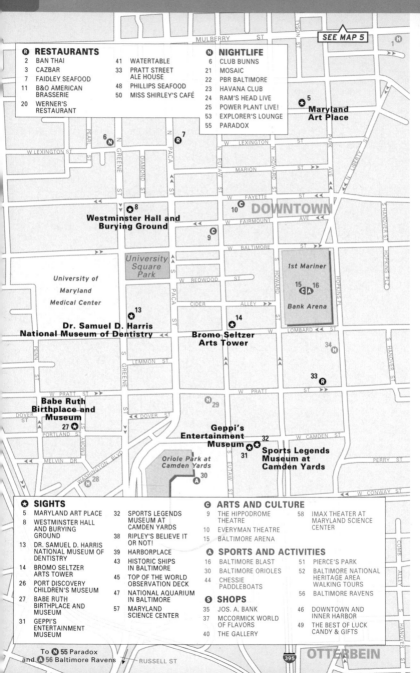

R RESTAURANTS

2	BAN THAI	41	WATERTABLE
3	CAZBAR	33	PRATT STREET ALE HOUSE
7	FAIDLEY SEAFOOD	48	PHILLIPS SEAFOOD
11	B&O AMERICAN BRASSERIE	50	MISS SHIRLEY'S CAFÉ
20	WERNER'S RESTAURANT		

N NIGHTLIFE

6	CLUB BUNNS
21	MOSAIC
22	PBR BALTIMORE
23	HAVANA CLUB
24	RAM'S HEAD LIVE
25	POWER PLANT LIVE!
53	EXPLORER'S LOUNGE
55	PARADOX

SEE MAP 5

Maryland Art Place

DOWNTOWN

Westminster Hall and Burying Ground

University Square Park

University of Maryland Medical Center

1st Mariner Bank Arena

Dr. Samuel D. Harris National Museum of Dentistry

Bromo Seltzer Arts Tower

Babe Ruth Birthplace and Museum

Geppi's Entertainment Museum

Sports Legends Museum at Camden Yards

Oriole Park at Camden Yards

O SIGHTS

5	MARYLAND ART PLACE
8	WESTMINSTER HALL AND BURYING GROUND
13	DR. SAMUEL D. HARRIS NATIONAL MUSEUM OF DENTISTRY
14	BROMO SELTZER ARTS TOWER
26	PORT DISCOVERY CHILDREN'S MUSEUM
27	BABE RUTH BIRTHPLACE AND MUSEUM
31	GEPPI'S ENTERTAINMENT MUSEUM
32	SPORTS LEGENDS MUSEUM AT CAMDEN YARDS
38	RIPLEY'S BELIEVE IT OR NOT!
39	HARBORPLACE
43	HISTORIC SHIPS IN BALTIMORE
45	TOP OF THE WORLD OBSERVATION DECK
47	NATIONAL AQUARIUM IN BALTIMORE
57	MARYLAND SCIENCE CENTER

C ARTS AND CULTURE

9	THE HIPPODROME THEATRE
10	EVERYMAN THEATRE
15	BALTIMORE ARENA
58	IMAX THEATER AT MARYLAND SCIENCE CENTER

A SPORTS AND ACTIVITIES

16	BALTIMORE BLAST
30	BALTIMORE ORIOLES
44	CHESSIE PADDLEBOATS
51	PIERCE'S PARK
52	BALTIMORE NATIONAL HERITAGE AREA WALKING TOURS
56	BALTIMORE RAVENS

S SHOPS

35	JOS. A. BANK
37	MCCORMICK WORLD OF FLAVORS
40	THE GALLERY
46	DOWNTOWN AND INNER HARBOR
49	THE BEST OF LUCK CANDY & GIFTS

To N 55 Paradox
and A 56 Baltimore Ravens

RUSSELL ST

395

OTTERBEIN

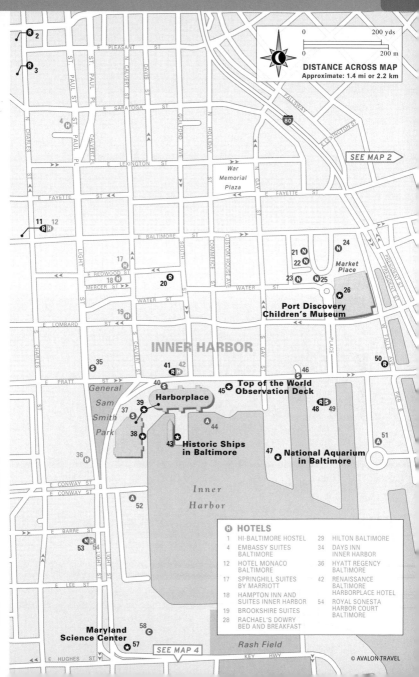

DISTANCE ACROSS MAP
Approximate: 1.4 mi or 2.2 km

SEE MAP 2

War Memorial Plaza

Market Place

Port Discovery Children's Museum

INNER HARBOR

Top of the World Observation Deck

Harborplace

Historic Ships in Baltimore

National Aquarium in Baltimore

General Sam Smith Park

Inner Harbor

Maryland Science Center

SEE MAP 4

Rash Field

KEY HWY

E HUGHES ST

© AVALON TRAVEL

HOTELS

1 HI-BALTIMORE HOSTEL	29 HILTON BALTIMORE
4 EMBASSY SUITES BALTIMORE	34 DAYS INN INNER HARBOR
12 HOTEL MONACO BALTIMORE	36 HYATT REGENCY BALTIMORE
17 SPRINGHILL SUITES BY MARRIOTT	42 RENAISSANCE BALTIMORE HARBORPLACE HOTEL
18 HAMPTON INN AND SUITES INNER HARBOR	54 ROYAL SONESTA HARBOR COURT BALTIMORE
19 BROOKSHIRE SUITES	
28 RACHAEL'S DOWRY BED AND BREAKFAST	

⊕ SIGHTS

1 PHOENIX (OLD BALTIMORE) SHOT TOWER
2 JEWISH MUSEUM OF MARYLAND
6 REGINALD F. LEWIS MUSEUM OF MARYLAND AFRICAN AMERICAN HISTORY & CULTURE
7 STAR-SPANGLED BANNER FLAG HOUSE
27 BALTIMORE CIVIL WAR MUSEUM
58 FREDERICK DOUGLASS-ISAAC MYERS MARITIME PARK
104 FELL'S POINT VISITOR CENTER
107 ROBERT LONG HOUSE

⊙ NIGHTLIFE

8 CLUB ORPHEUS
29 JAMES JOYCE IRISH PUB & RESTAURANT
62 DUDA'S TAVERN
68 THE HORSE YOU CAME IN ON SALOON
77 ONE-EYED MIKE'S
78 THE GET DOWN
89 BAD DECISIONS
95 MAX'S TAPHOUSE
97 RYE
105 THE CAT'S EYE PUB
109 THE WHARF RAT
110 JOHN STEVEN
114 V-NO

⊙ ARTS AND CULTURE

26 PIER SIX PAVILION
38 LANDMARK THEATRES
72 VAGABOND THEATER
102 ART GALLERY OF FELLS POINT
106 STEVEN SCOTT GALLERY
112 ROBERT MCCLINTOCK STUDIO & GALLERY

⊙ SPORTS AND ACTIVITIES

10 SEGS IN THE CITY
39 MAC HARBOR EAST
90 PATTERSON BOWLING CENTER
94 BALTIMORE GHOST TOURS
101 CHARM CITY FOOD TOURS
108 SECRETS OF THE SEAPORT WALKING TOUR
111 CHARM CITY YOGA
115 URBAN PIRATES
117 CAPT. DON'S FISHING CHARTER

⊙ HOTELS

3 1840S CARROLLTON INN
4 FAIRFIELD INN & SUITES
23 BLUE DOOR ON BALTIMORE
25 PIER 5 HOTEL
31 BALTIMORE MARRIOTT WATERFRONT
35 FOUR SEASONS HOTEL BALTIMORE
37 HOMEWOOD SUITES BY HILTON BALTIMORE
51 COURTYARD BY MARRIOTT
70 THE ADMIRAL FELL INN
100 CELIE'S WATERFRONT INN
116 THE INN AT HENDERSON'S WHARF

SEE MAP 5

Phoenix (Old Baltimore) Shot Tower

Jewish Museum of Maryland

Reginald F. Lewis Museum of Maryland African American History & Culture

Star-Spangled Banner Flag House

LITTLE ITALY

SEE MAP 1

Baltimore Civil War Museum

To Pier 5 Hotel

Inner Harbor

SEE MAP 4

Frederick Douglass-Isaac Myers Maritime Park

0   200 yds
0   200 m

DISTANCE ACROSS MAP
Approximate: 1.4 mi or 2.3 km

® RESTAURANTS

5 ATTMAN'S	19 HEAVY SEAS ALEHOUSE	36 TALARA	71 THE BLACK OLIVE
9 DA MIMMO	20 PIEDIGROTTA	42 LEBANESE TAVERNA	73 PITANGO
11 VACCARO'S	21 MY THAI	47 CINGHIALE	74 BRICK OVEN PIZZA
12 AMICCI'S	22 HENNINGER'S TAVERN	48 CHARLESTON	75 BERTHA'S
13 LA TAVOLA	24 SALT	49 GORDON BIERSCH BREWERY RESTAURANT	79 BLUE MOON CAFÉ
14 GERMANO'S PIATTINI	28 ROY'S	50 OUZO BAY	81 DING HOW
15 SABATINO'S	30 PABU	52 BAGBY PIZZA CO.	82 LOUISIANA
16 ALDO'S	32 LAMILL COFFEE	53 TEN TEN	86 ZE MEAN BEAN CAFÉ
18 LA SCALA	33 WIT & WISDOM	54 FLEET STREET KITCHEN	87 PETER'S INN
		55 CHAZZ: A BRONX ORIGINAL	88 PIERPOINT
		56 PAZO	91 CAPTAIN JAMES LANDING
		59 WATERFRONT KITCHEN	92 SIP & BITE RESTAURANT
		60 BOND STREET SOCIAL CLUB	96 JIMMY'S RESTAURANT
		63 KALI'S COURT	103 DAILY GRIND
			113 BONAPARTE BREADS

® SHOPS

34 THE SPA AT THE FOUR SEASONS HOTEL BALTIMORE	65 AMUSE
40 SASSANOVA	66 THE SOUND GARDEN
41 UNDER ARMOUR BRAND HOUSE	67 CORDUROY BUTTON
43 HANDBAGS IN THE CITY	69 FELLS POINT SURF CO.
44 HARBOR EAST	76 POPPY AND STELLA
45 URBAN CHIC	83 BABE
46 SOUTH MOON UNDER	84 A GOOD YARN
61 SU CASA	85 MAJA
64 FELL'S POINT	93 EL SUPRIMO
	98 CUPCAKE
	99 HATS IN THE BELFRY

SEE MAP 3

© AVALON TRAVEL

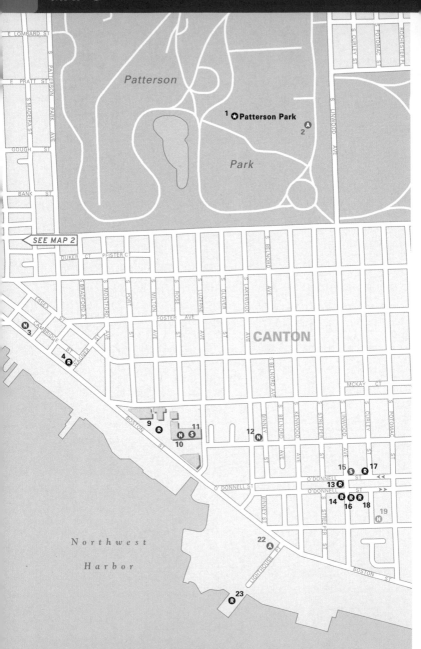

Patterson

1 ★ Patterson Park
                    A
                    2

Park

← SEE MAP 2

DUKER CT PFISTER C

S BELNORD AVE

S BRADFORD S
S MONTFORD
S PORT
S MILTON
S ROSE
S LUZERNE
S GLOVER
S LAKEWOOD AVE

FOSTER AVE

E LOMBARD ST
S PATTERSON PARK AVE
E PRATT ST
S MADEIRA ST

GOUGH ST

BANK ST

CANTON

ESSEX ST
CAMBRIDGE
N 3
CHESTER

4 R

S CURLEY ST
S POTOMAC ST
ROCHESTER S
S LINWOOD AVE

MCKAY CT

BOSTON ST
9 R
11
N S
10
12
N

BINNEY
S BELNORD AVE
BELNORD
KENWOOD
STREEPER
LINWOOD AVE
CURLEY
POTOMAC

15 S R 17

O'DONNELL ST
13 R
O'DONNELL ST
14 16 R R 18
19
N

BINNEY ST
STREEPER ST

Northwest

Harbor

22
A

LIGHTHOUSE P

BOSTON ST

23
R

© AVALON TRAVEL

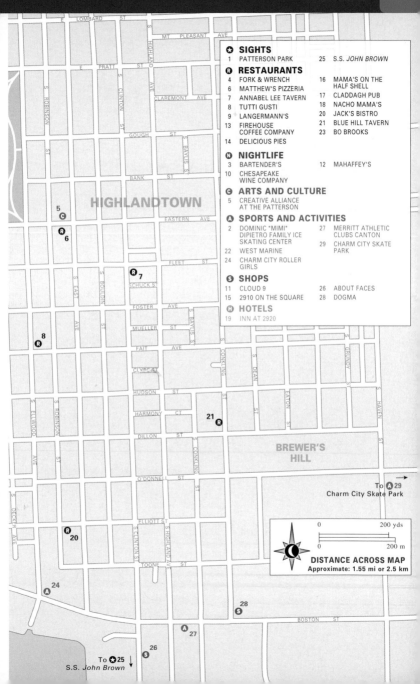

SIGHTS
1 PATTERSON PARK
25 S.S. *JOHN BROWN*

RESTAURANTS
4 FORK & WRENCH
6 MATTHEW'S PIZZERIA
7 ANNABEL LEE TAVERN
8 TUTTI GUSTI
9 LANGERMANN'S
13 FIREHOUSE COFFEE COMPANY
14 DELICIOUS PIES
16 MAMA'S ON THE HALF SHELL
17 CLADDAGH PUB
18 NACHO MAMA'S
20 JACK'S BISTRO
21 BLUE HILL TAVERN
23 BO BROOKS

NIGHTLIFE
3 BARTENDER'S
10 CHESAPEAKE WINE COMPANY
12 MAHAFFEY'S

ARTS AND CULTURE
5 CREATIVE ALLIANCE AT THE PATTERSON

SPORTS AND ACTIVITIES
2 DOMINIC "MIMI" DIPIETRO FAMILY ICE SKATING CENTER
22 WEST MARINE
24 CHARM CITY ROLLER GIRLS
27 MERRITT ATHLETIC CLUBS CANTON
29 CHARM CITY SKATE PARK

SHOPS
11 CLOUD 9
15 2910 ON THE SQUARE
26 ABOUT FACES
28 DOGMA

HOTELS
19 INN AT 2920

HIGHLANDTOWN

BREWER'S HILL

To 29 Charm City Skate Park

To 25 S.S. *John Brown*

0 200 yds
0 200 m
DISTANCE ACROSS MAP
Approximate: 1.55 mi or 2.5 km

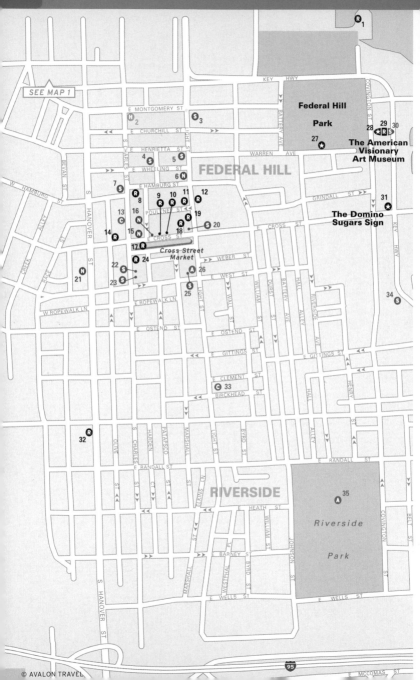

SEE MAP 1

KEY HWY

E Montgomery St

E Churchill St

E Henrietta St

E Wheeling St

E Hamburg St

W Hamburg St

Poultney St

E Cross St

Cross Street Market

Weber St

E West St

E Ropewalk Ln

W Ropewalk Ln

E Ostend St

E Gittings St

E Clement St

Birckhead

E Randall St

E Heath St

E Barney St

E Wells St

E McComas St

95

FEDERAL HILL

Federal Hill Park

The American Visionary Art Museum

The Domino Sugars Sign

RIVERSIDE

Riverside Park

© AVALON TRAVEL

SEE MAP 2

Inner

Harbor

**Baltimore Museum
of Industry**

LOCUST
POINT

Southside
Marketplace

To R 45
Hull Street
Blues

Latrobe

Park

SIGHTS
27 FEDERAL HILL PARK
28 AMERICAN VISIONARY
    ART MUSEUM

31 THE DOMINO
    SUGARS SIGN
38 BALTIMORE MUSEUM
    OF INDUSTRY

RESTAURANTS
1   RUSTY SCUPPER
8   AFTERS CAFÉ
9   SPOONS
10 RYLEIGH'S OYSTER
11 REGI'S
12 THAI ARROY
14 SOBO CAFÉ
17 NICK'S OYSTER BAR

18 ABBEY BURGER BISTRO
19 BLUE AGAVE
24 MATSURI
29 MR. RAIN'S FUN HOUSE
32 BLUEGRASS TAVERN
41 THE WINE MARKET
44 L.P. STEAMERS
45 HULL STREET BLUES

NIGHTLIFE
6   ZEEBA LOUNGE
15 8X10
16 PUB DOG PIZZA
    & DRAFTHOUSE

21 MUM'S
36 CAPTAIN LARRY'S
37 LITTLE HAVANA

ARTS AND CULTURE
13 CRYSTAL MOLL
    GALLERY

33 SCHOOL 33
    ART CENTER

SPORTS AND ACTIVITIES
26 LIGHT STREET CYCLES
35 RIVERSIDE PARK
39 BALTIMORE
    WATERFRONT
    PROMENADE

40 DOWNTOWN
    SAILING CENTER
42 MERRITT FORT AVENUE

SHOPS
3   THE BOOK ESCAPE
4   FEDERAL HILL
5   ALLIANCE COMICS
7   SHOFER'S
20 PANDORA'S BOX
    BOUTIQUE
22 M SALON
23 BRIGHTSIDE BOUTIQUE
    & ART STUDIO

25 DOGGIE STYLE
30 SIDESHOW AT THE
    AMERICAN VISIONARY
    ART MUSEUM
34 ANTIQUE CENTER
    AT FEDERAL HILL
43 STUDIO 921
    SALON & DAY SPA

HOTELS
2   SCARBOROUGH FAIR
    B&B

0   200 yds

0   200 m

DISTANCE ACROSS MAP
Approximate: 1.6 mi or 2.5 km

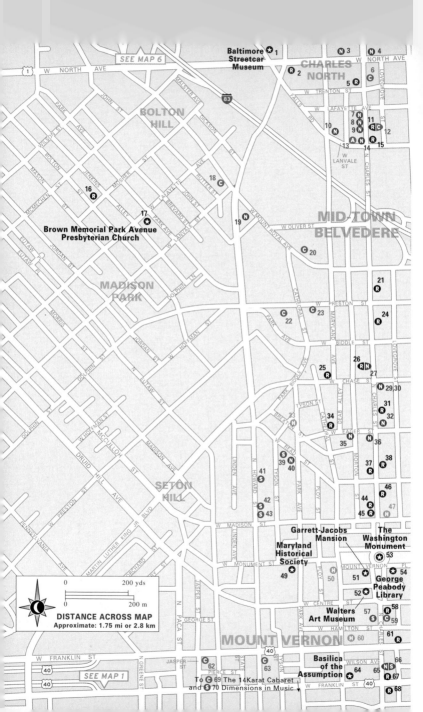

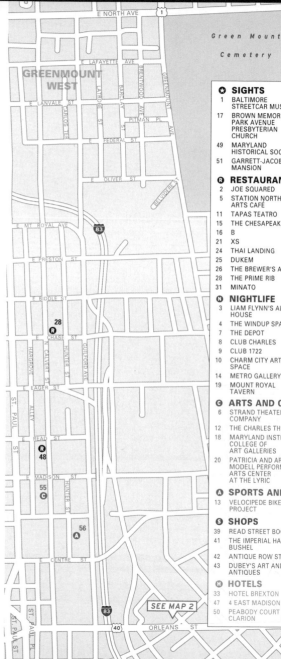

☉ SIGHTS

1 BALTIMORE STREETCAR MUSEUM
17 BROWN MEMORIAL PARK AVENUE PRESBYTERIAN CHURCH
49 MARYLAND HISTORICAL SOCIETY
51 GARRETT-JACOBS MANSION
52 WALTERS ART MUSEUM
53 THE WASHINGTON MONUMENT
54 GEORGE PEABODY LIBRARY
64 BASILICA OF THE ASSUMPTION

ℝ RESTAURANTS

2 JOE SQUARED
5 STATION NORTH ARTS CAFÉ
11 TAPAS TEATRO
15 THE CHESAPEAKE
16 B
21 XS
24 THAI LANDING
25 DUKEM
26 THE BREWER'S ART
28 THE PRIME RIB
31 MINATO
34 CITY CAFÉ
37 MARIE LOUISE BISTRO
38 KUMARI
44 THE HELMAND
45 THAIRISH
46 AKBAR
48 IGGIE'S
58 SASCHA'S 527 CAFÉ
61 TIO PEPE
67 SOTTO SOPRA
68 WOMAN'S INDUSTRIAL KITCHEN

ℕ NIGHTLIFE

3 LIAM FLYNN'S ALE HOUSE
4 THE WINDUP SPACE
7 THE DEPOT
8 CLUB CHARLES
9 CLUB 1722
10 CHARM CITY ART SPACE
14 METRO GALLERY
19 MOUNT ROYAL TAVERN
27 THE BREWER'S ART
29 THE 13TH FLOOR
30 THE OWL BAR
32 GRAND CENTRAL
35 THE HIPPO
36 RED MAPLE
40 THE DRINKERY
65 AN DIE MUSIK LIVE!

☉ ARTS AND CULTURE

6 STRAND THEATER COMPANY
12 THE CHARLES THEATER
18 MARYLAND INSTITUTE COLLEGE OF ART GALLERIES
20 PATRICIA AND ARTHUR MODELL PERFORMING ARTS CENTER AT THE LYRIC
22 JOSEPH MEYERHOFF SYMPHONY HALL
23 THEATRE PROJECT
55 CENTER STAGE
59 C. GRIMALDIS GALLERY
62 GALLERY FOUR
63 CURRENT GALLERY
69 THE 14KARAT CABARET

☉ SPORTS AND ACTIVITIES

13 VELOCIPEDE BIKE PROJECT
56 MERRITT'S DOWNTOWN ATHLETIC CLUB

Ⓢ SHOPS

39 READ STREET BOOKS
41 THE IMPERIAL HALF BUSHEL
42 ANTIQUE ROW STALLS
43 DUBEY'S ART AND ANTIQUES
57 A PEOPLE UNITED
66 AN DIE MUSIK
70 DIMENSIONS IN MUSIC

Ⓗ HOTELS

33 HOTEL BREXTON
47 4 EAST MADISON INN
50 PEABODY COURT BY CLARION
60 THE MOUNT VERNON HOTEL

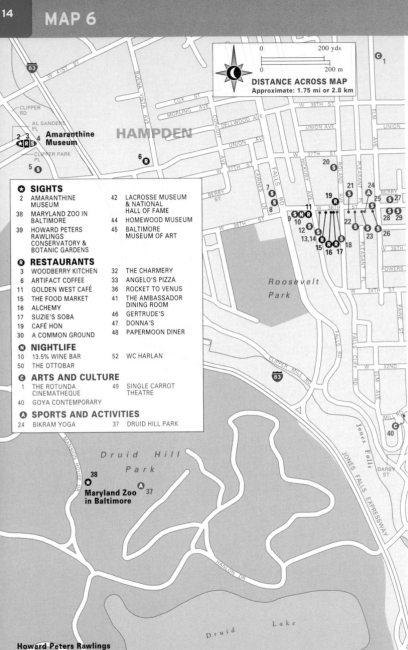

HAMPDEN

Amaranthine Museum

SIGHTS
2 AMARANTHINE MUSEUM
38 MARYLAND ZOO IN BALTIMORE
39 HOWARD PETERS RAWLINGS CONSERVATORY & BOTANIC GARDENS
42 LACROSSE MUSEUM & NATIONAL HALL OF FAME
44 HOMEWOOD MUSEUM
45 BALTIMORE MUSEUM OF ART

RESTAURANTS
3 WOODBERRY KITCHEN
6 ARTIFACT COFFEE
11 GOLDEN WEST CAFÉ
15 THE FOOD MARKET
16 ALCHEMY
17 SUZIE'S SOBA
19 CAFÉ HON
30 A COMMON GROUND
32 THE CHARMERY
33 ANGELO'S PIZZA
36 ROCKET TO VENUS
41 THE AMBASSADOR DINING ROOM
46 GERTRUDE'S
47 DONNA'S
48 PAPERMOON DINER

NIGHTLIFE
10 13.5% WINE BAR
50 THE OTTOBAR
52 WC HARLAN

ARTS AND CULTURE
1 THE ROTUNDA CINEMATHEQUE
40 GOYA CONTEMPORARY
49 SINGLE CARROT THEATRE

SPORTS AND ACTIVITIES
24 BIKRAM YOGA
37 DRUID HILL PARK

Roosevelt Park

Druid Hill Park

Maryland Zoo in Baltimore

Howard Peters Rawlings Conservatory and Botanic Gardens of Baltimore

Druid Lake

DISTANCE ACROSS MAP
Approximate: 1.75 mi or 2.8 km

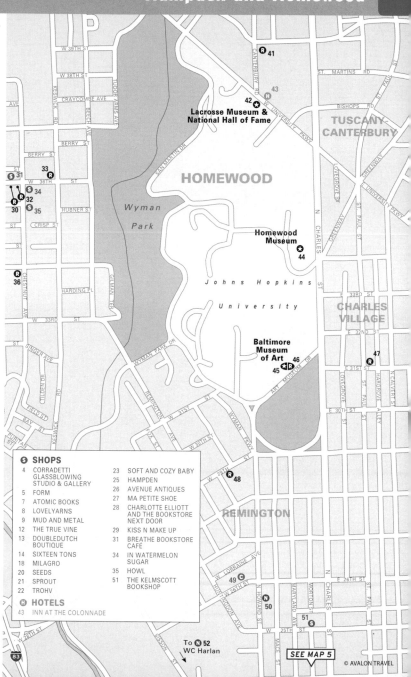

Lacrosse Museum & National Hall of Fame

TUSCANY-CANTERBURY

HOMEWOOD

Wyman Park

Homewood Museum

Johns Hopkins University

CHARLES VILLAGE

Baltimore Museum of Art

REMINGTON

S SHOPS

4	CORRADETTI GLASSBLOWING STUDIO & GALLERY
5	FORM
7	ATOMIC BOOKS
8	LOVELYARNS
9	MUD AND METAL
12	THE TRUE VINE
13	DOUBLEDUTCH BOUTIQUE
14	SIXTEEN TONS
18	MILAGRO
20	SEEDS
21	SPROUT
22	TROHV
23	SOFT AND COZY BABY
25	HAMPDEN
26	AVENUE ANTIQUES
27	MA PETITE SHOE
28	CHARLOTTE ELLIOTT AND THE BOOKSTORE NEXT DOOR
29	KISS N MAKE UP
31	BREATHE BOOKSTORE CAFE
34	IN WATERMELON SUGAR
35	HOWL
51	THE KELMSCOTT BOOKSHOP

H HOTELS

43	INN AT THE COLONNADE

To N 52
WC Harlan

SEE MAP 5

© AVALON TRAVEL

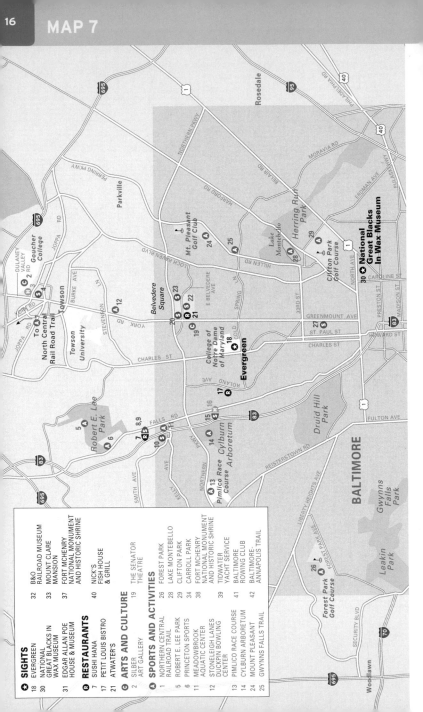

⊙ SIGHTS

18	EVERGREEN
30	NATIONAL GREAT BLACKS IN WAX MUSEUM
31	EDGAR ALLAN POE HOUSE & MUSEUM
32	B&O RAILROAD MUSEUM
33	MOUNT CLARE MANSION
37	FORT MCHENRY NATIONAL MONUMENT AND HISTORIC SHRINE

🍴 RESTAURANTS

7	SUSHI HANA
17	PETIT LOUIS BISTRO
21	ATWATER'S
40	NICK'S FISH HOUSE & GRILL

🎭 ARTS AND CULTURE

2	SILBER ART GALLERY
19	THE SENATOR THEATRE

🏃 SPORTS AND ACTIVITIES

1	NORTHERN CENTRAL RAILROAD TRAIL
5	ROBERT E. LEE PARK
6	PRINCETON SPORTS
11	MEADOWBROOK AQUATIC CENTER
12	STONELEIGH LANES DUCKPIN BOWLING CENTER
13	PIMLICO RACE COURSE
14	CYLBURN ARBORETUM
24	MOUNT PLEASANT
25	GWYNNS FALLS TRAIL
26	FOREST PARK
28	LAKE MONTEBELLO
29	CLIFTON PARK
34	CARROLL PARK
38	FORT MCHENRY NATIONAL MONUMENT AND HISTORIC SHRINE
39	TIDEWATER YACHT SERVICE
41	BALTIMORE ROWING CLUB
42	BALTIMORE-ANNAPOLIS TRAIL

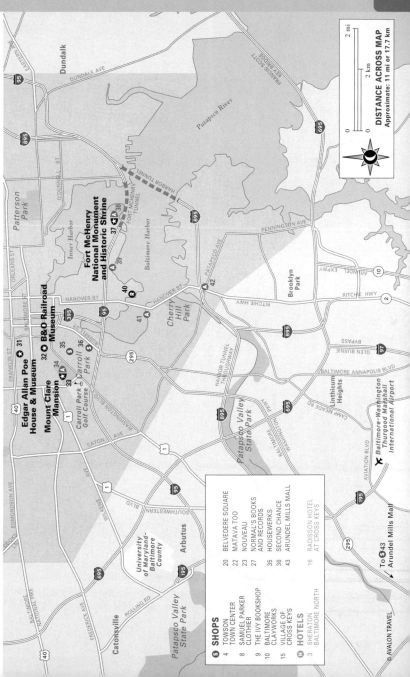

Dundalk

DUNDALK AVE

EASTERN AVE

Patapsco River

FRANCIS SCOTT KEY BRIDGE

Patterson Park

O'DONNELL ST

HARBOR TUNNEL

PENNINGTON AVE

Fort McHenry National Monument and Historic Shrine

FORT McHENRY TUNNEL

Inner Harbor

Baltimore Harbor

PATAPSCO AVE

Brooklyn Park

ARUNDEL EXPWY

RITCHIE HWY

ORLEANS ST

HANOVER ST

HANOVER ST

Cherry Hill Park

Edgar Allan Poe House & Museum

BALTIMORE ST

FRANKLIN ST

B&O Railroad Museum

Mount Clare Mansion

Carroll Park

RUSSELL ST

Carroll Park Golf Course

WASHINGTON BLVD

CATON AVE

HARBOR TUNNEL THROUGHWAY

GLEN BURNIE BYPASS

BALTIMORE ANNAPOLIS BLVD

Linthicum Heights

Patapsco Valley State Park

CAMP MEADE RD

WASHINGTON BLVD

Baltimore-Washington Thurgood Marshall International Airport

AVIATION BLVD

FREDERICK AVE

EDMONDSON AVE

WILKENS AVE

SOUTHWESTERN BLVD

University of Maryland-Baltimore County

Arbutus

BALTIMORE NATIONAL PARK

ROLLING RD

Catonsville

Patapsco Valley State Park

To Arundel Mills Mall

Arundel Mills Mall

DISTANCE ACROSS MAP
Approximate: 11 mi or 17.7 km

2 mi
2 km

⑤ SHOPS

4	TOWSON TOWN CENTER
8	SAMUEL PARKER CLOTHIER
9	THE IVY BOOKSHOP
10	BALTIMORE CLAYWORKS
15	VILLAGE OF CROSS KEYS
20	BELVEDERE SQUARE
22	MATAVA TOO
23	NOUVEAU
27	NORMAL'S BOOKS AND RECORDS
35	HOUSEWERKS
36	SECOND CHANCE
43	ARUNDEL MILLS MALL

ⓗ HOTELS

3	SHERATON BALTIMORE NORTH
16	RADISSON HOTEL AT CROSS KEYS

© AVALON TRAVEL

DISCOVER
Baltimore

Baltimore is a city with multiple personalities. There's the Baltimore of picture postcards, where ships glide along the water and crowds shop for souvenirs at the Harborplace pavilions. There's the gritty Baltimore from the HBO series *The Wire* that exists outside of the city's well-populated areas. And there's John Waters's Baltimore of beehive hairdos, cat-eye glasses, and residents calling each other "Hon," which can still be seen at least once a year at the annual HonFest in Hampden. All of these sides are a real part of Baltimore's landscape and culture, but in recent years, the city has become so much more.

Once the site of the first casualties of the Civil War and the penning of the lyrics of the U.S. national anthem, Baltimore was also an industrial city for years, with companies like Bethlehem Steel and the Holland Tack Factory making their homes here. Many of these companies' signs are still on buildings across Baltimore, even as new restaurants and shops have moved in—a visible reminder of the city's past.

Today, the steel mills and factories are long gone. Sophisticated restaurants and shops have taken over the upscale Harbor East neighborhood, joining the locally owned boutiques that have long lined "The Avenue" in quirky Hampden and the ballast-stoned streets in waterfront Fell's Point. There's also a great art scene, with premier theaters, alternative music venues, and artist-run galleries and performance spaces.

Despite all this, Baltimore can play second fiddle to the bigger cities that surround it. But the locals don't mind. There's a lot of pride and an infectious community spirit here. Come to Baltimore for its culture, its history—and its crab feats, but be prepared. Something about this sometimes wacky city just may get under your skin.

Planning Your Trip

Where to Go

Downtown and Inner Harbor

The result of an ambitious redevelopment project created to revitalize the City of Baltimore, the waterfront Inner Harbor has several kid-friendly museums like the National Aquarium in Baltimore and the Maryland Science Center. Paddleboating is a popular activity, the Harborplace pavilions are bursting with souvenirs, and the Orioles and Ravens stadiums are close by. To the west are theaters and art studios in the new Bromo Seltzer Art District.

Harbor East and Little Italy

The small but dense Harbor East neighborhood has exploded in recent years with a mix of upscale nationally and locally owned restaurants and shops, including the homegrown Under Armour Brand House. A couple of blocks north are Little Italy and its many traditional Italian restaurants. There are also four museums here: the Baltimore Civil War Museum, the Jewish Museum of Maryland, the Reginald F. Lewis Museum of Maryland African American History & Culture, and the Star-Spangled Banner Flag House.

Fell's Point

Fell's Point is still a working harbor where tugboats operate out of the old City Recreation Pier. It also is the Baltimore neighborhood with the richest history, so walking tours are abundant. Many bars and restaurants line the ballast-stoned streets and draw a lively crowd in the evenings. There are also several great boutiques

the Under Armour Brand House in Harbor East

along Thames Street and Broadway, making this a prime shopping destination.

Canton

Primarily a residential neighborhood with pretty row homes and new high-rises, Canton is also home to O'Donnell Square, a park surrounded by some notable shops and restaurants. Across the northern Canton border is Patterson Park, the city's most beloved green space, and the Creative Alliance at the Patterson, a multipurpose arts organization that hosts art exhibits, live music, and theater events.

Federal Hill

Named for the large hill that provides some of the best vantage points of downtown Baltimore and the Inner Harbor, Federal Hill also offers one of city's most bustling nightlife scenes on Cross Street. There are several bars and restaurants, a few boutiques and stores, and the Cross Street Market. The one-of-a-kind American Visionary Art Museum exhibits a range of rotating works, from a life-size sculpture of the late actress Divine to embroidered canvases that tell the story of a girl's life during the Holocaust.

Mount Vernon and Station North

With Center Stage, The Joseph Meyerhoff Symphony Hall, the Patricia and Art Modell Performing Arts Center at The Lyric, and the Walters Art Museum, Mount Vernon is known as the city's cultural district. The first monument erected for George Washington stands tall in Mount Vernon Place, beautiful 19th-century architecture abounds, and restaurants serving international cuisines are prominent. North of here, galleries and bars draw an artistic crowd in up-and-coming

a view of the Inner Harbor from Federal Hill

the Baltimore Museum of Art

Station North, where the historic Charles Theater, the city's only independent cinema, is also located.

Hampden and Homewood

Hampden, Baltimore's quirkiest neighborhood, also offers some of the best shopping in the city on "The Avenue," (36th Avenue), a four-block district of independently owned shops and restaurants. Woodberry Kitchen, the Baltimore restaurant with the most accolades, is in neighboring Clipper Mill. To the east, Homewood is known for Johns Hopkins University, as well as cultural attractions like the Baltimore Museum of Art and Homewood Museum.

Greater Baltimore

Recreational opportunities abound outside of Baltimore City, where some of the area's best trails for biking and running, such as the Baltimore-Annapolis Trail and the NCR Trail, are located. The Fort McHenry National Monument and Historic Shrine, B&O Railroad Museum, National Great Blacks In Wax Museum, and a couple of lavish old homes also surround the city limits. The historic and recently renovated Senator Theatre is a grand space for taking in a film, and Belvedere Square is a local favorite for dining and shopping.

old-school bar The Wharf Rat in Fell's Point

When to Go

The best seasons to visit Baltimore are spring and fall. May and June bring warm, bright skies and gardens in bloom, and there's lots to do from street festivals to baseball games to biking. September and October's cooler weather provide relief after a long, hot summer; fall is a great time to take advantage of the city's walkable terrain or go admire the changing leaves out in the country.

Summer is very hot and humid and can make being outside (during the worst days) unbearable. The heat doesn't last all summer, though, and beautiful, merely "warm" days are common. Winter usually begins mildly here, though cold spells in January and February are common (but brief), as is the odd February snowstorm.

The Two-Day Best of Baltimore

Day 1

► Start your day early with breakfast before the crowds arrive at a local favorite like Miss Shirley's Café downtown or Blue Moon Café in Fell's Point.

► Head over to the National Aquarium in Baltimore to see the new Blacktip Reef exhibit, and the mammals, reptiles, jellyfish, birds, and other animals that populate this wonderful attraction.

► Travel north (it's an uphill walk or a short bus ride) to see the towering and iconic Washington Monument in Mount Vernon. Wander among the stacks of books in the beautiful George Peabody Library, and admire the ancient collections at the Walters Art Museum.

► Continue your tour of Baltimore's cultural attractions at the Baltimore Museum of Art in Homewood, where you can gaze at huge works by Willem de Kooning and Robert Rauschenberg in the new contemporary wing, as well as the amazing postimpressionist paintings by artists like Matisse and Picasso in the Cone Collection.

► Hampden is one of Baltimore's great shopping districts. Have a light lunch at Artifact Coffee, then stroll along "The Avenue" by its many great independently owned boutiques and stores, where you can find clothes, home furnishings, souvenirs, books, and antiques.

view of the La Fayette statue by the Washington Monument

Crab Feasts

A seat on the water at Bo Brooks is a beautiful spot to crack open some steamed crabs.

Baltimoreans dine on this famous crustacean in four ways, and crab houses like **Phillips Seafood** in the Inner Harbor and **Bo Brooks** in Canton usually offer all of them. Try as many preparations as possible to see what you like best.

Also note that much of the crab served in Baltimore is no longer from the Chesapeake Bay. This prompted the Maryland Department of Natural Resources to start the True Blue campaign in 2012, which recognizes restaurants that serve only Maryland blue crab. If eating local crab is important to you, check the website (www.marylandseafood.org) for a list of dining options.

STEAMED CRABS

Cracking open a dozen steamed crabs crusted in Old Bay is a Baltimore tradition. If you want to try it, be prepared to work for your food (though it's work that Baltimoreans love). After you arrive at a crab house like **L.P. Steamers** (1100 E. Fort Ave.), a platter of crabs will be poured on your brown paper-covered table and served with wooden mallets, knives, and paper towels or wipes. Break them open, feast on the delicious white meat, and, to dine like a true local, wash it all down with a "Natty Boh," or National Bohemian beer.

SOFT-SHELL CRABS

Those who want to eat the whole crab (except the lungs) will love soft-shell crabs. They're made during the brief period of time between when a crab molts, or loses its hard outer shell, and when the shell grows back a few hours later. Around late May, many restaurants like **The Black Olive** (814 S. Bond St.), **Regi's American Bistro** (1002 Light St.), and **Fleet Street Kitchen** (1012 Fleet St.) offer specials to kick off the short season, while restaurants like **Nick's Oyster Bar** (1065 S. Charles St.) and **Mama's on the Half Shell** (2901 O'Donnell St.) usually offer soft-shell crabs throughout the summer.

CRAB CAKES

Crabs cakes come broiled or fried, either served simply with crackers or dressed up with accoutrements. For a simple fried version for lunch, try **Faidley Seafood** (203 N. Paca St.). **Woodberry Kitchen** (2010 Clipper Park Rd.) and **Heavy Seas Alehouse** (1300 Bank St.) serve more dressed up versions. To taste a different preparation, try **Pierpoint** (1822 Aliceanna St.), where the crab cakes are smoked.

CRAB SOUP

Maryland crab soup is made with a tomato or beef broth, vegetables like peas, carrots, and corn, and tons of Old Bay seasoning, but many restaurants also carry a rich, creamy crab soup, too. **One-Eyed Mike's** (708 S. Bond St.) has a good spicy version, **Nick's Fish House** (2600 Insulator Dr.) has well-received cream-of-crab option, and **Ryleigh's Oyster** (36 E. Cross St.) does both.

USCGC *Taney*, Historic Ships in Baltimore

▶ Take in a show (theater or symphony) in Mount Vernon, then have a tapas-style dinner at Tapas Teatro in the growing Station North Arts and Entertainment District.

▶ Finish the evening by enjoying some live music and drinks at Liam Flynn's Ale House or The Windup Space in Station North. Or, head back to Mount Vernon to have a beer with locals at The Brewer's Art or a cocktail at The 13th Floor in the grand Belvedere building that was once host to a slew of presidents and actors.

Day 2

▶ Have a light breakfast and an excellent coffee at LAMILL Coffee in Harbor East, then take a picturesque ride on the Water Taxi to Fort McHenry National Monument and Historic Shrine, where Baltimore's stout defense turned back a British invasion fleet during the War of 1812 and inspired Francis Scott Key to write the text of the "Star-Spangled Banner."

▶ Head north (it's about a two-mile trip that's very walkable, or a ride on the free Charm City Circulator's purple line) to the American Visionary Art Museum, the only museum in the country that exhibits work made by self-taught artists. Don't miss the giant whirligig and the bling-encrusted school bus outside.

▶ Walk to the top of Federal Hill for some sweeping views of the Inner Harbor. Eat like a local for lunch by enjoying a soft-shell crab sandwich from Nick's Oyster Bar or cracking open some steamed crabs on the rooftop deck at L.P. Steamers.

▶ Make your way to the Inner Harbor to board the four Historic Ships

jellyfish at the National Aquarium in Baltimore

- At the **B&O Railroad Museum,** little ones can play on huge iron locomotives and even board a train for a three-mile trip.

- Climb aboard the **Chessie dragon boats** and paddle around the Inner Harbor.

- Check out **Fort McHenry National Monument and Historic Shrine,** where, in 1814, U.S. troops held off a British invasion—and a flag that flew above the fort inspired "The Star-Spangled Banner."

- The **Maryland Science Center** has plenty of experiments, dinosaurs, and gizmos for kids to energetically embrace.

- Dive in to the **National Aquarium in Baltimore,** where options range from breakfast with the dolphins to overnight sleepovers.

- Burn off some energy in **Pierce's Park,** where kids can tap out a melody on the musical fence, run through a tunnel made of branches, or slide down a stainless steel cornucopia.

- Have a fun, crab-smashing dinner at **Bo Brooks** in Canton.

- Unleash your kids in the **Port Discovery Children's Museum,** where they can climb and crawl through a three-story tree house and immerse themselves in exhibits about everything from nature to robots.

- At **Ripley's Believe It or Not!,** kids can feel their way through a mirror maze, take a ride in the 4-D moving theater, and gawk at all the strange but true oddities in the museum.

- Dress up like a swashbuckling pirate, play games, and discover treasure while sailing around the harbor aboard the **Urban Pirates** ship.

Ripley's Believe It or Not!

Star-Spangled Banner Flag House

in Baltimore, including the Civil War-era U.S.S. *Constellation* (there's also a lighthouse). Or head to Little Italy, where you have a choice of three great museums to explore: the Jewish Museum of Maryland, the Reginald F. Lewis Museum of Maryland African American History & Culture, or the Star-Spangled Banner Flag House.

▶ Do some shopping in Harbor East, Baltimore's latest retail district, before having dinner and a local beer at the Heavy Seas Alehouse in Little Italy.

▶ Check out Fell's Point's bar scene and have a pint at the centuries-old The Wharf Rat under the holiday lights. Or, for a more boisterous atmosphere, head to Power Plant Live!, where you can ride a mechanical bull, join in with a sing-along at a piano bar, listen to live music, or have a late-night slice of pizza.

Sights

Downtown and Inner Harbor......32

Harbor East and Little Italy 43

Fell's Point 46

Canton 49

Federal Hill 50

Mount Vernon and Station North. .52

Hampden and Homewood........59

Greater Baltimore.................62

HIGHLIGHTS

★ **Most Awe-Inspiring Artifact:** Behind glass on the second floor of the **Babe Ruth Birthplace and Museum** is the Great Bambino's red-hued rookie card: a tiny piece of paper worth around $700,000 (page 32).

★ **Best New Exhibit:** It's hard to stop gazing at the black-tipped sharks, vibrant fish, and gigantic green sea turtle who swim in harmony in the **National Aquarium in Baltimore**'s Blacktip Reef, designed to look like an Indo-Pacific reef (page 37).

★ **Best Aerial View:** There's no finer way to get a completely 360° view of the city of Baltimore than from the huge glass windows around the **Top of the World Observation Deck** on the 27th floor of the World Trade Center. Go around sunset for the most dramatic photo opportunities (page 42).

★ **Best Gravestone:** It's an adventure walking through the **Westminster Hall and Burying Ground** looking for Edgar Allan Poe's gravestone—and a real thrill when you find it (page 42).

★ **Best One-of-a-Kind Museum:** Walking outside the **American Visionary Art Museum** among its giant whirligig, swan-topped bus, and mirrored mosaic egg is a treat itself, but be sure to go inside and climb the winding staircases to see the amazing paintings, sculptures, and mixed media pieces made by self-taught artists (page 50).

★ **Best Park for a Picnic:** Grab some cheese and bread or a crab cake from nearby Cross Street Market and walk a few blocks to **Federal Hill Park** for gorgeous views of the Inner Harbor (page 51).

★ **Best Cathedral:** America's first cathedral recently underwent a stunning renovation that makes the **Basilica of the Assumption** shine even more brightly than the day it was opened in 1821 (page 52).

★ **Best Iconic Landmark: The Washington Monument** was the first monument in the country built for George Washington; today, this 178-foot structure is the site of summer picnics and festivals, as well as a yearly holiday lighting ceremony (page 58).

★ **Best Museum for Contemporary Art:** The recently renovated contemporary wing at the **Baltimore Museum of Art** mixes works from big names like Willem de Kooning, Jackson Pollock, and Andy Warhol with rising stars in the field (page 59).

★ **Best Place to Rekindle Your Patriotism:** From a squat, star-shaped fortress perched on a spit of land southeast of downtown, some 60 brave soldiers held off an invading British fleet in 1814 and spared the city of Baltimore; from this conflict were born the U.S. national anthem, "The Star-Spangled Banner," and the legacy of the **Fort McHenry National Monument and Historic Shrine** (page 64).

Here's the first thing you should know about the aquatic part of Baltimore's most famous geographical feature, the Inner Harbor: The shimmering water you walk past, boat upon, and dine near is not part of the Chesapeake Bay. It's actually the Patapsco River, which eventually flows into the bay some 10 miles eastward. Still, Baltimore was founded as a New World port back in the late 1600s because of the Patapsco: The bounty of the bay and the fertile lands around that body of water led colonial European settlers to set up shop and shipbuilding operations along the banks of the river. That commerce led to the founding of many fortunes and the growth of Baltimore into one of young America's largest, most prosperous cities. Those early urban commerce and transport barons and civic leaders spread their wealth gradually away from the waterfront, and built themselves the businesses, homes, parks, houses of worship, and eventually universities and schools that helped Baltimore continue to grow for the next 300 years.

Around the waterfront, Baltimore is a very walkable city, though the distances between some destinations can be a bit daunting. The land rises gently—and constantly—from the Inner Harbor to the northern neighborhoods, but is basically flat in every other direction. As you walk through the city, you'll pass through different types of neighborhoods—historic, modern, working-class, upscale, and underprivileged—that sometimes share common boundaries, leading to striking contrasts. Still, passing through the streets offers the best view into the daily lives of Baltimoreans.

There are several don't-miss attractions in Baltimore, places where the history of the region and the United States was altered forever. Fort McHenry National Monument and Historic Shrine is one of those places; on a smaller scale, so is the gravesite of Edgar Allan Poe and even Fell's Point, where the legendary Baltimore clipper ship was built during the late 1700s. The city is also home to several magnificent art collections, such as those at the Baltimore Museum of Art and the Walters Art Museum, and unique attractions that have to be seen firsthand to really be understood (like the National Great Blacks In Wax Museum). That's part of the charm and mystery of Baltimore: Be prepared to be surprised by what you'll find here.

Downtown and Inner Harbor

Map 1

★ Babe Ruth Birthplace and Museum

Though he may have "built" Yankee Stadium with his herculean baseball exploits, George Herman "Babe" Ruth Jr. was born in 1865 in a humble redbrick row house on tiny Emory Street, about 10 blocks west of what would one day become Baltimore's Inner Harbor. The Ruth home (along with much of downtown Baltimore) fell into disrepair in the late 1960s, but was saved, protected, and restored; along with three adjacent row houses, the home opened as a museum in 1974. With Oriole Park at Camden Yards just a few blocks to the east, a stop at Ruth's birthplace is a must for die-hard baseball fans.

Today, the museum contains a cozy collection of Ruthian ephemera, exhibits, and authentic jerseys and gear worn or owned by the Babe, as well as replicas of two rooms in the Ruth home. On your tour, make sure to get a glimpse of the museum's valuable but sometimes overlooked artifacts. On the second floor is Babe Ruth's rookie baseball card when he played for the minor league Baltimore Orioles (estimated value: $700,000), although his time there was short-lived: He was traded to the Boston Red Sox that same year. There's also a 1910 baseball bat used by both the Babe and "Shoeless" Joe Jackson and a signed baseball on which Ruth promised a sick child in writing that he would "knock a homer" during a Wednesday game in the 1926 World Series (he actually hit three). This site is also part of the Sports Legends Museum at Camden Yards, which has a vast collection of Baltimore and Maryland sports memorabilia and exhibits.

MAP 1: 216 Emory St., 410/727-1539, www.baberuthmuseum.com; Apr.-Oct. daily 10am-5pm (7pm during Orioles game days); $6 adult, $3 child, $4 senior

In 1911, Isaac Edward Emerson decided to build a tower on the corner of Eutaw and Lombard Streets for his Emerson Drug Company, makers of Bromo-Seltzer, a fizzy medication for pain and fevers sold in a cobalt blue glass bottle for 10 cents a pop. The tower became a 14-story advertisement for that famous product: First, the four-faced gravity clock at the top of the building—still the world's largest today—was marked with the letters B-R-O-M-O-S-E-L-T-Z-E-R instead of numbers. Then a rotating, glowing 51-foot steel replica of the Bromo-Seltzer bottle was installed at the building's crown and even topped off with a froth of electric fizz. The company stayed here until 1967, when Warner-Lambert (since acquired by Pfizer) absorbed it and gave the tower to the City of Baltimore. Nearly four decades later, Sylvia and Eddie Brown bought the building, stipulating that it must be used for the arts; this wasn't a problem, considering that the Baltimore Office of Promotion & the Arts had been managing the tower since 2003.

Although the Bromo-Seltzer bottle was taken down in 1935 for safety reasons, the clock still stands atop the tower, and there is a great tour that takes visitors inside it. There are also three galleries here and more than 30 artist studios, some of which are open on summer Saturdays. After you leave, walk east on Lombard Street toward the harbor and stop to admire George Sugarman's **Baltimore Federal** sculpture, one of the more colorful pieces of public art in the city.

MAP 1: 21 S. Eutaw St., 443/874-3596, www.bromoseltzerarttower.com; May to Aug. Sat. 11am-4pm; clock tower tour $5, art studio tour free

Dr. Samuel D. Harris National Museum of Dentistry

It's difficult enough to get a person to visit the dentist regularly, so why would anyone want to go to an entire museum dedicated to the least favorite medical profession? But this museum has plenty of exhibits worth, um, chewing over. Most prominent in their extensive collection is one of George Washington's lower dentures (made of ivory, not wood), as well as four prints of Andy Warhol's portrait of St. Apollonia, the patron saint of dentistry (there's also a nearly 900-year-old stained-glass tribute to this plier-wielding saint). Sure, it's not as easy a sell to the kids as the National Aquarium, but where else are you going to see Queen Victoria's gilded dental instruments? In 2012, the museum merged with the University of Maryland School of Dentistry; those interested in visiting need to call ahead to schedule a tour.

MAP 1: 31 S. Greene St., 410/706-7461, www.dentalmuseum.org; by appointment, $7 adult, $6 senior, $5 child

The Harbor that Saved Baltimore

Bustling brick-lined walkways, pavilions filled with eateries and shops, and historic vessels in the middle of a major U.S. port city are common enough these days; but back in 1980, Baltimore's Harborplace was really the only place in the nation to experience such sights. Designed by the same team that created Boston's Faneuil Hall—another example of a repurposed urban space—Harborplace was a multimillion-dollar gamble taken by city leaders to stave off the urban blight of the 1960s and 1970s that threatened to destroy Baltimore.

The project was a big success for several reasons, some of which were not initially clear when construction began. One obvious force behind the Inner Harbor's popularity was James Rouse, a developer with a sense of purpose and history (he created the town of Columbia, south of Baltimore, which was America's first completely planned community). Working with dedicated city and community leaders, business tycoons, and architects from other cities, the team charged with turning an unpleasant industrial waterfront into a destination began with just a few buildings and features:

the National Aquarium, the World Trade Center, and the pavilions of Harborplace. Much of the waterfront was wide open and undeveloped when Harborplace opened, only filling in gradually as people realized it was not only going to work, but was going to be a huge success. National and international media attention focused on Baltimore's revolutionary new waterfront project, and cities from across the globe sent representatives here to learn how this gritty, industrial town managed to lure millions of visitors to its downtown each year with the creation of the Inner Harbor. It was dubbed "the Baltimore renaissance," and while much of the city continued to spiral into decay, the salvation of the downtown area helped keep Baltimore afloat long enough to reap the benefits of the booming economic growth of the late 1990s. Those gains can be seen in the new construction that's rising on property that was once littered with decaying warehouses, piers, and rubble: Today, luxe new residences built by developers like Ritz-Carlton and the Four Seasons rise along the waters of the Inner Harbor.

Geppi's Entertainment Museum

A more apt name for this amazing collection might be "The American Pop Culture Museum," because the items found here represent some of the finest examples of U.S. cartooning, comic books, and mass-market memorabilia in the nation. From colonial-era political cartoons to the golden age of comics and beyond, as well as grand movie posters from the 20th century to rare collectibles and toys, this museum (upstairs from the Sports Legends Museum at Camden Yards) is a treasure trove of U.S. culture. Founded by (and named after) Steve Geppi, a native Baltimorean who has made a fortune in the comic book distribution, collectible, and licensing business, the museum is a reflection of his love of comics and pop culture, and all of the memorabilia is from his personal collection. The 6,000-artifact strong exhibit will make giddy little kids out of visitors who find a favorite treasured comic book, doll, or decoder ring. The collections cover all the major and minor studios and publishers, from Disney to EC to Marvel, and they trace the development of simple line drawings in newspapers into the huge international marketing icons that permeate every aspect of our culture.

MAP 1: 301 W. Camden St., 410/625-7060, www.geppismuseum.com; Tues.-Sun. 10am-6pm; $10 adult, $7 child, $9 senior

Harborplace

It's difficult to imagine now, but the land occupied by Harborplace was, in the early 1960s, covered with huge, semi-rotting piers and abandoned industrial and warehouse space. No one came down to the harbor; in fact, people avoided it like the plague, because it was ugly and occupied by a variety of unsavory characters, many of whom, in fact, might have carried the plague. The real estate around the harbor was similarly undesirable, and in the 1970s, the city actually sold dilapidated houses in the Otterbein neighborhood (between Oriole Park and Federal Hill) for $1 if people promised to fix them up; houses in Otterbein now regularly sell for $300,000 or more. Short version: Things looked bad.

But city political and business leaders took a chance, and it paid off. Beginning with the nearby Charles Center project and then moving to the waterfront, the city gambled millions of dollars—and hired some of the nation's most visionary urban planners—to give Baltimore an anchor on which it could try to avoid complete collapse.

The pavilions of Harborplace, along with the National Aquarium and the World Trade Center (that pentagonal building), were the original occupants of the Inner Harbor, and they had the waterfront to themselves for a while. Although Harborplace houses traditional mall favorites like Urban Outfitters, H&M, Johnny Rockets, and Bubba Gump Shrimp; kitschy Maryland souvenirs shops, many touting wares emblazoned with crabs, also abound. In the Light Street Pavilion, stop by The Fudgery where music group Dru Hill, a quartet of Baltimore natives and former employees, once performed gospel and R&B music while making the store's namesake candy; today, staff continue the tradition by singing for passersby while cutting fudge on large marble slabs.

MAP 1: 201 E. Pratt St., 410/323-1000, www.harborplace.com; daily 10am-9pm

Historic Ships in Baltimore

This isn't a museum of dusty bells, sails, and sextants. In fact, there's no building at all: The museum consists of four historic oceangoing vessels and a fascinating "screw-pile" lighthouse. As a Civil War-era navy vessel—and the last surviving one, at that—the U.S.S. *Constellation* frequently sailed across the Atlantic, serving to hunt down slave ships leaving Africa; today, the three-masted warship makes its home across from Harborplace and features fascinating self-guided and staff-led tours, as well as daily cannon firings (which can be unsettling if you are walking close by). The Lightship 116 *Chesapeake,* parked next to the National Aquarium's entrance, served as a floating, illuminated beacon to shipping vessels around the Chesapeake Bay and Atlantic Ocean, twice surviving hurricanes so powerful they snapped the ship's anchor chain. Just behind the Chesapeake is the U.S.S. *Torsk,* a 1944 U.S. Navy submarine that sank the last two Japanese warships lost before that nation's surrender. Visitors can climb through the claustrophobic cabins and passageways of the sub, which was decommissioned in 1968.

Head next to the USCGC *Taney* (behind Phillips Seafood and the Power Plant Live! complex), which has its own connection to World War II: It's the last surviving ship to have been at Pearl Harbor during the Japanese attack in 1941. Last is the Seven Foot Knoll Lighthouse, which might seem a little short for a lighthouse. Not so for Maryland's coastal geography: The region around the Chesapeake Bay and Patapsco River's confluence is so flat that lighthouses didn't need to be particularly tall to be seen by ships in the late 1800s, so this design was used because it could be erected in the soft mud and sands of the bay.

MAP 1: Inner Harbor piers, across from Harborplace and the National Aquarium in Baltimore, 410/539-1797, www.historicships.org; daily 10am-4:30pm (USCGC *Taney* and Seven Foot Knoll Lighthouse Jan.-Feb. closed Mon.-Thurs.); one ship: $11 adult, $5 child, $9 senior; two ships: $14 adult, $6 child, $12 senior; four ships: $18 adult, $7 child, $15 senior

Maryland Art Place

Established back in 1981, Maryland Art Place (MAP) is an interesting creature: It's a nonprofit gallery and exhibition space for artists from Baltimore and the surrounding area to both show their work and have a direct conduit to the public. Sculpture, painting, drawing, and more technological media, many by new and up-and-coming artists, are on display here. Two well-regarded programs (Young Blood and Curators' Incubator) produce large shows of art by emerging talents, many from nearby art schools like the Maryland Institute College of Art. MAP's location in the Bromo Tower Arts and Entertainment District make this an ideal place to stop before taking in a show at the nearby theaters.

MAP 1: 218 W. Saratoga St., 410/962-8565, www.mdartplace.org; Tues.-Sat. 9am-5pm; free

Maryland Science Center

At the beginning of the 21st century, the Maryland Science Center underwent a welcome increase both in size and scope, and the

additions make this once somewhat dry attraction a must-see, **37**
especially if you're traveling with kids. The Dinosaur Mysteries
exhibit showcases huge re-creations of the prehistoric beasts, but
also lets kids dig through sand for fossils as the simulated roar
of *Tyrannosaurus rex* reverberates through the room. Newton's
Alley features lots of hands-on (and feet-on) exhibits that kids can
touch, punch, and climb from a laser harp to climbing and balance rigs. There's a planetarium that shows off the mysteries of the
universe. On clear Friday nights, head for the observatory, which
opens free of charge and also sets up smaller telescopes for peeks
up at the heavens. Older kids with a taste for experiments should
head to Wetlab, where they'll pull on some goggles and lab coats
and perform science projects involving glop, goop, and gunk. And
of course there's the requisite IMAX theater, showing both nature
and science-themed films. The entire center is awash in hands-on
computer stations and touchable, squeezable exploration stations
for visitors to sample and learn about biology, chemistry, and space
science (and even try on a mini-NASA flight suit). There's a popular
demonstration stage where experts explain everything from nano-
technology to black holes.

The Science Center is one of those attractions that kids go bon-
kers over, running from exhibit to exhibit, playing and touching
everything they can, while adults spend their time gently wrangling
the kids through the hallways. All the popular national touring exhibits about science (the kind that feature human bodies or artifacts
from shipwrecks) will stop here, usually requiring an additional fee.

MAP 1: 601 Light St., 410/685-2370, www.mdsci.org; Mon.-Fri. 10am-5pm, Sat.
10am-6pm, Sun 11am-5pm; longer summer hours; $16.95 adult, $13.95 child,
$15.95 senior

★ National Aquarium in Baltimore

When the National Aquarium in Baltimore opened in 1981, it was
one of the nation's first mega-aquariums, built after then-Balti-
more mayor William Donald Schaefer visited the New England
Aquarium in Boston. Baltimore's National Aquarium was the cornerstone of the Inner Harbor's redevelopment plan, meant to lure
both residents and, hopefully, tourists to the waterfront. In the
decades since that opening, the aquarium has expanded to keep
up with crowds both increasingly large and increasingly difficult
to impress.

Start your visit at the main building and the aquarium's newest exhibit, the coral-filled, Indo-Pacific-inspired Blacktip Reef.
The exhibit's namesake, the Blacktip Reef shark, named for the
coloring on its fins; has been designated as a near-threatened species; here, there are more than a dozen of them (try to catch the
regular shark feedings), along with a variety of colorful fish and

SIGHTS DOWNTOWN AND INNER HARBOR

Great Deals: Sightseeing

Purchasing a **Harbor Pass** (877/BALTIMORE, www.baltimoreorg/harborpass) is an economical option for visitors who are planning to see most of downtown's museums. At a cost of $49.95 for adults and $39.95 for children, the pass is good for four days and covers entry into the **National Aquarium in Baltimore,** the **Maryland Science Center,** and the **Top of the World Observation Deck**—a $57 value for adults and $40 value for kids alone—as well as admission to your choice of two other museums: either the **American Visionary Art Museum** or **Port Discovery Children's Museum,** and the **Reginald F. Lewis Museum of Maryland African American History & Culture** or the **Sports Legends Museum at Camden Yards.** Going to all five museums with the pass offers a savings of up to 37 percent.

In the fall and winter, the **National Aquarium in Baltimore** offers $12 tickets on Friday nights—a deeply discounted admission and one of the best deals in Baltimore. Go to the Maryland Science Center's **Crosby Ramsey Memorial Observatory** on Friday nights to gaze at the moon, planets, and stars through a refracting telescope for free. Once a month, the **Port Discovery Children's Museum** holds Target $2 Family Fun Nights on Fridays. On Thursdays in July and August, head to the **American Visionary Art Museum** for free evening admission followed by a movie screening on Federal Hill.

There are two wonderful museums that are always free: the **Baltimore Museum of Art,** which is undergoing a massive, $28 million renovation through 2015, and the **Walters Art Museum.**

October is also a great time to visit Baltimore because of **Free Fall Baltimore,** an annual event sponsored by The Baltimore Office of Promotion & the Arts that offers free admission to many museums.

the 490-pound green sea turtle named Calypso. Then head up the escalators to see a vast collection of exotic fish and environments, from an Amazon river forest to a North Atlantic seacoast (home to some terribly cute puffins). There's an impressive, if slightly fearsome, collection of sharks, which glide around their own massive 225,000-gallon circular tank. And there's an even larger tropical reef tank with dozens of brightly colored and oddly shaped residents. If the sharks are too creepy for you, check out the much cuddlier frogs exhibit, or sit down and hang on at the 4-D Immersion Theater, where high-definition, 3-D nature films are paired with "you-are-there" effects like sounds, smells, sea spray, and vibrations. Atop the main building is a living, walk-through tropical rainforest—if you've arrived early, head here first, as the birds and reptiles that scurry and flitter all around you are most active in the morning.

The Pier 4 pavilion is home to Dolphin Discovery, where you can watch the aquarium's Atlantic bottlenose dolphins perform impressive leaps and show off their balance skills. You'll also learn about these intelligent, curious animals, and maybe even get the chance to give them some hand signals to spur their performances. Afterwards, head to Jellies Invasion: Oceans Out of Balance to admire nine species of these fascinating (and oddly beautiful) creatures.

Another permanent attraction is Animal Planet Australia: Wild Extremes, a glass-enclosed mini-Australia, complete with a 35-foot waterfall and a variety of habitats found along a river gorge. As you wander through the gorge, you'll see all sorts of fish, birds, and reptiles, ranging from the laughing kookaburra bird to the not-half-as-funny snake known as the death adder.

If you're in town for a while, check out some of the aquarium's immersive tours, which include behind-the-scenes exploration of the inner workings of the facility. You can walk the narrow, wooden walkway above the huge shark tank, watch a dolphin training session, or (for kids) spend the night outside the shark tank or the dolphin amphitheater. Certified divers can guest dive in one of the aquarium's exhibits.

MAP 1: 501 E. Pratt St., 410/576-3800, www.aqua.org; Sun.-Thurs. 9am-5pm, Fri. 9am-8pm, Sat. 9am-6pm; longer summer hours; $34.95 adult, $21.95 child, $29.95 senior

Port Discovery Children's Museum

Just north of the Inner Harbor, this award-winning attraction is an immense hit with children because it seems like it was designed by kids. There are wacky rooms with mis-proportioned objects, lots of construction goodies and smart, creative playthings, and plenty of noisy, tactile toys for toddlers. In the center of everything is KidWorks, a huge, three-story climbing structure (and a big, dark, black slide through which kids can descend) for bigger kids; smaller fry can wander through Egyptian-tomb-themed mazes and play (and, amazingly, learn) in the Wonders of Water room, which lets kids make their own fountains and manipulate a river system, complete with dams and boat lock. (It's so hands-on that raincoats and rubber shoes are provided—but be aware it's closed on many summer Mondays.) There's Kick It Up!, an indoor soccer stadium with electronic goals; when soccer isn't in session, kids can ride bikes and challenge each other to dancing contests. There's even Tiny's Diner, where kids can pretend to cook up meals for their families who sit in nearby booths, and The Oasis, where you and your kids can read books and chill out between exhibits. Summertime afternoons can get a bit crowded, so plan on visiting early or late in the day.

MAP 1: 35 Market Pl., 410/727-8120, www.portdiscovery.org; Tues.-Fri 9:30am-4:30pm, Sat. 10am-5pm, Sun. noon-5pm, slightly different summer hours and Mon.; $13.95 for ages two and up

The namesake of this shrine to the wacky, Robert Ripley, published his first *Believe It or Not!* newspaper cartoon as a teenager in 1918, then traveled to 200 countries for the next two decades looking for "oddball" people, places, and customs to inspire his work. With the opening of this museum (of sorts) in 2012, Baltimore joins several cities around the world with similar attractions. Still, kids (and many adults, honestly) will love this place, which, contrary to its name, features art and exhibits that are completely true.

To find it, look around the Inner Harbor for the bright green dragon gracing Harborplace's Light Street Pavilion. Then enter for an exercise in sensory stimulation: There are many rooms with loud music, blinking lights, and tactile exhibits. There's an enormous replica of Hogwarts School of Witchcraft & Wizardry made of more than 500,000 matchsticks, and a larger than life-size robot built with old automotive parts; there is also a "toothpick city" room, an Egyptian room, and a few social statements, like the large portraits of Bill and Hillary Clinton "painted" with hamburger grease from fast-food chains. Much of this space is interactive, inviting guests to crawl through tunnels, walk on tightropes, gaze through microscopes, pull fingers, open chests, press blinking buttons, build gears, and more. There is also a small Mirror Maze and a 4-D Moving Image Theater that runs two short films complete with moving seats, gushing air, mist, and falling snow; both of these are a good bet for small children, who may be frightened by some pieces in the museum.

MAP 1: Harborplace, 301 Light St., 443/615-7878, www.ripleys.com/baltimore; Mon.-Sat. 10am-9pm, Sun. 10am-7pm, longer summer hours; $17.99 adult, $11.99 child, additional for 4-D Moving Image Theater and Mirror Maze

Sports Legends Museum at Camden Yards

Maryland has produced and worshipped an astonishing array of professional athletes, from George Herman "Babe" Ruth Jr. to Johnny Unitas to Cal Ripken Jr. to Michael Phelps. The now-destroyed Memorial Stadium, which hosted both football's Baltimore Colts (and, briefly, the Baltimore Ravens) and baseball's Baltimore Orioles, was occupied by fans so devoted and passionate that one national sportswriter dubbed it the "world's largest outdoor insane asylum." This obsession with sports is lovingly celebrated at the Sports Legends Museum, covering everything from the major league stars and teams to smaller sports and lesser lights who played just as hard.

Besides the big sports exhibits on the Orioles (including the team's Hall of Fame, and the numbers 2,131 that hung on the Camden Yards warehouse when Cal Ripken Jr. broke the consecutive-games-played streak), the now-residing-in-Indianapolis

clockwise from top left: cannons in Federal Hill Park; National Katyn Memorial, Harbor East; the American Visionary Art Museum, Federal Hill

Colts, and the recent Super Bowl-winning Ravens, there's plenty of other sports history in Baltimore as well. The museum showcases artifacts from the city's two Negro League baseball teams and highlights local legends of soccer and the less-well-known sport of lacrosse (there's even a lacrosse goalie simulation to see if you can block a virtual shot, which in real life can hit nearly 100 mph). There is also a simulated locker room where you can try on jerseys from several local teams, and a few stations where you can listen to or watch game day scenarios and make play calls. The museum is home to the Maryland State Athletic Hall of Fame.

Camden Station, the grand brick building that houses both the Sports Legends Museum and Geppi's Entertainment Museum, is an 1856 Baltimore & Ohio Railroad station and a key site in the first four deaths of the Civil War; a brief exhibit about the structure is on the first floor.

MAP 1: 301 W. Camden St., 410/727-1539, www.baberuthmuseum.org; summer daily 10am-5pm (to 7pm on Oriole game days), fall-spring Tues.-Sun. 10am-5pm; $8 adult, $4 child, $6 senior

★ Top of the World Observation Deck

Baltimore's World Trade Center, designed by architects at I. M. Pei's firm and completed in 1977, was one of the first new buildings to rise at the then-underdeveloped Inner Harbor. Today, it's merely one of many skyscrapers along the water, though it still claims one distinction: At a not-terribly-impressive 32 stories, it remains the world's tallest pentagonal building. On the 27th floor is the Top of the World Observation Deck, which is without a doubt the best vantage point for a 360-degree view of Baltimore. Wander around the room to get a sense of how Baltimore spreads out from the bustle, tourism, and commerce of the Inner Harbor to the far-ranging blocks of two-story row houses that make up so much of the city. There are mounted binoculars and maps to help orient visitors. An elevator ride to this deck around sunset is a great way to see Charm City in a whole new light.

MAP 1: 401 E. Pratt St., 410/837-8439; Wed.-Thurs. 10am-6pm, Fri.-Sat. 10am-7pm, Sun. 11am-6pm, summer hours include Mon. and Tues.; $5 adult, $3 child, $4 senior

★ Westminster Hall and Burying Ground

The main thing you should know about this eerie, historic church and graveyard is this: The dead came first. Generally, the establishment of a church leads to the founding of an attendant graveyard, but that's not the case with Westminster Hall and Burying Ground just west of downtown Baltimore. Built originally as a Presbyterian cemetery in 1786, its large, Gothic church didn't rise among the tombstones (and above several of them, resulting in

crude catacombs that riddle the church's foundation) until 1852.
The graveyard's most prominent occupant is the U.S. master of the macabre, Edgar Allan Poe, who in fact was buried in this same cemetery not once, but twice. (His wife and...cousin, Virginia, is interred with him.) Francis Scott Key's son Philip Barton Key is also buried here, as are several other prominent Baltimoreans of the 18th and 19th centuries. The current Poe family monument is right inside the graveyard's fence, at the corner of Fayette and Greene Streets, and is the scene each January 19 (Poe's birthday) of a visit from the Poe Toaster, a mysterious figure who leaves three red roses and a bottle of cognac on Poe's gravestone.

The entire property is owned by the neighboring University of Maryland School of Law, and run by a nonprofit; the church itself is no longer an active house of worship but rather an event space and hall available for rental. You can see the church and catacombs on the first and third Friday at 6:30pm or Saturday at 10am each month, but note that reservations are required and 15 people must attend for the tour to go on.

MAP 1: 519 W. Fayette St., 410/706-2072, www.westminsterhall.org; Burying Grounds: 8am-dusk; catacombs and Westminster Hall: Apr.-Nov., designated tour times; free for grounds; $5 adult, $3 child and senior for tours

Harbor East and Little Italy

Map 2

Baltimore Civil War Museum
On the edge of Harbor East's restaurant and shopping district sits this often-overlooked museum, a historical landmark that's most noteworthy for the building it calls home. Erected in 1850 as President Street Station, the brick structure is now the oldest U.S. train terminal still standing; it was also once a part of the Underground Railroad and a key site in the first four deaths of the Civil War. The story goes like this: Following the attack on South Carolina's Fort Sumter in April 1861, President Lincoln called up 75,000 New England militia volunteers to protect Washington DC, and a group of them had to pass through Baltimore on the way. Their trains arrived at President Street Station, where staff harnessed horses to the front cars. These horses would pull the train to Camden Station, the only railway stop between Baltimore and Washington DC (and today home to the Sports Legends Museum and Geppi's Entertainment Museum). But nearly 1,000 civilians—some supporting the North, others the Confederacy—blocked their passage. The soldiers left their horses behind and proceeded on

foot. But the crowd attacked them with weapons, and four militia volunteers were killed.

The museum itself—the bulk of which is filled with panels and text—tells the story of those deaths and the terminal's Underground Railroad history. It also has a small but interesting (and sometimes depressing) collection of memorabilia like touchable guns and hats and early 19th-century ankle irons that were worn by slaves. It's a small place though, ideal for history buffs or those who want to pop in when walking between Harbor East and the Inner Harbor.

MAP 2: 601 S. President St., 443/220-0290; Mon.-Sat. 10am-5pm, Sun. noon-5pm; free

Jewish Museum of Maryland

The location of the Jewish Museum of Maryland—just north of Fell's Point—was set by the path taken by Jewish immigrants to Baltimore and the path they took when they arrived here, in what was the nation's second-busiest immigration port (behind only Ellis Island). Most Jewish immigrants to Baltimore during the 19th century came ashore at the docks of Fell's Point and Locust Point (near Fort McHenry) and headed north to the area of east Baltimore between Baltimore and Lombard Streets and east of Central Avenue. The third-oldest synagogue in the nation, on Lloyd Street, was built in 1845, and a permanent exhibit in the basement tells the stories of its former congregations, one of them Roman Catholic. There were so many delicatessens that this part of town was known as "Corned Beef Row," though only a few delis now remain.

The main exhibit hall of the Jewish Museum re-creates the thriving Jewish community that made its home in this part of the city—showing the inside of houses (and an outhouse), as well as shops, businesses, and even busy street vendors and grocers. There's a small deli exhibit as well, and the audio played in the ersatz eatery uses snippets of real dialogue from typical deli patron conversations. A second display space hosts temporary exhibits that cover a wide variety of scenes from the Jewish experience, from the rise of Jewish comic book artists during the Great Depression to the role of Jewish cuisine in shaping identity.

MAP 2: 15 Lloyd St., 410/732-6400, www.jhsm.org; Sun.-Thurs. 10am-5pm; $8 adult, $3 child, $4 student

Phoenix (Old Baltimore) Shot Tower

The tall, unusual brick spire that reaches more than 234 feet into the air at the intersection of President and Fayette Streets, and dates from 1828, was an ingenious structure that was crucial to the U.S. military. It took more than one million bricks to build this tower, which is one of only a few left standing in the United States. So what's a shot tower, you ask? Old rifles (and modern shotguns) fired not bullets but round, spherical projectiles called shot: To create shot, bright armorers realized they could drop hot lead from a great height through a special sieve and into cool water, creating nearly perfectly spherical shot. This tower produced shot for the U.S. military through the Civil War and into the late 1800s, and was declared a National Historic Landmark in 1972. The interior remains as it was back in the 19th century, and guided tours leave from the Carroll Mansion twice a week. It's also a landmark worth recognizing during your travels.

MAP 2: 801 E. Fayette St., 410/605-2964, www.carrollmuseums.org; Sat.-Sun. 4pm tours only; $5 adult, $4 child

Reginald F. Lewis Museum of Maryland African American History & Culture

Clad in deep black granite and rising at one of the city's most historic intersections at a place where old Baltimore and new mingle together, this bold, monolithic museum examines the lives and history of Maryland's African American population. It examines the separate and very unequal societies that segregation created, and it also shows how African Americans made their own thriving and vibrant communities and culture, and created their own joys and futures when equality was an impossible dream. The three permanent exhibits here—Building Maryland, Building America, Things Hold, Lines Connect, and The Strength of the Mind—reveal the lives of African Americans from the days of slavery through the gradual gains made during the civil rights era.

There are great images and artifacts from the parallel communities and cultures that existed across Maryland, from waterfront resorts to radio stations to neighborhoods, all built because of segregation, both legalized and cultural. Videos of Maryland African Americans play throughout the exhibits, and the commentaries and histories told by those people help bring much of the museum's written displays to life.

A broad, crimson steel wall arcs through the center of the entire building and even extends outside. This Red Wall of Freedom serves to show the interruptions to the continuity of the culture of African Americans, and the tension that still surrounds race relations in the United States. The museum is named for, and was created, thanks to the estate of the late Reginald Lewis, a Baltimore native and prominent lawyer and venture capitalist who built Beatrice PLC into a multibillion-dollar company.

MAP 2: 830 E. Pratt St., 443/263-1800, www.africanamericanculture.org; Wed.-Sat. 10am-5pm, Sun. noon-5pm; $8 adult, $6 senior/student, free for children under age 6

This national historic site is based around the small, tidy brick home on the corner of Pratt and Albemarle Streets that was the residence of Mary Pickersgill, a flag maker and sewer of some renown. From a receipt found in the 1930s, we know that she was paid $574.44 when she delivered two flags for Baltimore's Fort McHenry in 1813. The larger flag was huge indeed, measuring 30 feet by 42 feet—the same size as the large, glass flag wall that lines one side of the museum—and it was this banner, fluttering slowly above Fort McHenry during the 1814 British bombardment, that inspired Francis Scott Key to pen the words to "The Star-Spangled Banner." The museum has some relics from the actual battle, including a fragment of the original flag (which now resides at the Smithsonian's National Museum of American History in Washington, D.C), and historic exhibits including an interactive kids' gallery, with 19th-century kid-size costumes to wear. In the Pickersgill house, actors in period costumes portray family members and residents of the home, welcoming guests and answering questions. The best days to visit include Flag Day (June 14) and Defender's Day (Sept. 12), a Baltimore-specific holiday that celebrates the defeat of the land and sea British invasion in 1814.

MAP 2: 844 E. Pratt St., 410/837-1793, www.flaghouse.org; Tues.-Sat. 10am-4pm; $8 adult, $6 child, $7 senior

Fell's Point   Map 2

Fell's Point Visitor Center

Tucked between the popular bars and boutiques on Thames Street (pronounced by lifelong Fell's Point residents not like the famous London river for which it's named, but with a soft "th" as in "thumb"), this onetime barn for horse-drawn trolleys now houses a well-stocked visitors center, where you can pick up abundant information about the historic waterfront community. There's also an exhibit that explains the importance of the Baltimore clipper privateer ships during the War of 1812 (and the anger they incurred from the British Royal Navy for their tactics and speed), as well as a collection of nautical artifacts and Baltimore-related souvenirs and gifts.

There are two things you should try to see here. First, stop by the restrooms. In the 1960s, when federal and state planners wanted to build a highway through Fell's Point that would essentially ruin the waterfront community, a group of local women formed a preservation society and fought to get the neighborhood designated as a historic district, effectively destroying the government's plans;

today, the map of the highway that would have ruined Fell's Point hangs next to the latrine. Then, as you leave the visitors center, walk a few steps to your left and open the green door that looks like it is off-limits (it's not): You'll head through a very cool, short tunnel known as a sally port to a small outdoor garden that few people know about, making this a nice place to take a break, especially during warm summer days.

MAP 2: 1724-26 Thames St., 410/675-6750, ext. 16, or 443/847-8738, www.preservationsociety.com; Apr.-Nov. Tues.-Thurs. noon-5pm, Fri.-Sat. 10am-8pm, Sun. 11am-5pm; winter hours Tues.-Sun noon-5pm; free

Frederick Douglass-Isaac Myers Maritime Park

This mixture of old and new buildings was once home to the Chesapeake Marine Railway and Dry Dock Company, a business founded in 1868 by African Americans to provide shipwright services to the bustling port city of Baltimore. Frederick Douglass lived as a slave here in Fell's Point, right near where Isaac Myers helped start the company. Douglass learned about shipwright work, which he said helped him fake his way to escape and freedom in 1838, and he was an inspiration to Myers.

Today, this building houses a variety of small exhibits about life for African Americans in Fell's Point and the business Myers ran. Kids can try their hand at some of the jobs the workers here would have performed, including "caulking," in which (now simulated) tar-soaked rope was pounded into the slots between boat hull planks to make the vessel watertight. The park is part of the Living Classrooms Foundation, which works with at-risk city youth to provide positive learning environments that include maritime activities and history.

MAP 2: 1417 Thames St., 410/685-0295, ext. 487, www.douglassmyers.org; Mon.-Fri. 10am-4pm, Sat.-Sun. noon-4pm; $5 adult, $2 child, $4 senior

Robert Long House

The Robert Long House is the city's oldest surviving urban residence, a good-size brick abode dating from 1765 (not that the house has made it easy on those who tried to preserve it). Long was a quartermaster for the fledgling Continental navy, and he built this building to serve as both his office and his house. For the next two centuries, it managed to stand, if in serious disrepair, until 1969, when it was slated for demolition as part of a project to level much of Fell's Point for a highway. The Fell's Point Preservation Society (now known as The Society for the Preservation of Federal Hill and Fell's Point) saved the home in 1975, and began a lengthy restoration of the building and its outdoor spaces. The repairs and rebuilding were then destroyed in a serious fire in 1999, but a second restoration has once again re-created Long's colonial home. The

clockwise from top left: The Washington Monument and Mount Vernon Place, Mount Vernon; Blacktip Reef Shark at the National Aquarium in Baltimore, Inner Harbor; the U.S.S. *Constellation* at Historic Ships in Baltimore, Inner Harbor

well-lit rooms (the windows in this home are quite large) are filled
with period furniture and tools of the quartermaster's trade; the
gardens at the side of and behind the house are small but splendid,
and many of the herbs grown there today are the same kinds Long
and his family would have cultivated. For Tuesday tours, reservations must be made by Sunday.

MAP 2: 812 S. Ann St., 410/675-6750 or 443/847-8738,
www.preservationsociety.org; tours Tues. at 1:30pm; $10

Canton

Map 3

Patterson Park

One of the city's oldest parks, the land now known as Patterson
Park used to be a 200-acre estate (owned by William Patterson) that
marked the far eastern edge of what was called Baltimore Town.
During the War of 1812, while soldiers at nearby Fort McHenry
were holding off a British invasion fleet, a second Redcoat force
moved on land toward Baltimore from the east. When they reached
Patterson Park, they found some 100 cannons and 20,000 soldiers
waiting for them; at the sight of such a massive defense, the British
withdrew. Today, the 155-acre park (which includes land east of
Linwood Ave.) is a thriving center of activity for the surrounding
residents, from lifelong Baltimoreans who grew up around the park
to newcomers. There are walking and jogging paths throughout the
hills, fields, and wooded areas of the park, a recently rebuilt boat
lake (which isn't as big as that name implies), and plenty of great
views of the city from the high ground at the north end of the park.
There's also a public swimming pool, tennis courts, soccer fields,
and a covered ice-skating rink. Patterson Park is host to a variety
of festivals, events, and sports leagues throughout the year.

The park's most notable feature is the pagoda, which is actually
a Victorian design, rather than an Asian one. Completed in 1892,
the 60-foot-tall observation tower (only open Apr.-Oct. Sun. noon-
6pm) was completely restored in 2002 and offers spectacular panoramic views of Baltimore. It's also a popular meeting place and
gathering spot for the park's many visitors.

MAP 3: Patterson Park and Eastern Aves., 410/276-3676, www.pattersonpark.com;
daily dawn-dusk; free

S.S. *John Brown*

Baltimore played a pivotal role in the national war effort during
World War II because of the mighty industrial production its factories and citizens could bring to bear for the United States. One
of the city's greatest contributions were medium-size cargo ships,

built at the Bethlehem-Fairfield Shipyards, known as Liberty ships. These mass-produced ships (some 2,750 were constructed) ferried huge amounts of cargo across the Atlantic to England to help it hold out against Nazi Germany.

The S.S. *John Brown* is one of only two surviving examples of this type of ship; built in Baltimore, the *John Brown* is now preserved as a piece of living history by a group of former sailors and history buffs. Climb aboard to explore the huge gray vessel, starting with a small history exhibit that explains the war and the role of the Liberty ships. Then head deep into the heart of the ship, where you can see (and hear) the massive machinery that moved the *John Brown* across the Atlantic. The ship makes occasional Living History cruises around the Baltimore waterfront, and even cruises up the Patapsco from its home pier in Canton to the Inner Harbor for special events.

MAP 3: Pier 1, 2000 S. Clinton St., 410/558-0646, www.liberty-ship.com; Wed. and Sat. 9am-2pm when the ship is in port; free, donation appreciated

Federal Hill   Map 4

★ American Visionary Art Museum

Drive past the large, old brick buildings that rise on the south side of the Inner Harbor, where Key Highway makes a hard right turn, and you'll see, in bright neon colors, the words "O Say Can You See." Or maybe you'll notice the enormous, 60-foot-high patchwork whirligig twirling overhead. Or maybe you'll spy the bead and sequin-encrusted bus topped with a flock of swans, or the glass mosaic egg, or...Well, there are plenty of ways to be entranced by the amazing, extraordinary, and unpredictable American Visionary Art Museum. The brainchild of local arts and social activist Rebecca Hoffberger, AVAM opened in 1995 and celebrates astounding works of art made by people who are not traditionally trained artists. Inside, you'll find a rotating series of exhibits (found by ascending a long winding walkway) showcasing painting, sculpture, and other types of art, all made with intense passion and incredible dedication. The newer barn building, to the south, contains larger works, including a great tribute to John Waters film regular Divine. The gift shop, run by famed Chicago retailer Ted "Uncle Fun" Frankel, is also an unexpected treat: You'll find the store shelves and alcoves packed with weird souvenirs and original artwork.

MAP 4: 800 Key Hwy., 410/244-1900, www.avam.org; Tues.-Sun. 10am-6pm; $15.95 adult, $9.95 child, $13.95 senior

Baltimore is a city that was largely built on the strengths of its industrial base—and the backs and sweat of the citizens who worked in the shipyards, steel mills, factories, shops, and industrial plants that used to pack the city and its waterfront. Those industries have, more often than not, fallen silent or been rendered obsolete, but the Baltimore Museum of Industry preserves the power of that history. Some of America's greatest products—from Noxzema and Bromo-Seltzer to gas lighting and aircraft innovations—were created, built, or perfected around Baltimore, and their stories are told here. Look for the enormous red crane out front as you head down Key Highway; it's a great place to stop, not just geographically, but culturally and historically, between a visit to Fort McHenry and the American Visionary Art Museum.

The first exhibits tell the story of Baltimore of the late 19th and early 20th centuries, with a re-created pharmacy, print shop, garment factory, and an original oyster cannery building. The large, waterfront Decker Gallery (named for one of the men who founded Black & Decker, the tool manufacturing giant based just north of the city) houses the museum's biggest items; just outside the window is the steam-powered tugboat S.S. *Baltimore,* built in 1906 and a stalwart of the once-thriving port that used to sprawl across this waterfront. Visual relics are a big part of the fun of this museum, from old painted metal signs to great glowing neon beacons for cars, insurance, and seafood.

MAP 4: 1415 Key Hwy., 410/727-4808, www.thebmi.org; Tues.-Sun. 10am-4pm; $12 adult, $7 child, $9 senior

The Domino Sugars Sign

The glowing red neon of this sugar processing plant's 120-foot-tall "Domino Sugars" sign has kept watch over Baltimore's harbor for more than 50 years. A few times a month, ships dock at the Domino plant in Tide Point to unload shipments of sugar, an interesting process that you may be able to see if you take the Water Taxi there at the right time. (The Tide Point complex's water promenade also offers some beautiful views of Fell's Point and the city.) But to really get a great view of this Baltimore waterfront icon, take a nighttime stroll west along the Inner Harbor into Federal Hill.

MAP 4: 1100 Key Hwy., 410/752-6150; 24 hours; free

★ Federal Hill Park

There's no better place to get a great view of Baltimore's Inner Harbor—and the city itself—than from the top of Federal Hill. Rising up dramatically from the waterfront along the south side of the Inner Harbor, this grassy mound was originally mined for paint pigment in colonial times and still has some old tunnels within it that occasionally give way, leading to saggy hillsides and sunken footpaths. The hill has been a public park since the late 1700s and was originally known as Signal Park, as observers could spot merchant and passenger ships on the Patapsco River as they approached the harbor. The park was renamed Federal Hill in 1789, after the news and celebration following the ratification of the U.S. Constitution (creating a "federal" government). Today, it's home to a park and a playground, and it's a great place for a scenic picnic that includes fresh food from nearby Cross Street Market. At the park's northern edge, several Civil War-era cannons are aimed right at downtown, symbolizing the weapons placed in a similar location by Union troops in 1861 to send a stern message to the Confederate-sympathizing residents of the city.

MAP 4: Battery Ave. and Key Hwy., 410/396-7900; daily dawn-dusk; free

Mount Vernon and Station North

Map 5

Baltimore Streetcar Museum

The location of this great little museum—tucked on a small, winding back section of Falls Road, at the base of a cliff and next to I-83—speaks volumes about the current standing of streetcars in civic importance. But from the late 1800s to the 1940s, more than a thousand streetcars crisscrossed Baltimore, carrying people to work, play, shop, and see the city. This museum, entirely volunteer-operated, has several good displays of the evolution of the railcar from glorified horse-drawn carriage to fully electrified modern conveyance, and working models and dioramas of streetcars. The best part (particularly for kids), though, is the salvaged, repaired, and working streetcars that leave about every 20 minutes for a clackety trip down the tracks. The train conductors (and the rest of the staff) obviously love their hobby and are thrilled to talk streetcars and Baltimore history with visitors. There's even a car barn down the tracks a bit that, if you ask nicely, they'll open up to reveal some of their works in progress (young kids may not be allowed in there, alas—too unsafe).

MAP 5: 1901 Falls Rd., 410/547-0264, www.baltimorestreetcar.org; Sun. noon-5pm, summer Sat. also; $7 adult, $5 child, $5 senior

★ Basilica of the Assumption

Maryland was founded by Lord Baltimore as a place of religious tolerance, at least in terms of the 17th century; this meant that Catholics (like Lord Baltimore) were more welcome here than in other English colonies. Fittingly, Baltimore is the nation's oldest

Catholic diocese, and the first Catholic cathedral in America was
the Basilica of the Assumption, completed in 1821. (The official
name of the cathedral is the Basilica of the National Shrine of the
Assumption of the Blessed Virgin Mary.)

The imposing building was designed and brought to life by two
men: John Carroll, the first American Catholic bishop (and a member of the storied Carroll family), and Benjamin Henry Latrobe, the
architect of the U.S. Capitol in Washington DC. The two wanted
to create a uniquely American cathedral, one that spoke of a new
architecture combined with Rome's building codes—but a building
that did not merely echo European designs. Latrobe's work in DC
gave him the experience and ideas that led to the basilica's massive
dome. The dome can be seen more clearly today than in recent decades, due to a massive, multimillion-dollar restoration, completed
in 2006, that gave the building new life and vitality.

The sweeping skylights, domes, rosettes, and curves of the interior of the basilica have a delicacy and stately nature that echoes
that of the Capitol, but the architecture has a more sacred style—
though it doesn't invoke the often ominous feel of European cathedrals. Tours offered Monday through Friday at 9am, 11am, and
1pm, and some Saturdays at the same times include the main chapel
and church, as well as the undercroft and crypt, where almost all
of Baltimore's archbishops are laid to rest.

MAP 5: 409 Cathedral St., 410/727-3565, www.baltimorebasilica.org; Mon.-Fri.
7am-4pm, Sat. 7am-conclusion of 5:30pm mass, Sun. 7am-conclusion of 4:30pm
mass; $2 donation requested for tour

Brown Memorial Park Avenue Presbyterian Church

As the basilica is the spiritual capital for Baltimore's Catholics,
Brown Memorial is the pinnacle of hallowed ground for the city's
Presbyterians. Built in 1870, and dedicated to George Brown, a
founder of the Baltimore & Ohio Railroad, this Gothic Revival
church rises above the stately row houses of Bolton Hill, long one
of the city's most exclusive neighborhoods (though today, art students from the nearby Maryland Institute College of Art occupy
many of the houses). The Gothic architecture gives the church a
spectacular vaulted ceiling, painted a dark, royal purple; there's
also a great 1930 pipe organ.

But the real reason to visit the church are the 11 Louis Tiffany
stained-glass windows, some of which are nearly three stories tall
and among the largest he ever created. Installed in 1905, each depicts a tale or re-creates a scene from the Bible; the craftsmanship
and scale of the works still inspire and astound visitors and wor-
shippers alike.

MAP 5: 1316 Park Ave., 410/523-1542, www.browndowntown.org; daily 9am-6pm;
free

Memorials and Public Art

The iconic Washington Monument in Mount Vernon may be Baltimore's most recognizable landmark. But there are other important memorials and public art pieces that you will likely come across during your stay.

9/11 Memorial
Maryland's **9/11 Memorial** is made from three steel beams from New York's World Trade Center that are twisted together; they sit on top of a thick marble box etched with the names of the 69 Marylanders who lost their lives that day. The memorial was dedicated on the tenth anniversary of 9/11, and it sits in front of Baltimore's World Trade Center and the Top of the World Observation Deck.

National Katyn Memorial
In the middle of Harbor East's President Street traffic circle, surrounded by a movie theater and several shops and restaurants, is the bronze **National Katyn Memorial** (www. katynmemorial.com) with its towering flame. It's a sad sculpture, a tribute to the 20,000 Polish officers who were executed after the Soviet Union invaded Poland during WWII. Artist Andrzej Pitynski made the piece in Poland and shipped it to Baltimore in 2000.

Crabtown Project
Visitors may notice a painted fiberglass crab sculpture or two around Baltimore, like the blue and gold crab in front of the National Aquarium in Baltimore. These 75-pound sculptures were part of the Crabtown Project, a 2005 campaign to raise funds for city schools. Artists painted about 200 crabs, and at one time they were scattered all over the city. Most of them

were auctioned off as part of the campaign, but a few of the winners chose to keep their crabs on city streets. Other good places for crab sculpture sightings are in front of the Inn at Henderson's Wharf in Fell's Point and on Hanover Street in Federal Hill about two blocks north of the Bluegrass Tavern.

Open Walls Baltimore murals
In 2012, the Station North Arts and Entertainment District managed the **Open Walls Baltimore street art project** (www.openwallsbaltimore. com), a three-month initiative in which about 20 artists—six from Baltimore; some from Argentina, the Ukraine, and other countries—painted about 20 murals around the neighborhood to, in part, inspire dialogue among residents and visitors. The nationally known street artist Gaia curated the project, and his mural of a hand holding a pigeon (1 W. North Ave.) near the Charles Theater is the one you're most likely to come across. But it's possible to tour of all the murals, too (the addresses are on the website).

Male/Female Sculpture
Jonathan Borofsky's 51-foot-tall *Male/Female* sculpture stands guard in front of Pennsylvania Station in the Mount Vernon and Station North neighborhood. It also happens to be the public art piece that has inspired the most discussion among Baltimoreans, both positive and negative. Still, whatever residents' feelings are about it, the $750,000 aluminum piece is here to stay. Recently, a seating area of blue and orange tables—a welcome pop of color—was added at the sculpture's base.

Garrett-Jacobs Mansion

John Work Garrett was president of the mighty Baltimore & Ohio Railroad during the growth of the United States during the mid- and late 19th century; the echoes of his fortune and fancies are still visible throughout the city of Baltimore. And there's no relic grander then the stately Mount Vernon home he bought for his son Robert. Admittedly, it was only somewhat grand when it was bought, but by the time Robert's wife and widow Mary Garrett (who would remarry Dr. Henry Jacobs) was through acquiring three other adjoining homes, hiring John Edward Pope to rework the architecture, installing a massive Louis Tiffany stained-glass dome and windows, and turning most of the block into a sprawling 40-room mansion...well, by then, it was the finest home in all of Baltimore.

Today, this enormous residence is home to the Engineer's Club, a private members-only society. Tours here are self-guided, and the home's entrance hall with its massive, elaborately carved pillars and sheets of dark mahogany is an impressive room worth seeing. But, because visits are limited to the first floor, it's best to treat the mansion as an already-in-the-area sight, and save the destination trip for another Garrett residence, Evergreen, just north of Loyola College in north Baltimore.

MAP 5: 11 W. Mount Vernon Pl., 410/539-6914, www.garrettjacobsmansion.org; Tues.-Fri., hours vary; free

George Peabody Library

The towering stacks room of the George Peabody Library is one of Baltimore's most recognizable and treasured spaces. Five stories tall and topped with a magnificent skylight, the library is home to 300,000 volumes covering history, architecture, art, and literature, all tucked within soaring columns and ornate cast-iron balconies and a dramatic marble floor. The library's collection is part of Johns Hopkins University's special collections and is located at the world-renowned Peabody Institute of Music, which means that the space hosts a variety of events, including lectures, concerts, and private affairs throughout the year. Note that this is a real, live working library, so please be considerate of those doing research.

MAP 5: 17 E. Mount Vernon Pl., 410/234-4943, www.peabodyevents.library.jhu.edu; Tues.-Thurs. 9am-5pm, Fri. 9am-3pm; free

Maryland Historical Society

Sprawling over two buildings (one new, one old) and home to a massive, seven-million-piece library that contains some amazing pieces of history (including "The Star-Spangled Banner" manuscript, as written by Francis Scott Key), the Maryland Historical Society is one of the city's hidden jewels. Start your tour with a look at the exhibit explaining the European settling of the Baltimore region, and explore the maritime history of Fell's Point and Baltimore (home to daring privateers the British regarded as little more than pirate scum).

Then head to the new building (it's the one topped by the statue of the dog Nipper, listening intently to a Victrola—a relic from a now-demolished RCA building) and its three stories of history; start on the first floor, which recounts the legacy of the region from Native American times to the present day. The exhibits don't flinch from the state's less admirable moments, including slavery and bigotry (even though the society's third president was Jewish).

There are some great items on display that cover the state's history, including an amazing shadowbox made using items from the horrific Civil War battle of Antietam, the 1763 contract that hired Mason and Dixon to survey the countryside, and a typewriter used by H. L. Mencken. Baltimore was once a renowned silverware city, and examples of intricate silversmith work occupy a landing between the two buildings.

The second floor houses an impressive portrait gallery, with much of it painted by a member of the vast Peale family of artists. The society's final gallery, on the third floor, is an amazing collection of Baltimore furniture from the past two centuries, including an assortment of Baltimore Painted Furniture from the 1800s. There's a semi-hidden wonder on this floor: By the elevators lurks an enormous, one-eighth-scale diorama of a fictitious 1930s-era circus called Bozo Brothers. There are more than 9,000 miniature people and animals in the work; its display here, among the fine oak and mahogany pianos, armchairs, and armoires, is a much-appreciated peculiarity that suits the character of Baltimore well.

MAP 5: 201 W. Monument St., 410/685-3750, www.mdhs.org; Wed.-Sat. 10am-5pm, Sun. noon-5pm (museum only); $9 adult, $6 child, $7 senior

Walters Art Museum

Think what you will about the ruthless American industrialists of the 19th century: They certainly knew how to leave a legacy. William Thompson Walters, a native of Pennsylvania who moved to Baltimore and made a fortune in wholesale liquor before the Civil War (and, postwar, another fortune in banking and railroads), moved to a grand home in exclusive Mount Vernon Place in 1858 and set about collecting paintings, sculptures, and antiquities. By the mid-1870s, Walters was allowing the public into his home to see his collection (for a fee—donated to charity, of course), which was an impressive trove of European and Asian artworks. His son, Henry Walters, helped in the acquisition of items, and expanded the breadth of the collection into new areas. His biggest score was the 1902 purchase (for $1 million) of the entire contents of a palazzo in

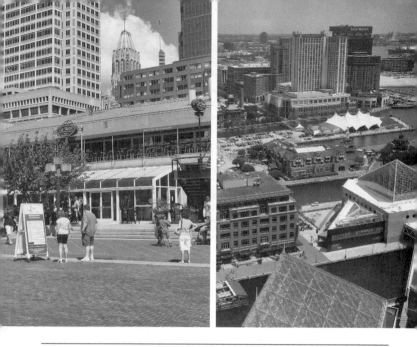

clockwise from top left: Harborplace, Inner Harbor; Top of the World Observation Deck, Inner Harbor; Maryland Science Center, Inner Harbor

Rome, including works by greats like El Greco, and seven astounding sarcophagi that are some of the museum's most amazing pieces.

Henry Walters left his incomparable collection to the city of Baltimore, and new construction and the donation of an adjoining mansion (Hackerman House) have made the Walters Art Museum one of the nation's finest small museums. It's rare to find such a incredibly deep and impressive collection from so many different cultures, epochs, and media in one place. The Walters amazes with every exhibit and never lets up throughout the various buildings' multiple levels and passageways. Egyptian mummies and burial items are one floor down from medieval European reliquaries; rows of Asian jade sculptures line the walls of Hackerman House, while the Chamber of Wonders in the original building re-creates a 17th-century nobleman's room of exotic animals, natural wonders, and heavenly observations. Tourists may often skip the Walters in favor of the bigger Baltimore Museum of Art, but the museums' collections complement one another, and the Walters should be considered a mandatory destination. Best of all, admission is free.

MAP 5: 600 N. Charles St., 410/547-9000, www.thewalters.org; Wed.-Sun. 10am-5pm; free

★ The Washington Monument

The first city to begin construction of a monument honoring the father of the United States was Baltimore; the 178-foot-high column and statue of a mounted George Washington now watch over Mount Vernon Place. Completed in 1829, this was the first real tribute to Washington that was built in the country, and it was designed by Robert Mills, the same man who would construct the enormous 555-foot-high obelisk dedicated to Washington in the capital city that bears his name. As of 2013, the monument was closed for construction for the foreseeable future, but visitors will one day be able to walk up the 228 narrow stone steps to the top of the column. For now, there are a couple of parks surrounding it, making this a good place for a picnic; many of the city's most popular festivals like the Baltimore Book Festival and the Flower Mart also take place here. There's also a wonderful, quirky, and still-active Baltimore tradition of stringing colored holiday lights from the monument in early December; an accompanying and well-attended lighting ceremony (complete with fireworks) helps mark the beginning of the holiday season.

MAP 5: 600 N. Charles St., 866/639-3526 or 410/396-0929; 24 hours; free

Hampden and Homewood Map 6

Amaranthine Museum
This is a museum in the way the encyclopedia is a book; the answer to "What's it about?" is "everything." A series of rooms, passages, and chambers, the Labyrinth at the Amaranthine (the word means eternally beautiful), created by the late Les Harris, charts "the history of art and the creative process in civilization, interpreted in inspired form by one of the foremost artists of our day," as the museum's website puts it. The best way to enter this museum is with no preconceptions; just go inside and begin the experience. This is a great companion visit to the American Visionary Art Museum because it encompasses Harris's vast vision, though he was a traditionally trained artist.

MAP 6: 2010 Clipper Park Rd., 410/456-1343, www.amaranthinemuseum.org; Sun. noon-3pm, other days by appt. (closed July and Aug.); $5 on Sunday, $25 for special appts.

★ Baltimore Museum of Art
One of the city's two great museums (along with Mount Vernon's Walters Art Museum), the Baltimore Museum of Art (BMA) has a world-class holding of works from across the globe and the centuries. Founded in 1914, the museum's grand, classical main building (designed by John Russell Pope) was opened in 1929, and today—along with a modest, more modern structure next door—is undergoing a massive $28 million renovation through 2015.

The contemporary wing, opened in late 2012, is the first newly renovated gallery. It now has smooth wood floors and gorgeous lighting designed to complement an impressive array of works from artists like Willem de Kooning, Jackson Pollock, Mark Rothko, Robert Rauschenberg, and Andy Warhol. There are also works from emerging artists that were made in the last couple of years and tend toward video and mixed media; seeing them next to a Rauschenberg or a Warhol gives a good picture of how contemporary art has evolved. While here, be sure to peer through Sarah Oppenheimer's architectural installations on the second floor and in the Cone Collection next door; made by cutting holes in the walls and the ceiling, they give visitors a new lens through which to view the galleries and artwork.

Also on display is the legendary **Cone Collection** donated by Baltimore sisters Claribel and Etta Cone upon Etta's death in 1949 (Claribel had passed away in 1929). Fueled by the profitable Cone textile business, the sisters personally amassed some 3,000 works from renowned artists (and, more often than not, close friends of the Cones) including Cézanne, Gauguin, Matisse, Picasso, and van Gogh. The collection, which includes 500 works by Matisse alone, is regarded as one of the most comprehensive samplings of post-impressionism in existence. Visitors can even take a virtual tour of the Cone sisters' massive, adjoining apartments and see how the artworks were displayed in their homes.

The BMA also boasts galleries devoted to European and English sporting art, and a large collection of early AD tile works called the Antioch Mosaics. Outside are Sculpture Gardens, which include 34 sculptures by artists like Auguste Rodin and Alexander Calder (the view of the gardens from the patio of the BMA's restaurant, Gertrude's, is a local favorite.) As for the renovation, there's more to come: New and much larger galleries for African and Asian works, as well as a brand-new interactive center, will be completed in 2015, while the museum's grand main entrance, unused since 1982, will reopen in the fall of 2014.

MAP 6: 10 Art Museum Dr., 443/573-1700, www.artbma.org; Wed.-Fri. 10am-5pm, Sat.-Sun. 11am-6pm; free

Homewood Museum

Homewood Museum is one of the rare surviving examples of what were once country homes for Baltimore's wealthy colonial-era residents. Charles Carroll, who had signed the Declaration of Independence, gave $10,000 to his son Charles Jr. in 1801 for the construction of a summer home on 130 acres north of Baltimore City. That home—called Homewood House, and finished at a final cost of more than $40,000—sits today on the eastern edge of the campus of Johns Hopkins University. It's a magnificent example of federal architecture that inspired copies and reproductions across the nation; the details of construction are revealed in the angry letters Charles Sr. wrote his son as the costs spiraled with every material and design upgrade Charles Jr. insisted upon. (Though, to be fair, it seems his siblings may have spent a good bit on their houses too.) Homewood Museum today is no drab historical drag; it's a riot of well-researched and proper colors, patterns, and furniture that makes the home feel lived-in and accessible. Some of Charles Jr.'s personal effects are still here, as is much of the home's original furniture. There's also a wine cellar downstairs for regular events, from dressmaking workshops to balls.

MAP 6: 3400 N. Charles St., 410/516-5589, www.museums.jhu.edu/homewood; Tues.-Fri. 11am-4pm, Sat.-Sun. noon-4pm; $8 adult, $5 child, $7 senior

Howard Peters Rawlings Conservatory & Botanic Gardens

In Druid Hill Park, this is the last remaining example of Baltimore's public conservatories, which once adorned many of the city's parks. The historic, Victorian-era complex includes two buildings from 1888 (the Palm House and the Orchid Room), as well as three newer buildings from the 20th century. Each of the five buildings is home to a distinct type of flora, representing five different climate types (Mediterranean, tropical, and desert join the palms and orchids of the original structures). There are also abundant outdoor gardens perfect for spring strolls, and several flower shows are held throughout the year. The five-story Palm House is the centerpiece of the conservatory; huge palm trees fill the grand and graceful glass dome, designed by the same architect who came up with City Hall.

MAP 6: 3100 Swann Dr., Druid Hill Park, 410/396-0008, www.rawlingsconservatory.org; Wed.-Sun. 10am-4pm; free

Lacrosse Museum & National Hall of Fame

Invented by Native North Americans as a combination sport/festival/warrior basic training regime (and called *baggataway* by the Iroquois, one of the dozens of tribes that played the sport), the modern game of lacrosse is Maryland's official team sport—and Baltimore has produced some of lacrosse's greatest players and teams. Popular throughout the Northeast for more than a century (official rules were adopted right after the end of the Civil War), the sport has grown across the country in the past decades and is a staple of prep school and Eastern college athletics. The museum traces the game from its role in Native American society (including the Ottawa/Ojibwe tribe's use of a game of lacrosse to distract British soldiers during a 1763 assault on Fort Michilimackinac, in what is now Michigan) to its popularity today. Photos, videos, and the evolution of the lacrosse stick from a well-bent branch into a specialized, carbon-fiber, goal-scoring tool help document the game's growth. The sport's national hall of fame is also here, showcasing the greatest men and women to ever play what is known as "the fastest game on two feet."

MAP 6: 113 W. University Pkwy., 410/235-6882, ext. 147, www.uslacrosse.org; Mon.-Wed. 10am-2pm, appts. available during other times; $3 adult, $2 child, free for U.S. Lacrosse members and children under age 5

Maryland Zoo in Baltimore

Within one of the city's largest parks (Druid Hill Park, to the west of Hampden), the Maryland Zoo in Baltimore was created by the state legislature back in 1876, and is the country's third-oldest zoo. The zoo is currently working on its latest new exhibit, a South African-inspired habitat for 100 African penguins scheduled to open in the fall of 2014.

But for now, a list of the most popular attractions and habitats should start with the Polar Bear Watch, where visitors take in the watery residence of bears Magnet and Anoki from an arctic-style buggy. Guests can also take a camel ride or feed a giraffe, tote their little ones to the Maryland Wilderness and Children's Zoo (where they can pet or even brush African pygmy and Nubian goats), or listen to a zookeeper discuss the details of one of the zoo's more than 1,500 inhabitants. There are even behind-the-scenes tours that take visitors inside several animal habitats like the polar bear dens and the rhino barns, and the zoo holds annual popular events for kids, like an Easter egg "hunt" (the eggs are simply laid out on the ground for little ones) and a Halloween costume contest.

An insider tip: As the zoo covers more than 160 acres of "natural" environments, full of water and animals, it's a good idea to wear bug repellent if you're visiting during Baltimore's warmer, more humid months (May-Sept.).

MAP 6: 1876 Mansion House Dr., Druid Hill Park, 410/396-7102, www.marylandzoo.org; Mar.-Dec. daily 10am-4pm, Jan.-Feb. Fri.-Mon. 10am-4pm; $17.50 adult, $12.50 child, $14.50 senior, half price admission fee Jan. and Feb.

Greater Baltimore   Map 7

B&O Railroad Museum

Historians make a pretty good case that railroads helped build the United States—and the birthplace of American railroading was in 1828, on Baltimore's Pratt Street, with the creation of the Baltimore & Ohio Railroad. This facility was first known as the Mt. Clare Shops and was a huge repair and maintenance center too, taking up some 100 acres. Now, though many of the original buildings remain, the museum is surrounded by row houses, but they're still in the shadow of the 123-foot-high roundhouse that is the centerpiece of the museum. Originally built in 1872, the structure served as an enormous turn-around point (a gigantic turntable was used) for steam locomotives and other railcars. Partially destroyed in 2003 by a huge blizzard, the now-restored roundhouse holds many of the historic train cars in the museum's collection, covering the growth of railroads from a small transportation option into a continental industrial behemoth. There's a short, 20-minute train ride on the same rail line first laid down nearly 200 years ago; the ride takes visitors past some of the outlying buildings still used to repair cars, as well as some of the decaying structures used in the past (and some of Baltimore's less-than-thriving neighborhoods). There are some impressive model train setups outside the roundhouse, and plenty of rolling stock everywhere on the grounds—even in the parking lot—to impress kids of all ages.

MAP 7: 901 W. Pratt St., Baltimore, 410/752-2490, www.borail.org; Mon.-Sat. 10am-4pm, Sun. 11am-4pm; $16 adult, $10 child, $14 senior

Now a museum, Edgar Allan Poe's onetime modest brick home on Amity Street, where he lived from 1833 to 1835, closed its doors in 2012. That's when its funder, the City of Baltimore, decided it couldn't continue to provide the $85,000 a year needed to operate the space. But the nonprofit Poe Baltimore came together shortly afterward, and fans of the writer will be happy to know that they plan to reopen the house in the spring of 2014. Here, visitors can learn about Edgar Allan Poe's brief life in Baltimore (he died here long after he had lived here, perishing in 1849 while passing through the city, and is buried at downtown's Westminster Hall). He lived in the house with his grandmother, his aunt, and his cousin Virginia (who, somewhat ickily, would go on to become Mrs. Poe), and it was while living here that Poe began to enjoy some success from the stories he wrote. The home is decorated as it would have been during the time Poe lived here, and a few of Poe's belongings, like a travel desk and telescope, are here, as are images of Poe. The house today shares the block (which is little more than an alley street) with a large public housing development named for Poe; the immediate area is not recommended for sightseeing, but visitors to the site should have no problems.

MAP 7: 203 N. Amity St., Baltimore, 443/327-9789, www.poeinbaltimore.org

Evergreen

Unlike Homewood House and Mount Clare Mansion, two surviving examples of early Baltimore summer estates, the vast, stunning home called Evergreen wasn't a warm-weather escape; it was a full-time residence. Bought by Baltimore & Ohio Railroad tycoon John W. Garrett in 1878 for his son T. Harrison Garrett, Evergreen was once a meager 12-room home; by the time it was given to Johns Hopkins University in 1942, it tallied some 48 rooms. It's a Gilded Age residence, built in 1857 and today perhaps the finest freestanding historic home in Baltimore City. T. Harrison's son John Work Garrett and his wife Alice, who were patrons of the arts and letters, inherited the house in 1920, and the home grew to house their collections and reflect their areas of interest. Paintings by Modigliani and Degas hang in the long living room; Louis Tiffany lamps and chandeliers abound; and one of the home's five libraries has murals that were painted on-site by Jose Miguel Covarrubias at the Garrett's request. The Victorian-era custom of displaying one's wealth is well represented here, most notably in the bathroom with the 24K gold-leafed toilet. But the Garretts were far more interested in knowledge, learning, and appreciating works of art; a gymnasium was converted into a small theater by Leon Bakst. Leave plenty of time to explore and learn about this amazing house, located just north of the Loyola University campus in north Baltimore—it's

Many cities can lay claim to notable innovations and inventions, but Baltimore's residents have been providing North America with a long and impressive list of firsts since before the formation of the United States. The Ouija board was created here in 1892, as was saccharine, the American Humane Society, and the world's first telegraph line, which ran from Baltimore to Washington DC. Many of the medical procedures used around the world today were developed by pioneering surgeons and physicians at Johns Hopkins Hospital. Here are just a few of the other pioneering people, moments, and ideas from Baltimore's history:

First stagecoach route—1773
This horse-drawn carriage service connected Baltimore to Philadelphia (some 90 miles north) across a series of rough, dangerous, unimproved roads.

First city to use hydrogen gas for streetlights—1816
Sure, hydrogen is kind of dangerous, but it beat the old oil-filled lamps and helped Baltimore maintain its role as a sophisticated, advanced city.

First U.S. umbrella factory—1828
Though the first person to come into Baltimore carrying an open umbrella was attacked for being strange, the rain- and sun-deflecting device was soon embraced by Americans.

First commercial and passenger railroad—1828
The debut of the Baltimore and Ohio (B&O) Railroad was the critical step in the growth of a still-young America; the quick, reliable routes to and from points west led to a huge growth in industry and commerce.

First ice-cream freezer—1848
Ice cream had been around for centuries, but it had to be eaten almost immediately after its creation or stored near blocks of ice; a Baltimore man patented a powerful electrically powered cooling device and compartment that could keep ice cream frozen indefinitely.

First African American on the Supreme Court—1967
Supreme Court Justice (and native Baltimorean) Thurgood Marshall's landmark decision and opinion in the 1954 *Brown v. Board of Education* case led to the gradual dismantling of legal segregation in the United States.

another hidden treasure that rewards visitors with its unexpected splendor.
MAP 7: 4545 N. Charles St., Baltimore, 410/516-0341, www.museums.jhu.edu/evergreen; Tues.-Fri. 11am-4pm, Sat.-Sun. noon-4pm; $8 adult, $5 child, $7 senior

★ Fort McHenry National Monument and Historic Shrine
In 1814, star-shaped Fort McHenry was the lynchpin in the defense of Baltimore during the War of 1812. The fort was squarely in the sights of the invading British army that had just burned Washington DC to the ground; a fleet of warships was bound and determined to pass the fort and attack the city, while a second prong of attack—an army of British soldiers—marched in from the east.

The British bombardment was massive, yet the defenders—numbering only 60 soldiers—managed to hold off the Brits after an evening of relentless fire. When the smoke cleared and the dawn came, the enormous U.S. flag sewn by Baltimorean Mary Pickersgill languidly flapped above the fort, letting a prisoner in one of the British vessels—Francis Scott Key—know that Fort McHenry remained in U.S. hands. The invasion failed; Key was released; and the verses he had written after realizing the battle's outcome would (eventually) become "The Star-Spangled Banner," the national anthem.

Start the tour with the obligatory, aged informational film (starring an actor in period attire playing a barely important character from the War of 1812) in the fort's visitors center. The only reason to endure the film is for what happens at the end, which is a manipulative but effective theatrical tool that cannot be revealed. Suffice to say, it will stir whatever patriotism lives within you.

Then head down the walkway to the fort itself, which is the only site in the United States designated as both a National Monument and a Historic Shrine. You can tour the bastions and barracks, which remain mostly as they were back in 1814, and see the powder magazine that was struck by a British shell during the bombardment—but did not explode, which would have probably turned the tide of the battle against the defenders. The surrounding waterfront park and trail is popular with locals for running and picnicking, and a stroll around the grounds gives a great view of Canton's working waterfront and the Francis Scott Key Bridge in the distance.

MAP 7: 2400 E. Fort Ave., Baltimore, 410/962-4290, www.nps.gov/fomc; daily 9am-6pm; $7 adult, children free

Mount Clare Mansion

It's hard to envision, but in the mid-18th century, much of Baltimore was still rolling countryside and woods. Many wealthy European settlers built grand summer homes far from the small downtown (which could get oppressively hot and smelly during summers). Charles Carroll, a prominent lawyer (but not the Charles Carroll who signed the Declaration of Independence), built Mount Clare at the center of Georgia, his 800-acre plantation west of the growing city of Baltimore. Completed in 1760, this grand colonial house would be home to Carroll and his wife, Margaret Tilghman Carroll; they hosted Martha Washington and the Marquis de Lafayette.

Today, Mount Clare is the city's oldest surviving house from this time period. Though much of it has been lost to the centuries, the central part of the home remains in amazingly undamaged condition. Paintings of Charles and Margaret by the famed artist Charles Wilson Peale hang in the vast living room, and the period furniture on display shows off some amazing craftsmanship. The Carrolls were one of early Maryland's most successful and prolific families, and about half of the period furniture in the house belonged either to Charles Carroll or a relative. The mansion occupies just over two acres in Carroll Park, which is now one of Baltimore's grittier neighborhoods, but don't let that keep you from visiting a truly remarkable piece of colonial Baltimore history.

MAP 7: 1500 Washington Blvd., Baltimore, 410/837-3262, www.mountclare.org; Thurs.-Sun. 11am-4pm, tours are on the hour; $6 adult, $4 child, $5 senior

National Great Blacks In Wax Museum

Opened in 1983, this amazing, unique, and powerful museum—built and guided by the vision of the late Dr. Elmer Martin and his wife, Dr. Joanne Martin—chronicles the indignities, tragedies, successes, and triumphs of Africans in the United States. It's also a very disturbing place if you're not ready for the incredibly graphic scenes of the slave trade (the Middle Passage) and violence against African Americans depicted in certain parts of the museum: Be warned, these are not for young children or those with delicate sensibilities. The majority of the museum charts the course of African Americans in the United States from their African heritage to the present day, using wax figures and mannequins to depict leaders, innovators, and common Americans throughout the centuries. The museum covers major events and movements in African American culture and history, as well as showing scenes from the lives of regular African Americans, from sharecroppers to a grim urban scene of crime and violence. One of the museum's most-cited exhibits explains the story of Henry "Box" Brown, who mailed himself to freedom in a packing crate sent from the slave state of Virginia to free Pennsylvania in 1848; his escape is re-created here.

This museum is a labor of love and duty to history, and is not the beneficiary of a huge endowment; the wax figures, displays, and scholarship are not slick nor seamless. But there's no other museum in the United States like this astonishing tribute and memorial to the struggles and achievements of African Americans, and though it's located far from the gleaming Inner Harbor, it's worth a visit for those who want to see how many African Americans view their role in American history.

MAP 7: 1601-03 E. North Ave., Baltimore, 410/563-3404, www.greatblacksinwax.org; Tues.-Sat. 9am-5pm, Sun. noon-5pm, slightly longer summer hours; $13 adult, $11 child, $12 senior

Restaurants

Downtown and Inner Harbor......70

Harbor East and Little Italy 75

Fell's Point........................85

Canton 92

Federal Hill 97

Mount Vernon and Station North..103

Hampden and Homewood.......112

Greater Baltimore.................119

HIGHLIGHTS

★ **Best Weekend Brunch:** It's a tie. If you're downtown, **Miss Shirley's Café** serves huge breakfasts with a Southern (and Baltimore) twist. If you're headed north, **Golden West Café** in Hampden takes great care in making every item on the varied menu, including Elvis pancakes with bacon, fried bananas, and peanut butter and the El Guapo sandwich made with chorizo or soy chorizo, jack cheese, and scrambled eggs (pages 70 and 118).

★ **Best Dressed-Up Crab Cake:** Named for the local Heavy Seas beer, **Heavy Seas Alehouse** also serves some amazing food, including a great crab cake with fried green tomatoes and bacon (page 75).

★ **Best Coffee:** One of three dining spaces to open in the Four Seasons Baltimore in Harbor East, **LAMILL Coffee** has spectacular coffee and the beautiful and delicious pastries to go with it (page 76).

★ **Best Scene: Pazo,** an immaculately designed and executed, vaguely Mediterranean-meets-the-Casbah-themed tapas restaurant and lounge has transformed an old machine shop in Fell's Point (page 83).

★ **Best Outdoor Dining:** Though it's not exactly waterfront, the large and cozy deck at **Bond Street Social,** complete with upright fireplaces and views of the people flocking to Fell's Point, is one of the best places to eat outdoors in the city (page 86).

★ **Best Crab House View:** Call ahead early to reserve a table on the west side of the outdoor crab deck at Canton's **Bo Brooks,** where you can look toward the Inner Harbor and watch the pleasure boats coming in for the night (page 95).

★ **Best Takeout:** Possibly the best curry in the city comes from tiny **Thai Arroy** in Federal Hill; order extra rice and save some of the sauce for an awesome early morning breakfast (page 99).

★ **Best Neighborhood Restaurant:** Basically the only restaurant in Bolton Hill, **b** also happens to be a charming place with a good selection of cheeses and seafood. Sit in the nice outdoor seating area to admire the neighborhood's stately homes (page 106).

★ **Best Late-Night Meal:** Located in prime spots for late-night revelers, **Joe Squared** satiates late evening (and early morning) cravings with gooey, flavorful slices of pizza (page 107).

★ **Best Restaurant Worth Searching For:** Located in an off-the-beaten-path location, **Woodberry Kitchen** has earned a coterie of feverishly loyal regulars who adore the locally sourced meals, prepared simply but with finesse (page 115).

PRICE KEY

$ Entrées less than $10

$$ Entrées $10–20

$$$ Entrées more than $20

Baltimore's culinary scene has really flourished in the past decade, and while the city may still reside in the not-quite-top tier of great American dining cities, it now stands much higher on that list than in years past. There are many smart, talented, and canny chefs doing great work in Baltimore, experimenting and reaching for new heights—while listening to the city's admittedly fickle dining public.

For too long, Baltimore's restaurants reflected the city's staid, traditional character a bit too well. Yet the city's dedication to the tried-and-true did have one delicious result: There are a plethora of diners and old-fashioned restaurants in Baltimore where you can sample some menu items that haven't changed in more than five decades. This is the city made famous by a movie called *Diner*, after all. There are a lot of great, unique, family-run places to grab a club sandwich or tuna melt (and you should always order fries, and get gravy on them if possible).

Alongside these beloved 24-hour joints and diners, gourmets today have a veritable cornucopia of new, intriguing restaurants from which to chose. Some are sleek new cathedrals to the modern art of food preparation and dining habits, while others are rehabbed row houses and old industrial buildings that reexamine classic meals. Several Baltimore restaurateurs and chefs have really hit their stride, and the hungry diners of Charm City have responded even more enthusiastically in recent years as a crop of restaurants serving creative, contemporary American cuisine have recently opened their doors across the city.

Still, if there's one food that defines the city of Baltimore, it's crabs. These crustaceans are the city's specialty, and though they once came from the bountiful Chesapeake Bay, most of the crab you'll eat in Baltimore is now imported from the Gulf of Mexico or Asia. There are a few restaurants in the city serving Maryland blue crab, and the Maryland Department of Natural Resources keeps track of those that do through its True Blue campaign (www.marylandseafood.org). As for the crab dishes themselves, if you want to get locals arguing, ask three strangers which restaurant has the best steamed crabs or the best crab cakes: Everyone has their own personal favorite, the more obscure the better. But you'll want to explore the city's menus on your own, eating your way to your own decision, because it's almost impossible to find a reputable restaurant in town that doesn't offer at least a decent crab cake.

Downtown and Inner Harbor

Map 1

AMERICAN

★ Miss Shirley's Café ⑤

This bustling eatery is a favorite breakfast spot of locals and tourists, primarily because of the stellar comfort food, often served with a Baltimore twist. There are dishes with crab, fried green tomatoes, and Old Bay, and some portions are more than generous, like the delicious and hard-to-finish French toast stuffed with cream cheese and flaked coconut. While it lacks a prime view, the spacious outdoor patio, which overlooks Pratt Street, is still a nice spot on sunny days. Late risers should note that waits can be quite long after 9:30am on the weekends. There are also locations in Roland Park and Annapolis.

MAP 1: 750 E. Pratt St., 410/528-5373, www.missshirleys.com; Mon.-Fri. 7am-3pm, Sat.-Sun. 7:30am-3:30pm

Werner's Restaurant ⑤

With booths, tables, decor (and, frankly, some of the staff) that hadn't changed in decades, Werner's Restaurant was a relic of old-school dining for Baltimore's denizens of City Hall (and Mayor Thomas Carcetti, the fictional character from the Baltimore-based HBO show *The Wire*) for 50 years before it abruptly closed its doors in 2011. But all was not lost: The restaurant reopened in 2012 under new management, and although the menu now features a few Greek specialties and a handful of wraps and paninis, old classics like hot turkey and roast beef are still around. You'll notice a lot of suits and

backslapping here during breakfast and lunch (no dinner is served), **71**
and the restaurant is still only open on weekdays.

MAP 1: 231 E. Redwood St., 443/842-7430; Mon.-Fri. 7am-3pm

ASIAN
Ban Thai $$

This unassuming Thai restaurant is a little gem in a part of town
that's dominated at night by empty office towers and a nearby Irish
pub. Walk up the long ramp to the dining room, past the portraits
of Thailand's royal family, and try to get a seat near the window
to watch people heading up Charles Street. The food here is quite
good (and can be ordered quite spicy), from the basics like pad thai
to crispy whole fish and soft-shell crabs. There are also a dozen entrées for vegetarians, though some contain fish sauces.

MAP 1: 340 N. Charles St., 410/727-7971, www.banthai.us; Mon.-Thurs.
11am-10:30pm, Fri.-Sat. 11am-11pm, Sun. noon-9:30pm

BREWPUB
Pratt Street Ale House $$

This alehouse is easy to spot: The brick building is trimmed in
bright blue and lined with wooden barrels along Hopkins Place
and Pratt Street. The main dining area and bar are filled with brick
archways and light wood; there are also several upstairs dining
areas, most with bars, and two outdoor spaces. The house-made
Oliver ales, 18 of which are on tap, are the main draw here, while
the menu offers burgers, sandwiches, and pizzas with many crab
options. Stop by for a pint on the third Thursday of each month
for the brewpub's Comedy Lab, a "raw" event held on the gray and
unadorned third floor that boasts a headlining act and six Open
Mic slots.

MAP 1: 206 W. Pratt St., 410/244-8900, www.prattstreetalehouse.com; daily
11am-11pm, bar open until 2am

CONTEMPORARY AMERICAN
B&O American Brasserie $$$

Once the headquarters of the B&O Railroad company, this restaurant, designed to evoke feelings of traveling on an upscale dining
car during the train's heyday in the early 1900s, embraces the structure's original beaux arts architecture. There is a grand wooden bar,
an open kitchen, leather chairs, and pops of cranberry and camel in
the decor downstairs; upstairs is filled with black leather banquettes
and golden lighting. Local critics have praised the restaurant's comfortable, if not daring, menu, which includes plenty of seafood options, as well as steak frites and brick oven pizzas. There are also
some creative cocktails here; try the Queen Bee made with vodka,
St. Germain elderberry liquor, yuzu, and honey syrup.

CRAB HOUSE

Phillips Seafood ❸❸❸

The Phillips name is synonymous with crabs in Maryland; from a
single crab house on the shore, the family has built what is today
a veritable mini-empire on the backs of the Chesapeake Bay's delicious crustaceans. Once housed in the Harborplace pavilions,
this restaurant has moved closer to the Power Plant Live! complex
and its 17-foot illuminated red sign is hard to miss. They also have
an outdoor deck with plentiful seating—an ideal spot for picking
steamed crabs. If you're a neophyte, the friendly servers will help
explain how to eat those crabs, but there are plenty of more conventional seafood (and a handful of meat and vegetarian) options
on the menu. This is a high-volume place designed to accommodate lots of tourists, so calling ahead for reservations is strongly
encouraged.

MAP 1: 601 E. Pratt St., 410/685-6600, www.phillipsseafood.com; Mon.-Thurs.
11am-10pm, Fri.-Sat. 11am-11pm, Sun. 11am-9pm

SEAFOOD

Faidley Seafood ❸❸

Don't expect fine silverware and tablecloths here; in fact, don't even
expect seats. Guests at Faidley Seafood on the west side of historic,
busy, and very ungentrified Lexington Market eat communally,
standing up at long wooden tables—surrounded by a winding line
of people waiting to order the city's famous crab cakes. Three styles
are available: Skip the cheapest option and decide between the mid-
range backfin (which consists of the less-prized meat of the blue
crab) and jumbo lump, the Cadillac of crab cakes. The cakes are
served fried and, when ordered as platters, adorned with a choice
of two sides like potato salad and coleslaw, as well as a two-pack of
crackers in a plastic wrapper, and served on red cafeteria trays. It's a
humble-looking meal, but once you taste the divinity of these mor-
sels, you'll understand the lines and the legend. The area around
Lexington Market is not one of the city's best, and visiting after
dark is not recommended.

MAP 1: Lexington Market, 203 N. Paca St., 410/727-4898,
www.faidleyscrabcakes.com; Mon.-Sat. 9am-5pm

Watertable ❸❸❸

On the fifth floor of the Renaissance Harborplace Hotel (a Marriott
operation), this sleek, smooth, modern restaurant offers some

Baltimore Farmer's Market & Bazaar

These days farmers' markets are hardly an anomaly, and yet **The Baltimore Farmer's Market & Bazaar** is still worthy of a visit. Here's why: Held on Sundays from April to December underneath the Jones Falls Expressway on Holliday and Saratoga Street, this beloved event has vendors who dole out some delicious prepared foods, so you can forgo a restaurant and have breakfast or lunch here. Those who want to avoid the throngs of people should hit the market before 10am (and even then, it's pretty crowded).

Once you're there, listen for shouts of "Best Fish on the Planet Earth!" That's the voice of Ollie Collier from **Konscious Kterers;** follow the sound until you see him, standing with freshly fried (and hot!) fish and a pair of tongs. Grab a sample, then join the line to feast on a simple but huge sandwich on white bread.

At the other end of the market, there's always a line at the literally named **Mushroom Stand,** and for good reason: Here, earthy mushrooms are perfectly paired with feta cheese and a squirt of bright red hot sauce. You can get them grilled or fried and on a salad or sandwich or with quinoa.

Now, for dessert look for **Dangerously Delicious Pies.** Owned by Rodney Henry, the runner-up on 2013's *The Next Food Network Star* who also has a store in Canton, the stand is stocked with some less-than-pretty but still delicious mini savory and sweet pies that are already wrapped up for you to take home.

RESTAURANTS DOWNTOWN AND INNER HARBOR

stunning nighttime views of the harbor and Federal Hill. The menu is very seafood-oriented with a few other options like short ribs, and has drawn solid, if uninspired, reviews; perhaps the fact that the clientele is predominantly tourists and businesspeople spending only a few days in town keeps the kitchen from pushing itself too hard. Having lunch here—for the view more than for the food—is probably your best option.

MAP 1: Renaissance Baltimore Harborplace Hotel, 202 E. Pratt St., 410/685-8439, www.watertablerestaurant.com; daily 6am-10pm

TURKISH

Cazbar ❶❸

The cuisine of Turkey—based heavily on Mediterranean ingredients like grape leaves, yogurt, seafood, and lamb—guides this fun, colorful restaurant, but there are plenty of other familiar items on the menu. Still, stick with the Turkish delights for the best the kitchen offers; their Mediterranean takes on pizzas are particularly interesting and very good. It's a great place for couples or small groups, particularly on Friday and Saturday nights, when reservations are recommended. That's because the belly dancers perform then, swirling through the dining room and making this well-designed space the most happening place on the block.

MAP 1: 316 N. Charles St., 410/528-1222, www.cazbar.pro; Mon.-Thurs. 11am-midnight, Fri.-Sat. 11am-2am, Sun. 4pm-midnight

Steamed Crabs 101

Gathering a group of friends, a few pitchers of beer, a couple dozen crabs, and sitting around pulling, smashing, and feasting on the steamed, seasoned critters is a nearly sacred Baltimore tradition, whether it's in a backyard or on a waterfront crab deck.

If you've never attempted to eat a steamed, hard-shell crab before, you're going to be pretty stumped about how to even start. The first hurdle you'll have to leap: What kind of crabs do you want? Mediums? Jumbos? Males? Females? And how many do you need?

Here are some good rules of thumb to use when ordering steamed crabs. Technically (and environmentally), it's better to order males only; the females need to be spared for future reproduction and harvests. For all the work you'll do cracking open a crab, there's not much meat, so figure on about four or five crabs per person. A crab's size determines the amount of meat and its cost. The price fluctuates with that week's harvest; at press time, a dozen large males went for about $38.

After you place your order, you'll be presented with a huge, hot heap of the crustacean critters, dumped in the center of a table wrapped in brown craft paper. You'll be issued a mallet and perhaps a knife, a roll of paper towels, and a stack of wet napkin packs. Now what?

Start with the claws (though some people save them for last, we'll start here). Tear them off and use the knife as a fulcrum to crack the shell open about one-quarter of the way down the claw, using the mallet to whack the knife and shatter the shell. Crack open the claw and get the meat out—you can eat everything in the claw.

Now comes the body. Flip the crab over and notice the "key," a long tab on the belly of the crab; the male's looks like the Washington Monument in DC, while the female's looks like the Capitol dome. Lift it up and use it to remove the top shell, exposing the interior of the crab. You'll notice some yellowish, fatty material on the sides and the crab's "lungs," more or less, which are also yellow. Do *not* eat anything yellow; scrape that stuff out! Crack open the shell some more, breaking the crab in half, and eat the white crabmeat.

Some of the best meat of the crab is the backfin meat; to get at it, notice the two small rear legs that have paddle-like flaps on them. The backfin meat is above those legs, in the crab's body.

Here are a few other tips from experienced eaters: Use plastic cups or cans for your beers (and drink beer or iced tea with crabs, please; chardonnay is preposterous). Don't accidentally wipe your eyes during crab eating; the spices and salts of the seasoning will hurt terribly. And don't wear a nice outfit or a bib (this ain't lobster) when eating crabs. It's going to be a delicious, loud, wonderful mess.

Here's a little secret: These days, the crabs you'll eat in Baltimore are almost definitely not from the Chesapeake Bay at all, but rather from the Gulf of Mexico or even farther afield. The bay's crab population is too low for major harvests right now; rejuvenation efforts continue to make small strides, but there's still plenty of work to be done.

Harbor East and Little Italy

Map 2

AMERICAN

Gordon Biersch Brewery Restaurant $$

This brewery has all the elements expected of a bar/restaurant: energetic crowds, multiple TVs, minimal lighting. But, this being affluent Harbor East, there are homegrown touches too: the German-inspired beers are made in large copper vats housed in the restaurant's far corner; nearly all of the dressings and condiments, like the bacon jam on the burgers, are made in-house too. The menu here is typically American, but walk-ins are generally accommodated when other nearby restaurants may have waitlists. The restaurant's best feature is the large outdoor seating area with its somewhat-obstructed-but-still-pretty view of the many boats docked on the water across the street.

MAP 2: 1000 Lancaster St., 410/230-9501, www.gordonbiersch.com; Sun.-Thurs 11am-1am, Fri.-Sat. 11am-2am

★ Heavy Seas Alehouse $$

One of the many restaurants to make its home in a former industrial space—in this case, the Holland Tack Factory in Little Italy—this alehouse celebrates the local Heavy Seas beer. (Hugh Sisson, a Baltimore celebrity when it comes to beer and the onetime owner of Maryland's first brewpub, created the Heavy Seas line, though he doesn't own the alehouse.) The interior embraces the rough wooden walls and beams of its former owner, but still manages to feel warm and polished. There is also a lovely enclosed beer garden out back with pots of vibrant green hops and glazed chess and checker boards mounted on barrels. And the food just happens to be really good. The crab cakes served with fried green tomatoes and bacon are amazing, as are the meltingly soft short ribs.

MAP 2: 1300 Bank St., 410/522-0850, www.heavyseasalehouse.com; Mon.-Wed. 4pm-9:30pm, Thurs. 4pm-10pm, Fri.-Sat. noon-10pm, Sun. noon-9pm

ASIAN

Pabu $$$

From its bamboo ceilings to the shelves of sake casks to the Japanese-style artwork that graces the walls, this eatery leads guests to feel they are in for a tranquil experience. Influenced by Japanese izakayas—pubs that also serve food—the menu is built around sushi (there's a long sushi bar in the back) and small plates. This being a Four Seasons establishment, the dishes here often come with special occasion prices ($19 for a sushi roll with shrimp tempura, avocado, spicy tuna, and pine nuts), but the space doesn't feel stuffy; the harmonious hum of patrons chatting amiably gives the dining rooms an energetic vibe. The most surprising aspect of this restaurant is the sheer number of sakes it has amassed: Tiffany Dawn Soto, beverage director and sake sommelier, has curated a list of more than 100 of them.

MAP 2: 725 Aliceanna St., 410/223-1460, www.pabuizakaya.com; Tues.-Thurs. 6pm-10pm, Fri.-Sat. 5:30pm-10:30pm

CAFÉS

★ LAMILL Coffee ⑤

LAMILL Coffee is the kind of place where you actually want to stay for a while, lingering over the European-inspired desserts and the excellent single-origin coffees, cappuccinos, lattes, and teas. This is an open and airy space with some fun decor choices, like the multicolored Edgar Allan Poe prints over the coffee bar and the red squiggle chandeliers bursting with lightbulbs; there is also outdoor seating during warm months. The fried beignets with a choice of dipping sauces and the Everything Cookie are not to be missed. *House of Cards* fans, take note: This is also the place where Robin Wright's character gets her coffee after her morning runs.

MAP 2: 200 International Dr., 410/576-5800; daily 7am-5pm

CLASSIC ITALIAN

Amicci's ⑤⑤

Many Little Italy restaurants have a signature dish: Amicci's features *pane rotundo,* a round, flat loaf of Italian bread that's been hollowed out and filled with garlic butter and scampi sauce, and then topped with enormous shrimp. Despite the daunting challenge presented by this and the other entrées here, this is perhaps the only restaurant in Little Italy where you can get a quick dinner and be on your way in 30 minutes. It's a casual, friendly eatery, decorated with large-size Italian film posters (of both Hollywood and Italian origin) and, in the front dining room, an at-home feel; Amicci's is perfect for those who don't have time for a two-hour, multicourse production.

MAP 2: 231 S. High St., 410/528-1096, www.amiccis.com; restaurant Sun.-Thurs. 11am-10pm, Fri.-Sat. 11am-11pm, bar daily 11am-midnight

Da Mimmo ⑤⑤⑤

Named for Domenico "Mimmo" Cricchio Sr., the late founder of this Little Italy landmark, this is a restaurant for those who eschew the subtle. The exterior is festooned with awnings, faux stones, and paint; the interior boasts plush red chairs, large paintings, and gilded everything. The signature dish here is the veal chop alla

Fiorentina, and it shares the decor's extravagance: a nearly three-inch thick slab of veal. Movie and stage stars have dined here in years past, which is fitting—as dining at Da Mimmo is an event unto itself.

MAP 2: 217 S. High St., 410/727-6876, www.damimmo.com; Sun.-Thurs. 11:30am-10pm, Fri.-Sat. 11:30am-midnight

Sabatino's $$
There's a charming, homey feel at this legendary restaurant that keeps diners returning for decades and decades. Things are done simply at "Sab's," from the basic house-made pasta dishes to the monstrous *brasciloe,* beef filled with veal, prosciutto, egg, and cheese, then topped with marinara. The experienced waitstaff here has seen it all (there's a brisk post-bar-closing weekend business here during the busy season, since it's one of the few places to serve late dinner), so they're happy to deal with pleasant inquiries and give recommendations. They can also handle anything from a couple to a large group with just a little advance notice.

MAP 2: 901 Fawn St., 410/727-9414, www.sabatinos.com; Sun.-Thurs. 11:30am-midnight, Fri.-Sat. 11:30am-3am

CONTEMPORARY AND NEW AMERICAN
Charleston $$$
Owners and operators of five top-notch establishments, chef Cindy Wolf and her husband Tony Foreman are, in many ways, the ultimate restaurateurs in Baltimore. Chef Wolf is a two-time finalist for the James Beard Foundation's regional award, and Charleston is her culinary flagship—and one of the city's top restaurants. It's a beautifully designed, completely unrestrained palace of fine American cooking, guided by the principles of the southern United States' "low country," which includes this establishment's namesake city in South Carolina. Low country-inspired dishes here (available in three- to six-course tasting menus) include pan-seared foie gras, grilled veal sweetbreads, and shrimp, andouille sausage, and grits unlike any you've ever tasted.

MAP 2: 1000 Lancaster St., 410/332-7373, www.charlestonrestaurant.com; Mon.-Sat. 5:30pm-10pm

Fleet Street Kitchen $$$
Many restaurants these days get a handful of their ingredients from herb or rooftop gardens, but this one actually has its own farm, Cunningham Farms in the nearby suburb of Cockeysville, which supplies much of the kitchen's herbs, vegetables, and greens. Part of the Bagby Restaurant Group—three side-by-side but distinctive restaurants located in a space that was once a furniture business—this restaurant serves dishes like a 30-day, dry-aged rib eye with

homemade sauerkraut in two dining rooms where fancy elements (white tablecloths, crystal chandeliers) mingle with more down-to-earth details like worn wood floors and plaid-covered booths. Be sure to stop by the brick bar to look at the reclaimed foot rails, made from the city's old trolley tracks.

MAP 2: 1012 Fleet St., 410/244-5830, www.fleetstreetkitchen.com; Mon.-Thurs. 5pm-10pm, Fri.-Sat. 5pm-11pm, Sun. 5pm-9pm

Germano's PIATTINI ⑤⑤⑤
Following the closing of three long-running restaurants in Little Italy, the classic Germano's Trattoria reinvented itself as the more modern Germano's PIATTINI in late 2013. Its menu now centers on *piattinis*, or small plates, along with a selection of pizzas, cured meats, cheeses, olives, and several vegetarian and vegan options. The restaurant has also shed its more serious ambiance in favor of casual dining spaces where after-work crowds can sip a craft beer while sharing *carciofi fritti* (prosecco-battered, long-stem artichokes) or *polpetti di kobe* (kobe meatballs). One thing hasn't changed though: The regular upstairs cabaret performances are still going strong. Check the website for a schedule of upcoming performances.

MAP 2: 300 S. High St., 410/752-4515, www.germanospiattini.com; daily 11:30am-11pm

Ten Ten ⑤⑤⑤
Of the three restaurants housed in the postindustrial Bagby Building in Harbor East, this quiet bistro, tucked behind the Bagby Pizza Co.—and the busy traffic of Fleet Street—feels the most romantic. Couples will enjoy the white leather seating, dim lights, and mellow music, which mixes with the brick walls and wood floors common in all of the Bagby Restaurant Group's restaurants. As expected, bistro food (steak frites, lamb ragout) is popular, as are dishes that offer contemporary American twists on classics (shrimp and grits with pork belly). The lunch crowd is a bit different, more professionals than groups of friends or starry-eyed lovers.

MAP 2: 1010 Fleet St., 410/244-6867, www.bagbys1010.com; lunch Mon.-Fri. 11am-4pm, dinner Mon.-Thurs. 5pm-10pm, Fri.-Sat. 5pm-11pm, brunch Sun. 11am-3pm

Wit & Wisdom ⑤⑤⑤
This warm tavern immediately stands out for its variety of seating options: you can relax at the large oval bar bathed in fiery orange light, on several leather chairs and couches (some in front of working fireplaces), or at traditional tables in a separate section of the restaurant. The crab cakes and octopus, as well as dishes with bone marrow, are popular, and the restaurant has also been

recognized for its desserts. The drinks are inventive and precise, at least in the case of martinis, which are stirred a nearly exact 75 to 80 times. In warmer months, the outdoor bar with nice harbor views is an energetic place to be. This is also the restaurant where Francis Underwood, Kevin Spacey's *House of Cards* character, power lunches with colleagues.

MAP 2: 200 International Dr., 410/576-5800, www.witandwisdombaltimore. com; breakfast Mon.-Fri. 7am-10:30am, Sat.-Sun. 7am-1pm, lunch Mon.-Sun. 11:30am-2:30pm, dinner Sun.-Thurs. 6pm-10pm, Fri.-Sat. 5:30pm-10:30pm

CONTEMPORARY ITALIAN
Aldo's ❸❸❸

It may look like a grand row house on the outside, but the inside of this upscale Little Italy restaurant is pure Italian piazza, with lots of natural light, marble, and open space. This is a special occasion restaurant, with all of the superlative service, fantastic wine selection, and rich, immaculately prepared food (like the tournedos Rossini) that such an excursion entails (and with a bill to match). There's also a great bar here, which provides a great reason to arrive a little early and admire the handmade cabinetry and woodwork of the place (it was built by the restaurant's owner, namesake, and executive chef, Aldo Vitale).

MAP 2: 306 S. High St., 410/727-0700, www.aldositaly.com; Mon.-Thurs. 5pm-10pm, Sat. 5pm-11pm, Sun. 5pm-9pm

Chazz: A Bronx Original ❸❸

The Vitale family, owners of the immaculate Aldo's in Little Italy, teamed up with actor Chazz Palminteri (*The Usual Suspects, A Bronx Tale*) to open this Harbor East eatery whose cuisine is inspired by the dishes served up on New York's Arthur Avenue. Both simple (clean lines, open spaces) and traditionally Italian (reds, whites, and blacks throughout), the restaurant specializes in hearty Italian American fare that has been well-received by local critics. Those who like to peek inside kitchens might enjoy sitting at the half oval bar counter that encases the white brick, faster-than-a-microwave, coal-fired oven—the Italian version of the sushi bar—where pizza pies are cooked for 90 seconds at 900 degrees.

MAP 2: 1415 Aliceanna St., 410/522-5511, www.chazzbronxoriginal.com; Sun.-Tues. 4pm-10pm, Wed.-Thurs. 4pm-11pm, Fri.-Sat. 4pm-midnight

Cinghiale ❸❸❸

Though it's built in the ground floor of a new condo and apartment building, Cinghiale could be an 80-year-old Italian restaurant, lifted right out of its beloved little town and placed gently just a few dozen feet from the Baltimore waterfront. There are two separate and beautiful dining rooms here; one is a less-formal, bistro-like *enoteca,* designed for casual diners who want small plates while they explore the immense wine collection. The more serious, mahogany and leather osteria is where the kitchen and menu aim for new heights (such as magret of duck with fennel, and veal tenderloin).

MAP 2: 822 Lancaster St., 410/547-8282, www.cgeno.com; Mon.-Thurs. 5:30pm-10pm, Fri.-Sat. 5:30pm-11pm, Sun. 5pm-9pm

La Scala $$$

The only Little Italy restaurant that boasts an indoor bocce ball court (with disco ball), this local favorite has a lively interior that is an open, airy mix of levels, stairways, exposed brick, subdued yellows, and warm woods. The real star here, though, is the food: Though the menu adheres to the basics you'll find at other restaurants, the quality of the kitchen here helps lift the fettuccine and spaghetti to delicious heights (simple ingredients used well seem to be the secret). Weekly specials let the chefs really show their mettle, though they can be very pricey. Make sure to save room (and money) for some cannoli, which are outstanding as well.

MAP 2: 1012 Eastern Ave., 410/783-9209, www.lascaladining.com; Mon.-Thurs. 4:30pm-10pm, Fri.-Sat. 4:30pm-11pm, Sun. 2pm-10pm

La Tavola $$$

This is one of the newest Italian restaurants in Little Italy, which means it's only about fifteen years old. The casual modern decor (lots of warm contemporary earth tones and matching furniture) is punctuated with tributes to classic Italy (check out the re-creations of vintage Italian ads on the walls), much like the menu. While many places offer a standard review of Italian American favorites, La Tavola has its own classics: Think linguine with truffles, taleggio cheese, and pioppini mushrooms, or black spaghetti tossed with Maryland crabmeat. This is a great place to go to sample modern takes on Italian food, though the basics are also available in fine form here.

MAP 2: 248 Albemarle St., 410/685-1859, www.la-tavola.com; lunch Mon.-Sat. 11:30am-3:30pm, dinner Mon.-Thurs. 4:30pm-10pm, Fri.-Sat. 4:30pm-10:30pm, Sun. 11:30am-9:30pm

DELI

Attman's $

Downtown's once-vibrant delicatessen culture has, alas, faded into distant, smoked and pickled memory. A few stalwarts survive; king of the bunch is Attman's, a modest deli and always-crowded, well-worn dining area (the no-frills Kibbitz Room). There's a panoply of meats, cheeses, side dishes, and breads to choose from. Corned beef here is always on the money—and a sign helpfully reminds

you how to order it (on rye with mustard only). Or you can order a combo sandwich, from the sedate New Yorker to the wackier
Tongue Fu. Jars offering pickled and preserved items line the back
walls, and if you're overwhelmed by all the choices, you can always
order a kosher hot dog.

MAP 2: 1019 E. Lombard St., 410/563-2666, www.attmansdeli.com; Mon.-Sat.
8am-6:30pm, Sun. 8am-5pm

DESSERTS
Piedigrotta $

Carminantonio Iannaccone, the man credited with inventing tiramisu, owns this unassuming bakery in Little Italy. Iannaccone
came up with the idea for the famous dessert more than 40 years
ago in Treviso, Italy. Although some cookbooks give another chef
the credit, *The Washington Post*'s Jane Black once pointed out
that this recipe did not contain marsala; Iannaccone's always has.
Walk past the sandwich counter and the gelato cases—and the locals, many of whom are regulars here—to the freezer cases, where
Iannaccone and his wife, Bruna, sell plastic containers of this boozy
dessert in three hefty sizes. Let it thaw in your hotel room (Bruna
will instruct you as to how long) before relishing this piece of local
history.

MAP 2: 1300 Bank St., Ste. 140, 410/522-6900, www.piedigrottabakery.com;
Tues.-Sat. 7am-8pm, Sun. 7am-6pm

Vaccaro's $

Though many of the restaurants in Little Italy excel at traditional
Italian desserts, it's a tradition to take a short stroll from wherever you ate dinner to Baltimore's temple of tiramisu and its cathedral of cannoli: Vaccaro's. The decor is more ice-cream parlor
than romantic nightcap stop, but that's because of the volume they
do here, mostly in their two stalwart sweet treats. There are plenty
of other cake and sugary options as well. There's also a location on
O'Donnell Street in Canton Square.

MAP 2: 222 Albemarle St., 410/685-4905, www.vaccarospastry.com; Sun.-Thurs.
9am-10pm, Fri.-Sat. 9am-midnight

GREEK
Ouzo Bay $$$

Walking into this restaurant swathed in cobalt blues and bright
whites is a bit like stepping onto a Mediterranean cruise ship; those
who sit on the handful of white wicker couches in the large outdoor
seating area can look across Lancaster Street at the docked boats
and actually pretend they're in Greece. Whole fish, offered up by
the pound or piece and most of it wild-caught, is a favorite here;
before eating, you can view the glistening dining room display of

RESTAURANTS
HARBOR EAST AND LITTLE ITALY

the day's offerings. There's Greek food too (dolmades, moussaka, lamb), all of which are easier on the wallet. Despite some of the menu's prices, the mood here is fun and lighthearted, a nice spot for dates, groups, or even families.

MAP 2: 1000 Lancaster St., 443/708-5818, www.ouzobay.com; dinner Sun.-Thurs. 4pm-10pm, Fri.-Sat. 4pm-midnight, brunch Sat.-Sun. 11am-2:30pm

HAWAIIAN
Roy's ⑤⑤⑤

Although the food at this national Hawaiian restaurant chain is always fresh and spot on—well worth the hefty price tags that come with it—the real standout here is the daily "Aloha Hour" at the bar. Then, wine, beer, specialty cocktails like Hawaiian martinis, and smaller but still generous appetizers like wagyu beef sliders and lobster pot stickers are offered at happy hour prices. Cross your fingers that the bar fills up; then, staff often open a smaller dining room where you can essentially have a sit-down meal that is also wallet-friendly. Those who come for dinner will find some romantic details like golden lighting and white tablecloth-covered tables, but the restaurant is just as popular for families as couples and the well-spaced tables are often filled, creating a bustling atmosphere.

MAP 2: 720 B Aliceanna St., 410/659-0099, www.roysrestaurant.com; Mon.-Thurs. 5pm-10pm, Fri.-Sat. 5pm-10:30pm, Sun. 5pm-9pm

LEBANESE
Lebanese Taverna ⑤⑤

This Baltimore outpost of the Washington DC-based chain is a big, modern, hip dining space (and bustling bar) that is popular with both locals and visitors looking to try new cuisines. There are great views of the water from the open, sweeping dining room (which still retains a few key Middle Eastern touches), making it a great destination for both dates and business. Start with hommos or *kibbeh* (little fried shells filled with meat), then try anything with lamb (the vegetarian kabob is quite good too). Wondering what to pair with *schawarma*? The hot tea here is delightful, as is the lemonade.

MAP 2: 719 S. President St., 410/244-5533, www.lebanesetaverna.com; Mon.-Thurs. 11:30am-10pm, Fri.-Sat. 11:30am-11pm, Sun. 11:30am-9pm

PIZZA
Bagby Pizza Co. ⑤

This pizza joint is the first in a trifecta of Baltimore restaurants founded by David Smith, CEO of the local Sinclair Broadcast Group, and housed in the Bagby Building, an old brick furniture factory that served the city for 12 decades. It also stands out among its slew of neighboring contemporary American restaurants because its one of the few places in Harbor East to get a quick meal.

Despite the kitchen's speed, the restaurant itself, with its ample natural light, warm landscape photographs on the walls, and bright green plants in the windows, is still a very nice place to eat pizza (the duck confit and pear pie is a popular choice). Those who can't find a table during the lunch rush can take a short walk to Lancaster Street and its many benches by the water if the weather is nice.

MAP 2: 1006 Fleet St., 410/605-0444, www.bagbypizza.com; Mon.-Wed. 11am-9pm, Thurs. 11am-9:30pm, Fri.-Sat. 11am-10pm, Sun. noon-8pm

TAPAS
★ Pazo ❸❸❸

Once a former machine shop, this upscale, beautifully renovated, industrial warehouse/Spanish tapas restaurant and lounge is one of the city's hottest places to both eat and drink and pose and be noticed. The city's well-dressed young turks come here to be seen while sipping wine from stemless glasses, noshing on ceviche or plates of cheese, and relaxing on circular couches beneath massive windows, iron chandeliers, and luxurious wall hangings. Less hedonistic city (and county) residents come to Pazo because of the food: There's a full menu of traditional Spanish-influenced entrées, best eaten at one of the upstairs tables across from the humming bar, giving foodies a fine perch from which to people-watch.

MAP 2: 1425 Aliceanna St., 410/534-7296, www.pazorestaurant.com; Mon.-Thurs. 5pm-10pm, Fri.-Sat. 5pm-11pm, Sun. 5pm-9pm, bar open until 1am

Talara ❸❸

Those looking for a party atmosphere would be wise to head to this lively South Beach-inspired tapas spot. From golden mustards to fiery reds to cooling turquoises, the interior is an explosion of color; this, combined with the upbeat music, makes it hard not to be in good spirits. The ceviche here is quite good, with six combinations to choose from, such as the popular fire and ice made with lime juice, jalapeños, habaneros, prickly pear granita, and your choice of seafood. On Monday, when there is little else going on, the restaurant hosts a happening salsa night with a free lesson, then dancing until midnight.

MAP 2: 615 S. President St., 410/528-9883, www.talarabaltimore.com; Mon.-Thurs. 4pm-11pm, Fri.-Sat. 4-midnight, Sun. 4pm-10pm

THAI
My Thai ❸❸

After its Mount Vernon location was destroyed by fire in 2010, this local favorite reopened a sleek, modern space in Little Italy's former Holland Tack Factory building, right next door to the Heavy Seas Alehouse. The staff are friendly here, and the space with its smooth blonde and chocolate floors and exposed beams feels organic and

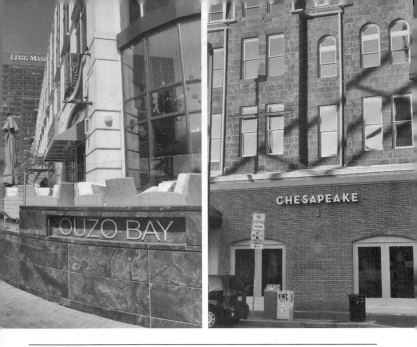

clockwise from top left: Ouzo Bay, Harbor East; The Chesapeake, Station North; Artifact Coffee, Hampden

inviting. One of the few Asian restaurants in the area, My Thai has the requisite curry and noodle dishes, as well as more adventurous choices made with brains and silkworm. There's also a 40-foot bar in front with a daily happy hour and interesting specialty cocktails that make use of Thai iced tea, lychee, and sugarcane.

MAP 2: 1300 Bank St., 410/327-0023, www.mythaibaltimore.com; Sun.-Thurs. 11:30am-10pm, Fri.-Sat. 11:30am-midnight

Fell's Point   Map 2

AMERICAN
Blue Moon Café $

This converted row house has nine tables—and a crowd waiting out front on most weekend mornings. The reason is that this bohemian, seat-of-the-pants operation makes some amazing breakfasts, from homemade biscuits to Cap'n Crunch French toast (featured on The Food Network's *Diners, Drive-Ins, and Dives*) and even Maryland crab eggs Benedict. Either arrive early in the morning (say, 7 or 8am), or very, very late: They are open 24 hours on weekends, the better to handle the area's nocturnal, booze-sodden hordes.

MAP 2: 1621 Aliceanna St., 410/522-3940, www.bluemoonbaltimore.com; Mon.-Thurs. 7am-3pm, Fri. 7am-midnight, Sat. all day, Sun. midnight-9pm

Captain James Landing $$$
It's not hard to find Captain James Landing; it's the huge white and blue building, shaped like a freighter, on the way from Fell's Point to Canton along Boston Street. What is hard is classifying it in a few words. First, it's a 24-hour carryout shop, with diner fare like cheesesteaks, sandwiches, and pizza—plus seafood and steak platters. In the nautically themed dining rooms of the ship-shaped main restaurant, food is served nearly all day long, with menus changing with each meal. Late-night dinner crowds can be a little intimidating, both in size and attitude. Then there's the crab house (more of a patio), across the street by the water, where the specialty, of course, is crabs (the menu explains how to pick them); there are also a few other seafood offerings like calamari and mussels.

MAP 2: 2127 Boston St., 410/327-8600, www.captainjameslanding.com; restaurant daily 7am-1am, crab house Mon.-Fri. 4pm-10pm, Sat.-Sun. noon-11pm, carryout daily 24 hours

ASIAN
Ding How $$
In a neighborhood packed with bars, taverns, and seafood restaurants that cater to tourists and weekend foot traffic, Ding How has

managed to remain a fixture in Fell's Point. Maybe it's because this always-busy restaurant turns out solidly good, reasonably priced Chinese food, year after year. Maybe it's the unadorned fish tank or the bamboo-backed chairs. Maybe it's that their more elaborate mixed and tropical drinks come with umbrellas in them. The only thing Baltimoreans—both Fell's Point diehards and suburban cocktail-seekers out for a night on the town—know for sure is that Ding How is a reliable place to get a lot of food and drinks and not break the bank.

MAP 2: 631 S. Broadway, 410/327-8888; Mon.-Thurs. 11am-10:30pm, Fri. 11am-11pm, Sat. 11:30am-11pm, Sun. 11:30am-10:30pm

CAFÉS
Bonaparte Breads $

The coolest thing about this airy bakery is what happens after hours. Around 1:30am, when bakers are kneading and baking for the next day, you can knock on Bonaparte's unmarked back door (look inside windows until you see the big mixer) and buy warm bread straight from the oven for a delicious and fresh post-bar snack. The warm, golden café is also a great place to savor a huge and buttery almond croissants or another pastry from the generously sized case while reading the newspaper or a book; French-inspired quiches, salads, and hot and cold sandwiches (croque monsieur, brie with walnuts) round out the lunch menu.

MAP 2: 903 S. Ann St., 410/342-4000, www.bonapartebreadsyolasite.com; daily 8am-6pm

Daily Grind $

Fell's Point's only coffeehouse is also one of the city's best, with two rooms of seating, well-made java, and a large variety of sandwiches and salads for lunch. You'll find a lot of locals here reading or working on computers, and the shop is a short walk from all of the area's hotels, making it a convenient place to stop for your morning joe before setting off on your travels.

MAP 2: 1720 Thames St., 410/558-0399, www.fellsgrind.com; daily 7am-8pm

CONTEMPORARY AND NEW AMERICAN
★ Bond Street Social $$

It's rare to find a restaurant as Jekyll and Hyde (in a good way) as this upscale hot spot, which manages to be both relaxed and a scene at the same time. The large outdoor patio with heaters and a prime view of a well-trimmed green space (a rare sight in Fell's Point) is a great spot for families, while the multiple fireplaces, golden lighting, and deep leather chairs inside draw a well-dressed, spirited crowd. The food offers modern twists on familiar favorites like chicken and biscuits and mac and cheese, always artfully presented and made for sharing. The bar is open until 2am, and the sangria and mojito "social drinks" served in 100-ounce jars are a fun choice for large parties.

MAP 2: 901 S. Bond St., 443/449-6234, www.bondstreetsocial.com; brunch Sat. 11am-3pm, Sun. 10am-3pm, dinner Sun.-Thurs. 4pm-10pm, Fri.-Sat. 4pm-11pm

Henninger's Tavern ❸❸

It's entirely possible to pass by the mild-mannered exterior of Henninger's a couple of times without noticing it, but make sure you don't give up trying to find it. Inside, there's a popular bar for locals and a charming dining room lined with old photos and older objets d'art. The variable menu takes some chances—such as maple and horseradish-glazed pork loin and Cornish hen with bread pudding—without ignoring the standards, like crab cakes and filet mignon. A trip to the restrooms reveals that the back of the restaurant seems like someone's house, which may help regulars feel even more at home.

MAP 2: 1812 Bank St., 410/342-2172, www.henningerstavern.com; Tues.-Sat. 5pm-midnight

Peter's Inn ❸❸

The short but comprehensive menu here changes weekly and is written on a chalkboard next to the tiny men's room; there's a huge swordfish mounted on the wall; and the music veers from old-school country to alternapop. Peter's Inn has been one of Baltimore's favorite restaurants for years because it pairs inventive cooking and fresh ingredients with an unpretentious, eclectic bar scene and a petite dining room (there's also outdoor seating). There are always steak, fish, and vegetarian-friendly options, and don't skip the legendary garlic bread. Weekend crowds and no reservations can mean a wait at the bar, but then again, it's a really great bar.

MAP 2: 504 S. Ann St., 410/675-7313, www.petersinn.com; Tues.-Thurs. 6:30pm-10pm, Fri.-Sat. 6:30pm-11pm

Pierpoint ❸❸❸

Chef Nancy Longo's open-kitchen Pierpoint restaurant, at the eastern outskirts of Fell's Point, has been a city favorite since 1989. She was one of the first in town to focus on using local ingredients, and still does today: Eastern Shore rabbit sausage and vegetables from nearby farms are a constant here, as are poultry, seafood, and an ample selection of vegetarian dishes (she also puts out a fine Sunday brunch). The restaurant's decor hasn't changed much since the 1990s, but it's a warm, modern look that has aged well. Longo is also known for her unique take on crab cakes: She smokes them, rather than broiling or frying. Note that although the restaurant closes at 9:30pm Tuesday through Thursday, the last seating is at 8:15pm

MAP 2: 1822 Aliceanna St., 410/675-2080, www.pierpointrestaurant.com; dinner Tues.-Thurs. 5pm-9:30pm, Fri.-Sat. 5:30pm-10:30pm, Sun. 4pm-9pm, brunch Sun. 10:30am-1:30pm

Salt ⑤⑤⑤

This modern bistro has become a neighborhood favorite that also draws diners from across the city. The owners spent some money on real interior design, and concocted a menu that has a bit of experimentation without being too daring. Stick with seafood here, like the coriander and pepper-crusted tuna, and don't skip the chance to try their famous Kobe beef and foie gras sliders and their perfectly crisped duck fat french fries. This is definitely a scene restaurant, and the staff can lean toward accommodating the innumerable regulars over first-timers, but not dauntingly so.

MAP 2: 2127 E. Pratt St., 410/276-5480, www.salttavern.com; Tues.-Sat. 5pm-close, Sun. 4:30-close

Waterfront Kitchen ⑤⑤⑤

Situated next to the Frederick Douglass-Isaac Myers Maritime Park— apart from the busy streets of Fell's Point proper—this relatively new restaurant has been praised for its outdoor dining area, which offers expansive views of the harbor and landmarks like the Domino Sugars sign (the views are pretty fabulous inside too). The dining room, designed in neutrals, feels classic, and the menu's seafood, poultry, and meat dishes served with creative accompaniments have drawn stellar reviews. In the summer and fall, there are also regular dinner cruises, which include a four-course meal at the restaurant.

MAP 2: 1417 Thames St., 443/681-5310, www.waterfrontkitchen.com; lunch Tues.-Sat. 11:30am-2:30pm, brunch Sun. 11am-3pm, dinner Tues.-Thurs. 5pm-10pm, Fri.-Sat. 5pm-11pm, Sun. 5pm-9pm

CREOLE

Louisiana ⑤⑤⑤

Though this luxurious restaurant bills itself as being French with a Creole flair, it's best to dine here with New Orleans in mind. The menu is undeniably French, but it's the Louisiana and Creole-inspired dishes that really stand out here. Simple beginning courses like blackened shrimp, collard greens, and grits lead the way to entrées like grilled pork tenderloin with roquefort bread pudding. The dining rooms are heavy on dark woods, thick fabrics, and quiet enjoyment—which is to say, the complete opposite of the Fell's Point bar scene just outside the massive door.

MAP 2: 1708 Aliceanna St., 410/327-2610, www.louisianasrestaurant.com; Tues.-Wed. 5pm-10pm, Thurs.-Sat. 5pm-11pm, Sun. 4pm-10pm

Pitango $

Frozen treats are a popular dessert choice in Fell's Point, and this tiny scoop shop serves up the best of the best. Containing less air than ice cream, the gelatos are made with fresh-squeezed juices and organic ingredients, the menu changes regularly with the seasons, and the dairy-free options are abundant. Mojito, chocolate noir, raspberry, and almond are popular flavors, but really you can't go wrong here. Although there are a few seats inside, taking your cup to the square across the street is a better option. On summer weekends, expect lines that go out the door, and strengthen your resolve knowing that this gelato is worth the wait.

MAP 2: 802 S. Broadway, 410/236-0741, www.pitangogelato.com; Sun.-Thurs. 11am-11pm, Fri.-Sat. 11am-midnight

DINERS

Jimmy's Restaurant $

Though you couldn't tell from the exterior, Jimmy's is a diner, serving breakfast all day and hot, gravy-laden dinners into the evening on weekends. Want a beer with breakfast? Not a problem here, though the waitress might eyeball you a little. This is a social hub for lifetime Fell's Pointers, as well as politicians, news anchors, tugboat crews, Hopkins medical staffers—you name it. The room is always alive with buzz, conversations, and action, whether it's romance or heated political debate. The food is genuine diner cuisine served up freshly made and at a bargain price; if you want to eat like a real local, ask for gravy on your french fries.

MAP 2: 801 S. Broadway, 410/327-3273; Mon.-Fri. 5am-4pm, Sat.-Sun. 5am-6pm

Sip & Bite Restaurant $

One of the landmark tiny diners of Baltimore's waterfront is the Sip & Bite, which has been dishing up American classics like grilled cheese sandwiches and no-frills burgers since 1948. As with most Baltimore diners (many of which are owned by Greek families), you can also get good salads, souvlaki, and gyros—plus a decent, cheap crab cake (featured on The Food Network's *Diners, Drive-Ins, and Dives*). This tiny eatery (there are tables and a lunch counter) bursts at the seams when the many nearby bars close at 2am and the hungry crowds realize they need greasy food; if you're planning on stopping in and don't want to face teeming hordes of properly inebriated folks, go early.

MAP 2: 2200 Boston St., 410/675-7077, www.sipandbite.com; daily 24 hours except Tues. closed 3pm-11pm

EASTERN EUROPEAN
Ze Mean Bean Café ⓢⓢ

Owing to Fell's Point's history as a haven for Polish immigrants, there are still a few places to get a great pierogi, and Ze Mean Bean is one of them. The best way to sample them is by ordering the pierogi dinner, which includes a trio—potato, sauerkraut, and sweet farmer's cheese—of this Polish staple. There are more than a few other Eastern European items on the menu too, including go-labki (cabbage rolls), chicken kiev, and goulash, all served in a cozy living-room-cum-dining-room, which features music on Friday and Saturday nights and during Sunday brunch. But the menu has plenty of surprises on it too, like smoked paprika short ribs and curried quinoa cakes with a coconut cream sauce.

MAP 2: 1739 Fleet St., 410/675-5999, www.zemeanbeancafe.com; Mon.-Thurs. 11am-11pm, Fri. 11am-midnight, Sat. 9am-midnight, Sun. 9am-11pm

ITALIAN
Brick Oven Pizza ⓢ

Whether it's for a quick lunch, a hearty dinner, or a couple of slices to soak up some beer, this eatery has been serving up extra-crispy pizzas (made in its wood-burning brick oven) for more than a decade. It's also one of the few places in Baltimore that serves pizza by the slice. A vast list of toppings lets diners concoct their own exotic pies (clams, pesto, and bacon!), but there are also pastas, salads, and wraps. The dining room is basic pizza shop utilitarian, but when it's bustling with customers, it's a great place to people-watch. Murals on the walls depict the neighborhood in a classic 1980s-style cartoon format, a reminder of the changes that lie outside the big windows.

MAP 2: 800 S. Broadway, 410/563-1600, www.boppizza.com; Sun.-Thurs. 11am-11pm, Fri.-Sat. 11am-3am

SEAFOOD
Bertha's ⓢⓢ

Perhaps best known for the "Eat Bertha's Mussels" bumper stickers seen all across America (and in abundance in the dark, welcoming bar itself), Bertha's is a great place to grab a beer and a pound of the aforementioned seafood and strike up a conversation with the quite possibly fascinating person seated at the next bar stool. Or you could eat in the dining room, choose something from the full menu, and take a quick tour of the bric-a-brac-filled old building. If you just want to hang out at the bar (open until 2am), the pub food here is great, there's live music most nights (generally blues), and there's always a good crowd in this tavern that many consider the heart of old Fell's Point.

MAP 2: 734 S. Broadway, 410/327-5795, www.berthas.com; Mon.-Thurs. 11:30am-10pm, Fri. 11:30am-11pm, Sat. 10:30am-11pm, Sun. 10:30am-10pm

clockwise from top left: Golden West Café, Hampden; LAMILL Coffee, Little Italy;
Heavy Seas Alehouse, Little Italy

The Black Olive $$$

One of the superlative moments when dining at the Black Olive comes when your waiter or waitress asks your table to please proceed to a marble display case near the kitchen in order to personally select the fish that will end up on your plate. It's an act that somehow engages the diner with the food in a more complete way, not that this Mediterranean-influenced restaurant needs it. Inside, the place feels like a small Greek eatery, albeit a very nice one (noncasual dress is recommended here). The fish is almost always spectacularly fresh, and what's on offer changes depending on what's the freshest at the market that week.

MAP 2: 814 S. Bond St., 410/276-7141, www.theblackolive.com; lunch Mon.-Fri. noon-2pm, dinner daily 5pm-10pm

Kali's Court $$$

Kali's Court is one of Fell's Point's truly exemplary seafood restaurants, and the kind of place where it's worth the risk to order something you've never had before. The posh, red-draped, wood-paneled dining room can seat a lot of diners, but the shape and layout keep it from seeming uninvitingly large. There's a strong Mediterranean hand guiding the kitchen here, and amazingly fresh whole fish and fillets alike are deftly executed. The owners of Kali's have two smaller restaurants nearby.

Next door is **Mezze** (1606 Thames St., 410/563-7600, www.kalis-mezze.com, Mon.-Fri. 4pm-close, Sat.-Sun. 11:30am-close), a contemporary-styled, two-story tapas eatery. At the foot of Broadway is **Tapas Adela** (814 S. Broadway, 410/534-6262, www.tapasadela.com, dinner Mon.-Wed. 4pm-10:30pm, Fri.-Sat. 3:30pm-midnight, Sun. 3:30pm-10:30pm, brunch Fri.-Sat. 11:30am-3pm), which serves Spanish tapas in a rich, warm setting.

MAP 2: 1606 Thames St., 410/276-4700, www.kaliscourt.com; daily 5pm-close

Canton

Map 3

AMERICAN

Annabel Lee Tavern $$

Only in Baltimore do you get a restaurant and bar with an Edgar Allan Poe theme. The walls here are purple and inscribed with the words of this tragic author (the bar is named for his last poem), and there is just the tiniest hint of the gothic here. But it's also a warm, fun place to grab a drink and eat at the bar, or head back to the small dining room and sample some of the bolder menu items, like seared duck breast with whiskey-braised apple sauce; order it with a side of duck fat fries.

MAP 3: 601 S. Clinton St., 410/522-2929, www.annabelleetavern.com; Mon.-Fri. 4pm-10pm, Sat. 4pm-11pm, Sun. 11am-10pm

Claddagh Pub $$

Many Canton taverns can get away with serving good pub grub and still pack in the customers every night. But Claddagh—while an immensely popular bar (open until 2am, and opening early for critical European soccer matches)—is also a genuine restaurant. You can tell someone in the kitchen cares about the food, even if it's just a burger or a Caesar salad; if you're in the mood for classic Baltimore food, try the Chicken Chesapeake—chicken breasts with jumbo lump crabmeat slathered in a creamy imperial sauce. There are a few good outdoor tables and a few good indoor seats right by the big windows overlooking O'Donnell Square (and lots of other perfectly nice tables, too).

MAP 3: 2918 O'Donnell St., 410/522-4220, www.claddaghbaltimore.com; Mon.-Fri. 11am-11pm, Sat.-Sun. 9am-11pm

CAFÉS
Firehouse Coffee Company $

Although there's a Starbucks a few blocks away, it's a much more charming experience to get your morning coffee at this café housed in a converted redbrick firehouse on the corner of popular O'Donnell Square. The food fulfills cravings for straightforward diner fare, like bacon, egg, and cheese sandwiches for breakfast, and shrimp salad and barbecued chicken sandwiches for lunch. Aside from the good coffee, locals come for the laid-back, inviting vibe; it's also fun to see decor that embraces the café's past: There's a firefighter mannequin sliding down a pole coming out of the ceiling, and black-and-white pictures of scenes from the Great Baltimore Fire of 1904 on the red walls.

MAP 3: 1030 S. Linwood St., 410/522-2199, www.firehousecoffeeeco.com; Mon.-Fri. 7:15am-5pm, Sat.-Sun. 8am-4pm

CONTEMPORARY AND NEW AMERICAN
Blue Hill Tavern $$$

Locals continually praise this Brewer's Hill restaurant's ambience: Accented in soothing ice blues and dark wood, the dining room feels inviting—a *Baltimore* magazine reviewer actually called this "one of Baltimore's most impressive dining spaces"—and there's a nice patio and a balcony, too, for those who prefer to have their meals outdoors. Most entrées are composed around seafood, chicken, and steak; appetizers like crispy escargot and grilled octopus are slightly more daring options. Save room for desserts like honey semifreddo with pistachio cake made by Bettina Clair, a pastry chef who has received a lot of local praise for her beautiful and delicious creations.

MAP 3: 938 S. Conkling St., 443/388-9363, www.bluehilltavern.com; lunch Mon.-Fri. 11:30am-2:30pm, dinner Mon.-Thurs. 5pm-10pm, Fri.-Sat. 5pm-11pm, Sun. 4pm-9pm

Fork & Wrench ❸❸❸

The owner of Fork & Wrench, a former set designer, took two years to transform the interior of a row home into a multistory restaurant space that celebrates the working classes of the early 20th century. The charcuterie and cheese plates are hallmarks of the menu; otherwise, offerings change with the seasons. There's also a vegetarian/vegan tasting menu, a welcome sight in a city with few upscale vegetarian offerings. But the big standout here is the restaurant's decor; after you order, wander around the space's four dining rooms and front bar area to look at the eclectic pieces like a card catalog, a chandelier made with Coca-Cola bottles, and a tobacco ad from the product's glory days.

MAP 3: 2322 Boston St., 443/759-9360, www.theforkandwrench.com; Mon.-Sat. 5pm-11pm, Sun. 10am-11pm

Jack's Bistro ❸❸❸

Nestled among row houses is this neighborhood bistro whose somewhat bland decor—rectangular tables with white cloths, a dull-looking tiled floor—hardly seems to matter after dining on the globally inspired and creative cuisine. Food adventurers will appreciate the appetizers, which include mac and cheese with dark chocolate and french fries with cheese curds and foie gras sauce. But even the more conventional entrées still have exciting twists (salmon with a cactus pear gastrique, sous vide Argentine steak, a coconut milk laksa curry with roasted chicken). There are a few weekly specials too, the best of which are the daily half-price bottles of wine.

MAP 3: 3123 Elliott St., 410/878-6542, www.jacksbistro.net; Wed.-Sat. 5pm-1am, Sun. 5pm-11pm

Langermann's ❸❸❸

Within the former Can Company building, this open restaurant is a great place to come if you have a craving for southern cuisine like roast chicken brined in sweet tea or catfish fingers. There's also standard American fare—salmon, mushroom ravioli—as well as gluten-free menus, a nice touch these days. The dining room is perfectly fine but not noteworthy, and there are a few tables outdoors that are popular on warm days. The Sunday brunch, which includes a fun side item buffet, is also a local favorite. There's another

location in **Federal Hill** (1542 Light St., 410/528-1200, Mon.-Thurs. **95**
4pm-10pm, Fri. 4pm-11pm, Sat. 10am-11pm, Sun. 10am-9pm) for
those staying across the city.

MAP 3: 2400 Boston St., 410/534-3287, www.langermanns.com; Mon.-Thurs.
11:30am-10pm, Fri. 11:30am-11pm, Sat. 10am-11pm, Sun. 10am-9pm

CRAB HOUSE
★ Bo Brooks ❺❺❺

Head for the once-operational lighthouse along Canton's water-front—home to yachts and condos—and don't wear your best shirt or blouse, because you're going to be working for your dinner. Crabs are available year-round at Bo Brooks, steamed and then seasoned with spices, then brought to your brown-paper-wrapped table, along with wooden mallets and knives and lots of napkins (there are other menu items to choose from as well). The great crabs and the stellar view mean this is one of the few restaurants in town that's popular with both locals and tourists, and it's hard to find an unhappy customer here. Reservations for one of the prime outdoor seats on the side of the restaurant are a must, especially during nice weather.

MAP 3: 2701 Boston St., 410/558-0202, www.bobrooks.com; Mon.-Thurs.
11:30am-9pm, Fri. 11:30am-10pm, Sat. 12:30pm-10pm, Sun. 12:30pm-8pm

DESSERTS
Dangerously Delicious Pies ❺

Fans of food TV will probably know Rodney Henry as the guitar-playing, "pie style" runner up on 2013's *Food Network Star*. But Baltimoreans just know him as the owner of this rockin' red-and-black pie shop in Canton. These are messy pies—filling breaking through the crust is common—but that's kind of the point: They're supposed to be edgy. For dinner, try a slice of steak pie with mushrooms, onions, and gruyère cheese, and for dessert, go for a fruit pie like strawberry rhubarb (à la mode, if you like). Order a frosty mug of milk, too, if that's your thing. And if it's after midnight and you're out at a bar on O'Donnell Square and craving pie, take heed: This shop is open late on weekends.

MAP 3: 2839 O'Donnell St., 410/522-7437, www.dangerouspiesbalt.com;
Sun.-Thurs. 7am-10pm, Fri.-Sat. 7am-2am

ITALIAN
Matthew's Pizzeria ❺❺

Sometimes, it's the humble little kitchens that make some of the most unforgettable, better-than-home cooking, and Matthew's Pizzeria is one of those places. Opened back in 1943 by Matthew Cacciolo, this pizza shop makes a very good and very classic pie, one best ordered with only a few choice toppings (the Crab Pie, with

RESTAURANTS CANTON

jumbo lump crabmeat, cheese, and caramelized onions, is a favorite of Baltimoreans) and eaten fresh out of the oven at one of the tables in the small, bright dining room. They also serve a variety of other Italian dishes, but it's the pizza that makes this place a city treasure.

MAP 3: 3131 Eastern Ave., 410/276-8755, www.matthewspizza.com; Mon.-Thurs. 11am-10pm, Fri.-Sat. 11am-11pm, Sun. noon-9pm

Tutti Gusti $$

Purveyors of probably the most New York City-like pizza in Canton, Tutti Gusti's owners celebrated their Italian (Neapolitan, specifically) roots by commissioning a huge pop-art mural of famous Italians on one interior wall. This place is a few blocks from the high-density O'Donnell Square area, so you're certain to bump into locals here; regulars know where to get a great pizza, saltimbocca, and cannoli, and the quattro stagione pizza (ham, red peppers, artichokes, and mushrooms) is a favorite.

MAP 3: 3102 Fait Ave., 410/534-4040, www.tuttigusti.net; Mon.-Thurs. 11am-10pm, Fri.-Sat. 11am-11pm, Sun. noon-10pm

MEXICAN

Nacho Mama's $$

Elvis was big in Baltimore—he embodied much of the city's Caucasian, southern, working-class sensibility—and The King lives on today at Nacho Mama's, out front (as a statue) and on the walls (in velvet). The food here is Mexican, served with a wink (chips and salsa arrive in old hubcaps, as do some of the margaritas) but also with a real eye toward balancing quality and quantity. Fajitas (from veggie to tenderloin) are popular, as are the enormous burritos, quesadillas, and enchiladas. There is also beer aplenty; to blend in, order a "Natty Boh," shorthand for National Bohemian, a once-locally-brewed cheap, cold brew that's still a big seller.

MAP 3: 2907 O'Donnell St., 410/675-0898, www.nachomamascanton.com; Sun.-Wed. 11am-midnight, Thurs.-Sat. 11am-12:30pm

SEAFOOD

Mama's on the Half Shell $$

Owned by the same proprietor as Nacho Mama's a couple of doors down, this more upscale (though not uptight) seafood restaurant is done up in New England-oyster house decor. There's nothing fake about the food here, though: the selection of oysters (available in preparations ranging from iced to oysters Rockefeller to stew) has quickly gained favor as the city's favorite. In fact, all the seafood here is exceptionally good, from crab cakes to shrimp to rockfish and salmon. Save room, though, for a slice of gooey, chocolate-oozing Derby pie. Despite two levels of seating and outdoor tables, this place is almost always packed (the raw bar serves until 1am and the bar is open until 2am), so plan accordingly.

MAP 3: 2901 O'Donnell St., 410/276-3160, www.mamasmd.com; Mon.-Thurs. 11am-11pm, Fri.-Sat. 11am-midnight, Sun. 9am-11pm

Federal Hill

Map 4

AMERICAN
Abbey Burger Bistro 💲💲

This burger joint hidden down a tiny alley off of bustling Cross Street—look for the yellow-and-blue crest—is also a sports bar (open until 2am) with multiple TVs, soccer banners hanging from the beams, and a laid-back crowd filling the high-top tables around the restaurant's two bars (there's also a small dining space for large parties). The real reason to come, though, is the varied burger menu. Most people create their burgers from a paper checklist, choosing their meat, type of bun, and cheese, as well as toppings from an extensive list with nearly 40 options. Want a kangaroo or bison burger with crab dip and a fried egg? Abbey can make that happen. Burger purists need not worry: Black Angus is always an option too.

MAP 4: 1041 Marshall St., 443/453-9698, www.abbeyburgerbistro.com; Mon. 5pm-midnight, Tues.-Sun. 11:30am-midnight

Hull Street Blues 💲💲

A local favorite long before the Locust Point neighborhood was awash in new condos and town houses, this big, well-aged restaurant (named for the street it's on and the 1980s TV show *Hill Street Blues*) is still a fixture in this part of town. An ample, hearty Sunday brunch buffet in particular draw crowds of Locust Point lifers and newcomers, so plan accordingly. At other times, you can stop by this inviting tavern and restaurant (it started as a saloon back in 1889) for lunch or dinner, from big sandwiches and burgers to steaks and seafood. Meals are best taken in the nautically themed Commodore Room, the adjoining formal dining area named for Commodore Isaac Hull, one of the heroes of the War of 1812.

MAP 4: 1222 Hull St., 410/727-7476, www.hullstreetblues.com; lunch Mon. 11am-10pm (light fare only), Tues.-Sat. 11am-5pm, dinner Tues-Thurs. 5pm-10pm, Fri.-Sat. 5pm-11pm, Sun. 4pm-9pm, brunch Sun. 10am-2pm

Spoons 💲

Located amongst Cross Street's bars and restaurants and bustling activity, this vibrant coffee shop with a carousel horse and rotating art on the walls is a welcome sight, particularly for coffee lovers

A Gathering of Food Trucks

Food trucks line up at the Gathering, which has quickly become a local favorite.

You can find Baltimore's food trucks by checking their social media accounts or just stumbling upon them in your travels. But the best way to try food from many trucks at once—and experience the great community spirit that is alive in Baltimore—is to attend the **Gathering** (www.thegathering-baltimore.com), a weekly food truck showcase held from March to November. The event sets up shop at some great locations, like West Shore Park in the Inner Harbor, the Baltimore Museum of Industry parking lot in Federal Hill, and The Castle in Keswick in Hampden and Homewood. There's always live music and a play area for kids, making this an event well-attended by both young professionals and families.

Some of the most popular trucks are the **Gypsy Queen Café,** whose specialty is a foil-wrapped waffle cone stuffed with french fries and topped with a crab cake, and **El Cuervo,** a taco truck that doles out amazing carnitas, smoked brisket, and tempura avocado varieties. Also try the **Komme Pig** for pulled pork and **Kooper's Chowhound** for burgers. There are usually trucks selling ice cream and cupcakes, too.

staying in Federal Hill. (There's also a beer, wine, and cocktail list.) The café serves great pancakes for breakfast along with a large list of omelettes and benedicts. For lunch, try the hearty skillets, a satisfying meal particularly on cold days; there's also the usual sandwiches, salads, and burgers.

MAP 4: 24 E. Cross St., 410/539-8395, www.spoonsbaltimore.com; Mon.-Sat. 7am-3pm, Sun. 7:30am-3pm

ASIAN

Matsuri ❸

Matsuri has one of the best locations in Federal Hill. Sushi here is very fresh and cut generously, and it's one of the city's best sushi bargains (which are generally two words you don't want to see together). They're imaginative here: Take their spicy tuna and avocado roll, deep-fried then topped with jumbo lump crabmeat. Other Japanese dishes, such as the lightly done tempura, are also prepared well. The spacious second floor, replete with origami cranes, has a much less hectic vibe than the bustling first floor and outdoor patio seats.

MAP 4: 1105 S. Charles St., 410/752-8561, www.matsuri.us; lunch Mon.-Fri. 11:30am-2:30pm, dinner Mon.-Thurs. 4:30pm-10pm, Fri. 4:30pm-11pm, Sat. noon-11pm, Sun. 4pm-10pm

★ Thai Arroy ❸❸

With its yellow awning and simple black metal tables out front, Thai Arroy doesn't look like much from the outside. But, in a tightly packed dining room surrounded by golden Buddhas and wallpaper murals, the kind staff happen to serve some of the best Thai food in the city. The curry here is fantastic; deeply flavored and spicy, it comes with your choice of vegetables and meats. The mock seitan "duck" is particularly satisfying, making the restaurant a good option for vegetarians. The restaurant can get crowded on weekends, so eat early or late to avoid the rush.

MAP 4: 1019 Light St., 410/385-8587, www.thaiarroy.com; lunch Tues.-Fri. 11:30am-3pm, dinner Tues.-Thurs. and Sun. 5pm-10pm, Fri. 5pm-11pm, Sat. noon-11pm

CONTEMPORARY AND NEW AMERICAN

Bluegrass Tavern ❸❸❸

A good five blocks from Federal Hill proper, Bluegrass Tavern is worth a short walk off the beaten path. A new chef recently came onboard, and he's added some classic lowbrow dishes with exotic twists to the menu, usually in the meats category. (Think rabbit and kidney corn dogs.) Entrées are more traditional seafood and steak plates, and the smoked fried chicken is very good. Bourbon drinkers will appreciate Bluegrass Tavern's extensive list of about 25 varieties. The outdoor patio is a nice spot to eat, even though it doesn't offer much in the way of people-watching or views.

MAP 4: 1500 S. Hanover St., 410/244-5101, www.bluegrasstavern.com; Mon.-Wed. 5pm-10pm, Thurs. 4pm-10pm, Fri. 4pm-11pm, Sat. 11am-11pm, Sun. 10am-9pm

Mr. Rain's Fun House ❸❸❸

Despite its name and its location on the third floor of the sometimes quirky American Visionary Art Museum, this restaurant is actually quite a sophisticated place. Sure, the chairs are covered in zebra print, the bar is overhung with long strands of glittering mirrors, and a few tables face a display case of Pez dispensers, but it never feels like too much. The outdoor seating area that overlooks Federal Hill (and the AVAM's giant whirligig) is a particularly lovely spot to enjoy the restaurant's simple chicken, seafood, and suckling pig dishes. Don't miss the craft cocktails, part of the city's latest culinary trend.

MAP 4: 800 Key Hwy., 443/524-7379, www.mrrainsfunhouse.com; lunch Tues.-Fri. 11:30am-3pm, dinner Wed.-Thurs. and Sun. 5:30pm-9pm, Fri.-Sat. 5:30pm-10pm, brunch Sat.-Sun. 11am-4pm

Regi's $$

This often-hopping bistro has been popular since before Federal Hill became one of the city's thriving next-generation neighborhoods, and part of the reason has been the consistently satisfying food. Mundane items like tater tots (a minor sensation in Baltimore) take on a new life when covered with brie and bacon—as do meatballs made with veal, provolone, and marinara. (There are also plenty of lighter entrées here.) The dining room is very cozy, but the outdoor seating right on busy Light Street is where the real social scene can be found (especially at Sunday brunch).

MAP 4: 1002 Light St., 410/539-7344, www.regisamericanbistro.com; lunch Mon.-Fri. 11am-4:30pm, dinner Sun.-Thurs. 5pm-10pm, Fri.-Sat. 5pm-11pm, brunch Sat.-Sun. 9:30am-3pm

SoBo Café $$

Taken over in 2012 by a former information technology specialist turned restaurant owner, SoBo (short for South Baltimore) Café offers great food in a space that manages to feel both vibrant and soothing with its red and orange walls, low music, and relaxed guests. This neighborhood spot is known for comfort food, particularly its chicken potpies and roasted half chicken entrées; there's also scallops, peach barbecued ribs, and steaks. Families with children, as well as diners who want a quieter atmosphere, will feel at home here, and there's always a good selection of works by local artists hanging on the walls to admire.

MAP 4: 6 W. Cross St., 410/752-1518, www.sobocafe.net; lunch Mon.-Fri. 11:30am-2:30pm, dinner Mon.-Sat. 5pm-10pm, Sun. 5pm-9pm, brunch Sat.-Sun. 10:30am-3pm

The Wine Market $$$

Situated in a renovated old foundry complex on Fort Avenue, this popular, modern restaurant (with exposed brick, bright corrugated air pipes) is the kind of place that wouldn't have flourished without Baltimore's somewhat recent influx of young urban professionals, particularly into the surrounding neighborhoods. You'll find a generally youthful crowd here that's as interested in hanging out as it is in the food, and a few foodie diehards who are all about the kitchen's creations (and the massive wine selection). There are a lot of lighter seafood entrées here worth trying, or you can create

Best Outdoor Dining

Not all of the best outdoor dining in Baltimore is at the Inner Harbor (though the views there are pretty darn great). There's also plenty of people-watching to be done around town in some of the city's historic neighborhoods.

At the Inner Harbor, those looking for the quintessential Baltimore experience should book an outdoor table at **Phillips Seafood** and get a couple dozen crabs, which should be devoured while watching the nighttime crowds who fill the streets in the summer.

In Fell's Point, you can get a great outdoor table at **Bond Street Social,** whose large patio with stand-up fireplaces has views of the rowdy crowds that roll into the neighborhood like the evening tide on warm weekend nights. Or head to the deck at the **The Waterfront Kitchen** for beautiful and unobstructed water views and a more appropriate romantic dinner atmosphere.

Federal Hill has only a few options, but they're quite good. First is **Regi's,** a longtime fixture on Light Street that serves classic American dishes. On the water, the Baltimore location of the **Rusty Scupper** chain doesn't have the city's most inventive menu, but the view (especially for brunch) is probably the best in the city. Almost-waterfront **Little Havana** is a loud, raucous bar and club where you can sip marvelous mojitos in the glow of the Domino Sugars sign, and south of Federal Hill proper is **Nick's Fish House,** a hard-to-find little water-front bar and restaurant that overlooks an inlet of the Patapsco (think Tampa, more than Miami).

There are some other outdoor dining gems in Baltimore, scattered across town. In Mount Vernon, **Marie Louise Bistro** gives its diners a look at Charles Street's bustle through the neighborhood, while **Sascha's 527 Café** offers a great view of the Walters and the Washington Monument. In the small Station North Arts District, and right next to the Charles movie theater, **Tapas Teatro** may not have a waterfront view, but it's a thriving, bustling scene for dinner and drinks (and great small plates). In Hampden and Homewood, **The Ambassador Dining Room** has a magnificent backyard lawn/dining area that offers seclusion among the neighboring apartment towers. At the Baltimore Museum of Art, the modern, tented patio at **Gertrude's** overlooks the museum's sculpture garden. And the lauded **Woodberry Kitchen** offers dining among the repurposed and restored mills and buildings of Woodberry's Clipper Mill complex of dwellings and stores.

a meal from small plates. Brunch here is a popular, well-booked event, particularly on nice days, when the outdoor patio is packed with happy eaters.

MAP 4: 921 E. Fort Ave., 410/244-6166, www.winemarketbistro.com; lunch Tues.-Fri. 11:30am-4pm, dinner Mon.-Thurs. 5pm-10pm, Fri.-Sat. 5pm-11pm, brunch Sun. 11am-4pm

CRAB HOUSE
L.P. Steamers 🟢🟢

This is a tavern that's devoted to making great, basic seafood, most notably steamed crabs. Thus, it can be counted a crab house (particularly since there's a rooftop crab deck), though it's unlike the others in town. All the seafood here is good, from crab soup to steamed shrimp to fried clams (just stick with the basics and you'll be thrilled). And even though gentrification has swept through this part of town, L.P. Steamer's remains a genuine, working-class-and-proud-of-it Baltimore joint, where locals go for a few beers and a dozen delicious crabs.

MAP 4: 1100 E. Fort Ave., 410/576-9294; daily 11:30am-10pm

DESSERTS
Afters Café $

This neighborhood make-your-own yogurt shop—complete with the requisite selection (albeit small) of rotating flavors, including at least one dairy-free option, and massive toppings bar—is notable because of the extras it offers: coffee well into the late-night hours and a small pastry case with precise and pretty desserts and good macarons. This is a local hangout with friendly staff, and it's close to the neighborhood's many bars, making it a good place to stop after a weekend night out (though be aware that the café closes at midnight).

MAP 4: 1001 S. Charles St., 410/752-8561, www.afterscafe.net; Mon.-Thurs. 7am-10pm, Fri. 7am-midnight, Sat. 11am-midnight, Sun. 11am-10pm

MEXICAN
Blue Agave $$

This is a pretty serious Mexican restaurant, where seafood, chicken, *cotija* cheese, and handmade moles rule; even better, it's also a serious tequileria, with about 100 tequilas on hand, including the mighty 1800 Reposado, which goes for about $35 a shot. The long, tiled bar dishes out libations until 2am. It's easy to focus on the delicious margaritas and tequilas here, but the exposed-brick and wood dining room is inviting, and the food here is worth paying some attention to as well; the small plates and basics are stronger here than some of the more grandiose entrées, and you shouldn't miss the in-house flan and *tres leches* cake for dessert.

MAP 4: 1032 Light St., 410/576-3938, www.blueagaverestaurant.com; daily 11am-1am

SEAFOOD
Nick's Oyster Bar $$

Located in the renovated west end of the historic Cross Street Market, this staple of Federal Hill living (and dining) has been serving up huge piles of mussels, steamed shrimp, fish and chips, and more for decades. Pull up one of the many stools and eat your catch at the counter (don't forget to order a big beer, served in a plastic cup). There's a fully stocked raw bar, as well as a sushi bar. Take in the loud, sometimes-raucous small crowd that gathers at

Nick's operation, watch sports on one of the many TVs, or just dig in to a big plate of deliciously spicy shrimp.

MAP 4: Cross Street Market, 1065 S. Charles St., 410/685-2020, www.nicksoysterbar.com; Sun.-Thurs. 11am-7pm, Fri. 11am-10pm, Sat. 11am-9pm

Rusty Scupper $$$

At the base of Federal Hill rises this longtime Inner Harbor eatery, which was one of the first big restaurants to take advantage of the great views of the then-new Harborplace gained from the south side of the harbor. The view is still the main reason to come to this big, corporate operation, though the (expensive) food can be surprisingly well-handled, and the Sunday brunches are a favorite of many locals. The best views are from the upper patio deck, so pass through the nautically themed main dining rooms and head for the stairs. There's live music most weekends (generally piano), and this is a lively, bustling place, so don't plan on a quiet, sedate evening here.

MAP 4: 402 Key Hwy., 410/727-3678, www.selectrestaurants.com/rusty; lunch Mon-Fri. 11:30am-4pm, Sat. 11:30am-3pm, dinner Mon.-Thurs. 4pm-9pm, Fri. 4pm-11pm, Sat. 3pm-11pm, Sun. 3pm-9pm, brunch Sun. 10:45am-2pm

Ryleigh's Oyster $$

This is one of the two best places to get seafood like oysters and steamed shrimp in Federal Hill (the other is Nick's Oyster Bar, in the Cross Street Market). Unlike the no-frills Nick's, Ryleigh's is a real restaurant, so in addition to their popular, blue-slate oyster bar (and the oysters here, no matter which variety you pick, are always very fresh), there's a full menu of gourmet seafood dishes, all artfully plated, along with hearty sandwiches and salads. It's also a great historic space, with lots of wood, exposed brick, large windowed dining areas that look out on bustling Cross Street, and an upstairs loft dining room.

MAP 4: 36 E. Cross St., 410/539-2093, www.ryleighs.com; daily 11am-2am

Mount Vernon and Station North

Map 5

AFGHAN

The Helmand $$

Few restaurants in Baltimore can boast of the family ties of The Helmand's owner, Qayum Karzai: His brother Hamid is president of Afghanistan. The Karzai name has been cherished in Baltimore for years, mostly because of the amazing, basic-yet-complex Afghan food served in this simple, white-walls-and-tablecloths restaurant. One of the city's most beloved appetizers is the *kaddo bourani*: fried and baked baby pumpkin served on garlic yogurt; popular entrées include lamb and beef meatballs and *mantwo*, hand-made pastries with onions and beef. There are plenty of vegetarian options here as well.

MAP 5: 806 N. Charles St., 410/752-0311, www.helmand.com; Sun.-Thurs. 5pm-10pm, Fri.-Sat. 5pm-11pm

AMERICAN
The Prime Rib $$$

If you want to know what going out to a no-holds-barred prime rib steak dinner with the boys in 1973 Baltimore was like, head to this well-preserved but still vital luxurious steak house in an unassuming building east of Mount Vernon. The chairs are huge leather thrones; the waiters are tuxedoed and battle-tested; the floors are cheetah-print; the piano lid is Lucite; the drinks are stiff and the wine list decadent. But the beef here (as well as the other food) is superlative. (The Prime Rib was once anointed by *Esquire* magazine for producing one of the best 20 steaks in America.) It's a place worth dressing up for, which is good, because jackets are required.

MAP 5: 1101 N. Calvert St., 410/539-1804, www.theprimerib.com; Mon.-Thurs. 5pm-10pm, Fri.-Sat. 5pm-11pm, Sun. 4pm-9pm

Woman's Industrial Kitchen $

Opened in 1887, this restaurant operated entirely by women holds an impressive title: longest continually running restaurant in the United States. This is even though it had to close its doors in 2002. But in 2011, the passionate Irene Smith, owner of the Souper Freak food truck (and mother of three girls) reopened the historic lunchroom with a menu that offers a few updated dishes like an asparagus, leek, and goat cheese wrap along with old favorites like chicken salad with aspic. It's a fun place to eat, mainly because everything about this hot-pink-and-gray restaurant celebrates women and their accomplishments. Just take a look at the tables: Each one tells the stories in pictures and words of famous women (Gertrude Stein, Rachel Carson) and not-so-famous women (advocates, scientists) who have made valuable contributions to society.

MAP 5: 333 N. Charles St., 410/244-6450, www.womansindustrialkitchen.com; Sun.-Fri. 11am-3pm

ASIAN
Minato $$

It's uncommon in Baltimore for a very good sushi restaurant to also be a very good bar, but Minato does both. The historic row house manages to incorporate modern, interesting design that

The Lunchroom from
Sleepless in Seattle

The story goes like this: In town to scout locations for *Sleepless in Seattle*, writer Nora Ephron had lunch at the Woman's Industrial Exchange in Mount Vernon, where she met Marguerite, an octogenarian who had worked at the kitchen since she was 17. In 1929, after the stock market crashed and the restaurant subsequently lost its professional staff, Marguerite and a group of young women stepped in to save the historic lunchroom. Ephron must have been impressed with her—or the menu of deviled eggs, green bean casserole, and tomato aspic—because she added a scene to the script in which Meg Ryan's character Annie has lunch with her editor at the Exchange. The addition made Marguerite a 30-second film star: She's the waitress who served Ryan her famous chicken salad. The lunchroom closed in 2002, but reopened in 2011 as the **Woman's Industrial Kitchen.** And although Marguerite has passed away, her recipes live on, so visitors today can still try her silver screen-ready chicken salad.

doesn't wreck the original space (though the huge lighting fixture is rather dominant). Maybe it's the confluence of these feats that makes Minato so popular, but it's probably the quality of the sushi and sashimi here; freshness is a constant, and the presentation (unless the place is swamped) is charming. There's a good selection of sake as well, making this a favorite for Mount Vernon residents and a destination for other Baltimoreans.

MAP 5: 1013 N. Charles St., 410/332-0332, www.minatosushibar.com; lunch Mon.-Fri. 11:30am-2:30pm, dinner Sun.-Thurs. 5pm-10pm, Fri.-Sat. 5pm-11pm

Thai Landing ⬤⬤

The neighborhood may have changed—upscale apartment and condo construction has embraced Thai Landing's much older three-story building—but this restaurant is still going strong, having earned loyal customers from all across the city. The decor in both the first- and second-floor dining rooms is unassuming, with several large Thai items and statuary, and a small shrine to family members in the back is particularly intriguing. The food is solid, if not the best Thai in town, and the staff is helpful and pleasant. Still, Thai Landing will cook up some mettle-testing spicy food (if requested, and double-checked if they don't know you), like the *goong khob pho* (grilled shrimp) appetizer or *pet pad kra-pao* (roast duck with vegetables).

MAP 5: 1207 N. Charles St., 410/727-1234, www.thailandingmd.com; lunch Mon.-Fri. 11am-2:30pm, dinner Sun.-Thurs. 5pm-9pm, Fri.-Sat. 5pm-9:30pm

Thairish ⬤⬤

Combine Thai and Irish and you get Thairish, a cozy little Thai restaurant/service counter with a tiny handful of tables. This is a one-man shop, for the most part, run by white-haired Thai native Kerrigan Kitikul (he's married to an Irish woman, and took an Irish-sounding name), and it's a personal dining experience to place your order with him from Thairish's small but complete menu. Curries are the way to go here, as are any of the Thai staples (like panangs and pad thai). Be warned: There's a no-cell-phones policy here, enforced with vigor that would make the East Germans envious.

MAP 5: 804 N. Charles St., 410/752-5857; lunch Tues.-Fri. 11:30am-3pm, dinner Tues.-Fri. 4:30pm-9:30pm, Sat.-Sun. 4:30pm-10pm

CAFÉS
Station North Arts Café ⑤
This small but vibrant café, a local favorite, is one of the few places to grab lunch if you're going to a matinee at the Charles Theatre across the street. Run by partners Bill and Kevin—fixtures in Station North before the area began its redevelopment—the food is simple sandwiches, soups, and salads, as well as breakfast favorites; the pulled pork is quite good, as is the pecan pie, if it's on the menu. You'll find lots of art inside, as well as a few photos and a bust of the owners (which sounds pompous, but it's really all in good fun). If you're in town in September, catch Kevin at the Baltimore Book Festival, where he is the MC of the always-fun Food for Thought stage.

MAP 5: 1816 N. Charles St., 410/625-6440, www.stationnortharts.com; Mon.-Fri. 8am-3pm, Sat. 10am-3pm

CONTEMPORARY AND NEW AMERICAN
★ b ⑤⑤
The Bolton Hill section of town has lots of grand and stately row homes and, sadly, very few places to eat. Luckily, it has b, a bright, tidy city bistro that is a cornerstone for the neighborhood's residents. The restaurant has a great, warm feel, and you'll see lots of people on dates—and longtime lovers having a great dinner. The menu features some particularly nice salads and seafood entrées, and delicate, inventive pastas and a selection of cheeses and charcuterie round out the bill. Sunday brunch (with omelettes, eggs, and pancakes) is immensely popular here, and reservations are highly recommended.

MAP 5: 1501 Bolton St., 410/383-8600, www.b-bistro.com; Tues.-Sat. 5pm-10pm, Sun. 5pm-9pm, brunch Sun. 10am-2pm

The Brewer's Art ⑤⑤
Though there are two outstanding bars in the building, the dining room at The Brewer's Art is a sometimes-overlooked star. Imaginative takes on old favorites are the standard fare here. The

deep, inviting dining room retains the early-20th-century charms
of this once-grand mansion, with wood details and floors and
grand fireplaces, updated with modern art hangings. The staff is
generally friendly and knowledgeable, and the wine list is solid and
not ridiculously marked-up. The rosemary garlic fries absolutely
must be ordered; they are one of the city's most beloved snacks.

MAP 5: 1106 N. Charles St., 410/547-6925, www.thebrewersart.com; Mon.-Sat.
4pm-1:45am, Sun. 5pm-1:45am

The Chesapeake $$$

It's not often that a once-beloved restaurant closed for two decades
is reborn in the exact same location, but that's what has happened to
The Chesapeake, which shut down in 1987, only to reopen in 2013
(with new owners) as one of two slightly upscale dining options (the
other is Tapas Teatro next door) in the artsy Station North neighborhood. Although local critics have pointed out that the menu
lacks focus, the food here (oysters, cheese and charcuterie boards,
grits with shrimp served with their heads on) is so flavorful that it
hardly seems to matter. The decor is sparse, though, and the restaurant is drawing an older crowd these days rather than a mix of
diners. Throwback Thursdays are worth checking out; that's when
the kitchen and the bartenders whip up dishes and drinks from the
restaurant's old days.

MAP 5: 1701 N. Charles St., 410/547-2760, www.thechesapeakebaltimore.com;
Mon.-Thurs. 4pm-10pm, Fri.-Sat. 4pm-11pm

City Café $$

Even if the food here weren't as good as it is—from lamb and
shrimp burgers and club sandwiches to steaks, roasted chickens,
salmon, and a few creative vegetarian options—there are other reasons to come to this longtime Mount Vernon favorite. There's a
great morning rush for coffee and bagels in the café section, which
is more informal than the bar/restaurant area. It's a good place to
come before going to a performance at one of the nearby theaters
and concert halls. And few restaurants in Baltimore cater to as
diverse a clientele, which makes the people-watching scene here
almost as interesting as the food.

MAP 5: 1001 Cathedral St., 410/539-4252, www.citycafebaltimore.com;
Mon.-Thurs. 11am-10pm, Fri. 11am-10:30pm, Sat. 10am-10:30pm, Sun. 10am-8pm

★ Joe Squared $$

Another standard on Baltimore's short list of good pizza purveyors, Joe Squared lives up to its name by serving squared-off pizzas
topped with everything from traditional pepperoni and vegetables to corned beef and Granny Smith apples. Surprisingly for a
pizza joint, the menu also includes a long list of excellent and rich

risottos. Owing to the eclectic live music, a great jukebox and CD selection, and cheap prices, this is a popular joint with cool, college-aged kids, though the only nearby school is the Maryland Institute College of Art. The restaurant is in the artsy Station North neighborhood, which, although changing, still isn't the best in the late hours. There's another location in the Inner Harbor's **Power Point Live! complex** (30 Market Pl., 410/962-5566, Sun. 11am-9pm, Mon.-Tues. 11am-5pm, Wed. 11am-10pm, Thurs. 11am-11pm, Fri.-Sat. 11am-1:30am).

MAP 5: 133 W. North Ave., 410/545-0444, www.joesquared.com; Sun.-Mon. 11am-midnight, Tues.-Sat. 11am-2am

Sascha's 527 Café ⑤⑤

The production begins with the entrance to Sascha's, which involves massive red velvet drapes that conceal an enormous, chandeliered Mount Vernon row house, with ceilings some 16 feet high and a red and gold color scheme that exudes warmth even in the dead of winter. A good selection of small plates is popular here (their take on croquettes involves crab, coconut, and curried bananas), but the entrées have some strong contenders as well (scallops with potatoes and pancetta, gnocchi with wild mushrooms). Sascha's is a place for those who like to eat and be seen eating, especially when it involves red velvet. Note that lunch is served here as well, but it's very light, with lots of salads, and done cafeteria-style.

MAP 5: 527 N. Charles St., 410/539-8880, www.saschas.com; lunch Mon.-Fri. 11am-3pm, dinner Mon.-Thurs. 5:30pm-10pm, Fri.-Sat. 5:30pm-11pm

XS ⑤⑤

This sleek, exposed-brick café (the name is pronounced "excess") and dessert favorite is the city's most vertical dining establishment; once you enter, you can continue to climb riserless stairs, choosing from one of the four floors of seating. This is a popular place with students from the nearby University of Baltimore; there are DJs every day of the week, and the crowd is young, cool, and energized. The first floor is home to the coffee bar, desserts, sushi bar, and a small outdoor dining area. The rest is restaurant and lounge, with a broad menu that covers everything from sushi to panini.

MAP 5: 1307 N. Charles St., 410/468-0002, www.xsbaltimore.com; Mon.-Thurs. 7am-midnight, Fri.-Sat. 7am-2am, Sun. 9am-midnight

CONTEMPORARY ITALIAN
Iggie's ⑤⑤

Any pizza place named for a dog is probably going to be good, and Iggie's is—just not in the ways you might expect. It's a bare-bones operation: You place your order, get your silverware and glassware, set your own table, open your own bottle of wine (bring-your-own only), and clean up your own mess. But it's worth the effort, because it makes you feel like you helped prepare the thin, gourmet pizzas made in Neapolitan style, with toppings like *sopressata,* roast duck, and dried tomatoes; there's also house-made gelato for dessert. It's a great environment, too, with lots of exposed ductwork, intriguing customers, and a few inexplicable pipes and big wheel valves springing out of the floor and ceiling.

MAP 5: 818 N. Calvert St., 410/528-0818, www.iggiespizza.com; Thurs. 11:30am-9pm, Fri.-Sat. 11:30am-10pm, Sun. 11:30am-8pm

Sotto Sopra $$$

For a city used to a certain type of Italian restaurant—that is, the kind in Little Italy—the arrival of Sotto Sopra was a bit jarring. Here was a modern, hip, exciting, and youthful-feeling restaurant, in a strange part of town for an Italian restaurant, serving interesting, delightful dishes with top-notch presentation. Their take on polenta comes with fennel, prosciutto, and a poached egg. Huge murals portraying diners line the expansive main dining room, curtains and gold-painted pillars accent the room, and there's a more intimate back bar as well.

MAP 5: 405 N. Charles St., 410/625-0534, www.sottosoprainc.com; lunch Mon.-Sat. 11:30am-2pm, dinner Sun. 5pm-9pm, Mon.-Thurs. 5pm-9:30pm, Fri.-Sat. 5pm-10:30pm

ETHIOPIAN
Dukem $$

Though the sign out front doesn't say it, this is Dukem #2; the flagship is in Washington DC. The Baltimore outpost is in a building barely two blocks from the Joseph Meyerhoff Symphony Hall and the Patricia and Arthur Modell Performing Arts Center at The Lyric. The oddly shaped first-floor dining room (very narrow and not very long) has been joined, thankfully, by a more traditionally laid-out second-floor room. Seating is provided both in traditional Ethiopian style (small stools and woven basket-tables to hold the communal tray) and with conventional tables and chairs. The food is delectably garlicky and designed to be eaten using pieces of a spongy sour bread called *injera;* utensils take away from the fun.

MAP 5: 1100 Maryland Ave., 410/385-0318, www.dukemrestaurant.com; daily 11am-10:30pm

FRENCH
Marie Louise Bistro $$

The first thing you will probably notice at Marie Louise Bistro is the tempting pastry case filled with rich domed delicacies and pretty fruit tars. But look beyond that, and you'll see that this restaurant actually has a very nice wrought-iron chandelier and some cool tin ceilings. Then check back outside, where you'll notice one of the nicest (and tiniest) outdoor dining areas in Mount Vernon. Though the food's reviews have been mixed—stick with the well-received quiches, bison burger, or mussels—the best reason to come here is the atmosphere. If you can't get a table outside, ask to sit by the pretty and isolated table by the window, an especially nice spot for couples out for a romantic evening.

MAP 5: 904 N. Charles St., 410/385-9946, www.marielouisebistrocatering.com; Sun.-Thurs. 8am-10pm, Fri.-Sat. 8am-11pm

INDIAN
Akbar $$

This place puts out a massive and renowned lunchtime buffet that always packs them in. But go at dinner, when the kitchen is not so focused on quantity, and you'll get even better versions of the Indian standards, like tandoori, palak paneer, and chicken tikka masala. The restaurant is in the basement of a large row house, so while it's a decent-enough sized room, it doesn't have the greatest views. But when the place is full, the candles are burning brightly, and the Indian music is rolling, there's a very good mood and feel here.

MAP 5: 823 N. Charles St., 410/539-0944, www.akbar-restaurant.com; lunch Mon.-Fri. 11:30am-2:30pm, Sat.-Sun. noon-3pm, dinner Sun.-Thurs. 5pm-11pm, Fri.-Sat. 5pm-11:30pm

NEPALESE
Kumari $$

Baltimore's only Nepalese restaurant opened a decade ago, and diners have supported it enough to keep it going. The menu includes a number of Indian standards, which are abundant in their popular lunchtime buffets. While the Indian staples are good here, take at least a small chance and order something you've never had before, like the *khaja* (chicken, rice, and homemade pickles) appetizer or *bhojan* (Nepalese lamb curry) entrée. The views of Charles Street are great from the second-story tables, which lie behind large plate-glass windows, and the decor is a mishmash of old Baltimore row-house-meets-restaurant and a simple white, red, and black color scheme.

MAP 5: 911 N. Charles St., 410/547-1600, www.kumarirestaurantnbar.com; daily 11:30am-2am

SPANISH
Tio Pepe $$$

A beloved Baltimore institution, this subterranean Spanish restaurant has been in business since 1968, and hasn't done much to change the decor or menu since. The walls are white stucco and

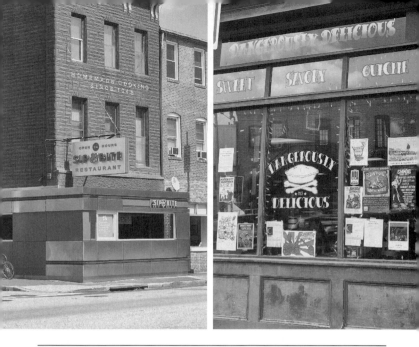

clockwise from top left: Sip & Bite Restaurant, Fell's Point; Dangerously Delicious Pies, Canton; Ze Mean Bean Café, Fell's Point

brick, there are plenty of wrought-iron sconces, and brightly painted sangria pitchers adorn many tables. Waiters in brightly colored tuxedo jackets glide through the room and linger at your table. The classic Spanish cuisine emphasizes seafood, starting with excellent shrimp in garlic and ending with two tours de force: roasted rack of lamb and a massive paella. Dining at the expensive Tio Pepe is an event; jackets are required for men, and reservations are a must.

MAP 5: 10 E. Franklin St., 410/539-4675, www.tiopepebaltimore.com; Mon.-Thurs. 11:30am-10pm, Fri. 11:30am-11:30pm, Sat. 5pm-11:30pm, Sun. 4pm-10pm

TAPAS
Tapas Teatro ⑨⑨

Once, the only reason to come to this stretch of Charles Street, just north of Pennsylvania Station, was to see a movie at the Charles Theatre or maybe grab a cocktail at the Club Charles across the street. But this area, known as Station North, is up-and-coming, and Tapas Teatro has become one of its social anchors, drawing hungry and thirsty crowds, especially during the warmer seasons for their expansive outdoor dining section and bar. It's a great place to stop before or after catching a film at the Charles, or to go just to eat. The plates are generally of Spanish and Mediterranean origin, and while quite good, dining at Tapas Teatro is about more than the food: It's about the scene.

MAP 5: 1711 N. Charles St., 410/332-0110, www.tapasteatro.com; Tues.-Thurs. 5pm-11pm, Fri. 5pm-midnight, Sat. 4pm-midnight, Sun. 3pm-10pm

Hampden and Homewood   Map 6

AMERICAN
Angelo's Pizza ⑨

This corner pizzeria and sub shop (owned by two brothers with the surname Pizza) has been serving pizzas and cheesesteaks to hungry Hampdenites for generations, but most people know Angelo's for one reason: their monstrous slices of pizza, cut from a colossal 30-inch pie. Best of all, it's not just quantity: Angelo's pizzas are among the city's better pies (although, alas, that's not saying much). There are a few outdoor tables that make for good people-watching and scene-observing, especially during the warmer months, and you can eat inside, but the basement-like space can get a tad claustrophobic and is a bit overstuffed with the kitchen, tables, pillars, equipment, and video poker machines—and that's all before you add people.

MAP 6: 3600 Keswick Rd., 410/235-2595; Mon.-Thurs. 11am-10pm, Fri.-Sat. 11am-11pm, Sun. noon-5pm

The two-story pink flamingo on the front of Café Hon is a tribute to local director John Waters's film of the same name and the "hon" culture that the restaurant's owner has helped build into a citywide brand (see June's HonFest). The café is always busy, serving up diner-style staples like meat loaf, slightly more upscale dishes like salmon, and Baltimore-peculiar entrées (like sour beef on Monday, and fries with gravy every day); a full brunch with eggs, pancakes, sandwiches (and another Baltimore favorite: cream chipped beef) is also served daily. There's even an adjacent tavern (Hon Bar) with karaoke on Friday and live music on Saturday.

MAP 6: 1002 W. 36th St., 410/243-1230, www.cafehon.com; Mon.-Thurs. 11am-9pm, Fri. 11am-10pm, Sat. 9am-10pm, Sun. 9am-8pm

ASIAN
Suzie's Soba 💲💲

If you're in Hampden and looking for Asian food, this is your best (and basically only) bet. A noodle house that doesn't play favorites, Suzie's has noodle dishes from Japan, China, Korea, and Vietnam, and lots of vegetarian and vegan options—which can be welcome in meat-centric Baltimore. The decorations are a mix of modern, leftover, and Asian, a conglomeration that might not make much sense, except that it fits the menu plan here. There's also a great little back patio and garden, perfect for grabbing a quick bite between rounds of shopping on "The Avenue."

MAP 6: 1009 W. 36th St., 410/243-0051; daily 5pm-10pm

CAFÉS
Artifact Coffee 💲

When Spike and Amy Gjerde, the owners of local farm-to-table favorite Woodberry Kitchen, opened Artifact Coffee in 2012, they gave Baltimore something it was lacking: a cozy bakery with a menu crafted around the ingredients available from local farms. The decor is homey; the seating options, from individual and family-style tables to long counters, are varied; and the changing pastry case is always beautiful. Try the gigantic cream-filled doughnuts or amazing savory and sweet scones; there are also soups, salads, and sandwiches for lunch. Even though this is a café first, don't overlook Artifact for dinner when you're in the mood for casual classics like burgers and pulled pork done well; a selection of light vegetarian small plates rounds out the evening menu.

MAP 6: 1500 Union Ave., 410/235-1881, www.artifactcoffee.com; breakfast and lunch Mon.-Fri. 7am-5pm, Sat.-Sun. 8am-5pm; dinner Wed.-Sun. 5pm-7pm

RESTAURANTS
HAMPDEN AND HOMEWOOD

A Common Ground $

Wedged into an exposed-brick row house that seems a little tight even by Baltimore standards, this homegrown coffeehouse and café is worth the squeeze. Great java and other drinks are their specialty, plus they have huge muffins, bagels, and freshly made sandwiches. If you can't find a seat in the tiny front area, there's another dining room in the back, and an outdoor deck past that. The small tables are usually taken by typical coffeehouse denizens—writers, students, artists, teachers, layabouts—and the songs selected by the staff, from every musical era, are always worth listening to.

MAP 6: 819 W. 36th St., 410/235-5533, www.commongroundhampden.com; daily 7am-5pm

Donna's $$

The Homewood (Charles Village, technically) branch of this local coffeehouse/café chain is one of the few places in the neighborhood to linger over a glass of wine and dine on ricotta gnocchi (or perhaps a lamb burger or fried oysters) in a modern, TV-free environment. There are plenty of students from nearby Johns Hopkins here, but they're the kind more interested in food and conversation than partying—this is an appropriate place to bring their parents for a quick, metropolitan meal. There's a popular (and small) outdoor sidewalk patio, too.

MAP 6: 3101 St. Paul St., 410/889-3410, www.donnas.com; Mon.-Thurs. 7am-9:30pm, Fri. 7am-10:30pm, Sat. 8am-10:30pm, Sun. 8am-9pm

CONTEMPORARY AND NEW AMERICAN

Alchemy $$$

Perhaps the most fine dining of the contemporary American restaurants to open on "The Avenue" in Hampden, Alchemy has a modern dining room filled with bright white leather and black and silver accents. The food is completely modern, too—hummus comes with a truffle mist, the béarnaise sauce atop two tenderloin medallions is torched, and the French toast is slathered with aloe syrup—and often inspired by international cuisines. There's also a more relaxed dining room upstairs with blue walls and several works of art; get a seat by the window to watch the varied crowds strolling down this popular street.

MAP 6: 1011 W. 36th St., 410/366-1163, www.alchemyon36.com; lunch Tues.-Fri. 11:30am-3:30pm, Sat. 11:30am-4pm, brunch Sun. 11am-3pm, dinner Tues.-Thurs. 5pm-9pm, Fri. 5pm-10pm, Sat. 4pm-10pm, Sun. 4pm-9pm

The Food Market $$$

This is one of a handful of sleek restaurants serving contemporary American food that have set up shop along quirky 36th Avenue in Hampden. The restaurant feels both industrial and modern with its exposed brick and beams and sleek open kitchen, and the menu, offering food in tasting, appetizer, and entrée sizes, changes so often that a new one is printed each day. Still, there's always lots of seafood and steak, and the friendly waitstaff are happy to offer recommendations. Although the restaurant prides itself on comfort food, the crowd is more hip than homey. Stop in for a seasonal cocktail and a tasting plate of buffalo fried pickles with gorgonzola and hot sauce, a crowd-pleasing favorite that is often on the menu.

MAP 6: 1017 W. 36th St., 410/366-0606, www.thefoodmarketbaltimore.com; dinner Sun.-Thurs. 5pm-11pm, Fri.-Sat. 5pm-midnight, brunch Fri.-Sun. 9am-3pm

Gertrude's ❸❸❸

Housed in the Baltimore Museum of Art, Gertrude's (named for chef John Shields's grandmother) is a showcase for classic Chesapeake Bay dishes, like oysters and fish, as well as Asian-style entrées, steaks, burgers, and some of the city's more exciting vegetarian dishes. There's also a popular Tuesday night fried chicken dinner, and a "make your own entrée" menu system that is great for both the indecisive and the adventurous. The restaurant's gorgeous, tented patio, overlooking the BMA's sculpture garden and grounds, with the city bustling just beyond the trees, is a local favorite. The patio fills up fast on fair-weather weekends and nights, so reservations, especially for brunch, are a necessity.

MAP 6: 10 Art Museum Dr., Baltimore Museum of Art, 410/889-3399, www.gertrudesbaltimore.com; Tues.-Fri. 11:30am-9pm, Sat. 10am-9pm, Sun. 10am-8pm

Rocket to Venus ❸❸

"RTV" has become one of the city's most popular and interesting places to eat, drink, and hang out. The menu seems to have been designed by a committee of hungry party-goers at 4am (fried pickles, pierogies, mini-burgers) and then burnished by inventive chefs (duck confit, tenderloin skewers with peppers and lemon ancho aioli). A great jukebox and free entertainment—there's a thriving see-and-be-seen scene with a hipster bent at the bar—are two other reasons to visit.

MAP 6: 3360 Chestnut Ave., 410/235-7887, www.rockettovenus.com; Mon.-Sat. 5pm-11pm, Sun. noon-9pm

★ Woodberry Kitchen ❸❸❸

The brains and talent behind Woodberry Kitchen belong to one of Baltimore's few culinary superstars, Spike Gjerde, a finalist for the 2013 James Beard award for Best Chef:Mid-Atlantic. This venture—a big, contemporary/rehabbed late-1800s-era industrial space with an open kitchen, in an old mill complex just west of Hampden—is one of the city's favorites (and hardest to get into

___

clockwise from top left: Miss Shirley's Café, downtown; Cross Street Market, home to Nick's Oyster Bar, Federal Hill; Vaccaro's, Little Italy

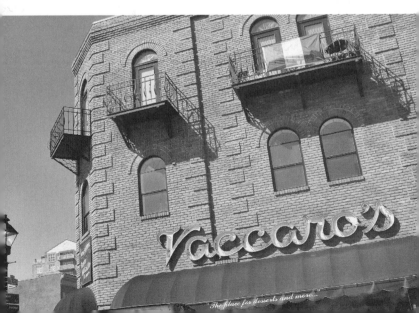

most nights of the week). Completely seasonal menus, based on as-local-as-possible purveyors, mean hearty regional dishes like meat loaf, braised beef, lamb sausage, and swordfish. Some of the crowd comes for the social status points, but is often distracted by the quality of the food. On weekend nights, the small bar is packed with slightly younger folks, along with hopeful walk-ins without reservations who will never see an empty table; there are a lot of serious eaters from across the region who plan their dinners here weeks in advance.

MAP 6: 2010 Clipper Park Rd., No. 126, 410/464-8000, www.woodberrykitchen. com; dinner Mon.-Thurs. 5pm-10pm, Fri.-Sat. 5pm-11pm, Sun. 5pm-9pm, brunch Sat.-Sun. 10am-2pm

DESSERT
The Charmery $

This new Hampden ice-cream shop has an ever-changing menu that incorporates a few foods that are completely Baltimore, like Berger cookies. In 1835, German immigrant Henry Berger began making these soft cookies covered in rich chocolate frosting in his East Baltimore bakery; today, The Charmery's Berger Cookies and Cream, a crowd favorite, has big, delicious chunks of those beloved cookies. There's also Old Bay caramel, a flavor that shouldn't work—it is seafood seasoning and caramel, after all—but does. (For purists, there's chocolate and vanilla, too.) If you plan to be back often, get a stamped card on your way out; once you collect 10 stamps, you can spin the retro wheel behind the counter for a prize.

MAP 6: 801 W. 36th St., 410/814-0493, www.thecharmery.com; Sun.-Thurs. noon-10pm, Fri.-Sat. noon-11pm, reduced winter hours

DINER
Papermoon Diner $$

This colorful, eclectic diner is adorned (on nearly every surface of the house-like space) with garish paint schemes, toys, mannequins, bric-a-brac, and junk. Take a stool at the long dining counter, or head for one of the utterly mismatched tables in one of two dining rooms. The sprawling menu covers almost every culinary base (though it's best with breakfasts and sandwiches), and this is one of the few places in town where the decor is more interesting than the clientele (a mix of moms, kids, artists, students, and businesspeople). The wait on weekend mornings can be severe, so come either early or late.

MAP 6: 227 W. 29th St., 410/889-4444, www.papermoondiner24.com; Sun.-Thurs. 7am-midnight, Fri.-Sat. 7am-2am

Vegetarian Dining

Finding an entirely vegetarian restaurant in the seafood-heavy city of Baltimore is a tough task. Still, several places do offer some creative meat-free options, from casual lunchtime fare to multicourse tasting menus.

For breakfast, try the toy-filled **Papermoon Diner** for an egg-free tofu scramble. The nearby **Golden West Café** is a great lunchtime option that offers vegetarian barbecued chicken and rib sandwiches.

For a more upscale dinner, **Gertrude's** at the Baltimore Museum of Art offers several vegetarian entrées like faux crab cakes made with zucchini and a vegetable curry. **Pierpoint** in Fell's Point serves eggplant cakes and pumpkin pierogies, and **Fork & Wrench** in Canton has a three-course vegetarian/vegan tasting menu.

Several global restaurants specialize in meat-free dishes. In Mount Vernon, **Akbar,** an Indian restaurant, and **The Helmand,** an Afghani restaurant, have large vegetarian sections on their menus; not-to-be-missed dishes include the bhindi masala (green okra) at Akbar and the mushroom lawand at The Helmand. And in Federal Hill, **Thai Arroy** can make curry, noodle, or rice dishes with their vegetarian duck, one of the most satisfying meat substitutes in the city.

ECLECTIC
★ Golden West Café $$

The decor is American Western kitsch (note the looming mounted moose head and barbed wire samplers), the waitstaff are unapologetically hipster, and the menu is...well, it's all over the place, but in the best way. Tex-Mex is sort of the guiding principle here (fantastic polenta with carne, Frito pie, and enchiladas), but there are also Asian influences, and other dishes inspired by a multitude of cuisines—all made fresh, to order, and with care. Huge and wholesome breakfasts are a specialty here, which makes the waits for Sunday brunch long but worthwhile. Also note that the kitchen closes midday, every day, before reopening for dinner; on weekends, it's brunch only until 3pm.

MAP 6: 1105 W. 36th St., 410/889-8891, www.goldenwestcafe.com; Mon.-Fri. 11am-3pm and 5pm-10pm, Sat. 9am-2:30pm and 5pm-10pm, Sun. 9am-3pm and 5pm-9pm

INDIAN
The Ambassador Dining Room $$$

In the back of a grand, gothic apartment building just north of Johns Hopkins University is, surprisingly, a grand, semi-upscale Indian restaurant, where waitstaff in tuxedos and saris watch over a sprawling, stately dining room. Best of all, though, is the backyard, where—during warm months—the restaurant expands onto the green lawn behind the building, and guests sit in large chairs as they dine on tandoori and naan. It's still worth a visit

here in the winter, as well: There's a large gas fireplace in the back
patio, which makes for a relaxing evening. The lunch buffet is a
big hit with locals and is a much less formal event than dinner.
MAP 6: 3811 Canterbury Rd., 410/366-1484, www.ambassadordining.com; lunch
Mon.-Fri. 11:30am-2:30pm, Sat.-Sun. noon-3pm, dinner Sun.-Thurs. 5pm-10pm,
Fri.-Sat. 5pm-11pm

Greater Baltimore Map 7

AMERICAN
Atwater's $

Though it's a bit outside of downtown Baltimore proper, locals
love this café in a bustling market in Belvedere Square. At first
glance, the food here may seem like traditional coffee shop fare,
but the sandwiches, salads, and soups are *really* good—they're
made with fresh ingredients from an on-site market, after all—
and it's fun to wander though the market looking at the produce,
meats, breads, and pastas afterward. Note, though, that tables can
be hard to come by on the weekends. The Grand Cru wine bar is
also in the market, making it possible to get a glass of wine and a
plate of cheese after your meal without ever leaving the building.
MAP 7: 529 E. Belvedere Ave., Baltimore, 410/323-2396, www.atwaters.biz;
Mon.-Sat. 8am-8pm, Sun. 8am-5pm

ASIAN
Sushi Hana $$

In the tiny and completely cute Mount Washington Village area
about seven miles north of downtown Baltimore, the interior of
this sushi restaurant is utterly perfect and calming, with lots of
light-colored woods, minimal and artfully displayed figurines,
and a welcoming sushi bar (there's a full menu of Asian specialties available). The fish here is always very fresh, which gives
Sushi Hana a good reputation among the city's sushi lovers. It's
popular with the younger crowd on the weekends (who go as
much for the sake and Sapporo as the sushi). There's also a few
great stores in the same shopping center like The Ivy Bookshop
and Samuel Parker Clothier.
MAP 7: 6080 Falls Rd., Baltimore, 410/377-4238, www.sushihanabaltimore.com;
Mon.-Thurs. 11am-10pm, Fri. 11am-11pm, Sat. noon-11pm, Sun. 1pm-10pm

FRENCH
Petit Louis Bistro $$$

Roland Park is one of Baltimore's most prestigious neighborhoods, but it's one where the concept of neighborhood

hasn't been lost; people know one another and interact on a regular basis. And a lot of that interaction goes on at Petit Louis Bistro in one of the nation's first tiny shopping centers. Though the restaurant looks like a century-old Parisian bistro—marble-topped tables, wrought-iron details and filigree—it's actually a modern installation. The service here is well-dressed and well-informed, and always willing to help and fulfill any request. The menu is, unsurprisingly, hardcore French bistro, with lots of fresh local ingredients and produce, an amazing selection of cheeses, and upscale fish, meat, and casserole dishes.

MAP 7: 4800 Roland Ave., Baltimore, 410/366-9393, www.petitlouis.com; lunch Tues.-Fri. 11:30am-2pm, brunch Sun. 10:30am-2pm, dinner Sun.-Thurs. 5pm-10pm, Fri.-Sat. 5pm-11pm

SEAFOOD
Nick's Fish House & Grill $$

Owned by the man behind the popular Nick's Oyster Bar in Federal Hill's Cross Street Market, this peculiar restaurant and watering hole is a short drive south of that neighborhood in an industrial area of the waterfront that doesn't get much tourist traffic. This bright yellow seafood house is popular with the young drinking enthusiast set and can get boisterous at night— but it's also a great place for an outdoor lunch with a view of the Hanover Street Bridge. The menu isn't noteworthy in concept or execution, so stick with the basics. After all, you're here for some cocktails and a bite to eat on the big deck, and to get the feel of being far from downtown—which is only a five-minute drive north.

MAP 7: 2600 Insulator Dr., Baltimore, 410/347-4123, www.nicksfishhouse.com; Sun.-Thurs. 11am-10pm, Fri.-Sat. 11am-11pm

Nightlife

Downtown and Inner Harbor.....124

Harbor East and Little Italy 127

Fell's Point.......................127

Canton 132

Federal Hill 133

Mount Vernon and Station North..136

Hampden and Homewood.......141

HIGHLIGHTS

★ **Best After-Hours Club:** In the dark shadows of elevated roadways and warehouses lurks **Paradox,** Baltimore's unstoppable, 13,000-square-foot late-night dance club (page 124).

★ **Best Old-School Bar to Have a Drink Amongst Ghosts:** A bar that is more than two centuries old should have some stories, and Fell's Point's **The Wharf Rat** doesn't disappoint; the lively nautically themed watering hole is said to be haunted by one of its former owners (page 130).

★ **Best Bar Food:** Locals love **The Brewer's Art,** which centers around about 20 house-made beers crafted by the bar's brewers. But this Mount Vernon institution is also a great restaurant that serves seafood and steak entrées and inventive appetizers (page 136).

★ **Best Performance Venue, Table Tennis Court, and Art Gallery in One: The Windup Space** offers a different experience every night, from table tennis and game nights to burlesque shows and dance parties (page 138).

★ **Best Gay and Lesbian Nightlife:** Mount Vernon's multiroomed **Club Hippo** and **Grand Central** have become the centers of local gay and lesbian nightlife, thanks to a variety of themed nights from bingo to karaoke to dancing (pages 138 and 139).

★ **Best Serious Jazz Club:** At some places the musicians are stuck in a corner so people can focus on their drinks and food and each other. Upstairs at **An die Musik LIVE!,** the audience is there to listen—and the performers respond with knockout sets (page 140).

★ **Best Lounge:** Though it was one of the first modern lounges to come to town, **Red Maple** is still one of the best, from the great bar, space, and music selections to the appealing small plates menu (page 140).

★ **Best Secretive Atmospheric Bar:** Lacking a phone number and sign on its door, the wonderful **WC Harlan** feels like a classy speakeasy. Sit on a velvet couch and drink a well-made cocktail surrounded by softly sketched portraits and red velvet curtains (page 141).

★ **Best Alternative Music Venue:** If you like being so close to a performer that their sweat can drip on you, the resolutely indie **The Ottobar** is the joint for you (page 141).

★ **Best Wine Bar:** With a prime location in Hampden's shopping and dining district, **13.5% Wine Bar** is a lovely spot to kick back with a glass of riesling and a plate of cheese while watching the often interesting crowds stroll by (page 141).

Going out on the town in Baltimore is easy; all you need to do is figure out what kind of evening you're looking to experience. Decadent cocktails and dancing to house music? Hot jazz upstairs at a music store? Innovative modern music in an art gallery? A huge mega-club or a tiny dive bar?

With the city's rejuvenation has come a wide variety of nightlife options to meet any taste or thirst—a big improvement over the (still charming) shot-and-a-beer joints that proliferated throughout the city for years.

Two neighborhoods are real standouts for their often over-lively nocturnal scenes: Fell's Point and Federal Hill. The waterfront bars and restaurants of Fell's Point entertain all sorts of folks, from those looking for a glass of wine and some dessert to college kids out for serious revelry. Federal Hill is very similar in character, though as there are a few less restaurants, there are more folks just out for some drinks. Closing time in both places (which is 2am in Baltimore) can be a little hectic, especially on warm summer nights, so plan wisely. Canton's small O'Donnell Square area is also very similar to Fell's Point and Federal Hill in character and crowd makeup, while Station North has a number of great new bars that often proffer live music and art.

The rest of the city can be categorized in some broad strokes: Downtown is where the city's big, sprawling clubs and bar complexes are found and more sophisticated-feeling lounges and gay and lesbian nightlife are in stately Mount Vernon. Unlike some cities, where music venues are congregated into certain areas,

Baltimore's live music scene is scattered all over town, which makes wandering into a club and hearing a great local band a bit tough; check the websites of some of the listed locations to find out what kind of music you'll find on each stage. So whether it's a night listening to traditional Irish music and hoisting a few Guinnesses, raising a well-shaken martini, or slipping into a small art gallery to catch a buzz-laden new band, nighttime in Baltimore is a great time to experience a different side of the city.

Downtown and Inner Harbor

Map 1

AFTER HOURS

★ Paradox

In the always-mercurial after-hours industry, Paradox has managed to survive for nearly two decades; it has done so by figuring out what the hordes of young people (it's an 18+ club) who head to this dark, industrial part of town want to do when their parents are asleep. They want to dance (two floors, lots of lights, smoke, and lasers), they want to eat (there's a full restaurant serving pizza, chicken, and more), and they want to hoop (a half-court basketball area is always packed, until the dancing gets going). Depending on the DJ and event, crowds here can vary from googly ravers to intimidating thugs, so a drive-by is recommended to see who has shown up.

MAP 1: 1310 Russell St., 410/837-9110, www.thedox.com; Fri. 11pm-5am, Sat. midnight-6am; $8-15, more for special events

BARS

Explorer's Lounge

Though there's a slightly Hollywood-set feel to this restaurant/ lounge—owing to the fact that it's in the 1970s-era architectural bore that is the Royal Sonesta hotel—it's still one of the city's best places to have a civilized cocktail or two. That's because it's got a spectacular, second-story view of Baltimore's Inner Harbor, enjoyed from your choice of stately chairs in a room filled with rugs, bookcases, huge plants, and murals depicting animals and scenery from Africa. Try the lounge's signature Honeysuckle, a combination of lemon vodka, elderflower liquor, and honey simple syrup made from honey harvested from the hotel's own apiary. There's often live jazz, and seats near the windows can go fast on weekends, so act quickly if you're looking to start your evening here.

MAP 1: Royal Sonesta Harbor Court, 550 Light St., 410/234-0550, www.sonesta.com; Sun.-Thurs. noon-midnight, Fri.-Sat. noon-2am; no cover

Those looking for more daring bar activities than darts will appreciate PBR Baltimore's large mechanical bull ring, the centerpiece of this spirited country bar in the Power Plant Live! complex. (Though, in actuality, Shania Twain and Jason Aldean share the airwaves with pop and hip-hop artists). Crowds gather around the ring to watch their friends take the reins and, inevitably, hurl to the padded floor. Otherwise, this place, which adjoins and shares cover fees with Angels Rock Bar, is popular with a young crowd, especially bachelorette parties (think skimpily dressed dancers cutting loose on the bars). Note that the bar is open only three days a week.

MAP 1: 2 Market Pl., Power Plant Live!, 443/680-9433, www.pbrbaltimore.com; Wed. 9pm-2am, Fri. 7pm-2am, Sat. 8pm-2am; $5 and up

Power Plant Live!

It's best to consider Power Plant Live! as a single entity, rather than trying to separate it into its many various food-and-alcohol-serving parts. This is a planned, managed congregation of eateries and bars, with a large center plaza area that hosts bands, DJs, and warm-weather crowds. There are restaurants here (like Joe Squared, MEX, and TATU), along with large bars (Angels Rock Bar, Luckie's Tavern), a comedy club (Baltimore Comedy Factory), and even a dueling-pianos establishment (Howl at the Moon). It's a reasonable option for an early dinner, but as the night goes on, the crowd gets younger and younger, and the music volumes and social high jinks increase. Although there is a cover to enter the main plaza after certain times on weekends, this includes two $5 vouchers that can be used at various bars, a trade-off which sort of makes everything even.

MAP 1: 34 Market Pl., 410/752-5483, www.powerplantlive.com; hours vary; most bars open at 5pm; $10 Fri. after midnight, Sat. after 11pm, extra for individual bars

GAY AND LESBIAN

Club Bunns

This dance club and bar is a popular hangout for gay and lesbian African Americans, though all are welcome here. The music tends toward more hip-hop and R&B tracks than the usual club and house music played at the city's other gay clubs. The neighborhood is not one of the city's best when visited after dark, so use caution and prudence when parking in the area.

MAP 1: 608 W. Lexington St., 410/234-2866; daily 3pm-2am; no cover

LIVE MUSIC

Ram's Head Live

This is the Baltimore outlet of a long-popular Annapolis-based nightspot; part of the bar/restaurant party complex called Power

Plant Live! (and yes, the exclamation point is part of the official name), this venue filled a most-needed niche in the Baltimore music scene. It's a medium-size performance space that can draw medium-size acts (and even top-name acts on their way down) and provide a slick, well-managed experience for everyone involved.

MAP 1: 20 Market Pl., Power Plant Live!, 410/244-1131, www.ramsheadlive.com; Mon.-Sat. from 10am; doors open 2 hours before showtime; $35 and under

LOUNGES

Havana Club

This richly appointed club and lounge—located above a Ruth's Chris Steakhouse, just a few steps from the monstrous Power Plant Live! complex—draws a crowd who likes to hang out in the big, leather chairs, have a few drinks, and get moving on the small dance floor. There are also pool tables and salsa dancing on some Friday nights. For a while, this was one of the few places in town to smoke, and the club offered an ample selection of stogies for guests to do so. Note that although smoking is no longer allowed because of Maryland's Clean Indoor Air Act, the club continues to pursue an exemption to the law that would allow use of tobacco products inside once again.

MAP 1: 600 Water St., 410/468-0022, www.havanaclub-baltimore.com; Thurs. 6pm-midnight, Fri.-Sat. 6pm-2am; $5 and up

Mosaic

At the back of the west side of the sprawling Power Plant Live! bar and restaurant complex is Mosaic, a medium-size lounge and club for those looking to get away from the hordes of beer-swilling patrons the venue attracts. This is a space to relax, have an adult cocktail, recline on some pillows, and let some ambient house music unwind (or entice) you. There's also a generous outdoor seating area. Later in the evening, the beats per minute accelerate, the generous outdoor seating area gains steam, and there is a lot more energy.

MAP 1: 4 Market Pl., Power Plant Live!, 443/468-5308, www.mosaic-baltimore.com; Fri.-Sat. 10pm-2am; $5 and up

Harbor East and
Little Italy

Map 2

BARS
James Joyce Irish Pub & Restaurant

Among all of Harbor East's restaurants/bars, which have created a thriving neighborhood, this is the one watering hole that feels like a bar first and a restaurant second. The pub itself is casual and largely swathed in wood, and the kitchen serves Irish specialties like beef and Guinness stew and bangers and mash, as well as standard American sandwiches, soups, and salads. There are regular theme nights (burgers on Monday; trivia on Tuesday) and live music on Friday and Saturday. With two hotels across the street, it can be hopping here even on a weekday night.

MAP 2: 616 S. President St., 410/727-5107, www.thejamesjoycepub.com; Mon.-Fri. 11am-2am, Sat.-Sun. 10am-2am; no cover

DANCE CLUBS
Club Orpheus

For those who enjoy slipping into leather, black lipstick, fishnet, and sorrow, Baltimore offers Club Orpheus, a very goth-centered venue just east of the candlelit pasta dinners of Little Italy. Fans of similar genres, like industrial and punk, will generally feel at home here as well; the sound system is not bad, and the atmosphere is relatively welcoming to new, like-minded people. Decor in this large, joy-free space is, unsurprisingly, black, minimal, and functional.

MAP 2: 1003 E. Pratt St., 410/276-5599, www.cluborpheus.webs.com; daily 9pm-2am; $8 18 and over, $6 21 and over

Fell's Point

Map 2

BARS
Bad Decisions

About six blocks east of the Fell's Point main drag is this dive bar that surprisingly stocks only about 10 beers. Instead liquor is the drink of choice here, and there are more than 800 varieties, providing plenty of options for cocktails. The spicy pickletini is popular, as is the bacon habanero mojito, a mainstay during the bar's regular bacon nights; the nice bartenders can also make special drinks depending on what you like. Just for fun, try to get ahold of the bar's "menu," a thick, tattered, slightly damp book where dozens of cocktails are handwritten on yellowing graph paper (though it may be easier to just ask for recommendations). There are also a few board games scattered around for late-night playing at one of the bar's deep booths.

MAP 2: 1928 Fleet St., 410/979-5161, www.makeabaddecision.com; Mon. 11am-2am, Tues.-Sat. 5pm-2am, Sun. 11am-2am; no cover

The Cat's Eye Pub

With the advent of new condos and upscale wine bars around Fell's Point, the survival of places like The Cat's Eye was sometimes in doubt. Never fear: This ramshackle turquoise tavern covered in holiday lights is a remnant of the older, grittier Fell's Point, where sailors, bikers, and boozers all mingled among the then-dirty wharves and streets. The Cat's Eye's tiny but serviceable stage is a great place to catch live music. It's a bar that wouldn't seem out of place in New Orleans, especially in the summertime.

MAP 2: 1730 Thames St., 410/276-9866, www.catseyepub.com; daily noon-2am; no cover

Duda's Tavern

This is what most of the bars in Fell's Point used to look like back in the pre-gentrification 1980s—well, actually, it's nicer than that, but Duda's is part of a vanishing breed of excellent old-school taverns (with great food, by the way). Grab a bar stool (or an outside table), order a beer, and tuck in to a huge burger, fantastic crab cake, or some crab soup to watch an Orioles game (note the tablecloths). It's a small enough place that you can listen in on the conversations of the nearby patrons; this place seems to be a favorite of National Aquarium workers. If you're a suds fan, Duda's has a fairly broad beer selection for a corner joint.

MAP 2: 1600 Thames St., 410/276-9719, www.dudastavern.com; Mon.-Fri. 11am-1am, Sat. noon-1am; no cover

The Horse You Came In On Saloon

This rowdy bar was founded in 1775, making it the "oldest continually operated saloon" in America, according to its website. That alone is reason enough to at least take a peek inside. But there's more: This was also the last place that Edgar Allan Poe was seen before he died in 1849. Today, a young and boisterous crowd come here for the daily live music that can be heard from the streets outside and the infused Jack Daniels cocktails kept in glass dispensers behind the bar. There's also a full menu of sandwiches, quesadillas, and pizzas.

MAP 2: 1626 Thames St., 410/327-8111, www.thehorsebaltimore.com; daily 11:30am-1:30am; no cover

There's a particular skill to getting the most out of a visit to this venerable, authentic, and well-used Fell's Point bar, where the crowd is a mix of lifers and tourists. First, get a couple of seats at the big bar (or one of the tables next to the small windows). Next, order from the ample, well-planned beer list. Third, order a pound of mussels or steamed shrimp. As you eat and drink, look around the room at the great wooden details on the bar and the pressed tin ceiling. Repeat until pleasantly full. Sure, there's a nice dining room and an enticing outdoor (and out back) dining patio, but the real fun is in the front bar (or at the outdoor tables).

MAP 2: 1800 Thames St., 410/327-5561, www.johnstevenstavern.com; daily 11am-2am; no cover

Max's Taphouse

Do you like beer? Really, *really* like beer? Do you like beer enough to brave an enormous mini-complex of three separate taverns, with five hand-pumped cask ales, 140 rotating draft beers, and about 1,200 bottled beers that will challenge your beer stamina? This brick and wood palace of hops and barley—in the heart of Fell's Point, just a block from the water—has a huge assortment of TVs, along with pool and foosball, a menu of burgers and sandwiches, and a regulation darts room (there's also a "lounge" upstairs that's a bit less beer-hall-like).

MAP 2: 737 S. Broadway, 410/675-6297, www.maxs.com; daily 11am-2am; no cover

One-Eyed Mike's

Some bars sell particularly large amounts of whiskey, or beer, or shiraz. One-Eyed Mike's sells Grand Marnier, and lots of it. Enough to cover many of the walls with bottles. Enough to have not a mug club, but rather a Grand Marnier club with more than 1,500 members and the perk of being able to keep personal bottles of the liqueur in vast glass cases. One-Eyed Mike's also serves food (which tends toward well-done, slightly upscale pub grub) to a loyal crowd, with a dining room in between the busy front bar and a popular back patio.

MAP 2: 708 S. Bond St., 410/327-0445, www.oneeyedmikes.com; Mon.-Sat. 11am-2am, Sun. 10am-2am; no cover

Rye

Locals describe this newcomer—named after the whiskey that was popular in Baltimore before Prohibition—as one of Fell's Point's more upscale bars. Indeed, the purple velvet banquettes and rich glazed wood ceiling in the front bar, large leather sofas in the back lounge, and menu of classic and modern craft cocktails do give the

Craft Cocktails and Local Beer

Baltimoreans are increasingly interested in what goes into their cocktails, and the city's mixologists have responded with drinks that have become a culinary art form. In Fell's Point, newcomer **Rye** offers craft cocktails in about four categories, from drinks inspired by the bartenders' ancestors to original creations, and **Bad Decisions** sometimes mixes drinks with a nod to the aperitifs and nightcaps popular during Prohibition. Craft cocktails can be found at several restaurants, too; try **Mr. Rain's Fun House** or **B&O American Brasserie**, both of which shake up modern versions of the classics and invent originals.

While craft cocktails are a relatively new trend, brewing beer in Baltimore goes back to the 19th century. Hugh Sisson may be the city's most popular brewmaster: He started Maryland's first brewpub in 1989 and is founder of the local Heavy Seas line of beers. The Heavy Seas brewery is in Halethorpe about 10 minutes outside of the city and gives regular tours (www.hsbeer. com), but the easiest way to sample the beer is to head over to the **Heavy Seas Alehouse** in Little Italy. Although Sisson isn't affiliated with the restaurant and bar, at least 10 varieties of Heavy Seas beer are available for sipping or pairing with the restaurant's menu.

Another pioneer of beer brewing is **The Brewer's Art,** a local favorite with a huge selection of house-brewed beers. Four popular varieties like Resurrection, the brewery's flagship brown ale, are always on tap, as are a few rotating seasonal offerings. Stay for dinner, if you can, either here or at Heavy Seas Alehouse, where the excellent food is several steps above your standard bar grub.

The inexpensive National Bohemian beer, or "Natty Boh," as locals like to call it, is also a Baltimore favorite: The beer was brewed here from 1885 until 1996. Though it's now produced in North Carolina and Pennsylvania, the one-eyed, mustachioed "Natty Boh" mascot can be seen on many a Baltimore souvenir, and you can find a cheap can of the pilsner in almost any city bar.

feeling that this is a place to have a drink among adults. But this being Fell's Point, the crowd is still relatively dressed-down and not the least bit stuffy. The decor has some cool artsy touches, like the fireplace adorned with rows of hanging lightbulbs in the lounge, and the bartenders teach informal cocktail classes one Sunday a month.

MAP 2: 807 S. Broadway, 443/438-3296, www.ryebaltimore.com; daily 5pm-2am; no cover

★ The Wharf Rat

Housed in a building from the late 18th century, this corner bar in Fell's Point is rumored to be haunted by one of its old owners (Baltimore Ghost Tours has the story). That hasn't deterred patrons though; The Wharf Rat is a favorite of many Baltimoreans, probably because of the character this dark, colonial-era room possesses: old wooden chairs and round tables decorated with beer caps and nautical charts, low ceilings filled with rowing oars and exposed wooden beams, and a grand back bar with a working fireplace. The crowd (which ranges from young to old) is a mix of regulars here for the beers and company, and tourists who peeked inside, saw the great atmosphere, and pulled up a chair.

MAP 2: 801 S. Ann St., 410/276-8304, www.thewharfrat.com; daily 11am-2am; no cover

DANCE CLUBS

The Get Down

Looking for a club with bright, blinking lights, a rotating book of DJs spinning house and electronica music, and a crowd who likes to dance? The Get Down is basically your only option in bar-heavy Fell's Point. Early in the evening when the club is still quiet and the cover is free, the small lounge with its white leather couches is a nice spot to have a drink and eye the crowd. But expect a small group then, as the place doesn't really get going until later, when the second floor opens up if needed and the dancing starts. Table reservations are offered here, and RSVP'ing on the club's Facebook page will usually get you in for free before 11pm.

MAP 2: 701 S. Bond St., 443/708-3564, www.getdownbaltimore.com; Thurs.-Sun. 8pm-2am; free before 10pm, $10-30 after 10pm

WINE BARS

V-NO

This small wine bar has some of the best real estate in town—waterfront in Fell's Point, best viewed from one of the cute outdoor tables. Inside, blonde-wood seating sections and an inviting bar are regularly filled with locals discussing the affairs of the historic neighborhood. Most wines for sale run under $30 per bottle (glasses are also available), and there's a selection of plates with cheeses, cured meats, breads, spreads, and desserts to quench your palate.

MAP 2: 905 S. Ann St., 410/342-8466, www.v-nowinebar.com; Mon.-Wed. 4:30pm-9pm, Thurs. 4:30pm-10pm, Fri.-Sat. noon-midnight, Sun. noon-7pm; no cover

NIGHTLIFE
FELL'S POINT

Canton

Map 3

BARS

Bartender's

Most of Boston Street in Canton is populated by clubs or hipster lounges; this homegrown establishment is run by gregarious local semi-celebrity Danny Coker, a lifelong bar and restaurant saint. The crowd at this well-sized, wood-rich bar is devoted, and they're open to strangers who appreciate the place as much as they do; the bargain-priced pizzas also have many devotees (try the Big Bill). It's a place that's popular with locals who want to grab a drink and some food and watch a little sports, or listen to another hilarious tale or theory from Coker.

MAP 3: 2218 Boston St., 410/534-2337, www.bartendersbaltimore.com; Mon.-Thurs. 4pm-2am, Fri.-Sun. noon-2am; no cover

Mahaffey's

It's nowhere near the often-boisterous O'Donnell Square that's the heart of Canton's nightlife scene, which may explain why this small corner pub has such a devoted following. (The great tin ceiling, huge back-room mural of an 1800s cityscape, and friendly atmosphere help, too.) Mahaffey's takes care to serve great beer correctly (not too cold, not too warm) from its often-rotated menu. There's also a grill right behind the well-stocked bar, where the chef may be turning intoxicatingly seasoned steaks over the fire.

MAP 3: 2706 Dillon St., 410/276-9899, www.mahaffeyspub.com; Sun.-Thurs. 3pm-2am, Fri.-Sat. noon-2am; no cover

WINE BARS

Chesapeake Wine Company

One of the many businesses retrofitted into the Can Company, a former canning facility turned into offices, shops, and restaurants, this open, airy wine and liquor store is also home to one of Canton's more popular little wine bars, found at the back of the store. There's a bar, good music, and lots of tables, often filled with neighbors (and their strollers) partaking of a pinot noir or a chardonnay, along with small plates of cheeses and pâté. Drinks are available by the glass or bottle.

MAP 3: 2400 Boston St., 410/522-4556, www.chesapeakewine.com; Mon.-Sat. 11am-9pm, Sun. 11am-6pm; no cover

Federal Hill

Map 4

BARS

Captain Larry's

The legendary founder and namesake of this South Baltimore watering hole may have sailed for warmer shores (Florida), but his fine bar and tiny restaurant still thrive, discovered by a new generation of residents. One room is a cluttered, eclectic bar; the other is the dining room, where your entrée of choice is the crab-cake sandwich, served on a roll or with saltines. A visit to this institution is a trip into the real South Baltimore, where pretension is forbidden and rooms filled with nautical memorabilia, random junk, and neon beer signs are celebrated.

MAP 4: 601 E. Fort Ave., 410/727-4799, www.captainlarrys.com; daily 11:30am-2am; no cover

Little Havana

Overlooking a couple of parking lots—and the Inner Harbor—this Federal Hill bar has been packing in crowds for years. The big, rear waterview deck is an ideal spot to partake of some cool mojitos and carne asada tacos under the glow of the Domino Sugars sign (and it's a great place to watch the fireworks that occasionally illuminate the Inner Harbor). Inside, this industrial-strength establishment has a huge central bar, lots of seats and TVs, and a faux-rickety "old Cuba" feel. If you're over 35, you might be in the minority here some weekends, but you won't be alone.

MAP 4: 1325 Key Hwy., 410/837-9903, www.littlehavanas.com; Mon.-Thurs. 4pm-midnight, Fri.-Sat. 11:30am-2am, Sun. 11am-midnight; no cover

Mum's

A town like Baltimore is going to have a few bars that are, to be polite, low-rent dives. Mum's is one of the city's greatest, meeting all of the requirements of a great cheap dive. Live music in a cramped back room? Check. Cheap drinks? Check. Surly, hilarious bartenders? Check. Great jukebox featuring exactly zero Top 40 hits of the past 10 years? Check. A couple of blocks from Federal Hill's more tony lounges and polished taverns, Mum's is where seasoned locals go for a drink and a stool near the TV to watch the O's or Ravens game.

MAP 4: 1132 S. Hanover St., 410/547-7415; Mon.-Fri. 2pm-2am, Sat.-Sun. 1pm-2am; no cover

clockwise from top left: Club Hippo, Mount Vernon; lively nightlife scene on Cross Street in Federal Hill; The Owl Bar and The 13th Floor in The Belvedere, Mount Vernon

Pub Dog Pizza & Drafthouse

Formerly one of the city's most popular "bring your dog while you go drinking" establishments (a now-outlawed practice), this bar, cozy and dark with lots of exposed brick, is still packing in regulars. Locals are drawn to the fireplace, brick-oven gourmet pizzas, and the good, cheap, microbrewed beer. Well-used booths and bar stools and a shuffleboard pub game upstairs let newcomers know that this place stays busy, especially on weekends.

MAP 4: 20 E. Cross St., 410/727-6077, www.pubdog.net; daily 5pm-2am; no cover

LIVE MUSIC
8x10

Though this rock and roots club has changed names and philosophies a few times over the years (it's back to the original 8x10 now, reflecting the addresses of the two buildings it occupies), this is still one of the city's great little venues that can pull in a full house with local reggae and hip-hop performers. It's a no-frills rock club, so don't expect anything too grandiose, but the beers are relatively cheap and the sound is not bad for such a narrowly shaped space.

MAP 4: 10 E. Cross St., 410/625-2000, www.the8x10.com; doors open approx. 1 hour before showtime; about $15-20

LOUNGES
Zeeba Lounge

This beautiful Federal Hill hookah bar and lounge really comes alive toward the end of the night, as it's one of the only late-night (until 4am on Friday and Saturday) options in the bar-heavy neighborhood. Lots of warm woods, rugs, tapestries, and pillows add to the vibe here, along with the heady smell of hookah smoke (which is the only kind of smoking allowed). There are belly dancers and live drumming, a pleasantly pre-inebriated crowd, and a great Mediterranean menu to help ward off a hangover. Note there are bottle fees; bringing a single bottle for a group is the best idea.

MAP 4: 916 Light St., 410/539-7900, www.zeebalounge.com; Wed.-Thurs. and Sun. 6pm-midnight, Fri.-Sat. 6pm-4am; no cover

Mount Vernon and Station North

Map 5

AFTER HOURS

Club 1722

Inside this unassuming Station North club, a stalwart of the Baltimore late-night party scene, there are two stories of rooms, dance areas, and couches. If there's a particularly popular DJ or themed party going on, there may even be a line out front. Generally speaking, this is a gay club, but the scene is tolerant of everyone who can follow the rules (this place is for grown-ups, and people sporting the youth "street" look are not allowed in). Friday nights are all about Top 40 music, while on Saturday, nearly anything goes, from techno and house to percussion and dance classics (although hip-hop doesn't make the list).

MAP 5: 1722 N. Charles St., 410/547-8423, www.club1722.com; Fri. 1:45am-5am, Sat. 1:45am-6am; about $10-15

BARS

★ The Brewer's Art

There are two completely different kinds of bars here (as well as a popular and inventive restaurant that you shouldn't miss). In the upstairs lounge, beneath an elaborate chandelier, you can have a cocktail and watch traffic glide past on Charles Street. After that, you can dine in the expansive, wood-paneled dining room, hung with contemporary paintings (don't skip the rosemary fries!). Then head downstairs to the dark, catacomb-like basement bar, and sample the beer that made this place infamous: Resurrection, a potent dubbel-style ale. This bar has gotten national attention as a must-patronize tavern, and once you're tucked into a dark, medieval brick corner with a well-crafted ale, you'll understand why.

MAP 5: 1106 N. Charles St., 410/547-6925, www.thebrewersart.com; daily 4pm-1:45am; no cover

Club Charles

One of Baltimore's premier, old-fashioned watering holes for discriminating drinkers, this art deco bar has hosted generations of city residents looking for some fine drinks, good music, and an artsy, metropolitan scene. The light here is very, very low, making it a great place to grab a booth and canoodle and people-watch over some martinis, either before or after a film at the Charles Theatre. The marvelous bartenders are unflappably kind, even when the crowds get two deep.

MAP 5: 1724 N. Charles St., 410/727-8815, www.clubcharles.us; daily 6pm-2am; no cover

This traditional Irish bar in Station North is most notable because it's so different from everything around it. While many of its watering hole neighbors draw a young creative crowd from the nearby Maryland Institute College of Art, Liam Flynn's attracts young professionals, social groups, and musicians looking to jam during the bar's regular bluegrass and Celtic music sessions. Inside, there's a lot of wood, the Guinness is flowing, and there's talk of the kitchen offering a full menu of Irish and Scottish favorites soon. There's also a band that plays jazz on Monday nights.

MAP 5: 22 W. North Ave., 410/244-8447, www.pintsizepub.com; Mon.-Fri. 5pm-2am, Sat. 10am-2am, Sun. 1pm-midnight; no cover

Mount Royal Tavern

There's really one reason to stop in at this well-worn and frankly dirty bar, long a favorite for the generations of art students from neighboring Maryland Institute College of Art, and one reason only: the ceiling. Rather, what's on the ceiling, which is a stunningly faithful recreation of Leonardo da Vinci's ceiling mural from the Sistine Chapel. Don't snicker: The quality and craftsmanship on this project is astonishing. Rotate around on your bar stool as you sip a beer and study the technique, the focus, and the preposterousness of the endeavor. Think it was a waste of time? Local legend has it that the mural's creator drinks for free, for life, here at the Mount Royal Tavern.

MAP 5: 1204 W. Mount Royal Ave., 410/669-6686; daily 10am-2am; no cover

The Owl Bar

The Belvedere building was once a hotel that hosted politicians like Woodrow Wilson and Hollywood stars like Clark Gable; more recently, Jon Hamm was here filming a scene for *Mad Men*. The building is now divided into condominiums, but it still has two bars, and this is one of them. With The Belvedere's history, it's not surprising that The Owl Bar initially feels opulent, thanks to gilded trim, deep green columns, and rich wallpaper that displays a scene between proper gents and ladies. But this is a fairly casual place, a favorite spot for locals who want to have post-work drinks at the long bar or dine on steak frites or pizzas at the white tablecloth-covered tables. There's also a front dining room for those who want a slightly quieter atmosphere.

MAP 5: 1 E. Chase St., 410/347-0888, www.theowlbar.com; Mon.-Thurs. 11:30am-midnight, Fri.-Sat. 11:30am-2am, Sun. 11am-midnight; no cover

The 13th Floor

Atop the looming historic Belvedere building—once a hotel where the likes of John Kennedy, Woodrow Wilson, and Clark Gable lodged in the first half of the 20th century—is this storied bar, which has survived a number of themes, crazes, and economic roller coasters. Its latest incarnation is as a lounge that serves steak, seafood, and old-school classics like baked brie and crab and avocado salad. But the amazing nighttime city views are still the best reason to visit, owing to the building's location at one of the city's highest points. Although jeans are allowed, upscale casual is the more accepted way to dress.

MAP 5: 1 E. Chase St., 410/347-0880, www.13floorbelvedere.com; Tues.-Wed. 5pm-10pm, Thurs. 5pm-11pm, Fri.-Sat. 5pm-1am; no cover

★ The Windup Space

Anything goes at this Station North bar and performance venue, from Wednesday night table tennis to occasional pie-making contests to burlesque shows, dance parties, and board game nights. This fun and varied schedule unfolds in a big, open room with a long bar on the right, plenty of artwork to admire on the left, several mismatched tables in the center, and a stage in back. There's usually a creative crowd here (the Maryland Institute College of Art is close by) that is generally welcoming, and the Charles Theatre is about a block away, making this a convenient stop for a post-movie drink.

MAP 5: 12 W. North Ave., 410/244-8855, www.thewindupspace.com; Tues.-Sat. 5pm-1am, occasional Sun. and Mon.; no cover

DANCE CLUBS
The Depot

If you miss the big hair and synthesizer-rich stylings of the 1980s music scene, The Depot is for you. Most nights, the sugary hits of the '80s are on heavy rotation in this dark, neon-lit, no-frills dance club; live bands and more modern DJs round out the bill the other nights. There's no food, and you should wear something you'll feel comfortable sweating through as you jump and twist the night away; it's a place for happy people with simple needs, not a place to show off your Jimmy Choo shoes.

MAP 5: 1728 N. Charles St., 410/528-0174, www.depotbaltimore.com; Wed.-Sun. 9pm-2am; cover varies

GAY AND LESBIAN
★ Club Hippo

Club Hippo is the other major gay and lesbian nexus of Baltimore; it's in a wonderful old building built as a nightclub in the 1930s. There are three main rooms here: a huge dance floor, where DJs and a sophisticated light show work the crowds into nonstop motion; a more traditional bar area, with pool tables; and a third lounge-ish area that's a video bar. Gay Bingo on Wednesday nights has become

There are two new(ish) schools of music in Baltimore, created by two different communities, that provide excellent examples of the music the city likes right now. First is Baltimore Club, a specific type of hip-hop club and dance music that originated in the early 1990s. It's fast: 130-beats-per-minute fast, which means you better know how to dance if you hit the floor. It's not terribly complex in terms of composition or structure, and the same sampled phrases or lyrics are repeated a lot, but if there's a good crowd and they like the song, it's a sight to behold as they all move in a sort of jittering unison.

More recently, a new group of young musicians and artists have gained attention. Bands like Beach House, Double Dagger, and Wye Oak have devoted and interested followings. One group of like-minded folks came together to form an operation known as Wham City, headed by Dan Deacon, who is something of a darling of the independent music press. This group is composed of artists and performers who like to include both costumes and strange sonic events in their shows, and they encourage crowd participation. As unlikely as it might sound, a lot of what comes out is really immediately fun and engaging; live shows are more like big parties than anything else.

a favorite for patrons of all persuasions, as it's generally led by a no-nonsense-tolerated, wickedly witted drag queen.

MAP 5: 1 W. Eager St., 410/547-0069, www.clubhippo.com; daily 4pm-2am; dance club opens at 10pm; cover varies

The Drinkery

This Mount Vernon institution is a gay bar in the most basic sense of the words: there's no glitz or glamour or club atmosphere here. It's just a regular city bar that happens to have purple walls and a gay clientele. There's a good jukebox, karaoke on the weekends, and a loyal crowd of regulars (most of whom are past their 20s and 30s). Drinks are cheap, the people are friendly, and there's no production required before a visit.

MAP 5: 205 W. Read St., 410/225-3100; daily 11am-2am; no cover

★ Grand Central

One of the two big gay and lesbian scenes in Charm City convenes nightly in this very large three-story bar and dance club in Mount Vernon. There are three separate areas in Grand Central (much like at Club Hippo across the street): a large bar area downstairs with karaoke and DJs; a massive dance floor with requisite light show and effects (plus a great sound system); and Sapphos, a second-floor, ladies-mostly area with a deck, pool, and dancing.

MAP 5: 1001 N. Charles St., 410/752-7133, www.centralstationpub.com; Mon.-Sat. 4pm-2am, Sun. 3pm-2am; no cover

LIVE MUSIC

★ An die Musik LIVE!

This is a fantastic classical and jazz CD and LP store, and it's also one of the most enchanting places to catch a jazz show. It's no smoky subterranean groove cellar, though; it's the second floor of a cool, modern renovation in the heart of downtown. Big, comfortable chairs are the standard here, and the acoustics of the room are outstanding. Owner Henry Wong also manages to lure a very high caliber of player, which draws the real cognoscenti.

MAP 5: 409 N. Charles St., 410/385-2638 or 888/221-6170, www.andiemusiklive.com; about $7-15

Charm City Art Space

This is not a quiet, subdued art space; it's a working, serious, do-it-yourself building for art and generally loud, unrestrained music. Upstairs are artworks and offices; rock shows take place in the totally rocker-friendly wood-paneled basement, which rapidly turns into an overheated swamp during well-attended gigs, but it all fits in with the ethos of the place. This is a DIY joint, so don't expect frills of any sorts, but do expect that, by coming to a show here, your money is going right to the artists and the space.

MAP 5: 1731 Maryland Ave., no phone, www.ccspace.org; doors open approx. 1 hour before showtime; hours and cover vary depending on performance times

Metro Gallery

Metro Gallery began as a basic art gallery; it's since evolved into a performance space and bar, and a great place to see some of the town's best new young bands. It's a nice big room, which hosts readings and art performances in addition to visual artworks. Best of all, there's a great big picture window behind the bands that let crowds watch the traffic on busy Charles Street blur by (though sometimes the management shuts the drapes) as the music plays. It's only open for special events, though, so check the calendar on the website before venturing out.

MAP 5: 1700 N. Charles St., 410/244-0899, www.themetrogallery.net; doors open approx. 1 hour before showtime; about $8-10

LOUNGES

★ Red Maple

Longevity in a lounge is something rare, especially in Baltimore, which has always favored bars or mega-clubs and little in-between. But Red Maple has succeeded because it got the basics right: great music, both from DJs and small live performances; a well-designed and nicely-appointed building with different areas for sitting, eating, and dancing; a tasty, modern menu (mostly Asian tapas) that's just right for the space; and even an out-back smoking patio featuring the club's namesake tree. Even the bathrooms, where many Baltimore lounges will cut corners, have smart design. Live flamenco bands and belly dancing balance out the house and trance DJs.

MAP 5: 930 N. Charles St., 410/547-0149, www.930redmaple.com; Mon. 8pm-2am (kitchen closed), Tues.-Fri. 5pm-2am, Sat.-Sun. 6pm-2am; $5 and up

Hampden and Homewood   Map 6

BARS
★ WC Harlan

When this bar opened in 2013, the owners wanted it to feel like a speakeasy guests could only hear about by word of mouth. Thus, there is no phone number or website, and the only sign outside is the word "Enter" written in chalk on the black door. All of this can sound a bit pretentious, but WC Harlan has quickly become a local favorite. Inside, the bar is really quite lovely and atmospheric, with soft music, red velvet curtains, sketched portraits, mirrors, chandeliers, and even an upright piano covered in a dainty white doily. The only draft beer options are dark and light (with a cordial, if you like), but there are also bottled beer, carafes of wine, a cocktail du jour, and a few snacks like bread with chorizo or olive tapenade. Note that the bar is on a quiet street with nothing else going on, but there is usually plenty of parking outside.

MAP 6: 400 W. 23rd St., no phone; Mon.-Sat. 5pm-1am; no cover

LIVE MUSIC
★ The Ottobar

It takes a special venue to host both underground rap and metal bands as well as '80s nights and more mainstream rock bands, but it all makes a strange sort of sense at The Ottobar. Upstairs is a great bar with lots of pool tables and a phenomenal jukebox; downstairs is a (relatively) huge stage (for a Baltimore rock club), a big main floor, and a side balcony with tables and chairs.

MAP 6: 2549 N. Howard St., 410/662-0069, www.theottobar.com; doors open approx. a half-hour to 1 hour before showtime; about $5-20

WINE BARS
★ 13.5% Wine Bar

This great Hampden wine bar, which carries about 40 wines by the glass and more than 200 bottles, feels more like a lounge with plenty of deep couches and big, comfortable chairs, as well as a full menu of small and large plates. The food—oysters, pork belly, pâté, cheese plates, and plenty of salads—is quite good, and there are a

NIGHTLIFE HAMPDEN AND HOMEWOOD

couple of tables outside, a rarity in Hampden. Although the bar's organic-feeling stone wall doesn't quite jive with the minimalist orange and gray decor, this is still a fine place to unwind with a glass of wine or to have dinner after shopping at the many nearby boutiques and stores.

MAP 6: 1117 W. 36th St., 410/889-1064, www.135winebar.com; Mon.-Thurs. 4pm-midnight, Fri. 4pm-2am, Sat. 1pm-2am, Sun. 3pm-midnight; no cover

Arts and Culture

Downtown and Inner Harbor.....147

Harbor East and Little Italy 149

Fell's Point.......................151

Canton 152

Federal Hill 153

Mount Vernon and Station North..153

Hampden and Homewood.......160

Greater Baltimore................161

HIGHLIGHTS

★ **Best Venue for a Broadway Show:** The immaculately restored **Hippodrome Theatre**—the jewel of the growing west side downtown—draws Broadway classics and the newest hit musicals (page 148).

★ **Best Multipurpose Arts Space:** A fabulous old movie marquee is the sign for **Creative Alliance at the Patterson.** Inside, it's possible to tour artist studios and admire art exhibits, listen to live music or see a play, and even have dinner at the farm-to-table restaurants without ever leaving the building (page 152).

★ **Best Independent Cinema:** The fare at **The Charles Theatre** can include foreign films, classics, and even a minor Hollywood hit or two (page 153).

★ **Best Small Gallery:** The 30-plus-year-old **C. Grimaldis Gallery** is the cream of the crop in Baltimore's contemporary art scene. The gallery exhibits paintings and sculpture from well-known local artists as well as rising stars (page 154).

★ **Best Theater:** For more than five decades, **Center Stage** has produced thoughtful, powerful performances—with a range of classic, reimagined, and contemporary shows (page 158).

Baltimore has long supported a variety of outstanding museums and collections, as well as talented artists, musical and theater companies, and bona fide legends. Lately, the city has gained fresh acclaim for its new wave of young artists. Singers, songwriters, rappers, DJs, painters, collectives—

there's a real, legitimate scene going on in Baltimore now, one that's being covered more and more by the national press. There are also plenty of things to do after dark; Baltimore's artists and musicians are working hard to make things happen, and to entertain and engage the public.

After years of having only a few outlets for young artists, there are more and more galleries (both traditional and ad hoc) displaying new and exciting works, and maybe having a band or two to liven up the party. The music being made by Baltimoreans is inventive, and the city's gritty nature and do-it-yourself attitude can be heard in the final product, no matter what genre.

But Baltimore's established artists and musicians—from the symphony to classical pianists like Leon Fleischer to modern abstract painters like the late Grace Hartigan—remain just as vital, if not more so now, because of the city's rising young stars. The Baltimore Museum of Art and the Walters Art Museum are world-class institutions, and the big-name venues like Pier Six, Ram's Head Live, and the Baltimore Arena draw a variety of national and international performers.

Spring and summer are when the small neighborhood festivals and larger big-scale events are held around town, creating up to two months' worth of event-rich weekends. There are longtime favorites, like the many neighborhood ethnic festivals, and new, totally independent shows, like the musical mayhem of Scapescape, in which more than 100 local bands and performers play in venues and bars across the Station North Arts and Entertainment District in August.

Ever since Baltimore's early days as a burgeoning metropolis, the arts have played an important role in the life of the city. From opera houses to art colleges to conservatories and art museums, Baltimore has always managed to maintain artistic voices, despite economic issues and changing tastes and mores. The city's biggest outdoor festival, Artscape, is a celebration of art and music that lasts for three days in July and draws a crowd of more than 100,000 each year. And there's recently been a resurgence in Baltimore's appreciation of the classical arts as well, particularly since the addition of maestra Marin Alsop to the Baltimore Symphony Orchestra. Her ascendance to the podium of the BSO—and her enthusiastic cheerleading for Baltimore, the BSO, and music—has garnered the city a lot of positive attention.

Mount Vernon is the cultural heart of Baltimore City. From its elegant, European-influenced architecture and landscaping to the symphony hall, performing arts center, and Walters Art Museum— not to mention the prestigious Peabody Institute, one of the finest music schools in the nation—it's impossible to not be influenced and affected by the arts in this wonderful neighborhood. Mount Vernon and nearby Station North are also rich with a new crop of artist-run art galleries. And between these two neighborhoods lies Bolton Hill, home to the amazing and nationally recognized Maryland Institute College of Art and its many galleries exhibiting student, faculty, and national and international works by artists creating in all mediums.

As to contemporary art and music, Baltimore's East Coast location, urban energy, and low rents have attracted a variety of creative people to the city. This new vanguard of artists and musicians has set up their own spaces, galleries, and performance areas in Station North and in the Westside's Bromo Tower Arts & Entertainment District. There are two other centers of the contemporary art scene. The first is School 33 Art Center in Federal Hill, an arts and education center run by the Baltimore Office of Promotion & the Arts that holds regular openings for its solo and group shows, as well as studio tours and classes. The other is Highlandtown's Creative Alliance, a little north of Canton; this converted movie theater hosts art exhibitions, performances, films, and bands on a regular basis, as well as offering classes and lectures on the arts.

Baltimore has also had a wave of artists like the bands Animal Collective and Beach House and musician Dan Deacon who are getting attention and garnering fans from all over. The city also isn't slacking in the classical music department; celebrated violinist Hilary Hahn is a Charm City native.

Many of Baltimore's independent musicians and artists have formed loose (or more solid) collectives to help each other get shows and exhibit their works. The Scapescape, a four-day musical extravaganza in which artists aim to introduce attendees to as many local bands as possible, is the most recent example of this.

This is a great time to explore Baltimore's arts and cultural landscapes, as rarely before have there been so much energy, talent, and enthusiasm at both ends of the scale, from the classical to the experimental. The high quality of artists in Baltimore these days makes taking a chance on a show or event not only a worthwhile risk; it should be considered a requirement.

Downtown and Inner Harbor

Map 1

CINEMA
IMAX Theater at Maryland Science Center
There's nothing like walking into a five-story tall, 400-seat IMAX theater and preparing to have your senses blown away by surreally clear building-high images and gut-shaking sound. Like most IMAX theaters that are associated with science centers, this venue shows a healthy slate of nature and science documentaries, blended with kid-friendly Hollywood fare like animated films and Disney features. This theater can also show IMAX 3-D films, making for an even more engrossing experience. Most showings are in the morning and afternoon.
MAP 1: 601 Light St., 410/685-5225, www.mdsci.org; $8 after 4pm

CONCERT VENUES
Baltimore Arena
This midsize stadium/performance venue was built way back in 1962, and though a series of upgrades and improvements have been made, this space is showing its age. Still, at 13,500 seats, it's the only game in town for a variety of performers. Early on, the arena hosted bands and performers like the Beatles, the Rolling Stones, the Supremes, and Led Zeppelin. Today, the bigger names in country, hip-hop, and rock stop here on tours geared toward second-tier cities; it's also where the TV-created next generation of performers (like Nickelodeon's The Fresh Beat Band) stop as they head across the United States.
MAP 1: 201 W. Baltimore St., 410/347-2020, www.baltimorearena.com

Accessible Theater

Baltimore has many wonderful theaters that run top-notch performances for very reasonable prices. Mount Vernon's **Center Stage** offers half-price rush tickets an hour before scheduled performances; seats with slightly obstructed views are also a great deal at around $20. **Everyman Theatre** sells half-priced rush tickets 30 minutes before shows, as well as $10 student seats. Tickets to performances at **Vagabond Theater** in Fell's Point and **Theatre Project** in Mount Vernon cost around $20. Even at **The Hippodrome Theatre,** one of the only places to see traveling tours performing Broadway productions, seats with obstructed views are less than $40 and prime seats in the center aisle can be less than $100, depending on the performance.

THEATERS

Everyman Theatre

The bright purple walls covered in old costume sketches—they're actually stickers—in the lobby of the renovated Everyman Theatre are a tribute to the resident company's 20-year history in Baltimore's Station North neighborhood. In 2013, the theater moved to the Bromo Tower Arts & Entertainment District on the Westside into a bigger space that was a perfect fit: It was at one time the Empire Theatre, a vaudeville house, and an "E" still marks the top of the building. (The building has also, at various times, been a movie theater and a parking garage.) In its new home, Everyman continues to stage top-notch productions of both venerable classics and Baltimore debuts of interesting modern works. The theater is also barely a block away from the Hippodrome Theatre, creating a mini Broadway of sorts in Baltimore.

MAP 1: 315 W. Fayette St., 410/752-2208, www.everymantheatre.org; $35-60

★ The Hippodrome Theatre

In the 1940s, the western side of downtown was home to the city's thriving arts scene, with movie theaters, stages, music halls, and nightclubs on every street. As Baltimore declined, this neighborhood was hit particularly hard, but recent rebirths have included wonderful rehabs like this project. The original Hippodrome Theatre, which opened in 1914 as a movie house and vaudeville palace, saw stars like Frank Sinatra, Bob Hope, and Benny Goodman take the stage. In 2004, a larger complex (The France-Merrick Performing Arts Center) was opened here, and the heart of the operation is the gorgeously renovated and rebuilt Hippodrome. There's an enormous mural above the stage, incredible detail in everything from the seats to the ceiling, and a sense of ceremony

for the audiences who fill the 2,286-seat auditorium for musicals,
holiday performances, comedians, and other entertainers.

MAP 1: 12 N. Eutaw St., 410/837-7400, www.france-merrickpac.com; $50-130

Harbor East and
Little Italy

Map 2

CINEMA
Landmark Theatres
Tucked into one of the towers of the Harbor East neighborhood, this seven-screen art-house chain theater shows both standard Hollywood fare as well as more thoughtful films from documentaries to foreign features. This is a theater for grown-ups who like their movies; there's a full bar where cocktails can be purchased and taken into the theater, the projection and sound is spectacular, and the plush leather seats are some of the best in town.

MAP 2: 645 S. President St., 410/624-2622, www.landmarktheatres.com; $12 adult, $8.50 senior and child, $8.50 all ages before 4pm

CONCERT VENUES
Pier Six Pavilion
The large, white wave-meets-tent-like structure you may glimpse in your travels around the Inner Harbor is this waterfront performance venue. The 4,200-capacity space (there is also lawn seating) plays host to a variety of smaller (and sometimes larger) big-name acts during the season (as it's an outdoor space, shows run normally from spring to fall each year). All kinds of performers have played here, including OneRepublic, Toni Braxton, The Beach Boys, Sting, and Daughtry. The acoustics can be less than stellar, as with most outdoor venues, but the location—right on the water, with views of Baltimore's downtown in every direction—somehow excuses any sonic sins. If you're a casual fan of the night's entertainers, it's also nice to stand for a song or two in front of the nearby Baltimore Marriott Waterfront hotel, where the sound is quite clear, before going on your way for the evening.

MAP 2: 731 Eastern Ave., 410/783-4189, www.piersixpavilion.com; $35-100

Plenty of celebrities have once called the greater Baltimore area home, including Tupac Shakur, Josh Charles, Tori Amos, and Edward Norton. But Charm City's most famous director, writer, and actor is none other than the wacky John Waters. Waters is best known for pushing the boundaries way past vulgar in films like *Pink Flamingos,* where the late actor and transvestite Divine (whose real name was Harris Glenn Milstead) famously munched on dog feces. Scenes like this no doubt prompted the writer William S. Burroughs to contribute this thought to the book jacket of *Crackpot: The Obsessions of John Waters:* "John Waters is the Pope of Trash and his taste in tacky is unexcelled."

Waters began directing in the 1960s with two short films, including *Roman Candles,* which marked the first time he worked with Divine. He would go on to direct his friend in *Mondo Trasho* and *Polyester,* along with several other feature movies and shorts. But perhaps his most successful film during the Divine era was 1988's *Hairspray.* The movie's heroine is Tracy Turnblad (played by Ricki Lake), who wins fame dancing on a local TV show and decides to use her celebrity to fight racial segregation. This may be the Waters film that has reached the widest audience, helped in part by its PG rating—his only movie to receive this classification—and its spin-off into a musical and a 2007 movie remake starring Michelle Pfeiffer and John Travolta, who reprised Divine's role as Tracy's mother.

After Divine passed away in 1988, Waters directed five more films, such as *Cry-Baby* starring Johnny Depp, *Serial Mom* with Kathleen Turner, and *Pecker* starring Edward Furlong and Christina Ricci. He directed his last movie, the sex addict tale *A Dirty Shame* starring Tracey Ullman, a decade ago, but Waters has kept busy with other projects. These include his traveling one-man show, *This Filthy World,* and acting and voice gigs in *Suburban Gothic* with Kat Dennings and the animated holiday horror film *Mugworth.* He also has told media that he's been working on a book about his adventures hitchhiking from his home in Baltimore to his home in San Francisco.

But no matter what the 60-something legend has planned for the future, Waters will always be an icon in Baltimore. He has set all of his movies here, and he has a home here. He can still be found on the town, too, most recently at the historic Senator Theatre. There, when the movie house reopened its doors after a year-plus-long renovation, he attended the opening night screening and 25-year anniversary celebration of *Hairspray.*

Tributes to Waters and his work can be seen throughout the city. His autograph graces the "Walk of Fame" outside of the Senator Theatre and a gigantic sculpture of Divine stands tall at the American Visionary Art Museum. His biggest fans may want to consider visiting Atomic Books in Hampden, where visitors can admire the wall display of holiday cards that Waters has sent to the store, then scribble a letter for him to leave behind. (Atomic Books is the official collector of John Waters's fan mail.)

Fell's Point

Map 2

GALLERIES

Art Gallery of Fells Point

A collective of about 50 artists runs and operates this gallery, which shows work ranging from paintings and drawings to sculpture, jewelry, and ceramics. There's a new show every month, and much of the work is affordable, making this a great place to stop for gifts. Perhaps because the gallery has so many members, the collective makes use of every inch of wall space, a design decision that may throw off gallerygoers who are used to looking at well-spaced work at eye level. Still, there's something for everyone here, and the collective's artists—who also take turns working behind the desk during gallery hours—are friendly, passionate about what they do, and more than willing to talk to you about the works on hand.

MAP 2: 1716 Thames St., 410/327-1272, www.fellspointgallery.org; Mon.-Fri. 11am-6pm, Sat.-Sun. 10am-6pm

Robert McClintock Studio & Gallery

Robert McClintock has often said that he's an artist who knows how to market his work, and the richly colored canvases and prints that fill every inch of this Fell's Point gallery have sold well enough to earn him impressive gross annual sales. McClintock describes his art as "photo-digital illustrations." He takes photographs then paints over them with Adobe Photoshop. If you've fallen in love with a bar or museum or stadium in Baltimore, McClintock likely has a piece of artwork to help you remember it in his more than 300-image-strong "Baltimore Seen" collection. There are also collections celebrating dogs, cats, and firefighters, and prices range from around $10 for a small, un-matted print to upward of $1,000 for a signed, limited edition canvas.

MAP 2: 1809 Thames St., 410/814-2800, www.robertmcclintock.com; Mon.-Sat. 11am-7pm, Sun. 11am-5pm

Steven Scott Gallery

Housed in a brick building on Ann Street, this gallery represents about 20 American artists who create paintings and works on paper. The outdoors are a theme of many of the exhibitions, so it's common to see works with flowers, animals, and scenes from nature. But there may also be pieces created by established artists like photographer Annie Leibovitz and painter Francesco Clemente. With 25-foot ceilings and several skylights, it's a pleasant place in which to admire art. This gallery is also just steps away from the

Robert McClintock Studio & Gallery and the Art Gallery of Fells Point, creating a mini gallery row.

MAP 2: 808 S. Ann St., 410/902-9300, www.stevenscottgallery.com; Tues.-Sat. noon-6pm

THEATERS
Vagabond Theater

Among the bars, taverns, and boutiques of Fell's Point is this enchanting little shoebox theater, whose performers have been taking to this and other local stages for nearly a century. The Vagabond stages about six plays each season, leaning toward easily enjoyed fare like light comedies and musicals, but there are some heavy dramas on the bill as well. Best of all, after the show, you've got about two-dozen options nearby for a nightcap.

MAP 2: 806 S. Broadway, 410/563-9135, www.vagabondplayers.org; $15-20

Canton   Map 3

THEATERS
★ Creative Alliance at the Patterson

Housed in the former Patterson movie theater—and, thankfully, still under its massive neon marquee—the Creative Alliance is a community-based arts group that works to both help local artists pursue their goals and get nonartist Baltimoreans involved with the arts. Their HQ is this wonderful repurposed space, which includes a theater that holds about 200 people for movies, performances, and lectures; two galleries for artworks; and a variety of labs, offices, and rooms for the Alliance's staff, students, and eight resident artists. (These artists often open their studios during exhibits, providing a glimpse into some interesting environments.) There's also a new farm-to-table restaurant called Clementine at the Creative Alliance, making it possible to have dinner, view an art show, and experience a theater performance in one space.

MAP 3: 3134 Eastern Ave., 410/276-1651, www.creativealliance.org

Federal Hill

Map 4

GALLERIES

Crystal Moll Gallery

Take a stroll through Federal Hill and you may see urban land-scape artist Crystal Moll, who paints on location on the city streets. (Federal Hill is a favorite stop.) Her gallery in the same neighborhood—a lilac storefront with two narrow rooms for exhibitions—shows her paintings and prints, as well as work by mainly local artists during regularly themed exhibitions. Much of Moll's work captures Baltimore scenery, from favorite attractions to the city's popular row homes. The gallery also participates in Federal Hill's Third Thursdays evening event by offering snacks like wine and cheese and sometimes live music.

MAP 4: 1030 S. Charles St., 410/952-2843, www.crystalmoll.com; Wed.-Sat. noon-6pm

School 33 Art Center

This former city school building—a sturdy brick Richardsonian Romanesque structure in Federal Hill—is now a city-sponsored collection of artists' studios and exhibition areas. The contemporary art on display is often abstract and made of found and created materials, though traditional paint and sculpture are also regularly featured. Regular gallery openings and studio walk-throughs, and a great annual fundraiser held every April ("Lotta Art"), make this a feature on the art social circuit.

MAP 4: 1427 Light St., 443/263-4350, www.school33.org; Wed.- Sat. 9am-5pm during exhibitions

Mount Vernon and Station North

Map 5

CINEMA

★ The Charles Theater

Once a cable car barn and a powerhouse, the two beaux arts buildings that are now the Charles Theater are a great warren of open, exposed-brick spaces—with winding hallways into four smaller theaters that hold from 115 to 230 people, and one large auditorium that accommodates 485. Independent, art-house, and revival shows are the staples at this popular theater, with a smattering of more popcorn-oriented fare as appropriate. There's a popular

Cinema Sundays series that includes bagel breakfasts and guest speakers. This was once (along with the Club Charles) the only reason to come to this part of town; now, the Station North Arts and Entertainment District has added theaters, bars, restaurants, and galleries.

MAP 5: 1711 N. Charles St., 410/727-3456, www.thecharles.com; $9.50 adult, $8.50 senior, $7.50 before 6pm

CONCERT VENUES

Joseph Meyerhoff Symphony Hall

Opened in 1982, this graceful building—a series of rising, curved structures—is named for one of the Baltimore Symphony Orchestra's most generous patrons and officers. The curves on the exterior carry over to the interior, as the outer areas and hallways gently sweep around the 2,443-seat concert space. In addition to traditional classical music, the BSO orchestra pays tribute to popular performers like The Bee Gees and accompanies screenings of famous movies like *Casablanca* and *West Side Story* during some of its performances. The Joseph Meyerhoff Symphony Hall also occasionally hosts celebrities like comedians Jerry Seinfeld and Daniel Tosh.

MAP 5: 1212 Cathedral St., 410/783-8100, www.bsomusic.org; $15-100

Patricia and Arthur Modell Performing Arts Center at The Lyric

It's difficult to appreciate the splendor of this opera house from the drab, 1980s-era exterior that was constructed around the original 1894 building. But get past the unappealing brownstone and glass, and you'll be swept back to an era of grand theaters, red velvet chairs, and detailed craftsmanship. A recent and huge renovation and the new lighting and sound systems that came with it have also greatly improved the audience experience. The center hosts a wonderful and varied schedule of performances and events, including Broadway shows, dance competitions, stand-up comedians, pop and country stars, and children's shows. Following the sad demise of the Baltimore Opera Company, which was once housed here, the center started a series of Lyric Opera Baltimore performances, some of which are accompanied by the famed (and nearby) Baltimore Symphony Orchestra.

MAP 5: 140 W. Mount Royal Ave., 410/685-5086, www.lyricoperahouse.com; $30-90

GALLERIES

★ C. Grimaldis Gallery

Open since 1977, this renowned Mount Vernon stalwart (named for owner Constantine Grimaldis) is the grande dame of Baltimore's contemporary art gallery scene. Grimaldis exhibits many paintings

The Rise of Station North

Station North was a vibrant arts community in the early 20th century, according to **Baltimore Heritage** (www.baltimoreheritage.org), a nonprofit that offers fascinating tours of many Baltimore neighborhoods. The Aurora Theatre movie house was the first cultural attraction to open in 1910, followed in 1915 by the Parkway Theatre, a treasured entertainment venue for the locals who flocked there to see vaudeville shows and silent films. Two decades later, school principal and chocolate shop owner Morris A. Mechanic opened the Centre Theatre, another movie house, in a complex that was also home to a radio station and bank. Over on Charles Street, the Times Theatre was the city's first newsreel-only movie house. So this was quite a lively part of town, helped in part by the 12-store North Avenue Market and its 22-lane bowling alley across the street.

But somewhere around the mid-19th century, things began to change. Mechanic closed his theater in 1959, while a fire shuttered up the North Avenue Market, which would remain vacant for the next 40 years. Although the Aurora Theatre eventually began showing risqué movies, and the Parkway Theatre was reinvented as a live theater and a movie house/performance space, both venues were closed by the late 1970s. Only the Times Theatre—renamed **The Charles Theater** (1711 N. Charles St.) in the mid-1950s—remained, and it was the only reason to come to this part of town for decades.

Fast-forward to 2002. The Station North area, which encompasses Charles North, Greemount West, and Barclay, is poised to become a center for the arts again. It was the first neighborhood to receive Maryland's Arts & Entertainment District designation. And ever since then theaters and galleries have sprouted up here.

Today, the **Strand Theater Company** (1823 N. Charles St.) has a five-show season that showcases works primarily by female playwrights. The Maryland Institute College of Art (MICA) has a brand-new **Graduate Student Center** (131 W. North Ave.) complete with a beautiful gallery that exhibits student work in all mediums. **Area 405** (405 E. Oliver St.) and **D center Baltimore** (16 W. North Ave.) are galleries that have regular exhibits, film screenings, and events. And the old **Centre Theatre** may soon get a new life: MICA has partnered with a local developer and foundation to reopen the historic building as a multipurpose arts space for film screenings, live music, artist studios and galleries, and even a restaurant.

This area also has one more storied arts space: the **Copycat Building** (1501 Guilford Ave.), the onetime headquarters for the Crown Cork & Seal Company. In the last two decades, a prolific and ever-changing group of artists and musicians have worked here. Although you may not have an occasion to go inside, it's an important part of Baltimore's industrial and cultural history that is worth admiring if you're in the area.

ARTS AND CULTURE MOUNT VERNON AND STATION NORTH

and sculptures by several of the city's most prominent artists (like Raoul Middleman, Kim Manfredi, and the late Grace Hartigan), as well as a wide range of European and North American modern artists. There's also intriguing work by new young painters and sculptors on display here.

MAP 5: 523 N. Charles St., 410/539-1080, www.cgrimaldisgallery.com; Tues.-Sat. 10am-5:30pm

Current Gallery

This artist-run gallery is across the street from Gallery Four and Nudashank in the H&H Building, making this area the closest thing Baltimore has to a gallery row. Paintings, prints, and photographs dominate the exhibitions here, and the gallery is divided into two small spaces so multiple collections can be shown at once. Current also recently came up with an interesting way to make art collecting affordable: You can buy a portfolio of eight limited edition prints made by Baltimore artists, along with a 64-page catalog filled with local work, for a couple hundred dollars.

MAP 5: 421 N. Howard St., 410/343-9295, www.currentspace.com; Sat.-Sun. noon-4pm

Gallery Four

Housed in the H&H Building—named after H&H Outdoors, a military surplus, camping, and hunting store on the first floor—Gallery Four feels like a contemporary art gallery you might find in New York. Visitors are buzzed into the huge, open, loftlike space, and, once they get there, cracked windows and chipping paint show the building's age. Still, this is a fine artist-run contemporary art gallery, one of the only art spaces in Baltimore to show primarily large works and installations. There are also six live-in studios surrounding the main exhibition space, and the resident artists often collaborate to plan programming.

MAP 5: H&H Building, 405 W. Franklin St., 410/962-8941, www.galleryfour.net; Sat. noon-5pm and by appt.

Maryland Institute College of Art Galleries

Baltimore is home to the Maryland Institute College of Art (MICA), one of the nation's top art schools, and the small campus has a number of galleries that feature some great art exhibitions throughout the year. On the main campus, the large and extremely nice Decker Gallery and Meyerhoff Gallery in the Fox Building, a former shoe factory, host student and faculty shows and exhibit work by local, national, and international artists. The building is also home to two smaller galleries that exhibit student work, from paintings, prints, and graphic design to photography and electronic media. Next door, the Bunting Center's Pinkard Gallery features solo exhibitions from faculty and visiting artists.

On the other side of the Fox Building, the open and airy Brown Center (it's the glass building) has several exhibition spaces, including the Leidy Atrium downstairs for large, three-dimensional work, and the Rosenberg Gallery for shows boasting work from national and global artists. Down the street is a very cool space that was once a train station; today, the **Mount Royal Station Building** (1400

Grassroots Art and Performance

In recent years, a few of Baltimore's great arts spaces have closed, and a new wave of artist-run galleries and performance venues have opened in their place. Some of these grassroots operations like **Gallery Four** (405 W. Franklin St.) and **Current Gallery** (421 N. Howard St.) are open every week. But it's more likely that the dedicated and passionate creators who manage the space keep by-appointment or event hours only. Still, these galleries and venues have become a vibrant part of the city's young arts scene, and most of them do hold frequent and lively openings and events that are well worth a visit if you happen to be in town.

In the Bromo Tower Arts & Entertainment District, a group of artists called the **EMP Collective** manage **EMP** (307 W. Baltimore St., www.empcollective.org/calendar), a 5,000-plus-square-foot multipurpose space housed on the first floor of a former shoe factory. There are several interesting events a month here; recent happenings have included performances by the **Glass Mind Theatre** (www.glassmindtheatre.com), live music, art exhibitions and markets, readings, a beer brew-off, and a fashion show. About a half-mile away is **Nudashank** (405 W. Franklin St., 3rd fl., 203/273-8289 or 443/415-2139,

www.nudashank.com), a contemporary art gallery popular with the city's hipster contingent and housed in the H&H Building along with Gallery Four. Run by artists Seth Adelsberger and Alex Ebstein, who have both received some local recognition for their work, the gallery hosts regular and well-attended openings and also has occasional hours for viewing.

Farther north, the Station North Arts and Entertainment District is home to the nonprofit, volunteer-run **Area 405** (405 E. Oliver St., www.area405.com), a 66,000-square-foot building that was once a brewery and window blind manufacturer (at different times) and is now a space for 30 artist studios and regular exhibitions. Area 405 also hosts a fun dinner-and-a-movie film series in the spring and winter. Then farther west is **D center Baltimore** (16 W. North Ave., www.dcenterbaltimore.com), a gallery and event space whose mission is to use design as a means to enhance the lives of city residents; exhibitions here often focus on some aspect of Baltimore or city living and convey a social message.

The best way to find out about upcoming events or exhibits at any of these spaces is to check the venue's Facebook page. EMP in particular also has a regularly updated calendar on its website.

Cathedral St.) is home to MICA's ceramics, sculpture, and fiber department, as well as the Middendorf Gallery on the first floor.

If you're still eager to see more art after touring the main campus, head across the bright yellow Howard Street bridge to Station North and turn right. Next to the Joe Squared pizza shop is the just-renovated **Graduate Studio Center** (131 W. North Ave.) with the brand-new and beautiful Sheila & Richard Riggs Gallery, which presents a variety of student work in several mediums throughout the year.

With so many galleries, MICA holds regular art openings and receptions as well as annual events like art walks and huge Commencement shows in the spring. It's best to check the

ARTS AND CULTURE
MOUNT VERNON AND STATION NORTH

frequently updated website to find out about all that is going on during your visit.

MAP 5: 1300 Mount Royal Ave., 410/225-2280, www.mica.edu; Mon.-Sat. 10am-5pm, Sun. noon-5pm

THEATERS
★ Center Stage

Started more than fifty years ago by local actors and performance enthusiasts, Center Stage is Baltimore's premier theater with two performance spaces: the 540-seat Pearlstone Theater downstairs and the newer 320-seat Head Theater upstairs. In both places the seats are often filled, and the playbill is a smart mix of standards, crowd favorites, and even a few offbeat shows. The plays and performances, which have always reflected the city's diversity, are leaning even more in this direction since British playwright and director Kwame Kwei-Armah became artistic director in 2011, while low ticket prices also contribute to the Center Stage's mission of making theater accessible for all.

Once you arrive, there are a couple of features worth seeing. First, stop by the media wall to the left of the entrance. This is where the theater shows interactive videos such as live streamings of plays in London (though it's still a work-in-progress). Then, if you're seeing a performance at the upstairs theater, head to the pretty chapel-turned-bar before the show. Notice the stained-glass windows? They're actually painted. Now have a drink admiring this rare piece of pastoral history.

MAP 5: 700 N. Calvert St., 410/986-4000, www.centerstage.org; $20-60

The 14Karat Cabaret

This subterranean performance venue hosts a wide variety of fringe, weird, peculiar, delightful, and (rarely) rather normal artists and shows, ranging from performance artists to bands to vaudeville-like revues to dance parties. It's a nonprofit venture run and organized by artists, so the program schedule is generally pretty interesting. There are more than a few regular performers (like founder Laure Drogoul) and shows (like Shattered Wig Night).

MAP 5: 218 W. Saratoga St., 410/962-8565, www.the14karatcabaret.org; around $10

Strand Theater Company

Jayme Kilburn founded this small theater company in 2008 to provide opportunities for women in all aspects of theater production, from acting and directing to writing and set design. That mission is still the foundation of the Strand's work, and the 55-seat theater, housed inside a renovated row home in Station North, runs

clockwise from top left: The Charles Theater, Station North; The Hippodrome Theatre, downtown; Joseph Meyerhoff Symphony Hall, Mount Vernon

about five shows each season, most of which are Baltimore comedy premieres written by female playwrights. The theater also has a small claim to fame: In 2012, Rain Pryor, Richard's daughter, came onboard as artistic director for a year before stepping down after a successful run of her one-woman show took her career in new directions.

MAP 5: 1823 N. Charles St., 443/874-4917, www.strand-theater.org; around $20

Theatre Project

This is the Baltimore theater where, often, risks are taken and boundaries are pushed (though not to unreasonable ends). Performances here at this 150-seat theater, which recently celebrated its 40th anniversary, range from drastic reimaginings of traditional tales to experimental works, sometimes dances, that aim to break new ground. The stage itself is a simple wooden platform that's about 35 feet on each side; that and the small size put the performers and audience in very close company. There's a good selection of more accessible works, some that will amaze through their inventiveness, and then a few that will prove challenging to all but the most avant-garde.

MAP 5: 45 W. Preston St., 410/539-3091, www.theatreproject.org; $22

Hampden and Homewood   Map 6

CINEMA

The Rotunda Cinematheque

This smaller two-screen theater is on the northern edge of Hampden in the Rotunda, a large, historic office and retail complex that looks more like a college hall than a shopping mall. There's usually one mainstream film and one independent or art-house film being shown at any given time. Both theaters are cozy, with about 120 seats each. It's not a great choice for a big-budget blockbuster, but smaller films and character-driven movies fit perfectly. The $5 Tuesday movies here are also a great deal.

MAP 6: 711 W. 40th St., 410/235-4800, www.horizoncinemas.com; $9 adult, $8 senior, $7 child, $7 all ages before 4pm

GALLERIES

Goya Contemporary

This is the gallery side of Martha Macks's Goya operations (the other is Goya-Girl Press, geared toward artists in need of high-quality printing options); housed in an old mill building at the base of Hampden, this brick and wood gallery shows works by all sorts of artists (females are well-represented) working in paint and print, but photography and sculpture are also part of the palette here.

MAP 6: 3000 Chestnut Ave., Mill Center, Studio 214, 410/366-2001, www.goyacontemporary.com; Tues.-Fri. 10am-6pm, Sat. noon-5pm

THEATERS
Single Carrot Theatre

Several University of Colorado graduates who wanted to dive right into the theater industry rather than move to New York or L.A. and take their chances started this grassroots company in 2005. Anything goes during Single Carrot's roughly five-show season, from Shakespeare to sketch comedy to slam poetry and puppetry. Although the theater has bounced around—it's been housed in the now-closed Load of Fun building, as well as the Everyman Theatre's former space in Station North—the company found a new home on Howard Street in early 2014, in the same building as an arts education nonprofit; the owners of the beloved Woodberry Kitchen plan to open a restaurant and butcher shop here too.

MAP 6: 2600 W. Howard St., 443/844-9253, www.singlecarrot.com; $15-25

Greater Baltimore

Map 7

CINEMA
The Senator Theatre

Just south of the city line with Baltimore County is this historical 1939 theater that's led a charmed life, escaping demolition, repossession, financial strife, and a myriad of other disasters. The Senator Theatre's most recent obstacle came when its longtime owner foreclosed in 2009. The building was then leased to the owners of the beloved Charles Theatre in Station North, who later proceeded with a much-needed $3.5 million renovation. The art deco movie palace reopened at the end of 2013 with four screens—the main 750-seat auditorium plus three smaller theaters—and a brand-new restaurant. The Senator shows major Hollywood blockbusters and often hosts Baltimore premieres of films shot in the city or those that star (or were directed by) Charm City natives or fans, like John Waters and Edward Norton.

MAP 7: 5904 York Rd., Baltimore, 410/435-8338, www.thesenatortheatre.com; $11.50 adult, $9 senior and child, $9 all ages before 6pm

GALLERIES
Silber Art Gallery

The crisp and clean Silber Art Gallery on the Goucher College campus near the Towson Town Center mall has quickly become a favorite art space among Baltimore creatives. A wide range of contemporary works are showcased here, from paintings and drawings to sculpture, video, and interactive installations. With its 21-foot ceilings, the white-walled and wood-floored gallery can present large pieces too. Artists on view may be students or emerging or mid-career professionals, and recent exhibitions have centered on the themes of nature, water, relationships, and power struggles. Works from Goucher College's permanent collection may also be on display.

MAP 7: Goucher College Athenaeum, 1021 Dulaney Valley Rd., Baltimore, 410/337-6477, www.goucher.edu; Tues.-Sun. 11am-4pm.

Sports and Activities

Downtown and Inner Harbor.....168

Harbor East and Little Italy 174

Fell's Point........................174

Canton 178

Federal Hill 180

Mount Vernon and Station North..182

Hampden and Homewood.......183

Greater Baltimore.................183

Various Locations.................188

HIGHLIGHTS

★ **Best Interactive Park:** Children and adults alike have fun at the new **Pierce's Park,** an ideally located and pristine green space that invites guests to play songs on the musical fence, slide down a steel horn, and crawl through a tunnel made of interwoven branches (page 169).

★ **Best Duckpin Bowling Alley:** Duckpin bowling is one of those great Baltimore traditions. Give it a try at the **Patterson Bowling Center,** the only duckpin alley downtown that also happens to serve some great snacks (page 175).

★ **Most Beautiful Scenic Run:** Because the **Baltimore Waterfront Promenade** follows the harbor, the views on this seven-mile, relatively flat run are hard to beat. The path also crosses through

four of Baltimore's best neighborhoods, so it's a nice way to get oriented with the city (page 181).

★ **Best Serious Bike Ride:** Get to BWI Airport (the Dixon Observation Area, to be specific) with your bike, and you can cruise down the flat 25 miles from there to beautiful downtown Annapolis along the **Baltimore-Annapolis Trail.** The way back is uphill, but not dauntingly so (page 184).

★ **Best Baltimore Tour Guide:** It's not just that **Zippy Tours with Zippy Larson** shares things about Baltimore that almost no one else knows, it's that your guide's quirky, unstoppable personality can get her tour groups into places no one else can go (page 189).

Whether it's cheering the Ravens at the landmark M&T Bank Stadium, learning the difference between a jib and a tack while sailing on the Inner Harbor, or taking a serious bike trip down to Annapolis, there are countless ways to get out and enjoy the lands and waters that surround Baltimore

City. There are also several high-tech gyms and athletic centers that have opened up across town if you're looking for an indoor workout that will challenge your limits. And there are even a couple of unique city golf courses worth checking out.

If you're the kind of person who prefers to watch the pros handle all the sweating, there's the storied Baltimore Orioles baseball team (the lifelong squad of Hall of Famer Cal Ripken Jr.) and the newer but perhaps even more beloved Baltimore Ravens (winners of Super Bowl XLVII during the 2012 season and XXXV during the 2000 season). There's also the multiple-championship-winning Baltimore Blast of the National Indoor Soccer League. Lacrosse is Maryland's state team sport, and the high schools and universities around Baltimore play some of the best "lax" in the world. And there's the Pimlico Race Course, where you can play the ponies and spend the day at the track, catch some rays, and sip on a Black-Eyed Susan cocktail while the horses and jockeys do all the work.

Baltimore may not be known as the fittest city in the United States (though surprisingly, *Men's Fitness* magazine rated it as such back in 2006), but a nice, flat jaunt around the seven-mile-long Waterfront Promenade, which runs from the Inner

Harbor to Canton, will show that runners, bicyclists, and walkers are coming out in droves these days. The Baltimore Marathon draws some 25,000 runners a year for a long course that ambles throughout most of the city. There are also several other wonderful road races held during the year, the best of which include the Baltimore 10-Miler and the Charles Street 12. All of these running events can be the best ways to see the city and get acquainted with Baltimore's various neighborhoods. Bicyclists have some great new paths and trails, including the NCR Trail that runs from Baltimore County into Pennsylvania and the Baltimore-Annapolis Trail. Swimmers can head to several local gyms or aquatic centers (including the same pool where 18-time-Olympic-gold-medal-winner Michael Phelps once trained). And there are several great city parks for simple walks, tennis, or jogs. State and county parks outside the city offer great opportunities for hiking and trail running.

No matter what kind of physical challenge you prefer—from aerobics to trail riding to yoga—there's a place in Baltimore where (with all due respect to the late, great Baltimore sportscaster Jim McKay) you can pursue the thrill of victory, and hopefully avoid the agony of defeat.

Unlike many great cities, Baltimore is without a single defining park. Patterson Park, in Canton, has become the city's favorite park in many ways, but it's not quite the same as New York City's unsurpassed Central Park. And while Federal Hill Park offers some stunning views of the city (and has a great playground for toddlers), it's not large enough to be Baltimore's main park. Druid Hill Park has the size and the majesty to have been the city's premier park, but with much of the surrounding neighborhoods having fallen into disrepair over the past 40 years—and the physical separation created by I-83—the park, while popular (and home to the Maryland Zoo and Rawlings Conservatory), is not a central public space.

Despite this, many neighborhoods have smaller parks that are important parts of those communities, offering some needed green space to row-house dwellers who may have a backyard made of concrete. There's also a newer, centrally located park called Pierce's Park. Nestled between the Inner Harbor and Pier Six Pavilion, this gem combines recreation and art: The slide is an enormous stainless steel cornucopia sculpture, the tunnel is made of intertwining branches, and parts of the fence are actually steel xylophones ready for music-making. And in many ways, the Inner Harbor area serves as an unofficial (and very concrete-laden) main public space for Baltimoreans, as does much of the waterfront. The green lawns and shade trees of Fort McHenry are popular for picnicking and just lying under the sun (no ball- or

Frisbee-playing is allowed; it's a hallowed national shrine, after all). Patterson Park is the main sports park in town, if that's what you're looking for; it includes tennis courts, a covered ice rink, a public pool, and lots of space for softball, football, and—more and more often—soccer games.

Baltimore came into existence thanks to the waters of the Patapsco River (the Inner Harbor) and the Chesapeake Bay; it's a shame that, for so many years, the city thanked those giving waters by dumping pollutants and garbage into them. A recent review of the harbor's water quality received a "C," a grade that isn't surprising if you see the few floating islands of debris that creep up, especially following torrential downpours when many of the city's storm sewers empty into the water. Advocacy groups and nonprofits are working toward a harbor that's clean enough for swimming and fishing, but that goal won't be achieved until 2020, if it's reached at all.

The water is perfectly fine to boat on, however, and on warm, sunny spring days, you'll see all sorts of sailboats, motorboats, and other watercraft taking to the waters of the Inner Harbor (but no personal watercraft, as it's not the best water in which to plunge). If you want to join them, you can take a spin on a kayak or sailboat through the Baltimore Rowing Club or the Downtown Sailing Center, though it will cost you (in both time and money). Some organizations will also let you use their vessels if you join their clubs or sign up for lessons. For kids, the colorful Chessie dragon paddleboats in the Inner Harbor are a hit, as is the Urban Pirates ship, which offers swashbuckling adventures complete with games, treasure, and even a rival pirate.

There are a slew of die-hard bicyclists in Baltimore, and the larger community comes together once a month for the Baltimore Bike Party (baltimorefamilybikeparty.wordpress.com) evening rides across the city. Recent years have even brought some dramatic gains: New bicycle lanes have been added to many streets, more buses have been outfitted with bicycle-carrying racks, and even more places to lock up a bike have been added at major area attractions and throughout the city. Still, this ain't Portland, Oregon; many main streets are narrow enough with two lanes of traffic, and the addition of a bicyclist can lead to honking horns (at best) and peril (at worst). Still, it's a relatively easy city to get around in by bike, though heading north to Mount Vernon and Homewood is a long uphill trip that can take a cumulative toll on the less-than-fit. But just pedaling around the waterfront, from Canton over to Federal Hill, is predominantly flat and often doesn't even involve crossing major thoroughfares. Tour du Port is the city's big bike event, held in early fall and offering a few different routes.

North and south of the city are two great trails, both of which are pretty flat and cover some serious ground. To the south, there's the Baltimore-Annapolis Trail, which runs from BWI Airport all the way to the state capital, about a 25-mile trek. And to the north is the NCR Trail, a rail-to-trail bike path that starts in Baltimore County and rolls northward into Pennsylvania. If you're looking for a shorter ride, there's the Gwynns Falls Trail. Find out about riding in Baltimore at **Bikemore** (www.bikemore.net).

A waterfront city as old as Baltimore has so much history, so many secrets, and so many tall tales associated with its neighborhoods and residents that it's worth considering signing up for a guided tour (or at least one of the self-guided walking tours) of the city's neighborhoods. Head to the Baltimore Visitors Center in the Inner Harbor—it's the building with the roof that looks like a wave—and consult with one of the staffers there for suggestions about which tour is best for you, and pick up some brochures detailing the routes through neighborhoods like Mount Vernon. With its long and storied history, Fell's Point is an idea neighborhood for tours, and options vary from the historical Secrets of a Seaport Walking Tour to the eerie Baltimore Ghost Tours to the cuisine-and-history-focused Charm City Food Tours. Though it's an easy city to walk, you can also take a powered tour aboard a Segway personal transporter.

If you're looking for a really personalized way to learn about the city, there are two famous people to consider. For a one-of-a-kind experience, contact historian Zippy Larson, whose Zippy Tours take you wherever you want to go, and often into private homes and places the general public can't access. Then there's Wayne Schaumburg, another historian of renown who can reveal many of the city's hidden mysteries and legends on his own guided tours; he's the recognized expert on Green Mount Cemetery.

Downtown and
Inner Harbor

Map 1

GUIDED AND WALKING TOURS
Baltimore National Heritage Area Walking Tours

From May through November, this guided walking tour leaves from the Baltimore Visitor Center in the Inner Harbor at 10am (and also on Saturday and Sunday at 1pm) and heads for many of the city's greatest neighborhoods and landmarks. The 90-minute walk covers about half of the entire Heritage Walk (about three miles), and is led by an Urban Park Ranger. Featured areas and stops include the Inner

Harbor, Little Italy, Jonestown, the Carroll Mansion, and the Star-Spangled Banner Flag House. Private group tours can be scheduled.

MAP 1: Baltimore Visitor Center, 410/878-6411, www.nps.gov/balt; $10 adult, free child, $7 senior

KAYAKING, PADDLING, AND ROWING
Chessie Paddleboats

To get on the water from a central location like the Inner Harbor, your best (and only) bet is to hop on a paddle boat, which you'll find docked between Harborplace and Baltimore's World Trade Center. Kids tend to like the brightly colored green and purple "Chessie" boats, named after the dragon that, according to legend, lives in the Chesapeake Bay. The downside is that you can't paddle that far, but the Inner Harbor's backdrop provides enough ambience for a short ride. The best time to go is in morning; later, lines build up, which can make for congested waters.

MAP 1: 301 Pratt St., 410/528-1060; Apr.-Nov. Sun.-Thurs. 10am-11pm, Fri.-Sat. 11am-10:30pm; $11 for regular boats, $18 for "Chessie" boats per half hour

PARKS
★ Pierce's Park

This new green space is part public art, part children's playground, and it's ideally situated in the thick of downtown right between the Inner Harbor and Harbor East. Named after local businessman Pierce John Flanigan III, Pierce's Park was built with sustainability in mind; thus, there are indigenous trees, native plants, and three rain gardens to educate children about the benefits of capturing runoff rainwater. But naturally, kids find more pleasure in the park's stainless steel xylophone known as the "musical fence," aboveground tunnel made of interwoven branches, and sculptures designed for play, such as the huge stainless steel cornucopia for them to run through.

MAP 1: Behind 701 E. Pratt St., www.piercespark.org; free

SPECTATOR SPORTS
Baseball
Baltimore Orioles

There have been a couple of incarnations of the Baltimore Orioles throughout baseball history; the current club came to Baltimore in 1954 from St. Louis, where they had been the Browns. The American League East Orioles have won three World Series, in 1966, 1970, and 1983. The last World Series win was the first (and only) for a young shortstop named Calvin Edwin Ripken Jr.; Cal would go on to break the Major League Baseball consecutive game streak in 1995, a milestone and celebration that many critics cite as the first step baseball took back into America's hearts after the players' strike of 1994 (a year in which there was no World Series).

The early years of the Orioles (known affectionately as the O's) were a mixture of good and bad, with the majority of their games played in the now-demolished Memorial Stadium. Loyal crowds packed the house during the team's glory years, which ran from that 1966 championship year until the World Series in 1983. The team was made up of All-Stars who played hard and led by a mean, foulmouthed, happy-go-lucky, and fearless manager of short stature and massive confidence named Earl Weaver; naturally, they had the undying loyalty of the city's fans.

The opening of Oriole Park at Camden Yards in 1991 was a revelation to American baseball fans; the stadium wasn't one of the typical huge, monolithic, concrete bowls that had became de rigueur throughout American cities. It was a throwback to storied stadiums like Wrigley Field in Chicago and Fenway Park in Boston—built downtown, and not out in the suburbs where the fan base lived, designed to hold about 48,000 fans, and crafted of brick and wrought iron, meant to evoke the feeling of old-time baseball and Americana (and this was done even before the steroid scandals of the 2000s). A few years after the Orioles moved downtown, they became the powerhouse of the A.L. East, reaching the American League Championship Series in both 1996 and 1997, but falling short both times.

Recent years had been less kind to this club—that is, until 2012, when the Orioles made it to the postseason for the first time in 15 years. The team beat the Texas Rangers in the Wild Card games before falling to the division rival New York Yankees in five games. Still, the Orioles surprise playoff run rekindled a passion for baseball among loyal Baltimore fans, a phenomenon dubbed "Orioles Magic." In terms of attendance though, Camden Yards still hasn't reached the heights of its early days, unless the neighboring Boston Red Sox, New York Yankees, or Philadelphia Phillies come to town; then their boisterous, proud fans help fill the seats.

If you're planning to pay a visit to the park, take some time for a behind-the-scenes tour of the facility ($9 adult, $6 child), including the luxury boxes, the press box, the broadcasting booths, and the Orioles dugout. Getting to see the stadium from the field is a real thrill, no matter how old you are.

Then to attend an Orioles game like a real Baltimorean, here's a simple guide. First, pay a visit to the Babe Ruth statue outside the main gate on Camden Street. Notice anything strange about this tribute to George Herman Ruth Jr.? If you did, you're a real seamhead: the sculptor gave Ruth a left-handed glove, but Ruth was a lefty. You can get a decent ticket (prices run from $9 on bargain nights for nosebleeds to $95 for the primo

Charm City Sports Heroes

Not only has Baltimore given the sporting world some amazing athletes, it's also contributed some great sportscasters and sportswriters. Obviously, the best-known athlete of them all is celebrated baseball "Ironman," Hall of Famer, and lifelong Baltimore Oriole **Cal Ripken Jr.**—but note that he is technically from Aberdeen, a small town about 25 minutes northeast of Baltimore, though he's called Baltimore home for most of his adult life. Late sportscasting legend **Jim McKay** (who famously intoned the intro of the *ABC Wide World of Sports* that touted "the thrill of victory and the agony of defeat") was a Philadelphia native who moved to Baltimore in 1935 and never left. On a more recent note, NBA All-Star and Olympic gold medalist **Carmelo Anthony** hails from New York City originally, but moved to Baltimore at age eight; and 18-time Olympic gold medalist swimmer **Michael Phelps,** grew up just north of the city.

Here are some more well-known men and women from the Baltimore area who have distinguished themselves on the fields of sport (or chronicled those who have done so):

- Tyrone "Muggsy" Bogues—Former NBA player

- Frank DeFord—Prominent sportswriter and broadcaster

- Juan Dixon—NBA player

- Antonio Freeman—Former Pro Bowl NFL player

- Joe Gans—Legendary boxer, died 1909

- Rudy Gay—NBA player

- Al Kaline—MLB Hall of Famer

- Mel Kiper Jr.—Television football analyst

- Bucky Lasek—Skateboard superstar

- Kimmie Meissner—Olympic figure skater

- Anita Nall—Olympic gold medal-winning swimmer, 1992

- Travis Pastrana—Motocross magician

- Bill Ripken—Cal's brother; had 12 seasons in the major leagues

- Cal Ripken Sr.—Cal's dad; spent 36 years with the Orioles, three as manager

- George Herman "Babe" Ruth Jr.—Possibly the greatest baseball player of all time

- Mark Teixeira—MLB player

- Bernard Williams—Olympic gold medal-winning relay runner, 2000

behind-the-dugout seats for division rival games) at the ticket booth right before the game. Once inside, stop by former Oriole great Boog Powell's barbecue stand (just follow the plume of beefy smoke) and grab a barbecued pork, beef, or turkey sandwich and a beer. Get to your seat in time for the national anthem; there's a peculiar Baltimore tradition to follow during the song, with its local roots. When the singer reaches the "O say does that Star-Spangled Banner" line, everyone in the stadium yells "O!" in tribute to the beloved O's.

MAP 1: 333 W. Camden St., 888/848-2473, http://baltimore.orioles.mlb.com

Football
Baltimore Ravens

Baltimore football fans' hearts were broken one snowy night in 1984 when the Colts stole away into the dark and reappeared in the exotic city of...Indianapolis. Sure, Baltimore ended up getting a Canadian Football League team (the Baltimore CFL Stallions won the Grey Cup in 1995), but the black hole where NFL football had once lived was a wound that wouldn't heal for many residents. So it was with bittersweet rapture that, in 1995, it was announced that the Cleveland Browns—another beloved blue-collar football team—would be moving to Baltimore to take advantage of a big new taxpayer-financed stadium, one that Cleveland would not provide. The Ravens stunk in those early years, but it wasn't for lack of fan support, as the city got used to not only the return of real NFL action, but the black and purple uniforms, and the fact that their team was named, in part, to honor a poem by the tragic figure of Edgar Allan Poe.

But the team gradually got better and, led by a devastating defense, won its first Super Bowl in 2001. This triumphant win was followed by a decade of ups and downs, but fans stayed devoted, selling out games regularly and turning downtown purple on many fall and winter Sundays.

Then, in 2013 and about to enter the playoffs for the fifth straight year under coach John Harbaugh and quarterback Joe Flacco, the Ravens had something big to play for. Seventeen-year veteran Ray Lewis, a Raven since the team's inaugural 1996 year, announced his retirement at season's end, and the team clearly wanted to send him off in a big way. The Ravens deemed themselves "A Team of Destiny," a moniker that most certainly got under the skins of other fans but was wholeheartedly embraced by Ravens Nation. In the first round, they decisively beat the Indianapolis Colts, then went on to face the Denver Broncos as big underdogs. Things did look grim when, with 31 seconds remaining, the Ravens were down by a touchdown. Then Flacco threw a soaring 70-yard pass to wide receiver Jacoby Jones to unexpectedly tie the score. Hailed as "epic" and "thrilling" by sportswriters, the game lasted for an exhilarating two overtimes before the Ravens won 38-35. The team went on to beat the rival New England Patriots before heading to Super Bowl XLVII, a contest significant, in part, because it pitted coaching brothers (John Harbaugh for the Ravens, Jim Harbaugh for the San Francisco 49ers) against each other for the first time. The Ravens had a strong start and held on to an early lead in the second half to win 34-31. A few weeks later, the team's victory parade was a raucous event, drawing 200,000 fans to downtown Baltimore and setting the city awash in purple.

Baltimore's Spectator Sports

Baltimore's glory days were heady times indeed; both major sports teams—baseball's Orioles and football's Colts—regularly went to the playoffs and notched their share of championships. Players lived around town, weren't paid sums that dwarfed many countries' GDPs, and there was a (perhaps) naive joy taken by Baltimoreans in their star athletes and teams.

Times are different today, though not as grim as they were back in the mid- to late 1980s; the Orioles couldn't get back to the playoffs, and even worse, the Colts were moved to Indianapolis by their owner in the dead of night, and they continue to play there today. While the Colts are still loathed in town, the Baltimore Ravens (née the Cleveland Browns, and first playing in Baltimore under the Ravens moniker in 1996) have become the city's number-one sports franchise, making tickets a little tough to come by. After more than a decade of losing baseball seasons, the Orioles made it the playoffs

in 2012; their success has reignited the city's love of baseball, and fans are packing Camden Yards once again. Still, on most days it's still easy to walk up to the game and get tickets. The Baltimore Blast of the National Indoor Soccer League regularly vies for the title, and play in the friendly confines of the Baltimore Arena.

Baltimore has no major colleges or universities (save one, but it's Johns Hopkins), so NCAA Division I basketball and football are only watched via TV here. There is one sport, however, where several local schools—not sports powerhouses by any means—compete at the nation's top level: lacrosse. Rivalry games between Johns Hopkins, Towson University, Loyola College, and the University of Maryland Baltimore County can draw tens of thousands of fans; the NCAA Division I Men's Lacrosse Championships, often held at M&T Bank Stadium, has drawn some 48,000 fans for the championship game.

Game day (single tickets range from $50-345) at M&T Bank Stadium (most locals still call it Ravens Stadium) begins with tailgating, whether or not you've driven. Just wander through the cars, SUVs, vans, and customized RVs in purple and black, meeting some very happy, beverage-hoisting fans who are cooking up some great-smelling foods. There's usually an "NFL Experience" set up outside the stadium, on the walkway to Oriole Park, where fans can try their hand at accurately throwing a football, or have their face painted, or get some free giveaways. Before heading inside, wish for luck for the Ravens and rub the left foot of the Johnny Unitas statue at Unitas Plaza, on the north side of the stadium. Once inside, it might be a long walk to your seats; as the stadium was wedged into a tight urban footprint, it's quite steep, and if you've got nosebleed seats, you might want to get in shape before hiking up to the top of the stadium. Fans here also cheer with the "O" in the "O say does that Star-Spangled Banner" line in the national anthem, though not at heartily as at Orioles games.

MAP 1: 1101 Russell St., 410/261-7283, www.baltimoreravens.com

Indoor Soccer
Baltimore Blast

The Baltimore Blast are perennial contenders in indoor soccer, a bit of a niche sport, which is played in small arenas across the country; they're now in the seven-team Major Indoor Soccer League. The Blast have been in existence since 1980, with a few years on hiatus here and there as various indoor soccer leagues have come and gone. The team plays fast, captivating soccer, using boards to keep the action going and the scoring high (a typical indoor soccer game score can be 15-9).

MAP 1: Baltimore Arena, 201 W. Baltimore St., 410/732-5278, www.baltimoreblast.com

Harbor East and Little Italy
Map 2

GYMS AND HEALTH CLUBS
MAC Harbor East

This cosmopolitan palace of fitness offers just about every conceivable piece of exercise equipment, instructor-led class, and even a five-lane, 25-meter lap pool, which is impressive as this new gym is located on the second floor of one of Harbor East's towers. There are a yoga/Pilates studio and two squash courts here, plus a Whole Foods supermarket right across the street for some post-workout healthy eats.

MAP 2: 655 President St., 410/625-5000, www.macwellness.com; Mon.-Thurs. 5am-11pm, Fri. 5am-10pm, Sat.-Sun. 7am-7pm; $20 for single-day guest pass

Fell's Point
Map 2

CRUISES
Capt. Don's Fishing Charter

You don't want to fish, much less eat, anything from the Inner Harbor; that said, there is a lot of great fishing to be done in the waters of the upper Chesapeake Bay—all you need to do is get out of the city. Captain Don will take out groups of up to six people on two-, three-, six-, and eight-hour fishing (or just sightseeing) charters that leave right from Henderson's Wharf in Fell's Point. His boat, the *Lady Luck* is a 46-foot Chesapeake Bay-built, low-slung, and wide-beamed fishing vessel, designed to be able to handle the rough chop that can spring up on the bay. This is the only major all-day, full-time fishing charter in town.

MAP 2: Henderson's Wharf Marina, Fell's Point, 410/342-2004, www.fishbaltimore.com; 90-minute and two-hour sightseeing cruises, $350, $450; three-, six-, and eight-hour fishing tours, $260, $450, $500-600

Urban Pirates

While you're walking around the Inner Harbor, there's a good chance you'll see the black skull flags of the Urban Pirates ship, an adventure cruise that is a hit with kids. It's easy to see why: There are games like the limbo and conga line; cannons for shooting water at a rival pirate, One-Eyed Mike; and a chest full of plastic jewelry from which they can choose two pieces of treasure. A half hour before the ship departs, the staff, who expertly play the role of swashbuckling adventurers themselves, dress their young crew as pirates with tattoos, beards, and mustaches. Thursday through Saturday there are also adults-only "Bring Your Own Grog" cruises (the pirate version of the booze cruise).

MAP 2: 913 S. Ann St., 410/327-8378, www.urbanpirates.com; family cruises, $22 adult or child over three, $11 child under two; adult cruises $25

DUCKPIN BOWLING

★ Patterson Bowling Center

Duckpin bowling is regular bowling on a much smaller scale: The pins are under a foot high and the ball is the size of a softball. In the early 1960s, the sport was so popular in Baltimore that there were two television shows devoted to it. But today, the only downtown duckpin bowling alley remaining is the Patterson Bowling Center, which opened in 1927 on the Fell's Point/Canton border, just a few blocks west of Patterson Park. There are 12 lanes on two levels here and a full-duty snack bar that churns out great salty snacks.

MAP 2: 2105 Eastern Ave., 410/675-1011, www.pattersonbowl.com; open play Mon.-Thurs. 1pm-9:30pm, Fri.-Sat. 1pm-12:30am, Sun. 2pm-9pm

GUIDED AND WALKING TOURS

Baltimore Ghost Tours

Fell's Point was once filled with brothels and drunken and morally corrupt sailors, which makes great fodder for a ghost tour. The owners of Baltimore Ghost Tours uncovered the best of these stories, and after two years of research, The Original Fells Point Ghostwalk was born. You'll hear tales about the onetime bar owner who was shot at The Wharf Rat, the little girl who haunts Bertha's, and the massive graveyard that may lie under Fell's Point. The tour guides, performers at heart, are often funny despite their grim subject matter, and it's great fun to visit some of the restaurants and bars afterward to look for signs of the ghosts who reportedly haunt them. There's also a haunted pub walk and another ghost tour in Mount Vernon.

MAP 2: Meets in front of 731 S. Broadway, 410/357-1186, www.fellspointghost.com; $13-20

Charm City Food Tours

These 3.5-hour adventures are a fascinating and fun way to learn about the history and food cultures of Baltimore's varied neighborhoods. The Fell's Point tour is the most popular, and it covers the history of the Fell family, who founded the neighborhood, as well as the stories behind the markets and centuries-old bars. But the real highlight is the food: You'll sit down at five restaurants to sample some well-known dishes, which may include crab soup, pit beef, and pierogies. Accommodations are made for vegetarians and those with food allergies. The tour guides are energetic and knowledgeable, and, because there is food and often drink involved (though most beverages cost extra), there is generally a convivial spirit among the group. There are also tours of Federal Hill, Little Italy, and Mount Vernon.

MAP 2: Near Broadway Market, exact meeting location provided upon ticket purchase, 202/638-8847, www.baltimorefoodtours.com; $58 plus $3 ticketing fee, purchase in advance

Secrets of the Seaport Walking Tour

Held on some Saturdays (and occasional Sundays) at 10am from April until November, this tour—led by a living history performer—takes visitors on a 90-minute stroll through the stone streets of Fell's Point. The history of the region, from its upstanding merchants and captains to its more scurvy sea dogs, is revealed with flourish; other historic characters, including shipwrights, immigrants, and the less-fortunate members of 18th-century Fell's Point life are also discussed. It's best to call about a week ahead to reserve a space and make sure the guide is available.

MAP 2: 1732 Thames St., 410/675-6750 or 443/847-8738; $12 adult, $8 child, $11 senior (reduced group rate available)

Segs in the City

Based in Fell's Point (and part of a regional chain), this Segway tour operation takes visitors on a "safari" (as they call them) through a good chunk of Baltimore's neighborhoods, including the Inner Harbor, Harbor East, Fell's Point, Federal Hill, and Little Italy. Tours leave at 10am, 12:15pm, 2:30pm, and 5pm; guides use headset microphone systems to discuss historical and important sights. Learning to ride a Segway takes about two minutes, and while you may draw some chuckles from the "cool" Baltimore kids

clockwise from top left: Urban Pirates cruise, Fell's Point; Baltimore Waterfront Promenade, Federal Hill; Chessie paddle boats, Inner Harbor

as you go whirring past, you'll cover a huge amount of ground in no time flat.

MAP 2: 207 S. Albemarle St., 800/734-7393, www.segsinthecity.com; $60 for a 90-minute tour

YOGA
Charm City Yoga

One of Baltimore's most popular yoga studios is Charm City Yoga; even though it's not large, this Fell's Point location has a great view of the neighborhood and water. There's also an outdoor deck for practicing during the nice months, a great and rare opportunity in Baltimore. Charm City Yoga does a version of hot yoga, as well as other routines (including a vinyasa yoga routine set to rock & roll music), and offers regular community classes for $6. There are also locations in **Federal Hill** (37 E. Cross St., 800/336-9642, ext. 11) and **Mount Vernon** (107 E. Preston St., 800/336-9642, ext. 13).

MAP 2: 1807 Thames St., 800/336-9642, ext. 12, www.charmcityyoga.com; $17 for a drop-in class

Canton

Map 3

BOATING SUPPLIES AND FACILITIES
West Marine

This Canton store, part of the nationwide West Marine boating supply chain, sells just about every piece of boating gear you might need in case you forgot it or broke it. From basics to more obscure gear, Baltimore's busy boating community keeps this shop busy and well stocked. They're also just a short drive (or sail) from the Inner Harbor.

MAP 3: 2700 Lighthouse Pt., #100, 410/563-8905, www.westmarine.com; Mon.-Sat. 9am-7pm, Sun. 9am-5pm

GYMS AND HEALTH CLUBS
Merritt Athletic Clubs Canton

An enormous facility on the outskirts of Canton, this hugely popular gym (also the official club of the Baltimore Ravens cheerleaders) has so many pieces of equipment that waiting is almost never a concern. There's a full-size basketball court, two squash courts, and a good-sized outdoor lap pool covered with a heated tent in winter (unlike the club though, it's not open 24 hours), in addition to several fitness rooms and a yoga studio. A day spa and massage area are also available for those who want to relax after they feel the burn. This is a popular place for young urban professionals to

MAP 3: 3401 Boston St., 410/563-0225, www.merrittclubs.com; 24 hours; $25 for single-day guest pass

ICE SKATING

Dominic "Mimi" DiPietro Family Ice Skating Center

Dubbed "The Mimi Dome" by wiseacre city wags, this inflated, pale yellow structure on the eastern side of Patterson Park contains a large rink (big enough for hockey games) beneath a latticework of metal arms. So while the view's not much, the skating is sure fun, and after you leave the ice, the concession stand has hot chocolate and a fireplace. Hours change frequently; check website for an updated schedule.

MAP 3: 200 S. Linwood Ave., 410/396-9392, www.pattersonpark.com; Tues. noon-2pm, Fri. 7pm-9pm, Sat. 3pm-5pm and 7pm-9pm, Sun. 3pm-5pm, closed Mon., Wed., and Thurs. for league use; $4; skate rental $2

SKATEBOARDING

Charm City Skate Park

This semi-respectable private skate park is in an old warehouse under a highway overpass (which is pretty punk rock). Charm City Skate Park has re-created (in plywood and metal) a mini-city of steps, ramps, and rails, then decorated the walls with graffiti and artwork. Regular events and pro skaters on tour stop by this Canton fixture.

MAP 3: 4401 O'Donnell St., Ste. B, 410/327-7909, www.charmcity.tv; Mon.-Sat. 12:30pm-8:30pm, Sun. noon-6pm; $10 before 5pm, $5 after

SPECTATOR SPORTS

Roller Derby

Charm City Roller Girls

This four-team league of talented young women plays to packed houses across Baltimore, and fields an All-Star team that goes up against the crème de la crème from other cities. Founded in 2005, this rejuvenation of the concept of all-female roller derby (a hit in the 1950s and '60s) mixes the thrill of competition, the knowledge that the matches aren't rigged, and a black-fingernailed dose of punk rock fearlessness and pride in the ability to perform a thunderous takedown without drawing a penalty.

MAP 3: DuBurns Arena, 1301 S. Ellwood Ave., 443/475-0088, www.charmcityrollergirls.com

Federal Hill

Map 4

BICYCLE RENTALS AND RESOURCES
Light Street Cycles
The city's premier bicycle shop is also the only place near the Inner
Harbor to rent a ride; you can pick it up at their bustling Federal
Hill location. Costs vary according to the type of bike rented (all
rentals come with helmets and a bike map, and they try to accommodate pedal choices too): Mountain bikes and road bikes are $60
for the first day, $50 for each additional day, while hybrids are $30
for the first day and $25 each day after.

MAP 4: 1124 Light St., 410/685-2234, www.lightstcycles.com; Mon.-Fri.
10am-8pm, Sat. 10am-6pm, Sun. 11am-4pm

BICYCLE TRAILS
Riverside Park
This small park is a big hit with the many residents of this neighborhood south of Federal Hill, where the row houses are a little
less stately and the streets a little less crowded. There's a popular
public pool here that draws sweltering residents from all around,
and the paths are popular for the many dog owners who call this
area home. There are also some ball fields and basketball courts, a
good little playground, and a pavilion that hosts small community
gatherings and other events. Lots of big, broad trees make for great
shade in the summer.

MAP 4: 1800 Covington St., 410/396-8059

GYMS AND HEALTH CLUBS
Merritt Fort Avenue
The lap and exercise pool is out back and outdoors, a welcome change from the inside swim centers of many local gyms
(though it means no swimming in the winter months, alas). This
long, well-stocked Federal Hill gym is always busy, peopled with
young professionals from the neighborhood who are hitting
the huge assortment of treadmills, bikes, elliptical machines,
Stairmasters, and free weights. A nice variety of classes is offered (including Zumba and hot yoga), and regular lunchtime
sessions are available.

MAP 4: 921 E. Fort Ave., 410/576-2004, www.merrittclubs.com; Mon.-Thurs.
5am-10pm, Fri. 5am-8:30pm, Sat. 8am-7pm, Sun. 9am-6pm; $25 for single-day
guest pass

Although Baltimore hasn't been recognized as a top running city, a quick glance at the many runners getting in their miles around the waterfront will show that there is a passionate community here. The premier running event is the Baltimore Marathon in October, which regularly draws about 25,000 runners each year. But there are lots of races all year long, and participating in one is a great way to see many Baltimore neighborhoods.

In mid-June, Corrigan Sports Enterprises' **Baltimore 10-Miler** (410/605-9381, www.baltimoretenmiler.com) starts at the Maryland Zoo, passes through Homewood and Johns Hopkins University, and ends at Lake Montebello on the other side of the city. It's a popular course, but a tough one with lots of hills and challenging warm temperatures. This race often has one of the best premiums like vests or jackets, and it covers parts of Baltimore that visitors often don't get to see.

In August, the **Charles Street 12** (www.charlesst12.com) course takes runners down this historic street, starting in the suburb of Towson (where Elaine Benes on *Seinfeld* was from) and ending at Power Plant Live! downtown. You'll pass through several neighborhoods like Homewood, Station North, Mount Vernon, and the Inner Harbor, and there's a lively postrace party at Power Plant Live!

If you've ever yearned to run through a highway tunnel, the **Fort McHenry Tunnel 5K Run/Walk** (410/242-1515, www.somd.org) will take you right through it during this mid-September event. The race benefits Special Olympics Maryland so premiums and postrace parties are minimal. But the course is so unique (and the cause worthwhile) that it doesn't really matter.

Check out the website of **Charm City Run** (www.charmcityrun.com/listofevents), a mini-chain of five local running stores, for an updated list of other running events in the city and beyond.

Running
★ Baltimore Waterfront Promenade

The best thing about this seven-mile, nearly entirely flat path is that it passes through four of Baltimore's best neighborhoods and many of its major attractions. Running on the path is easy, just follow the harbor and occasional signs. If you want to run the full route, the ideal place to start is by the Baltimore Museum of Industry in Federal Hill, making your way through the Inner Harbor, Harbor East, and Fell's Point to Canton. You'll pass the Maryland Science Center, the National Aquarium in Baltimore, the Frederick Douglass-Isaac Myers Maritime Park, the shops and restaurants of Harbor East and Fell's Point, and the row homes and boats that dominate Canton. But really you can jump on the promenade from any of these neighborhoods. It's a beautiful run, and a great way to orient yourself to the city.

MAP 4: Start at Federal Hill across from the Baltimore Museum of Industry (1415 Key Hwy.)

SAILING
Downtown Sailing Center
A few dozen yards east of the Baltimore Museum of Industry, this nonprofit organization exists to teach sailing and provide sailboats to anyone who wants to learn, but with an eye toward letting city residents who can't afford sailing get a chance to try their hand aboard a real vessel. The nearly 40-strong fleet consists primarily of fast, safe J-22s, Sonars, and Access 303Ws. Visitors new to the sport can start with the three-hour "Introduction to Sailing" course for $90; there's also a two-hour harbor tour that covers some sailing basics (and Baltimore history) for $45, as well as regular specialized skill classes and other options for more experienced sailors.

MAP 4: 1425 Key Hwy., Ste. 110, 410/727-0722, www.downtownsailing.org

Mount Vernon and Station North

Map 5

BICYCLE RENTALS AND RESOURCES
Velocipede Bike Project
This collective nonprofit group of bicyclists, mechanics, and socially minded folks in the Station North Arts and Entertainment District works to repair, restore, and provide bicycles to people who want to use them for transportation. The main goal is to get bikes into the hands of low-income folks who need to get to work or get around the city. To that end, this group rescues bikes from all sorts of near-fatal ends, spiffs them back up, and makes them available to Baltimoreans who need them.

MAP 5: 4 W. Lanvale St., 410/244-5585, www.velocipedebikeproject.org; Wed.-Thurs. 6pm-10pm, Sun. 2pm-6pm

GYMS AND HEALTH CLUBS
Merritt's Downtown Athletic Club
The local Merritt Athletic Club chain now operates this venerable health club, which is one of the city's two 24-hour gym facilities (the other is also a Merritt operation in Canton). This sprawling building (66,000 square feet) was once a train depot, and has been a gym for decades, though it's been renovated repeatedly. There are plenty of machines, plus basketball and squash courts, group workout classrooms, an indoor track, and a small aquatic center.

MAP 5: 210 E. Centre St., 410/332-0906, www.merrittclubs.com; 24 hours; $25 for single-day guest pass

Hampden and Homewood Map 6

PARKS
Druid Hill Park
Covering some 745 acres of woods, fields, ball fields, basketball and tennis courts, and paths, Druid Hill Park is also home to a large lake, the Maryland Zoo in Baltimore, and the Howard P. Rawlings Conservatory. This is one of the oldest major parks in the United States (along with New York City's Central Park and Philadelphia's Fairmount Park), and though it's showing its age in some places, it's still a major part of the lives of west Baltimoreans. Not all of the park is open, and that's probably for the best, as this is not a place to visit after dark. During the day, however, it's perfect for jogging around the reservoir and the main, open areas.

MAP 6: 900 Druid Park Lake Dr., 410/396-7900, www.bcrp.baltimorecity.gov; free

YOGA
Bikram Yoga
This Hampden center is dedicated to the practice of Bikram yoga (the hot kind); the 8,000-square-foot studio can accommodate many practitioners, and there's a nice recovery room to help reacclimate to normal temperatures. The studio also offers One, a wellness spa that can provide massages, acupuncture, and even "talk therapy" by appointment.

MAP 6: 911 W. 36th St., 410/243-2040, www.bikramyogahampden.com; $18 for a drop-in class

Greater Baltimore Map 7

BICYCLE RENTALS AND RESOURCES
Princeton Sports
Head north to the outskirts of the city on Falls Road, past the Mount Washington neighborhood, and you'll find this big, well-stocked sporting goods store in a bucolic little office building in the woods. Rentals available here include road, mountain, and hybrid bikes (all come with helmets).

MAP 7: 6239 Falls Rd., Baltimore, 410/828-1127, www.princetonsports.com; Mon.-Fri. 10am-8pm, Sat. 10am-6pm, Sun. noon-5pm; $25 per day, Thurs.-Mon. weekend $45, weeklong $75

SPORTS AND ACTIVITIES
GREATER BALTIMORE

BICYCLE TRAILS

★ **Baltimore-Annapolis Trail**

This trail technically starts in the town of Glen Burnie, so plan to begin your ride at BWI Airport, and take the BWI Trail about 12 miles to the northern end of the 13-mile long Baltimore-Annapolis Trail (maps of both trails are available on the website). The ride crosses only a few roads, and mostly takes you through woods and behind lots of residential areas. Built on a former railroad line, this is a flat trail that challenges riders with distance, not elevation gain. There are plenty of places to stop for food and drink along the way, including (during the summers) a great snowball stand at the halfway point of the B-A Trail.

MAP 7: Access trail via various trailheads: B & A Trail Ranger Station, 51 West Earleigh Heights Rd., Severna Park, Jonas Green Park and the South Lot at Boulters Way (southern end of the intersection of Route 450 and Boulter's Way in Annapolis), Glen Burnie Parking Lot, near Glen Burnie Courthouse (7500 Ritchie Hwy., Glen Burnie), www.aacounty.org/recparks

Gwynns Falls Trail

What's coolest about this 15-mile trail, which starts on the west side of town, is that if you ride it from its beginning at the I-70 Park & Ride near the I-695 Beltway and follow its winding paths across bridges, past baseball fields, and through deep woods, you'll have passed through some 30 city neighborhoods. At the end, you'll be in the heart of the city, long past the trees and streams, but the voyage from wilderness to concrete jungle is transformative in a lot of ways. This is part of two greenways projects: the East Coast Greenway and the Chesapeake Bay Gateways Network. The trail does pass through some less-than-thriving sections of town, but there's never been any trouble for riders.

MAP 7: Access trail via various trailheads: 70 Park and Ride, Winans Meadow Trailhead, 4500 North Franklintown Rd., Windsor Mill Road Trailhead, 4500 Windsor Mill Rd., Leon Day Park, 1200 North Franklintown Rd., Gwynn Falls Park, 2700 Frederick Ave., 410/396-0440 or 410/448-5663, ext. 113, www.gwynnsfallstrail.org

Lake Montebello

This bike and pedestrian path follows the shoreline of this 54-acre lake (actually one of the city's reservoirs) and is popular with joggers, inline skaters, and bicyclists. The loop is 1.35 miles, and the smooth, low-traffic road that hugs the bike path is no worry for bikers. During the early morning and early evening, many residents take their daily constitutionals around the waters of the lake.

MAP 7: Between Harford and Hillen Rds. at 32nd St., Baltimore

This trail, which connects with the York (Pennsylvania) Heritage Trail after it crosses the border some 20 miles from its starting point in Ashland in rural northern Baltimore County, is extremely popular with Baltimore bicyclists. If you take the trail all the way to York, it's a 41-mile ride one-way, mostly flat until you hit the Pennsylvania border; then, it's a long gradual climb uphill (which becomes a pleasant downhill on the way home). A former railroad bed, this trail runs through almost entirely rural countryside, with big shade trees and beautiful scenery. There aren't many facilities around, though, so you'll need to pack all your own food and water.

MAP 7: Ashland, 410/592-2897, www.dnr.state.md.us

BOATING SUPPLIES AND FACILITIES
Tidewater Yacht Service

If you're a boater in need of some service or repair, Tidewater is your best bet in town, though it is located well to the south of the Inner Harbor, in the industrial area of Port Covington, south of Federal Hill. This marine shop offers everything from engine and hull repair and electrical work to painting and woodworking. They can handle craft ranging from small boats to huge yachts (they've got a 77-ton crane), and have even implemented environmentally friendly business practices.

MAP 7: 321 E. Cromwell St., Port Covington, 410/625-4992, www.tysc.com

DUCKPIN BOWLING
Stoneleigh Lanes Duckpin Bowling Center

Of the dedicated duckpin lanes that remain in the Baltimore area, this one is probably in the best shape; the decor, lanes, and equipment are all wonderfully retro and in kind-of good repair. Located in the basement of a 1950s-era shopping strip, Stoneleigh is like a time capsule of crazy carpeting and jet-age industrial design—and 16 lanes of duckpin action.

MAP 7: 6703 York Rd., Baltimore, 410/377-8115, www.stoneleighlanes.com; Mon. and Wed. 11am-9pm, Tues., Thurs., and Fri. 11am-1am, Sat. 10am-1am, Sun. 10am-10pm

GOLF
Carroll Park

Carroll Park, just a short drive west from downtown, is a modest nine-hole course that's perfect for getting in a few quick holes. Next to the lumbering Montgomery Park office building right off of I-95, this is a quirky course that is often used by office workers to fire off a few drives during conferences and lunchtimes.

MAP 7: 2100 Washington Blvd., Baltimore, 410/685-8344, www.bmgcgolf.com; weekdays $16, weekends $18.50

Clifton Park

Though the course is not as good as Mount Pleasant, Clifton Park (formerly the site of Johns Hopkins' summer mansion) is a favorite because it provides some amazing views of the city, particularly as you play back to the clubhouse. Challenges here include some unforgiving out-of-bounds—and the occasional city resident who stops on a walk past the course to provide blunt criticism of your game.

MAP 7: 2701 St. Lo Dr., Baltimore, 410/243-3500, www.bmgcgolf.com; weekdays $34, weekends $40

Forest Park

On the far west side of the city is Forest Park, a short course that makes up for lack of distance with an increase in obstacles and hazards. The front nine are tight, tough holes, while the back nine are more modern and open. There's a relatively new clubhouse here, with locker rooms, a pro shop, and a small restaurant.

MAP 7: 2900 Hillsdale Rd., Baltimore, 410/448-4653, www.bmgcgolf.com; weekdays $34, weekends $40

Mount Pleasant

The pinnacle of Baltimore City's golf courses is Mount Pleasant, rated four-star by *Golf Digest;* it was also *Golf Week*'s onetime pick as the 12th-best municipal course in the country. It's the most expensive weekend morning course, at $49—but that's still peanuts compared to what most courses charge. Arnold Palmer won a tournament here (his second) back in 1956, and throughout the 1950s and '60s, this course was host to many major tournaments. It's aged well (it was built back in 1934), and is a good example of early pro golf course design and tests.

MAP 7: 6001 Hillen Rd., Baltimore, 410/254-5100, www.bmgcgolf.com; weekdays $42, weekends $49

GYMS AND HEALTH CLUBS

Meadowbrook Aquatic Center

This Mount Washington pool complex, located under a bridge, doesn't give visitors much to see from the outside, but within these walls (and in these waters), Olympic gold has been forged. These lanes are home to the phenomenal Michael Phelps, as well as other swimming gold medalists like Katie Hoff, Teresa Andrews, Anita Nall, and Beth Botsford. The center has indoor and outdoor pools (including one for kids), and indoor exercise facilities as well as outdoor tennis courts. Alas, you can't just walk in and use the pool for a day; you've got to purchase a season pass.

MAP 7: 5700 Cottonworth Ave., Baltimore, 410/433-8300, www.mbrook.com

Baltimore Rowing Club

From a boathouse in the shadow of the Hanover Street Bridge in south Baltimore, this group of rowers (and coxswains) takes to the waters of Baltimore in a collection of shells ranging from singles to fours and eights. The club competes against other groups at regattas up and down the East Coast, and offers serious, weeks-long lessons to newcomers ($200) and the chance to row with the pros.

MAP 7: 3301 Waterview Ave., Baltimore, 410/355-5649, www.baltimorerowing.org

PARKS

Cylburn Arboretum

No, it's technically not a park, but the lovely grounds of this 207-acre arboretum make it one of the city's most beautiful urban retreats. There are more than three miles of paths running through the rolling hills and dense woods here (self-guided cell phone tours are available), and the majestic, Victorian-era Cylburn Mansion (1888) provides a strong anchor for the site's superlative grounds. There are gentle lawns and well-tended gardens around the mansion, while tall trees provide shade for the pathways that wind around the property.

MAP 7: 4915 Greenspring Ave., Baltimore, 410/367-2217, www.cylburn.org

Fort McHenry National Monument and Historic Shrine

With a couple of acres of flat, green lawns and tall, shade-giving trees overlooking the Inner Harbor as it becomes the Patapsco River again and heads toward the Chesapeake Bay, the grounds surrounding historic Fort McHenry are a favorite for Federal Hill residents, who bike, jog, and picnic here regularly (but no ball playing). It's one of the most peaceful spots in town (if you tune out any activity at the heliport across the water), and a great way to escape the heat and noise of downtown Baltimore. Do take a look around before you put your blanket down, however; the large geese who make their homes around the fort tend to use the grassy areas as their toilet.

MAP 7: 2400 E. Fort Ave., Baltimore, 410/962-4290, www.nps.gov/fomc

Robert E. Lee Park

This is *the* city park (though it lies in Baltimore County, Baltimore City owns it) for dog lovers, despite what you might think having been to some other parks. Acres of wooded trails and the Jones Falls (plus the shores of Lake Roland) are a paradise for a stroll and a frolic, though the light-rail trains blow through the park and are not behind a fence, so use caution when crossing the tracks. If you're not a fan of dogs, this is probably not the best place to get away from it all, as this park is usually teeming with happy-go-lucky (and often illegally un-leashed) canines and their owners. And yes, it's named for the Confederate general; Baltimore's Confederate-sympathizing proclivities are always lurking around.

MAP 7: 1000 Lakeside Dr., Baltimore

SPECTATOR SPORTS
Horse Racing
Pimlico Race Course

The nation's second-oldest horse racing track (behind New York's Saratoga) opened in 1870, covering 70 acres of what was then countryside north of Baltimore City. Although there was a period (1889-1904) when there was no flat-track racing here, Pimlico has now been running the horses for more than 100 years. The first Preakness Stakes was run here in 1873, two years before the first Kentucky Derby. "Old Hilltop," as it's called by old-timers, runs races throughout the spring, sharing the state's racing season with another track in Laurel, south of Baltimore (check the website for schedules). Weekday attendance is pretty sparse, so if you're looking for a quiet day at the races, Pimlico is a lock. Crowds erupt, however, on the third Saturday in May, when the Preakness draws over 100,000 fans.

MAP 7: 5201 Park Heights Ave., Baltimore, 410/542-9400, www.pimlico.com

Various Locations

GUIDED AND WALKING TOURS
Wayne Schaumburg

Wayne Schaumburg is one of those little-appreciated civic re-sources that makes a city a better place to live, even if few peo-ple know about him or what he does. Though he's most famed for his fascinating walking tours of Green Mount Cemetery (offered in May and Oct.), his knowledge of the city doesn't end with its dead; let him know what you're interested in, and maybe you can work out a personalized tour that might mix walking and a little driving. His website is also one of the best ways to find out about the various tours, open houses, lectures, and historic walks that are taking place in Baltimore in upcom-ing months.

VARIOUS LOCATIONS: 410/256-2180, http://home.earthlink.net/~wschaumburg; $15

When you sign up for a guided tour with Zippy Larson, you're getting one of the city's great personalities to go along with its history. Larson was born in Baltimore and educated at the city's public schools and the University of Baltimore; today, she lives a few blocks from where she was born. As a lifelong Charm City resident, Larson has amassed hundreds of contacts across the city, allowing her to create custom tours for groups; she can accommodate 28 people on walking tours and more on driving tours. Although she never gives the exact same tour twice, her previous voyages have covered the sites that inspired *Hairspray*, and the Duchess of Windsor (Wallis Warfield Simpson was a Baltimore girl), as well as more standard sites across the city. Larson has access to lots of one-of-a-kind areas, and her irrepressible charm and demeanor open those few doors that are initially closed to her.

VARIOUS LOCATIONS: 410/522-7133, www.zippytours.com; $100 per hour, two-hour minimum

SPORTS AND ACTIVITIES

VARIOUS LOCATIONS

Shops

Downtown and Inner Harbor.....193

Harbor East and Little Italy 195

Fell's Point.......................197

Canton 201

Federal Hill 203

Mount Vernon and Station North..207

Hampden and Homewood.......210

Greater Baltimore................217

There are two great reasons to set aside some time to go shopping in Baltimore: The city has lots of cool stuff, and a lot of it is still pretty cheap. That's not always true, of course—there are plenty of boutiques, galleries, and high-end stores throughout town. In fact, that's a third great reason to make shopping part of your trip: New retail districts have literally sprung from the ground in the past few years. Harbor East's upscale stores are a very welcome addition to a downtown shopping scene that was, to put it kindly, sparse, and Broadway and Thames Street in Fell's Point have welcomed some popular boutiques. But part of Baltimore's charm for shoppers is also found in its quirky, independently owned shops, especially in neighborhoods like Fell's Point, which has a lot of women's boutiques and children's stores, and Hampden, where a large percentage of the stores are owned and operated by women.

Downtown, shoppers looking for a single location to handle lots of shopping need head no farther than the Gallery at the corner of Pratt and Calvert Streets just across from Harborplace, which has its own collection of shops and gift stores. Outside of the city, there are a few truly massive palaces of retail wonder. First and foremost is the Arundel Mills Mall, south of BWI Airport: Not only does it have more than 225 stores, there's a Cinemark Egyptian 24 movie theater, which sometimes ranks as the nation's number-one theater in terms of ticket sales. To the north of town is Towson Town Center, a more upscale mall that's recently undergone yet another expansion.

Highlights

★ **Best Homegrown Fitness Store:** The headquarters for the popular fitness company Under Armour is in Baltimore and the new **Under Armour Brand House** stocks all the clothing, shoes, and accessories you need to power through workouts in functional style (page 195).

★ **Best Shopping District with National Chains and Local Shops:** Upscale national stores join independently owned shops like Urban Chic in the small but dense **Harbor East** shopping district (page 196).

★ **Best Toy Store:** The staff at Fell's Point's **aMuse** really know their toys, making it easy to find the best (and often the cutest) baby teether, board game, or fun educational item for the kids in your life (page 197).

★ **Best Music Store Run by Musicians:** Motor down to Fell's Point's **The Sound Garden** for not only the big new sounds, but the obscure old ones (page 200).

★ **Best Pet Shop:** From luxurious little coats to delicious treats and chew toys, Canton's **Dogma** has everything for your precious pooch or kitty (page 203).

★ **Best Day Spa:** If you need a break from a grueling schedule of brunch, sightseeing, and shopping, take the edge off at **Studio 921 Salon & Day Spa,** near Federal Hill (page 207).

★ **Best Bookstore That Also Sells Art Toys and Drinks:** Need one bookstore to sell you the latest Jonathan Lethem novel, a Batman Trexi figure, and a glass of wine? Head to Hampden's **Atomic Books** (page 210).

★ **Best Independently Owned Women's and Men's Clothing Stores:** Located on separate floors in the same storefront, the lovely and atmospheric **Sixteen Tons** (for men) and **Doubledutch Boutique** (for women) are great places for couples looking for contemporary, vintage, and indie apparel (pages 213 and 214).

★ **Most Artfully Displayed Home Furnishings:** Gather inspiration for your home while looking at the beautiful displays of books, children's wares, furniture, home decor items, and cards at **Trohv,** a sweet-smelling, two-floor store in Hampden (page 214).

★ **Best Place to Try on Shoes While Eating Chocolate:** There's no better way to spend a Saturday than trying on shoes from Miz Mooz while eating a Vosges chocolate bar from **Ma Petite Shoe.** A new café next door means that you now get a latte, too (page 215).

It's pretty easy to find what you're searching for in Baltimore, whether it's an item of apparel, jewelry, art, or a unique handmade gift. Between the big-name stores at the malls, the upscale boutiques around town, and the charming little single-proprietor shops tucked into neighborhoods, shoppers have a great hunt waiting for them in Charm City.

Downtown and Inner Harbor

Map 1

CLOTHING AND ACCESSORIES

Jos. A. Bank

For Baltimore's upper class, the sensible khakis, blue blazers, tweed suits, and tattersall shirts of Joseph A. Bank clothiers (not as fancy as Brooks Brothers, but just as preppy) have been de rigueur since 1905, when the company was founded. After some lean years in the recent past, this clothing company has become a real mover in the U.S. men's clothing world, and while you won't be setting any trends with the conservative attire here, you will be able to gain entry into any of the city's more elite restaurants and clubs. This is the city's flagship store in the same building as one of Baltimore's most storied financial companies (T. Rowe Price), which means while it's no marble and walnut shopping Shangri-la, you can feel the heavy billfolds of some of the shoppers here.

MAP 1: 100 E. Pratt St., 410/547-1700, www.josbank.com; Mon.-Sat. 9am-8pm, Sun. 10am-6pm

GIFT AND SPECIALTY

The Best of Luck Candy & Gifts

Next to the enormous Phillips Seafood in the Inner Harbor is this cute and colorful sweet shop that stocks current and vintage candies like the Charleston Chew, Pop Rocks, and Big League Chew gum, along with popcorn, ice pops, and more. This is also a great place to try specialty foods from several local producers, like Taharka Bros. ice cream and Zeke's Coffee. There's a small old-fashioned lunch counter inside, but guests should take their sweets to one of the many benches or green spaces along the Inner Harbor to enjoy dessert while watching the often-heavy foot traffic pass by.

MAP 1: 601 E. Pratt St., 410/752-2500, www.thebestofluck.com; Mon.-Sat. 11am-8pm, Sun. noon-8pm

Founded in Baltimore in 1889 by then 25-year-old entrepreneur Willoughby M. McCormick, global juggernaut McCormick & Company produced its spices, seasonings, and flavorings on the Inner Harbor's Light Street from 1921 to 1989. Today, its headquarters is in nearby Hunt Valley, but this new store—the company's only retail outlet—lies in the recently renovated Light Street Pavilion in Harborplace. McCormick & Company's line of 88 spices is available, including the seafood seasoning Old Bay, so popular in Baltimore that you'd be hard-pressed to find a steamed crab that isn't covered in it. (And, really, you wouldn't want to.) There are also T-shirts, cooking utensils, and gift baskets, as well as several interactive elements, including a fun "Guess that Spice!" game that rewards winners with coupons.

MAP 1: Harborplace, 301 Light St., 443/853-1355, www.harborplace.com; daily 10am-9pm

SHOPPING CENTERS AND DISTRICTS

Downtown and Inner Harbor

Pratt Street, which runs through downtown and along the north side of the Inner Harbor, is the prime shopping artery in this part of the city. There is the Gallery, a small shopping center with clothiers and apparel merchants directly across from Harborplace, which itself is filled with gift shops and locally themed stores that are perfect for souvenirs and mementos. Farther east lies a huge Barnes & Noble bookstore in the old Power Plant building (look for the four tall smokestacks).

MAP 1: Pratt St. between Light St. and Market Pl.

The Gallery

Across Pratt Street from the waterfront pavilions of Harborplace is the Gallery, an open, airy, indoor mall that caters to both tourists and downtown office workers with a mix of shops and even a food court (with some great views of the city). Shops here include Ann Taylor, Banana Republic, Brooks Brothers, Coach, Forever 21, Nine West, and The Children's Place—your typical mall basics. There's also the wellness center Access Health, which offers acupuncture and reflexology services, and a nail salon. If you're staying downtown, the convenience of this shopping center can't be beat, even if it's all national chains.

MAP 1: 200 E. Pratt St., 410/332-4192, www.thegalleryatharborplace.com; Mon.-Sat. 10am-9pm, Sun. noon-6pm

Harbor East and Little Italy

Map 2

CLOTHING AND ACCESSORIES

Handbags in the City

There's more to life than purses, to be sure, but if handbags are a big part of your life, it's worth a visit to this modern boutique along Harbor East's main shopping drag. Expect to find handbags (and clothing) from must-have labels like MCM, Michael Kors, Longchamps, Diane von Furstenburg, Nicole Miller, and Kate Spade. There's also a nice selection of accessories and a small area devoted to shoes.

MAP 2: 840 Aliceanna St., 410/528-1443, www.handbagsinthecity.com; Mon.-Fri. 10am-7pm, Sat. 10am-8pm, Sun. noon-5pm

South Moon Under

If you find yourself in need of a swimsuit—either for the pool or a trip to the beach on Maryland's Eastern Shore—you'd be smart to head straight to the bright, sunny corner occupied by South Moon Under, where you'll find suits from classic makers like Quiksilver and Billabong as well as creations from L*Space, Trina Turk, and Seafolly. There's also a wide variety of casual clothes for men and women, including denim and shoes. If you're in need of a small gift, South Moon Under has plenty of great options (it's a big, modern store with several well-stocked sections).

MAP 2: 815 Aliceanna St., 410/685-7820, www.southmoonunder.com; Mon.-Sat. 10am-8pm, Sun. noon-5pm

★ Under Armour Brand House

This well-known sports apparel company began in 1995 with Kevin Plank, then a University of Maryland football player; four years later, its global headquarters opened in Baltimore's Locust Point. This is the company's first Baltimore retail store, filled with accessories, workout clothes, and graphic tees for men, women, and youth, including some fun designs that celebrate Baltimore. There's also a good collection of shoes, displayed in the center underneath four large TV screens. If you need workout inspiration, approach the store from the side closest to the water to walk past enormous signs showing local sports heroes like Michael Phelps in full training mode.

MAP 2: 700 S. President St., 410/528-5304; Mon.-Sat. 10am-9pm, Sun. 11am-7pm

This small local chain gained popularity for stocking modern clothing brands that weren't always easy to find in Baltimore. Their sleek, modern, yet warm store (there are some nice real-world objects tossed in as decor to keep things grounded) features denim from makers like Hudson, Joe's Jeans, and Paige. Urban Chic has a good variety of men's and women's apparel and shoes (including Hunter Wellington Boots), featuring brands like Vineyard Vines, Yosi, and Samra. There's also a good assortment of skin and beauty products from makers like Kai, and even toddlers' clothes.

MAP 2: 811 Aliceanna St., 410/685-1601, www.urbanchiconline.com; Mon.-Sat. 10am-8pm, Sun. 11am-5pm

SHOES
Sassanova

A shoe lover's paradise, this shop features high-end models from houses like Stuart Weitzman, L.K.Bennett, Michael Kors, and Bettye Muller. Mid-price shoes by makers like All Black and Andre Assous round out the footwear selection, and there are also handbags, jewelry, and accessories. Shoppers (and guests) can relax while seated on the plush pink couch in front of the store's mirrored mantel.

MAP 2: 805 Aliceanna St., 410/244-1114, www.sassanova.com; Mon.-Sat. 10am-8pm, Sun. 11am-6pm

SHOPPING CENTERS AND DISTRICTS
★ Harbor East

Harbor East has grown in bona fide shopping hub in recent years as more big-name retailers have come to town. There are still several wonderful independently owned shops on Aliceanna Street, as well as new Lululemon Athletica and MAC stores. Around the National Katyn Memorial (and the traffic circle) are new Anthropologie and J. Crew stores, and a block south, by the water, is the recently opened Under Armour Brand House; the company's headquarters are across the harbor in Locust Point.

MAP 2: Aliceanna St. between President St. and Exeter St.

SPA, BATH, AND BEAUTY
The Spa at the Four Seasons Hotel Baltimore

When you come upon the white stone entryway on the fourth floor of the Four Seasons Hotel Baltimore, you've arrived at The Spa, a relaxing oasis in Harbor East where voices are hushed and the rolling sound of water fills the air. Quench, a three-hour treatment that starts with a salt and sugar scrub and ends with a hot oil scalp massage, is the signature experience; the traditional massages, nail services, and skin and body treatments are also offered. Those who

book spa treatments or stay in the hotel can also use the relaxation
room and the "heat experience" space with its shallow soaking tubs, a nice touch for guests.

MAP 2: 200 International Dr., 410/576-5800, www.fourseasons.com/baltimore; facilities daily 8am-9pm, appts. daily 9am-9pm

Fell's Point

Map 2

ARTS AND CRAFTS

A Good Yarn

The resurgence of knitting in the United States—picked up by a new generation of needle-twirlers, and re-embraced by their parents—has led to the opening of a couple of great yarn and knitting shops. A Good Yarn is Fell's Point's center of knit culture; yarns both pedestrian and exotic are available at this cozy little shop (which always smells divine), and the helpful staff has an astonishing array of tricks and tips available for both newcomers and old purlers.

MAP 2: 1738 Aliceanna St., 410/327-3884, www.agoodyarn.com; Wed.-Fri. noon-6pm, Sat. noon-7pm, Sun. noon-5pm

CHILDREN'S STORES

★ aMuse

If you're in need of a birthday present or baby shower gift, this welcoming store is the place to go, mainly because the staff know their toys so well. The well-stocked shelves hold toys that are made to grow with your child (at least for a while), including games, crafting kits, and art supplies (there are a couple of fun baby teethers made by local moms too). Not sure what to get? Tell the staff a little bit about the gift recipient, and they'll have plenty of helpful suggestions. The store also holds occasional events on topics important to parents, such as traveling with children, as well as toy demonstrations.

MAP 2: 1623 Thames St., 410/342-5000, www.amusetoys.com; Mon.-Sat. 10am-7pm, Sun. 10am-5pm

Corduroy Button

Looking for some cool kids' clothes and toys for your cool friends (or for your own kids)? This funky and upscale Fell's Point infant and toddler shop has plenty of traditional, high-quality apparel choices, as well as a great selection of the clothes you wish you could have worn as a youth from makers like Tuff Cookie and Zutano. You'll find fun graphic prints, great hats and jackets, and lots of other gear for the cool kids in your life.

MAP 2: 1625 Thames St., 410/276-5437, www.thecordbutton.com; daily 11am-7pm

First Fridays, Third Thursdays

Several of Baltimore's shopping districts have special weekly evening events where stores offer discounts, refreshments, and live music for customers.

The most creative event is the relatively new **Ladies' Night Out in Fell's Point** on the third Thursday every month. The organizers have set up the evening as a fun "shop crawl": Check in at The Admiral's Cup on Thames Street to receive a bag full of the participating stores' discounts and gifts with purchase, then start shopping until 9pm. Refreshments like sangria are flowing in many of the boutiques, too.

First Fridays on "The Avenue" (36th Avenue) in Hampden is another great event. The wonderful boutiques here stay open until 9pm and offer some combination of discounts, food, drinks, and music. While you're here, don't miss Chocolate Happy Hour at Ma Petite Shoe, a weekly Friday evening event where you can sample the latest confections to hit the store.

Federal Hill also has a **Third Thursdays** event, where the nice (if fewer) independently run stores (and some restaurants) in this area serve refreshments, host live musicians, and provide discounts until 8pm. It's a good event to attend before checking out Federal Hill's bar scene.

You can find details about all of these fun evenings on the events' Facebook pages.

CLOTHING AND ACCESSORIES

Babe

Recently bought by the owners of the popular shoe store Poppy and Stella, this hip and youthful Fell's Point store was designed for cost-conscious (but fashion-starved) Baltimoreans who wanted better clothing options without the SoHo prices. You'll find tops, pants, and dresses by Blaque Label, Hourglass Lilly, and Ella Moss, plus handbags by makers like Deux Lux and basic and patterned camisoles from the store's own clothing line called Betties.

MAP 2: 1716 Aliceanna St., 410/244-5114, www.babeaboutique.com; Mon.-Sat. 11am-7pm, Sun. 11am-5pm

Cupcake

Right on Fell's Point's main square, at the foot of Broadway, this boutique draws regulars for its upscale selection, which includes labels like Yoana Baraschi, Black Halo, and Parker. This clean, sunny, and unobtrusively decorated store (with white walls and neutral decor) is the perfect place to look for a great little dress destined to liven up an event or a night on the town. If you're not in the market for a knockout outfit, there are plenty of jeans and more day-to-day apparel here as well.

MAP 2: 813 S. Broadway, 410/522-0941, www.cupcake-shop.com; Mon.-Sat. 11am-8pm, Sun. 11am-6pm

Although the harbor offers limited water activities (due to the fact that the water, while lovely to sail on, is not suitable for swimming), the city does have an air of surf culture, thanks to its proximity to Eastern Shore beaches. This store embraces that laid-back lifestyle with easy, casual clothes for men and women in addition to the expected bathing suits, flip-flops, and sunglasses, as well as a decent selection of skateboards and surfboards. This is also a good spot to pick up some sunscreen or lip balm on hot summer days.

MAP 2: 1631 Thames St., 410/276-7873, www.fpsurfco.com; Mon.-Thurs. 11am-7pm, Fri.-Sat. 10am-8pm, Sun. 11am-6pm

Hats in the Belfry

Maryland's premier event for hat culture is the Preakness Stakes, the Triple Crown race held at the Pimlico Race Course in May, and this Fell's Point store, part of a five-store, mid-Atlantic mini-chain, is well-stocked with contemporary men's and women's styles (hats even hang on the chandelier and lamps). Fedoras and cloches are popular options. Many of the offerings are adorned with jewels, feathers, and other accoutrements, and about half of them are designed by Hats in the Belfry. There's also a location in **Harborplace** (201 E. Pratt St., 410/528-0060).

MAP 2: 813 S. Broadway, 410/342-7480, www.hatsinthebelfry.com; Mon.-Wed. 10am-8pm, Thurs. 10am-9pm, Fri.-Sat. 10am-10pm, Sun. 10am-7pm

FURNITURE AND HOME DECOR

Su Casa

One of the first stores to embody the new Fell's Point—the one where people can walk from their house to a contemporary furniture store, instead of having to drive somewhere—Su Casa has a vast array of home goods, most in the modern Americana school of design, with faux-distressed pressed tin stars and heavy wooden construction. Su Casa is packed with beds, lamps, tables, love seats, armchairs, and all sorts of objects for decorating, both for adults and kids. There are also dishes and glassware.

MAP 2: 901 S. Bond St., 410/522-7010, www.sucasa-furniture.com; Mon.-Thurs. 10am-9pm, Fri.-Sat. 10am-9:30pm, Sun. 10am-7pm

GIFT AND SPECIALTY

Maja

Jewelry, clothing, bags, masks, and fair trade crafts from all over the world, but primarily the United States, South America, Africa, and East Asia, line the walls and fill the cases of this inviting Fell's Point store. There are also blouses, handbags, and hats, from places like Madagascar and Cambodia. Incense is a big part of this store;

you can buy everything from sticks to Buddhist holders, plus soaps and oils.

MAP 2: 1744 Aliceanna St., 410/327-9499, www.majacollections.com; Wed.-Sun. 11am-7pm

MUSIC

El Suprimo

This basement-based vinyl paradise mostly eschews the CD in favor of racks and racks of black (and sometimes other hued) vinyl, covering the weird, the awesome, and the inexplicable (the store's label issued a title called "Cambodian Psych-Out"). There are also turntables for sale, along with other DJ equipment, books, and even some musical instruments. Call to make sure they're open before stopping in.

MAP 2: 1709 Aliceanna St., 443/226-9628, www.elsuprimo.com; Mon.-Sat. noon-7pm, Sun. noon-6pm

★ The Sound Garden

Getting the name out of the way first: Although this store has received worldwide recognition—in 2010, *Rolling Stone* named it the second-best record store in the U.S.A.—it is not associated with the famed Seattle grunge band. What it is associated with is a very broad selection of CDs and a decent vinyl collection, covering both the big hits of the day and more obscure rock, hip-hop, and country artists. There's a big used CD collection, which can be full of dreck but may also contain some hidden gems. The DVD wall has a lot of really fantastic finds, from TV boxed sets to strange foreign films to anime and horror. There are a few listening stations to try before you buy, and the in-store music selection is usually right on.

MAP 2: 1616 Thames St., 410/563-9011, www.cdjoint.com; Sun.-Thurs. 10am-10pm, Fri.-Sat. 10am-midnight

SHOES

Poppy and Stella

After quickly attracting a loyal clientele, this popular footwear shop recently expanded into the building next door. It now offers a small selection of clothing from makers like Lani, Olive & Oak, and Very J, as well as a good selection of handbags and accessories. It's the shoes, though, that keep people coming in; from perilous and artsy heels to sneakers and boots, from cobblers like Frye, Jeffrey Campbell, and Pour La Victoire, this welcoming shrine to the shoe is worth a walk-through. The owners also run the great clothing store **Babe** (1716 Aliceanna St.) a couple of blocks away.

MAP 2: 728 S. Broadway, 410/522-1970, www.poppyandstella.com; Mon.-Thurs. 11am-7pm, Fri.-Sat. 11am-8pm, Sun. noon-6pm

Fell's Point

One of the city's most popular shopping areas, the charming waterfront and paving-stone streets of Fell's Point are perfect for an afternoon of poking into the wide variety of shops that line both the main thoroughfares and the tiny side streets. From jewelry and clothing to home goods to music to toys, this quirky, busy neighborhood has a store for every shopper, from high-end connoisseurs to bargain hunters.

MAP 2: Thames St. between Bond St. and Broadway, Broadway between Thames St. and Fleet St.

Canton   Map 3

CLOTHING AND ACCESSORIES

Cloud 9

This Baltimore-based women's (and some men's) clothing and accessories merchant has built a loyal following because it has great taste and doesn't charge a fortune for its wares. There are two Baltimore locations; this Canton outlet, and another in **Hampden** (1111 W. 36th St., 410/889-1330). In addition to denim and tops, there are dresses for work, play, and special events; handbags and jewelry round out the options here. This is a fun, airy store, with good music playing. Allow plenty of time to browse and discover items on the racks and tables.

MAP 3: The Can Company, 2400 Boston St., 410/534-4200, www.cloud9clothing.us; Mon.-Sat. 11am-9pm, Sun. 11am-7pm

GIFT AND SPECIALTY

2910 on the Square

This whimsical store, located on Canton's O'Donnell Square between the bars, restaurants, and hair salons, is a good place to find gifts for a wide range of people. There are lots of fun toys and clothes for kids, for example, and chewable goods for pets, glassware boxes for the office, and so on. This multicolored, multiethnic shop also carries a few local items, such as trivets and ornaments made by children from St. Elizabeth School, a special education institution. It is also one of the only places in the area for Judaica, so if you're in need of a Jewish-themed gift or maybe a mezuzah, this is probably your best bet.

MAP 3: 2910 O'Donnell St., 410/675-8505, www.2910onthesquare.com; Tues.-Thurs. noon-8pm, Fri.-Sat. noon-9pm, Sun. 10am-4pm

clockwise from top left: Brightside Boutique & Art Studio, Federal Hill; A People United, Mount Vernon; Sixteen Tons and Doubledutch Boutique, Hampden

★ Dogma

Though most pets will never appreciate just how cute these chew toys, food bowls, jackets, or collars are, owners go ga-ga over the huge selection of colorful, fuzzy, and sleek items at this Canton emporium of pet accessories (they also sell lots of brands of healthy food and snacks). Bright corrugated metal, pastel colors, and industrial touches like exposed I-beams and ductwork surround displays filled with more leashes and collars than you have ever seen. There are also self-serve baths here, as well as groomers, if your little Fido needs a sprucing up before leaving town.

MAP 3: 3600 Boston St., 410/276-3410, www.dogmaforpets.com; Mon.-Fri. 10am-8pm, Sat. 9am-8pm, Sun. 10am-6pm

SPA, BATH, AND BEAUTY

About Faces

This locally run chain of hair salon and day spa centers has been around for more than four decades, giving them the claim to the title of grande dame of the Baltimore spa circuit. There are roughly five kinds of massages, five types of spa treatments (from salt scrubs to green coffee wraps), and a vast array of hair, nail, and makeup services available. This is a huge, blonde-wood and glass filled facility, with lighting plans and flow decisions to help guide the traffic between the stations. The location, on the third floor of a Canton office tower, gives clients some great views of the city as they get a manicure or soak in a huge whirlpool tub.

MAP 3: Canton Crossing, 1501 S. Clinton St., 410/675-0099, www.aboutfacesdayspa.com; Mon.-Tues. 10am-7:30pm, Wed.-Thurs. 9am-8:30pm, Fri. 8am-7:30pm, Sat. 8am-6pm, Sun. 10:30am-5:30pm

Federal Hill

Map 4

BOOKS

Alliance Comics

Expect to overhear conversations about a patron's most treasured issue or the estimated worth of his entire collection at this Federal Hill store devoted to comic books, graphic novels, and memorabilia like posters and action figures. The well-stocked store attracts diehard fans of the genre, but people who are new to comic books are welcomed too. The location is great for those who also want to see the cases and cases of comic book memorabilia at **Geppi's Entertainment Museum** (301 W. Camden St.), which is a nice 15-minute walk away.

MAP 4: 904 Light St., 410/685-0021, www.alliancecomicsonline.com; Mon.-Sat. 11am-7pm, Sun. 11am-5pm

The Book Escape

This musty but lovely store has amassed an astonishing number of books: 30,000 that are displayed, as well as 40,000 in storage. The general-interest collection includes fiction and books about cooking, religion, gardening, and history; many of the volumes are sold at great discounts; and there are a couple of comfy chairs for perusing. Don't miss walking through the pretty courtyard in back to see more books, as well as a second store, **Trade Stone Gallery** (803 Light St.), which sells intricate lacquered boxes, dolls, and artwork from Russia.

MAP 4: 805 Light St., 410/504-1902, www.thebookescape.com; Mon.-Sat. 10am-6pm, Sun. noon-6pm

CLOTHING AND ACCESSORIES
Brightside Boutique & Art Studio

Founded by a New York-based couple—one with a penchant for fashion, the other tattoo artistry—the Brightside Boutique (in a hard-to-miss bright yellow building) is a store where you can have the rare Baltimore experience of listening to a buzzing tattoo gun (a tattoo parlor is in back) while flipping through racks of dresses, tops, and pants from designers like BB Dakota and MINKPINK. The clothing is influenced by edgy New York fashion and well priced, and there's a good selection of sunglasses, scarves, and other accessories. There's also a brand-new clothing-only store in **Fell's Point** (732 S. Broadway, 410/522-1337).

MAP 4: 1133 S. Charles St., 410/244-1133, www.brightsidebaltimore.com; Mon.-Fri. 11am-8pm, Sat. 10am-8pm, Sun. 11am-5pm

FURNITURE AND HOME DECOR
Shofer's

Many of Baltimore's storied companies of yore—Hamburger's, Hochschild Kohn—have long vanished. But Shofer's, first opened in 1914 in part of the same Federal Hill location (five floors and now some 70,000 square feet) it occupies today, has managed to hang on, probably because it's helped establish Baltimore's taste in furniture and home decor for almost a century. No matter your style, be it over-the-top leopard print or staid, proper leather, Shofer's probably has something for you. Looking for a bargain? Don't miss checking the large outlet center on the left side of the store.

MAP 4: 930 S. Charles St., 410/752-4212, www.shofers.com; Mon. 10am-9pm, Tues.-Sat. 10am-5:30pm, Sun. noon-5pm

GIFT AND SPECIALTY
Pandora's Box Boutique

At the edge of Cross Street and its many bars and restaurants is this cute gift shop filled with brightly colored jewelry, sunglasses, pillows, key chains, painted glassware, bags, and purses; there's also a small selection of baby toys and onesies. But the best items may be local artist Linda Amtmann's painted brick and wood "row homes" designed to look like Baltimore businesses and landmarks. Although the store is tiny, it's quite pleasant shopping here, thanks to the lovely scents wafting through the air.

MAP 4: 50 E. Cross St., 410/244-1442; Mon.-Fri. 10am-7pm, Sat. 10am-8pm, Sun. 10am-6pm

Sideshow at the American Visionary Art Museum

As befits a museum like AVAM that celebrates the genius of the off-kilter, this gift store is run by Chicago's legendary Uncle Fun (Ted Frankel), who travels from Second City to Charm City to keep the place stocked. You won't find boring old coffee cups and coasters here; instead, be prepared for original folk art, crazy glasses with guitars and flamingos (as well as more standard options), funky jewelry, blast-from-the-past toys, junky bric-a-brac, gimmicks, jokes, puns, and all sorts of other perfectly peculiar items.

MAP 4: AVAM, 800 Key Hwy., 443/872-4926, www.sideshowbaltimore.com; Tues.-Sun. 10am-6pm

PET SUPPLIES AND GROOMING
Doggie Style

This big, open pet store—with somewhat classy-looking turquoise walls and wood floors, no less—carries everything you could possibly need for your beloved dog or cat. The bakery treats that look like tiny frosted cookies are popular, as are the several displays of dog and cat toys, which are either soft or rubber (and sometimes interactive). There's also a good selection of vibrant collars and leashes, several displays of cute clothing, and shelves of pet food and grooming products; grooming services are offered too. With Federal Hill and Riverside Park close by, this is also a good area for taking your pet on a scenic walk.

MAP 4: 1130 Light St., 410/347-7575; Mon.-Wed. 9am-8pm, Thurs.-Sat. 9am-9pm, Sun. 11am-7pm

SHOPPING CENTERS AND DISTRICTS
Federal Hill

Along Charles Street and Light Street, small clothing boutiques and housewares stores have found a happy home in this historic neighborhood, making it not only a popular social destination but also a cool place to shop. There are a couple of places to pick up some hot new styles, from jeans to dresses and shoes, plus some fun gifts for friends. For those looking for something old, there's the huge Antique Center at Federal Hill a few blocks east on Key Highway.

Looking for handmade gifts that support Baltimore's local artists? Several of the boutiques carry at least a couple of locally made items, but your best bet for finding handcrafted products is an art market. There are several good ones, especially around the holiday season.

A small group of artists and crafters known as the **Charm City Craft Mafia** (www.charmcitycraftmafia.com) host two juried craft shows a year at **St. John's Church** (2640 St. Paul St.), a beautiful stone building with high ceilings and arched columns that's a few blocks south of Johns Hopkins University in Homewood. First, there's **Pile on Craft,** the spring show in late June, then **Holiday Heap** in December. Both shows host more than 50 crafters who sell prints, jewelry, pillowcases, clothes, notebooks, decorative items, and more. It's a festive atmosphere in which to shop for gifts or something special for yourself.

The American Visionary Art Museum's (AVAM) **BAZAART** (410/244-1900, www.avam.org) is in late November on the third floor of the Jim Rouse Visionary Center (that's the building with the large sculpture of the late actress Divine downstairs). This event also draws more than 50 crafters selling mixed media works, metalwork, jewelry, textiles, and, in true AVAM fashion, "other works that defy categorization."

But the biggest event is the Maryland Institute College of Art's **Art Market** (410/225-2280, www.mica.edu) in December. This is when 250 vendors—all MICA students, faculty, staff, and alumni—converge on three floors of the open and airy Brown Center in Bolton Hill for four days of crafts-selling merriment. Here, you'll find mosaics, ceramics, paintings, stationery, prints, toys, wrapping paper... you get the idea. This being an art school, there's also lots of work—possibly from the next Jeff Koons—hanging on the walls, too.

And there are plenty of weird finds at the American Visionary Art Museum's interesting gift shop.

MAP 4: Light St. and S. Charles St. between Montgomery St. and West St.

SPA, BATH, AND BEAUTY
M Salon

This is Federal Hill's most popular salon for getting a haircut that looks as good in the boardroom as it does at a nightclub—or just a regular trim and highlights, if that's all you need. A variety of other hair and beauty services (like conditioning treatments, extensions, and eyebrow waxing) are available at this luxe-appointed power salon (gold walls, cranberry drapes). There's even an in-salon store, M Vanity, that stocks a huge variety of beauty products from all the major makers.

MAP 4: 1131 S. Charles St., 410/685-0089, www.msalonfederalhill.com; Wed.-Fri. 10am-9pm, Sat. 8:30am-6pm

★ **Studio 921 Salon & Day Spa**

This popular full-service salon and spa occupies the same former foundry building as a restaurant (The Wine Market), creating the potential for an afternoon spent in the huge, sun-lit rooms of this enormous historic brick and wood building. The hair salon area is large, with lots of chairs and stations, so there's never a long wait. There are eight spa treatment rooms, offering everything from massages to microdermabrasion, hair removal, and body scrubs; the comprehensive services list is one reason for Studio 921's popularity. The other is the staff, who have developed rabidly loyal (and satisfied) customers and clients who keep the store bouncing and busy.

MAP 4: 921 E. Fort Ave., Ste. 108, 410/783-7727, www.studio921spa.com; Tues.-Thurs. 11am-8pm, Fri. 10am-6pm, Sat. 9am-5pm, Sun. 10am-5pm

VINTAGE AND ANTIQUES
Antique Center at Federal Hill

Unlike some of the other antiques operations in town, this enormous warehouse (some 30,000 square feet) doesn't mess with old beer trays and yellowed Orioles programs. The furniture here is European, American, large, and expensive; it's also beautiful enough, and so resplendent with old-world craftsmanship, that the prices don't seem that ludicrous. In addition to the well-arranged and well-displayed items and rooms from multiple dealers here, there is a good selection of smaller items, from porcelain and silverware to clocks and watches.

MAP 4: 1220 Key Hwy., 410/625-0182; Fri.-Sat. 11am-6pm

Mount Vernon and Station North

Map 5

BOOKS
Read Street Books

Located on an appropriately named street, this independent bookstore carries a little bit of everything, as long as it's not expected. There's a big selection of used paperbacks, new books of note, and even vintage magazines and art folios. There's also a good selection of lesbian works. And like most smart bookstores in Baltimore, Read Street has branched out to offer coffee and, on Friday and Saturday, singer/songwriter performances, all inside a European-feeling and charming, historic Mount Vernon storefront.

MAP 5: 229 W. Read St., 410/669-4103, www.readstreetbooks.com; Tues.-Fri. 10am-6pm, Sat.-Sun. 10am-8pm

CLOTHING AND ACCESSORIES

A People United

Designed to both showcase and help craftspeople from developing nations, A People United features handmade and small-scale production clothing for women in a variety of ethnic styles and formality levels. In addition to clothing, there's also a selection of Tibetan and Indian furniture and rugs and statuary from several cultures. The store is a treat for senses besides the eyes and touch, too, as there's always incense burning, and exotic scents from teas and aromatic products. The store's longevity (it was opened by a Johns Hopkins public health expert and his photographer wife in 1994) shows that being able to learn about the people who made your clothes definitely helps foster sales, which directly helps the creators of the clothing, rather than a multinational corporation.

MAP 5: 516 N. Charles St., 410/727-4471, www.apeopleunited.com; Mon.-Sat. 10am-6pm, Sun. 11am-6pm

MUSIC

An die Musik

Located (fittingly) within a couple of blocks of the Peabody Institute, Baltimore's renowned music school, An die Musik is the city's finest store for classical, jazz, and world music. No rock, no rap, no country or western here—just the finest highlights in the recorded canon of classical music and the milestone moments in jazz. And it's all sold and discussed without any attitude, which makes this a great place to either start exploring these great genres or continue your journey. The second floor hosts a wide variety of jazz and classical performances all year long. The store is only open during these performances.

MAP 5: 409 N. Charles St., 410/385-2638, www.andiemusiklive.com; open during shows only

Dimensions in Music

Be it on CD, tape, or wax, Dimensions in Music has the best selection of hip-hop, R&B, rap, and house music in town, along with plenty of jazz, gospel, and oldies recordings. This three-story store keeps bargain records on the third floor, a huge selection of records on the second floor, and DJ gear on floors one and two. If you're looking to grab some homegrown Baltimore music, ask one of the staffers—or maybe one of the DJs browsing the vinyl, though they're not always up for sharing their inside info on Charm City's best beats.

MAP 5: 233 Park Ave., 410/752-7121; Mon.-Sat. 10am-6pm

VINTAGE AND ANTIQUES

Antique Row Stalls

Look for the red awning (and big sign on the building) on Howard Street; it signals the entrance to this sprawling 10,000-square-foot showcase for some 20 different antiques dealers. One plus about this collaboration is that, unlike at some antiques superstores, there's not a great deal of overlap in the offerings here; instead, most of the dealers stick to their specialties, though decorative arts and objects are in abundance. Pottery, porcelain, paintings, and books are also prevalent, but there are also textiles, furniture (from the past two centuries, including some great 1960s Mod finds), and toys.

MAP 5: 809 N. Howard St., 410/728-6363, www.antiquerowstalls.com; Wed.-Mon. 11am-5pm

Dubey's Art and Antiques

Dubey's collections focus on elegant ceramics from the world's best makers in Asia and Europe, from delicately painted vases to ornately festooned plates and other tableware (the Japanese selections are often the most visually striking). The big, sprawling store showcases its porcelain offers mixed in with its other wares in simple tableaus; there generally are also many pieces of early American furniture, chandeliers, and European paintings on display at this quiet storefront.

MAP 5: 807 N. Howard St., 410/383-2881, www.dubeysantiques.com; Wed.-Mon. 11am-5pm

The Imperial Half Bushel

One of Baltimore's lesser-known accomplishments began back in the 1800s, when the city joined the ranks of the finest silver-crafting cities in the United States (Kirk-Stieff, one of the last great Baltimore manufacturers, closed its business in 1999). The Imperial Half Bushel specializes in the great heyday of the city's silverware makers, providing an important resource for people looking to replace specific items in sets, pick up an antique platter for a gift, or even acquire an entire silver service for 12 in one fell swoop. You can learn more about the city's great craftspeople from the helpful owners and staff, and see some of the great items here (like the personalized silver business and calling card holders).

MAP 5: 831 N. Howard St., 410/462-1192, www.imperialhalfbushel.com; Wed.-Sun. 10:30am-5pm except August, which is by appt.

SHOPS
MOUNT VERNON AND STATION NORTH

ARTS AND CRAFTS
Corradetti Glassblowing Studio & Gallery
Anthony Corradetti is one of several artists who have set up shop in the sturdy, stone, late-1800s-era mill buildings of Clipper Mill. His beautiful and innovative glass sculptures and creations are renowned throughout Baltimore and the region. This large, reclaimed industrial space is both his rough and tumble studio (complete with Hades-hot furnace) and sedate and beautiful gallery. Try to time your visit with a meal at Woodberry Kitchen next door.

MAP 6: 2010 Clipper Park Rd., Ste. 119, 410/243-2010, www.corradetti.com; Tues.-Fri. 1pm-9pm, Sat.-Sun. 11am-3pm and 5pm-9pm

Lovelyarns
This Hampden store is the city's other fine knitting supply shop. A bit less polite than A Good Yarn (there's a regular Saturday "Stitch N Bitch"), this is where the more "punk rock" knitters head for their yarns, patterns, and supplies, though many perfectly upstanding knitters also do their shopping here. There's a couch in front for folks to sit and stitch, the selection of yarns and other craft essentials is wide and varied, and the owner and staff are full of great suggestions and ideas. There's also a full class schedule for beginning knitters.

MAP 6: 3610 Falls Rd., 410/662-9276, www.lovelyarns.com; Mon.-Fri. 11am-5:30pm, Sat. 11am-6pm, Sun. 11am-4pm

BOOKS
★ Atomic Books
This alternative, independent bookstore is actually two side-by-side stores, one devoted to books, the other records and overstock. The bookstore features tomes on culture, politics, humor, and music, as well as a thorough compendium of graphic novels and books, plus gag gifts, 'zines, CDs, crafts, and outsider DVDs, and there's a new bar in back that serves wine and beer. It's also where director (and frequent shopper) John Waters gets his fan mail delivered—be sure to look at the collection of charmingly unnerving holiday cards he's sent the store. They also stock an amazing selection of art toys and figures from creators like Cartoon Network and Kidrobot. In the other store there's lots of vinyl and discounted books, comics, and magazines; those inspired by the art figures can also make their own three- or seven-inch plastic toy with the very cool 3-D printer.

MAP 6: 3620 Falls Rd., 410/662-4444, www.atomicbooks.com; Sun.-Mon. 11am-7pm, Tues.-Thurs. 11am-9pm, Fri. 11am-midnight, Sat. 11am-10pm

This calming store specializing in books, music, and gifts about spiritual awareness and personal growth is a nice complement to the neighboring Seeds and its menu of massages, acupuncture, and other wellness services. There are events nearly every day, ranging from psychic readings and Ayurvedic consultations to meditation practices and book clubs. A new café—one of the only establishments in the city serving only vegetarian, vegan, and raw food made without white flour or sugar—offers sandwiches, soups, tarts, juices, teas, and desserts. You may notice a few dishes bearing people's names: Through the café's former Indiegogo campaign, some funders have a dish named after them for a month, a cool perk of supporting the healthy cause.

MAP 6: 810 W. 36th St., 410/235-7323, www.breathebooks.com; Mon.-Sat. 9am-8pm, Sun. 9am-5pm

The Kelmscott Bookshop

Baltimore's tiny fine books district—numbering fewer than a half-dozen shops—lies along a stretch of 25th Street where most residents and passersby favor loud hip-hop music instead of rare first editions. Kelmscott is the largest of the group, though all are worth a browse for the dedicated bibliophile. This isn't an old London bookshop, dark and dusty and encased in dark woods; it's bright, clean, and simple. Within this store's selection are some 30,000 rare, unique, and fascinating books (there are many first-edition H. L. Mencken tomes), and some rarer works dating back to the 1600s. Kelmscott also sells prints, manuscripts, and assorted book-reading paraphernalia (they also repair and rebind books).

MAP 6: 34 W. 25th St., 410/235-6810, www.kelmscottbookshop.com; Mon.-Fri. 10am-6pm, Sat. by appt. only

The True Vine

If you're the kind of music lover who, instead of the latest Top 40 pop CD, would rather find a treasure trove of obscure Turkish recordings from the 1930s, psychedelic Japanese pop from the 1970s, or underground new crazy blues from some Baltimore musicians, the True Vine is for you. The weirder the better is the mantra here, but the music is always good, even if the provenance is peculiar. In-store performances at this off-the-Avenue Hampden shop are frequent and often captivating.

MAP 6: 3544 Hickory Ave., 410/235-4500, www.thetruevinerecordshop.com; Sun.-Mon. noon-6pm, Tues. and Thurs.-Sat. noon-9pm, Wed. noon-8pm

clockwise from top left: Harbor East shopping district; boutique-lined Thames Street, Fell's Point; Under Armour Brand House, Harbor East

CHILDREN'S STORES

Soft and Cozy Baby

This primarily cloth diapering and baby wear store started by a wife-and-husband team also stocks some adorable clothing, toys, books, teething jewelry, diaper bags, and other baby essentials. Staff are clearly passionate about natural parenting and the products and are more than willing to spend time explaining them. Classes and moms' groups are held on the big couch in the back room (next to the small bookcase of sale items), and there's even a train table to keep little ones entertained. Note that the store is closed on Saturday.

MAP 6: 915 W. 36th St., 410/467-2229, www.softandcozybaby.com; Mon.-Thurs. 11am-7pm, Fri. 11am-4pm, Sun. 11am-6pm

CLOTHING AND ACCESSORIES

★ Doubledutch Boutique

Featuring an excellent range of women's modern design lines from well-known designers and even some indie talent, this shop stocks contemporary clothing, handbags, shoes, and accessories. Doubledutch recently moved into this lovely second-floor store (the men's clothing store Sixteen Tons is downstairs) on "The Avenue" in Hampden; it's a long, lovely space with turquoise walls that is enjoyable to wander around, checking out designs from makers like Dear Creatures, Kling, and Sugarhill Boutique, and shoes from B.A.I.T. and Mel by Melissa.

MAP 6: 1021 W. 36th St., 410/554-0055, www.doubledutchboutique.com; Mon.-Thurs. 11am-6pm, Fri.-Sat. 11am-7pm, Sun. noon-5pm

Form

The opening of Form marked a definitive step up for Hampden's retail game. In the Clipper Mill complex's Poole and Hunt Building, Form is a sleek, upscale boutique (housed in a stone building with exposed beams and well-tended display racks) that offers women's clothing, accessories, and shoes from makers like Diane von Furstenberg, Shoshanna, and Alexis Bittar; the store has its own clothing and jewelry line, too. If you're looking for a complete wardrobe retooling, Form also offers one-on-one consultations. The boutique has studio hours on Tuesday and Wednesday; if the designers are working (it's best to call ahead to find out), you're welcome to shop.

MAP 6: 2002 Clipper Park Rd., 110-C, 410/889-3116, www.formtheboutique.com; Thurs.-Fri. noon-7pm, Sat. 11am-7pm, Sun. noon-4pm

Milagro

Milagro (Spanish for "miracle") features modern, hip clothing, handbags, and accessories from Mexico and all over the world, almost always from fair-trade makers and suppliers. There are plenty

SHOPS HAMPDEN AND HOMEWOOD

of items for your home, too, from pottery to mirrors to wall hangings. Baltimore's savvy shoppers are particularly fond of the dresses and extensive jewelry selection in this warm-colored, whimsical, and friendly store where the cash register station is in a large, hand-carved wooden cantina from Mexico.

MAP 6: 1005 W. 36th St., 410/235-3800, milagrobaltimore.tumblr.com; Sun.-Wed. 11am-6pm, Thurs.-Sat. 11am-7pm

★ Sixteen Tons

This is a men's shop where deer heads are mounted on the walls and honky-tonk music fills the air, where old-fashioned shaving brushes look cool inside a glass display case and vintage and classic button-down shirts and pants from designers like Benjamin Sherman, Farah Vintage, and Fidelity hang on racks or are neatly folded on tables. There are also shoes, belts, wallets, eyewear, bags, and toiletries for men. The selection is still somewhat limited, but the store has a nice vibe and the owner has been known to make helpful suggestions. Sixteen Tons is owned by Daniel Wylie; his wife, Lesley Jennings, owns the Doubledutch Boutique upstairs.

MAP 6: 1021 W. 36th St., 410/554-0101, www.shop16tons.com; Sun.-Mon. noon-5pm, Tues.-Thurs. 11am-6pm, Fri.-Sat. 11am-7pm

FURNITURE AND HOME DECOR
★ Trohv

This sprawling retailer offers everything from tiny earrings to enormous wardrobes and beds, all in well-thought-out displays that might make you want to redo your own bedroom and living room. Two stories display new, traditional-yet-cool furniture, decorations, lamps, books, cards, jewelry, art, and even clothing and toys for babies and toddlers. The place smells like rose hips (there's a fill-your-own potpourri basket on the first floor), and the owners and staff are well known for their friendliness.

MAP 6: 921 W. 36th St., 410/366-3546, www.trohvshop.com; Mon.-Wed. 11am-7pm, Thurs.-Fri. 11am-8pm, Sat. 10am-8pm, Sun. 11am-6pm

GIFT AND SPECIALTY
In Watermelon Sugar

Like many of Hampden's successful stores, this charming, warm shop has stocked a little bit of everything—skin care and beauty products in the big bright front room, while the back room contains glassware, decorative boxes, pet snacks and trifles, pottery, candles and holders, and more. Be sure to spend some time ogling the great window displays that change throughout the year to reflect the seasons.

MAP 6: 3555 Chestnut Ave., 410/662-9090, www.watermelon-sugar.com; Mon.-Sat. 10am-6pm, Sun. noon-4pm

This is a pleasant and whimsical store with marbleized orange walls, an intricate ceiling, and a large array of colorful gifts like jewelry, frames, rugs, a large rack of cards, plates, knobs, and outdoor decorations. Many of the items are funny (like Rachel Allen's clocks) or covered in inspirational quotes, and about half of them are made by local artists. Upstairs is a brand-new art gallery; the first exhibit was a mixture of paintings, sculpture, and photography inspired by Baltimore.

MAP 6: 1121 W. 36th St., 410/467-8698, www.mudandmetal.com; Wed.-Sat. 10am-6pm, Sun.-Mon. 10am-5pm

PET SUPPLIES AND GROOMING
Howl

You won't find any Snausages here: This bare-bones pet food store stocks the most popular noncorporate and naturally made brands of dog and cat food, as well as a good array of treats, toys, dietary supplements, and other animal accessories. Folks bring their dogs in to chat with the owner and other customers, so plan on making some new canine friends if you stop by. Plus, there's a self-serve pet washing area in the back of the building (also out back: plenty of free parking).

MAP 6: 3531 Chestnut Ave., 410/235-2469, www.howlbaltimore.com; Mon.-Fri. 10am-7pm, Sat. 10am-6pm, Sun. 11am-5pm

SHOES
★ Ma Petite Shoe

It's a combination so obvious that it's surprising no one else in town came up with it. Talk about a brilliant retail concept: Sell women's shoes and gourmet chocolate. Sure, they have men's shoes, too, and accessories, but its selection of footwear for the ladies (think Nicole, Jeffrey Campbell, and Miz Mooz), including a large selection of vegan shoes, and its chocolate delights (from makers like TCHO and Vosges) make this a paradise for many Baltimore shoppers. Displayed on pedestals, mantels, racks, and stands, the offerings at this tiny two-room store (it's in a converted row house with a nice front porch) are treated like the artistic designs they are. And now it's possible to have coffee, pastries, and even lunch while you shop, since Ma Petite Shoe has opened the CHOUX café next door.

MAP 6: 830 W. 36th St., 410/235-3442, www.mapetiteshoe.com; Mon.-Thurs. and Sat. 11am-7pm, Fri. 11am-8pm, Sun. noon-5pm

SHOPPING CENTERS AND DISTRICTS
Hampden

Hampden's 36th Street—known as "The Avenue"—is one of Baltimore's best shopping areas for several reasons. There are four blocks of stores, selling everything from clothing to furniture, from high-end name brands to cut-rate quirky. No matter your style, you'll find at least three spots that match your aesthetic, and since they're all locally run and owner-operated, you can get great service and ideas. There's a real buzz on the sidewalks as people flock to Hampden for antiques, health and beauty products, clothes, and just to be part of the shopping scene.

MAP 6: 36th Ave. between Chestnut Ave. and Falls Rd.

SPA, BATH, AND BEAUTY

Kiss N Make Up

This Hampden shop offers a broad selection of top contemporary cosmetic lines (Beauty Buffet, Pop Beauty, Too Faced) to cleanse, buff, cover, and improve just about every place on your epidermis, as well as a great bunch of gag items (such as Happy Childhood Memories Breath Spray). The festively decorated and fun store—there's an oversized lip sculpture, bright fabrics and colors everywhere, and inventive little displays, though all have a down-to-earth feel—also provides a complete line of cosmetic services, from facials and manicures to waxing.

MAP 6: 827 W. 36th St., 410/467-5477; Tues.-Wed. 11am-5pm, Thurs.-Sat. 11am-6pm, Sun. noon-4pm

Seeds

A collection of six practitioners of natural medical arts have joined forces at this Hampden location to offer services like acupuncture, craniosacral therapy, several more conventional types of massage, naturopathy, and Reiki. This calm, tranquilly decorated space is housed in the building with the pink flamingo on it (the Café Hon restaurant is on the first floor). There are even organic teas in the waiting area, which adds to the relaxing ambience of the place.

MAP 6: 3600 Roland Ave., Ste. 4, 410/235-1776, www.seedswellness.com; call or visit the website for appt.

Sprout

In a bright space filled with exposed brick and wood, this all-natural hair salon really goes the extra mile to make sure everything used on your hair and head is as chemical-free as possible. The staff here is young, talented, and artsy (you'll see plenty of gorgeous tattoos), but they can cut, dye, highlight, extend, and spruce up any kind of hair, whether you're going on a power job interview or a monthlong stint at a New Mexico painter's colony.

MAP 6: 925 W. 36th St., 410/235-2269, www.sproutsalon.com; Tues.-Fri. 10am-7pm, Sat. 10am-5pm

VINTAGE AND ANTIQUES

217

Avenue Antiques

A vast, three-story collection of wares offered by more than 60 antiques dealers, this sprawling shop offers everything from Victorian jewelry and glassware to pop art collectibles and Americana to pianos and jukeboxes. There are some good items from Baltimore's past here (old Preakness memorabilia, for example), as well as furniture, signage, and clothes. The basement is home to Decades, a mid-century modern wonderland of groovy furniture, "art," and clothing.

MAP 6: 901 W. 36th St., 410/467-0329, www.avenueantiques.com; Mon.-Sat. 10am-7pm, Sun. 10am-5pm

Charlotte Elliott and The Bookstore Next Door

It's hard to classify exactly what type of store Charlotte Elliott is because there's a little bit of everything here, from vintage clothes and furniture to jewelry and African art. There are antiques too, like Herend porcelain from Hungary, silver, and even sewing machines (though the selection is always changing). And, as the name says, there is a bookstore next door filled with used books and first editions about history, art, and photography, as well as fiction. The shop itself is a delight to walk through, mostly because you never know what kind of amazing pieces you'll find.

MAP 6: 837 W. 36th St., 410/243-0990, www.charlotteelliott.com; Wed.-Fri. 11am-5pm, Sat. 11am-6pm, Sun. noon-4pm

Greater Baltimore

Map 7

ARTS AND CRAFTS

Baltimore Clayworks

A working studio and gallery and school, Baltimore Clayworks has 12 resident artists who take humble clay and transform it into everything from working home furnishings to fantastic, creative visions. Located in the New England-like village center of Mount Washington, this store/gallery/education center has a great home in an old library surrounded by tall pines, right by the waters of the Jones Falls. Demonstrations, classes, and lectures are held throughout the year and draw healthy crowds. There's even a tiny outdoor community space that has a great mosaic and clay fountain.

MAP 7: 5707 Smith Ave., Baltimore, 410/578-1919, www.baltimoreclayworks.org; Mon.-Fri. 10am-5pm, Sat.-Sun. noon-5pm

BOOKS

The Ivy Bookshop

Baltimoreans who want to attend a reading or literary event on any given evening know that The Ivy Bookshop with its packed schedule of around 100 events a year will likely have something great going on. Located in Lake Falls Village next to Samuel Parker Clothier, this cute and independently owned shop—bought a few years ago by New Yorkers Ed and Ann Berlin—stocks about 30,000 titles, mainly biographies, children's books, and volumes about cooking and interior design, as well as fiction and nonfiction. In the future, the Berlins will also sell e-books and offer a great list of benefits for book clubs.

MAP 7: 6080 Falls Rd., Baltimore, 410/377-2966, www.theivybookshop.com; Mon.-Fri. 10am-7pm, Sat. 10am-6pm, Sun. 11am-5pm

Normal's Books and Records

About seven blocks east of Johns Hopkins University, Normal's has survived every literary and musical trend of the past two decades and continues to persevere in a world it feels has gone utterly corporate and foul. The collectively run shop has stacks of used books, from classics to obscure oddities. There's also music galore (spanning the range of must-have hits to never-heard-of-'em obscure tunes), and the Red Room, a performance space for generally nonstandard music.

MAP 7: 425 E. 31st St., Baltimore, 410/243-6888, www.normals.com; daily 11am-6pm

CLOTHING AND ACCESSORIES

Samuel Parker Clothier

Travel up Falls Road, past Mount Washington's tree-canopied stores, and you'll find this Baltimore institution for traditional men's clothing in a tasteful little shopping center. This is the kind of quiet, sturdy store that's a bit like a private club; once you're done relaxing and browsing, you'll actually want one of the knowledgeable salespeople to help you figure out your sartorial style and be walked through a variety of suits, materials, and cuts to find the piece of haberdashery that is "you." You won't find any Prada or Hugo Boss here; brands tend toward the conservative qualities of Polo Ralph Lauren and Samuelsohn of Canada.

MAP 7: Lake Falls Village, 6080 Falls Rd., Baltimore, 410/372-0078, www.samuelparker.com; Mon.-Fri. 10am-6pm, Sat. 10am-5pm

FURNITURE AND HOME DECOR

Housewerks

This delightful store lives up to its mission by inhabiting a former natural gas pumping station (Bayard Station), a beautifully decaying old building with an enormous cupola-topped center room where many of the store's salvaged items reside. Outside are huge signs, marble pieces, and sculpture; downstairs, in the spooky catacomb-like basement, there are neon signs, store relics, decorative sconces and lights, and all sorts of peculiar wonders. Many items are huge and carry similar price tags, but there are also amazing finds for around $20. If it's a neat or cool or interesting piece of a house or building, it's probably in this store.

MAP 7: 1415 Bayard St., Baltimore, 410/685-8047, www.housewerksalvage.com; Fri.-Sat. 10am-6pm, Sun. noon-4pm, other days by appt.

Nouveau
This is a big, modern furniture store, but one geared toward pieces that are practical, inspired, and actually usable. Various room configurations—living rooms, dining rooms, bedrooms—are set up throughout the large showrooms of the store. You won't find much in the way of abstract chairs or for-display-purposes-only tables here; everything is built for regular everyday use and enjoyment, from overstuffed couches to icy, sleek dining room sets. Nouveau's furniture, artworks, and other home goods adorn many a Baltimore house.

MAP 7: Belvedere Square, 514 E. Belvedere Ave., Baltimore, 410/962-8248, www.nouveaubaltimore.com; Mon.-Fri. 11am-7pm, Sat. 11am-6pm

SHOES
Matava Too
Another homegrown mini-chain, this two-store-strong collection of women's shoe stores covers Baltimore County's horse country and their sole (pun intended) Baltimore City location, in the popular and bustling Belvedere Square. Featuring brands of shoes, sandals, clogs, heels, and boots as diverse as Jessica Bennett, Dansko, Butter, and Frye, this busy footwear shop manages to still provide great customer service when things get hectic.

MAP 7: Belvedere Square, 521 E. Belvedere Ave., Baltimore, 410/235-1830, www.matavashoes.com; Mon.-Sat. 10am-6pm, Sun. noon-5pm

SHOPPING CENTERS AND DISTRICTS
Arundel Mills Mall
About 20 minutes south of downtown on Route 295 (the Baltimore-Washington Parkway), this huge shopping center draws people from across the state. One of the national chain of Simon Malls, it's home to more than 200 stores, including Saks Fifth Avenue, H&M, rue21, and a Banana Republic outlet, plus everything from jewelry kiosks to the massive Bass Pro Shops Outdoor World facility, where you can climb a rock wall, practice some archery, or gawk at the 23,000-gallon aquarium. There's also a Best Buy, a Bed

Bath & Beyond, an Old Navy, and a Medieval Times. Still not sold? Visit the Cinemark Egyptian 24 movie theater, one of the busiest cinema palaces in the nation.

MAP 7: 7000 Arundel Mills Cir., Hanover, 410/540-5100, www.simon.com; Mon.-Sat. 10am-9:30pm, Sun. 11am-7pm

Belvedere Square

Far from the waterfront (and far from the peculiar charms of Hampden) is Belvedere Square, a shopping center that's become a social anchor for the far northern part of Baltimore City (where there are far more single-family homes, lawns, and wide avenues). There's a collection of outdoor shops, boutiques, home decor stores, the popular Market at Belvedere Square, and regular music events on spring and summer Friday nights. There's a real family-friendly feel to the whole place and the crowd is also diverse and reflects the neighborhood. The Market is home to great produce-sellers, soup-makers, delis, and other food and gourmet purveyors. The historic Senator Theatre, which now has four screens and a new restaurant after a 2013 renovation, is across the street, making this a great destination if you're looking to get out of the city without actually leaving the city.

MAP 7: 518 E. Belvedere Ave., Baltimore, 410/464-9773, www.belvederesquare.com; shops: Mon.-Sat. 10am-6pm, Sun. noon-5pm; market: Mon.-Sat. 10am-8pm, Sun. 10am-5pm

Towson Town Center

Once a small, intimate mall serving the quiet town of Towson (about a 15-minute drive north of downtown), this massive shopping complex is now one of the busiest malls in the region, and parking can be a bit of a pain—despite the addition of several attached garages. There are about 200 stores here, including anchors like Macy's and Nordstrom, plus an Apple store and several upscale cosmetics shops like Aveda, bareMinerals, Lush, MAC, and Sephora. The mall also has four new stores: Marbles: The Brain Store, Sur La Table, Lilly Pulitzer, and L'Occitane.

MAP 7: 825 Dulaney Valley Rd., Towson, 410/494-8800, www.towsontowncenter.com; Mon.-Sat. 10am-9pm, Sun. noon-6pm

Village of Cross Keys

This interesting little upscale mall is just one part of the Village of Cross Keys, a planned mini-community north of Hampden. Tucked into the ground level of a sprawling building, there are about 30 shops and boutiques here, almost all upscale, ranging from shoes to ladies apparel (both classic and trendy) to jewelry to cookware. There are also a couple of cafés and restaurants for hungry shoppers, and the tree-lined grounds are a pleasure to stroll through.

VINTAGE AND ANTIQUES

Second Chance

This 200,000-square-foot warehouse lies south of M&T Bank
Stadium in the southern part of the city. Inside, you'll find antique toilets, claw-foot bathtubs, and glass doorknobs, as well as a
huge selection of antiques and plenty of smaller items that make
great keepsakes, like brass items and art deco curiosities and detail pieces. It's a fun place to hunt for items—Second Chance has
salvaged pieces from the Philadelphia Civic Center's facade and
procured some leftover sets and props from *The Wire* in the past—
but you can tell the helpful staff what you're looking for and they'll
point you in the right direction. It's also nice that by shopping here,
you're contributing to Second Chance's social mission: With the
revenue from the store, the nonprofit provides job training to high-
need Baltimore residents.

MAP 7: 1700 Ridgely St., Baltimore, 410/385-1700, www.secondchanceinc.org;
daily 9am-5pm

SHOPS
GREATER BALTIMORE

Hotels

Downtown and Inner Harbor.....226

Harbor East and Little Italy 230

Fell's Point........................233

Canton 235

Federal Hill 235

Mount Vernon and Station North..236

Hampden and Homewood.......237

Greater Baltimore................239

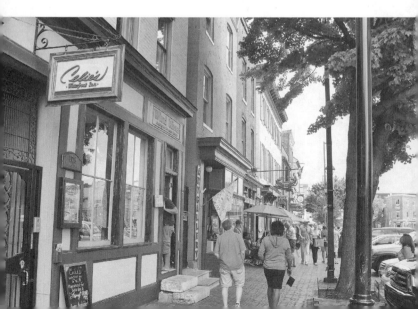

F rom the massive, looming big-name hotels that line the waters of the Inner Harbor to the cozy owner-operated inns and bed-and-breakfasts scattered throughout Baltimore's classic neighborhoods, there are enough lodging options here to satisfy any traveler. The most commanding views of the city can be found on the top floors of the downtown mega-hotels, and these venues also offer some of the best locations from which to set out and explore the city. Just a few blocks away from the harbor, though, it's possible to tuck into a historic B&B in a neighborhood like Fell's Point or Federal Hill, and spend your mornings wandering narrow streets and waterfronts.

About five years ago, Baltimore added more than 1,000 new downtown hotel rooms to help lure more national conventions to town, and most of the rooms were supplied by the huge new Hilton located just north of Oriole Park at Camden Yards. Baltimore's big hotels are designed to provide lots of rooms, rather than make an artistic statement. Still, the swanky Four Seasons Hotel Baltimore recently opened in the growing-by-the-minute shopping and dining district of Harbor East; there's also the Kimpton hotel chain's modernist Hotel Monaco Baltimore downtown and the Pier 5 Hotel, a locally grown boutique lodging choice. Looking for opulence in the Inner Harbor? Though the Royal Sonesta Harbor Court Baltimore isn't much to look at from the outside, the interior appointments are some of the best in town. Guests who prefer intimate lodging may consider Rachael's Dowry Bed and Breakfast, a home that George Washington once visited seeking assistance after he fell off

HIGHLIGHTS

★ **Best Place to Meet Other Travelers over Pancakes: HI-Baltimore Hostel,** the city's only hostel, lays out the fixings for make-your-own pancake breakfasts in its nice common areas, a good way to get the conversation rolling among guests (page 227).

★ **Best Hotel for Baseball Fans:** One-third of the rooms at the **Hilton Baltimore** have views of Oriole Park at Camden Yards, a few suites overlook center field, and the stadium is just steps away (page 228).

★ **Best Historical-Meets-Hip Hotel:** In the entrance to the **Hotel Monaco Baltimore** there is a grand marble staircase from the building's days as the B&O Railroad headquarters, but upstairs is all modern, from the funky and colorful lobby to the quirky amenities (like a companion goldfish) the hotel offers (page 228).

★ **Best Bed-and-Breakfast with Ties to George Washington:** Roam the house that George Washington once visited by staying at the historic **Rachael's Dowry Bed and Breakfast** (page 229).

★ **Best Fitness Center and Lounge with a View:** Play tennis on the roof of the **Royal Sonesta Harbor Court Baltimore,** then have a drink in the Explorer's Lounge, all while enjoying prime, hard-to-beat views of the Inner Harbor (page 230).

★ **Best Place to See Stars:** The New York Yankees and the Boston Red Sox have stayed at the **Four Seasons Hotel Baltimore,** and the Netflix series *House of Cards* films some scenes here, making this the best spot for celebrity sightings (page 232).

★ **Best Fell's Point Hotel:** If you want to stay in this charming waterfront neighborhood, head for **The Inn at Henderson's Wharf,** a small independent hotel in a huge old warehouse (page 234).

★ **Best Contemporary Boutique Hotel:** Just a block off of Canton's busy O'Donnell Square is a corner row house with an intriguing olive green door. Behind it lies a modern, cozy, five-room mini-hotel: the **Inn at 2920** (page 235).

★ **Best Historic Inn:** If you're planning on spending a lot of time among the cultural wonders of Mount Vernon, plan on staying at the historic **4 East Madison Inn,** a massive 1845 townhome full of mahogany, stained glass, and period furniture (page 236).

his horse; it's also in a great location near Oriole Park at Camden Yards and a short walk from the Inner Harbor and Federal Hill.

Away from the busy Inner Harbor, Baltimore offers several interesting and unique hotels and a handful of B&Bs scattered in some of the city's prettiest neighborhoods. Fell's Point has the widest variety of small hotels, with Mount Vernon a close second. Staying in these neighborhoods has some benefits (you'll really get to experience Baltimore city life) and some downsides (you're pretty far from other attractions, though not prohibitively so). One other bright spot—for young backpackers and bargain hunters—is the HI-Baltimore hostel housed in a 19th-century brownstone with full modern sleeping and bathing quarters. The bad news is that, in many of the other neighborhoods covered in this guide, there are at most one or two lodging options: It's not that there are others that aren't recommended, it's that they don't exist.

Travelers do have options in Baltimore, from brand-new, modern lodgings in the heart of downtown to charming little inns and B&Bs tucked into the city's most fashionable and beloved neighborhoods. Take some time to figure out what you want to do in Baltimore, and let that plan help you pick the best place to stay.

CHOOSING A HOTEL

The first rule of real estate applies to Baltimore's selection of hotels, inns, and few bed-and-breakfasts: it's all about location, location, location. That means waterfront, preferably, and downtown. The views and convenience of staying at one of the big chain hotels facing the Inner Harbor can't be beat, though you'll pay for both. If you're looking for a centrally located hotel, you'll probably want to stay around the Inner Harbor and downtown, as it makes it much, much easier to travel to other parts of the city. Just be ready to fork over a hefty fee; most of these hotels are geared toward convention and business travelers with expense accounts and big budgets. Also note that parking can add considerably to your costs (free parking at downtown hotels is nonexistent, unless there's a special), and that some hotels charge you whenever you enter and exit the lot, so carefully research each hotel's policy. Some of the smaller hotels don't have parking, so you may be on your own in looking for a lot or space.

Fell's Point is a solid choice for those looking to experience a bit of real Baltimore. There are two small, independent hotels here, as well as a couple of bed-and-breakfasts. Staying here gives you the chance to leave your lodging and walk along the working waterfront, watching pleasure boats, tugs, and the Water Taxis scoot across the water—it's an opportunity you shouldn't pass up.

Mount Vernon is another old city neighborhood with a large chain hotel and a few independent options too; it's a great place

HOTELS

to walk around during the day, it's loaded with cultural attractions, and Charles Street has lots of restaurants and bars for evening activities.

Finding a bargain hotel in Baltimore can be a little tricky; do your due diligence on discount websites like www.priceline.com, which can cut the list price of some rooms by more than 50 percent (which makes a merely acceptable $250 room a *fantastic* $109 room). Also check the city's official tourism website, www.baltimore.org, for regular specials and bargain packages. That site—run by Visit Baltimore—also has a very user-friendly search function for hotels all across the city, and even points beyond, including BWI Airport. Weekend rates are always higher, so consider a midweek stay if you're trying to save some cash. There are a few great inns out in northern Baltimore County's horse country, about 20 minutes from downtown Baltimore.

The rates you'll find listed here are summer season rates, the highest charged by each hotel. These top rates may also apply during holidays and major weekend-long events (like May's Preakness Stakes horse race and weeklong celebration).

Downtown and Inner Harbor

Map 1

The best part about staying downtown, or (better yet) in the Inner Harbor, is the central location—allowing easy exploration of the rest of the city with, at most, a 10-minute car ride. Yet there's so much to do in this part of town that guests might not even need to leave. It's the easiest place to find a cab, and Harborplace has a wide selection of restaurants and bars for nighttime diversions.

Brookshire Suites ⑤⑤

Just a block from the Inner Harbor, this semi-boutique, 11-story, 97-room hotel has one of the most recognizable exteriors in the city, a geometric pattern of horizontal white and black plates. The common spaces have some interesting modern touches, and the rooms will, too, after a planned renovation replaces the traditional decor with black and white furniture and furnishings and abstract art. Prices here tend to be fairly low, so it's a good option for the bargain hunter who wants to stay downtown.

MAP 1: 120 E. Lombard St., 410/625-1300, www.brookshiresuites.com

Days Inn Inner Harbor ⑤⑤

A bargain-priced hotel with a very good location, this Days Inn is especially convenient for people coming to town for a convention (the Baltimore Convention Center is right across the street), or an Orioles game at Camden Yards. This is a basic hotel, with 250 perfectly fine rooms and a small heated outdoor pool that's not particularly picturesque.

MAP 1: 100 Hopkins Pl., 410/576-1000, www.daysinnerharbor.com

Embassy Suites Baltimore ●●●

Formerly the Tremont Suites Hotel, the 300-room, all-suite Embassy Suites (with recently refurbished bathrooms) offers the usual amenities, such as coffeemakers, refrigerators, microwaves, and free wireless Internet access, as well as a nice daily evening reception with free snacks and drinks. This is the city's tallest hotel at 37 stories, and, because it's a bit of a walk to the Inner Harbor, prices are generally lower. There's also a new, Chesapeake Bay-inspired restaurant, B'more Bistro and Lounge, which serves crab cakes, rockfish, and other seafood specialties.

MAP 1: 222 St. Paul Pl., 410/727-2222, www.embassysuitesbaltimore.com

Hampton Inn and Suites Inner Harbor ●●●

Retrofitted into the former USF&G insurance company building, this hotel scores points for location and amenities. The regal lobby, done in plums, metallics, and dark wood, has several dedicated spaces with couches, tables, and individual TVs, and free coffee and tea all day long. There are 116 rooms here (the suites include a wet bar and sofa bed), most of which look out over the heart of Baltimore's downtown district, a place that is pretty deserted after dark. But the Inner Harbor is just three blocks south, and there are plenty of attractions and destinations within walking distance. Note that there is a basic Hampton Inn just across from Oriole Park at Camden Yards; cab drivers sometimes confuse the two.

MAP 1: 131 E. Redwood St., 410/539-7888 or 800/426-7866, www.hamptoninn3.hilton.com

★ HI-Baltimore Hostel ●

This 1857 brownstone has gained positive reviews from all sorts of travelers—mostly those looking for a cheap, clean place to spend a night or two. Just across the street from the Basilica of the Assumption, this modern Hostelling International-affiliated lodging has 44 beds in various-sized rooms, a lot of great perks (free wireless Internet, free make-your-own pancakes, a place to make tea and coffee), and a solid location that makes accessing both the Inner Harbor and Mount Vernon a breeze for motivated walkers.

MAP 1: 17 W. Mulberry St., 410/576-8880, www.hiusa.org/baltimore

★ Hilton Baltimore $$$

With its connecting walkway to the Baltimore Convention Center
and 757 rooms—more than any other downtown hotel—this hotel
is an ideal pick for business travelers (though plenty of families
stay here too). Baseball fans will also appreciate that one-third
of the rooms have views of nearby Oriole Park, with 10 hospitality suites actually overlooking center field. Although the boxy
metallic building has drawn flak for being too boring and big,
a 2013 renovation should reveal a main lobby swathed in softer,
more homey colors and complete with conveniences like ample
outlets, a wireless printer, and a new coffee and sandwich shop.
When you exit the south lobby and turn right, you're greeted
with a wonderful view of Oriole Park, which is literally a couple
dozen steps away.

MAP 1: 401 W. Pratt St., 443/573-8700, www.hilton.com

★ Hotel Monaco Baltimore $$

This majestic old 13-story beaux arts building, built in 1906 as the
headquarters for the B&O Railroad company, lies at the "center"
of the city on the corner of Charles and Baltimore Streets. While
there are numerous grand, century-old architectural touches, this
202-room Kimpton hotel is completely modern. On the ground
floor, walk up the marble staircase, just in front of the massive
chandelier, to the refreshing lobby with its abstract art and eclectic and colorful furniture. There are many exciting and unusual
amenities here, including free bikes for riding, a yoga mat in every
room, a hosted wine hour, and a companion goldfish upon request;
there are also seven bunk bed suites with two TVs and an Xbox.
B&O American Brasserie, the hotel's restaurant, serves modern
American cuisine that is consistently considered among the best
food in the city.

MAP 1: 2 N. Charles St., 888/752-2636, www.monaco-baltimore.com

Hyatt Regency Baltimore $$$

This is another of the Inner Harbor's original wave of major hotels
that went up in the 1980s—not that the mirrored exterior and dated
architecture of the building gives it away. Get past that, and inside
you'll find one of the city's top upscale chain hotels. Unlike the
exterior, the interior is up-to-date and modern, from the lobby to
the newly upgraded Bistro 300 restaurant, which has a large indoor
water feature complete with floating flowers and leaves. There are
488 guest rooms, all appointed with upscale contemporary furniture. Location is the big sell here; the entire Inner Harbor is steps
from the door, and Federal Hill is a short walk to the south.

MAP 1: 300 Light St., 410/528-1234, www.baltimore.hyatt.com

A recent survey showed that free wireless Internet, breakfast, and parking are the amenities guests most want from their hotels. While free parking is still pretty hard to come by in Baltimore, plenty of hotels and inns offer some truly outstanding (and sometimes unique) amenities that go beyond the other options.

The fabulous **Hotel Monaco** downtown is loaded with one-of-a-kind perks, the best of which is the companion goldfish, available upon request for those who would like some company. There's also a hosted wine happy hour every day, bikes that guests can "rent" for free, a yoga mat in every room, and the new bunk bed rooms come equipped with an Xbox for the gamers in your group. In the Inner Harbor, guests who want to be close to shopping (or are traveling with teenagers) might consider the **Renaissance Baltimore Harborplace Hotel,** which is connected to The Gallery, the only mall in the city.

On the other side of Harbor East is the **Four Seasons Baltimore** and its outdoor infinity pool, probably the best pool in the city because of its breathtaking harbor vistas. There's also a whirlpool that's heated and a shallow "reflecting" pool with the same amazing views. Farther east, in Fell's Point, **The Inn at Henderson's Wharf** has a verdant interior courtyard that may be the best breakfast room in town.

As for more budget-friendly options, the **Courtyard by Marriott** in Harbor East has a cozy movie room and three "media pods" with personal TVs in the lobby, the historic **Hotel Brexton** in Mount Vernon has six first-come, first-served free parking spots, and the **HI-Baltimore hostel** has free make-your-own pancakes with toppings.

★ Rachael's Dowry Bed and Breakfast $$$

In the midst of downtown's multistory, big-name hotels is this small bed-and-breakfast with a big history: The basement of this house, built in 1798, may have safely harbored slaves who were fleeing the South, and George Washington once came here looking for help after he fell off of his horse. Now run by a brother-and-sister team, the four suites and two rooms, many of which have arched doorways, marble mantelpieces, and antique furniture, combine federal and Victorian styles; some also have fireplaces and iPhone/iPod docking stations.

MAP 1: 637 Washington Blvd., 410/752-0805,
www.rachaelsdowrybedandbreakfast.com

Renaissance Baltimore Harborplace Hotel $$$

This 622-room building, clad in green glass and a few dozen steps from all of the attractions of the Inner Harbor, is a favorite for many regular Baltimore visitors. Let's start with location: A quick jaunt across Pratt Street puts guests next to Harborplace and within walking distance of the Inner Harbor's cultural attractions like the National Aquarium in Baltimore; an even shorter walk to the adjoining Gallery mall next door should delight even discerning teenagers. Next are the views: On the upper floors, the panoramic views of the Inner Harbor are unbeatable. Guest rooms are modern in decor, the comforters are down, and the fully loaded gym has huge windows overlooking Pratt Street and the waterfront—as does Watertable, the property's upscale restaurant.

MAP 1: 202 E. Pratt St., 410/547-1200 or 800/535-1201, www.marriott.com

★ Royal Sonesta Harbor Court Baltimore $$$

Although the exterior is made of unassuming (and uninspired) brick, this hotel's main lobby is all opulence, from its grand staircase to the rich gold and burgundy library that also serves as the concierge room. But, after a 2014 renovation, the 195 rooms, which are really big, will be more modern with black and white decor and clean lines. There are 22 suites as well, offering various degrees of luxury (and cost). Rooms overlook either the Inner Harbor or the hotel's courtyard, which is also an apiary for 30,000 bees whose honey is used in some of the hotel's dishes and drinks. The rooftop health club has an outdoor tennis court with great views, as well as indoor racquetball courts and fitness classes. And the Explorer's Lounge is one of the city's best places for enjoying an opulent cocktail while looking at a grand view of the Inner Harbor.

MAP 1: 550 Light St., 410/234-0550 or 888/424-6835,
www.sonesta.com/baltimore

Springhill Suites by Marriott $$

This is another relative bargain that, even though it's just a short walk from the Inner Harbor, demonstrates how prices drop off as you move away from the waterfront. In this all-suite hotel, the 99 rooms use some tricks (like wall-mounted flat-screen TVs) to maximize space, and have microwaves and refrigerators. Since it is housed in a former bank building, one of the conference rooms here is called "The Vault"; entry is gained between two enormous half-round vault doors.

MAP 1: 120 W. Redwood St., 410/685-1095, www.marriott.com

Harbor East and Little Italy

Map 2

Due to its location right between the Inner Harbor and Fell's Point, Harbor East is an ideal place to lodge for those who want to walk to the attractions, restaurants, shopping, and nightlife in both neighborhoods. New shops and restaurants are sprouting up in Harbor East all the time, too—not to mention the traditional Italian

restaurants in Little Italy—so it's easy to end your evening here,
conveniently next to your hotel.

Baltimore Marriott Waterfront ⑤⑤
This 32-story hotel towers over Harbor East, a burgeoning area of restaurants, shops, and hotels tucked between the Inner Harbor and Fell's Point. There are a whopping 750 rooms (and 21 suites) here, making it the second-largest hotel in town. If you're planning on doing a few things at the Inner Harbor and a few in Fell's Point, this might be a good choice, as it's equidistant from both. There are amazing views of the city from the upper floors and Keurig coffeemakers in every room.
MAP 2: 700 Aliceanna St., 410/385-3000, www.marriott.com

Courtyard by Marriott ⑤⑤
Thanks to a recent renovation, this hotel—a little sibling of sorts to the looming Baltimore Marriott Waterfront that's just two blocks to the west—is now decked out with modern technology. Families and business travelers alike should enjoy the updates: a new ground-level bistro with three media pods equipped with laptop hookups and personal TVs, a movie room on the first floor, and a big, interactive computer screen in the lobby where you can get directions to local restaurants and attractions (and even send them to your phone). The traditional accommodations (205 rooms, 10 suites) have fresh carpeting and wallpaper, and the hotel's neutral decor has been brightened with splashes of blue and orange. The location is also great for walks to Little Italy and Fell's Point, as well as the Inner Harbor.
MAP 2: 1000 Aliceanna St., 443/923-4000, www.marriott.com

1840s Carrollton Inn ⑤⑤⑤
You wouldn't expect to find these historic homes in the shadows of an office tower and contemporary town houses—but this part of Baltimore, known as Jonestown, was one of the original settlements incorporated into what became Baltimore Town. This collection of row houses has been turned into an inn; there are 13 rooms ranging from the opulent (like the $350-per-night Annapolis Suite) to the merely very nice (generally ranging $155-250). All are furnished with period antiques or reproductions, and many have fireplaces and whirlpool tubs. There's a large, tree-covered brick patio that backs to President Street, historic Carroll Mansion is next door, and most of the city's popular tourist attractions are within a 10-minute walk.
MAP 2: 50 Albemarle St., 410/385-1840, www.1840scarrolltoninn.com

Best Water Views

If you're willing to pay for it, there are some truly spectacular views of Baltimore's Inner Harbor available at many of the big downtown hotels. Starting on the west side of the water, the luxurious **Royal Sonesta Harbor Court Baltimore** has one of the most commanding views of the entire waterfront, and lots of rooms facing Harborplace. To the north, the **Hyatt Regency Baltimore** also boasts lots of water views, and it's much taller than the Royal Sonesta, so you can get some great bird's-eye panoramas. Moving east down Pratt Street, the **Renaissance Baltimore Harborplace Hotel** (it's a Marriott) is also tall enough (12 stories) to offer some outstanding scenery; just make sure you're high enough to not end up staring at the pavilions of Harborplace. And on the other side of the harbor, in Harbor East, most rooms at the new **Four Seasons Baltimore** overlook the water and the city skyline, including Pier Six Pavilion and the National Aquarium. There's also another Marriot here, **Baltimore Marriott Waterfront,** which, at 31 stories, offers some of the best vantages in the city; if you're in Baltimore during one of the several weekends when there's a fireworks show at the Inner Harbor, this is one of the most Olympian heights from which to behold the colorful spectacle.

Fairfield Inn & Suites $$

This 156-room hotel was the first in the city to obtain LEED-Gold certification, the highest level of ecofriendliness. The designers helped achieve this by integrating the construction into the historic row houses and buildings that surround it in the historic Jonestown neighborhood, just a block from Little Italy. Built on the site of the Baltimore Brewing Company and Brewer's Park, the hotel uses some of the materials from that famed business (like bricks, metals, the massive brewing silo, and even the signage); inside, the interior showcases basic building materials like wood and brick; amenities include a tavern/restaurant and 26 suites.

MAP 2: 101 President St., 410/837-9900, www.marriott.com

★ Four Seasons Hotel Baltimore $$$

Opened in 2011, this 256-room, 45-suite hotel has brought luxury to the burgeoning Harbor East neighborhood. The decor is modern but minimal with a few artistic touches, from the three chandeliers made of handblown Italian Murano glass in the entranceway to the abstract art on every floor. Rooms have floor-to-ceiling windows and TVs in the bathrooms; most also have amazing water views and some have marble soaking tubs. There are many excellent amenities here, including an infinity pool overlooking the harbor and a relaxation room in the spa that is open to guests. The New York Yankees and the Boston Red Sox stay here when they're in town, and the Netflix's series *House of Cards* has been filmed in two of the hotel's restaurants.

MAP 2: 200 International Dr., 410/576-5800, www.fourseasons.com/Baltimore

Homewood Suites by Hilton Baltimore ⑤⑤

Hilton's brand of all-suite hotels has a Baltimore outpost in the Harbor East neighborhood between the Inner Harbor and Fell's Point. The suites aren't always huge, but they often have separate bedrooms with doors, and all have basically complete kitchens and a generally high level of other amenities. There's plenty to do right outside the door in the surrounding area, and guests can use the huge, glitzy Maryland Athletic Club (MAC) gym located in the same building.

MAP 2: 625 S. President St., 410/234-0999, http://homewoodsuites1.hilton.com

Pier 5 Hotel ⑤⑤

Keep your eyes peeled for the turn into the Pier 5 driveway from Pratt Street—there's a large sign, but the feeling that you'll be driving on a sidewalk can be tough to override. Part of this independent, modern boutique hotel's charm is that it's off the main thoroughfares and tucked down on the water, surrounded by waterfront walkways. The 66 guest rooms are heavy on purples and golds; the modern, swooping furniture takes some chances without being too risky. There's a Ruth's Chris Steak House on the premises, but you can also walk to dozens of other restaurants at the harbor and Harbor East and Little Italy in about five minutes.

MAP 2: 711 Eastern Ave., 410/539-2000 or 800/584-7065, www.harbormagic.com

Fell's Point Map 2

The cultural opposite of downtown, this delightful, real-life, working waterfront neighborhood is perfect for visitors who want to get some real Baltimore experiences—the sights of boat traffic in the harbor, the sounds of the water lapping against piers and wharves, and the feel of paving stones under your feet.

The Admiral Fell Inn ⑤⑤

The oldest of the seven buildings that now constitute the Admiral Fell Inn dates from the late 18th century; such history gives the place a storied feel that the modern upgrades can't obscure. And that's for the best because this wonderful collection of 80 rooms looks out over the well-worn stone streets, taverns, and piers of Fell's Point. The decor is early nautical America, with modern touches and improvements. The Water Taxi stops a few yards from the front door, and the shops, pubs, and restaurants of Fell's Point are no more than three blocks away. The only catch? The place is reputed to be haunted by the inn's previous inhabitants, a salty collection of mariners and ne'er-do-wells (there's a ghost tour).

MAP 2: 888 S. Broadway, 410/522-7380, www.harbormagic.com

Blue Door on Baltimore ⑤⑤

A good seven-block walk north of Fell's Point proper in Butcher's Hill, this three-room bed-and-breakfast is worth considering if you're looking for a real Baltimore neighborhood experience. It's a totally rehabbed brick row house (dating from the early 1900s), and the rooms are done in a modest, modern style; all have claw-foot tubs and separate showers, and two have private decks with great views of the water, which lies nine blocks south. Parking in this area can be among the toughest in town, but the owners have some smart tips.

MAP 2: 2023 E. Baltimore St., 410/732-0191, www.bluedoorbaltimore.com

Celie's Waterfront Inn ⑤⑤

In between the art galleries, bars, restaurants, coffee shops, and other businesses along Thames Street, it's possible to stroll right past the door to this charming little bed-and-breakfast. It's even somewhat hidden behind a tall tree. But inside, there's a warren of brightly painted hallways, rooms, and passageways leading to nine guest rooms. Amenities run from wood-burning fireplaces to new massage tubs and showers; the common areas of Celie's are furnished with simple, Arts and Crafts-style furniture. The rooms that face Thames Street can get a little loud late on weekend nights, so either request a room in the rear of the building, or stay out late yourself.

MAP 2: 1714 Thames St., 410/522-2323 or 800/432-0184, www.celiesinn.com

★ The Inn at Henderson's Wharf ⑤⑤⑤

This looming brick building and wharf date back to 1893, and in a way they mark the geographic eastern end of Fell's Point. Today, this huge structure is broken up into condominiums, a conference center, and the inn; there's also a large marina, which gives guests even more to look at from their gorgeous waterfront rooms, decorated with plush, heavy, colonial-style contemporary furnishings. There's a lovely interior courtyard where guests can have their complimentary breakfasts, and visitors can stroll along the wooden planks of the waterfront promenade into the heart of Fell's Point, close enough to enjoy but far enough to keep the late-night revelers out of your slumber plans. The biggest problem here? With only 38 rooms and a devoted clientele, it's sometimes hard to book a room.

MAP 2: 1000 Fell St., 410/522-7777, www.harbormagic.com

Canton

Map 3

There's very little modern about much of Canton; most of the re-cent improvements are rehabbed brick row houses and taverns, along with repurposed factories and canneries that are now wa-terfront condos. There aren't a lot of short-term accommodations here, as it's a very residential neighborhood (though it's one with a good variety of dining and nightlife options). If you want to stay relatively far from the bustle of downtown and some of the other neighborhoods, this is a good choice, though you'll be traveling 10-15 minutes for attractions.

★ Inn at 2920 $$

Venture just a block south of bustling, bar-and-restaurant-filled O'Donnell Square and you'll find a regular-looking row house with a white stone corner entrance and a suspiciously contempo-rary olive green door; this is the Inn at 2920, a hidden gem of a boutique hotel. The inn's five guest rooms feature lots of exposed brick, sleekly designed (but comfortable) furniture and bedding, and an inviting sitting and common area. There's also free park-ing, a big plus in Canton, where finding a spot can be a nightmare on Saturday nights. It's probably the coolest little hotel in the entire city, and a great place to blend into Baltimore like a local—one who lives in a fantastic, modern rehabbed row house. It's a short walk to the water, and Fell's Point is a good 15- to 20-minute walk to the west (or a very short, and flat, bike ride away).

MAP 3: 2920 Elliott St., 410/342-4450, www.theinnat2920.com

Federal Hill

Map 4

Though many people only know the Federal Hill of shops, bars, and Cross Street Market, it's a vibrant neighborhood full of historic homes, devoted residents, and small, tree-lined streets. Real estate in this part of town is so valuable that you won't find many places to stay here—in fact, there's really only one option. This is a great neighborhood to stay in because it's only a five-minute walk from the Inner Harbor; avid walkers can also make the long walk to Fort McHenry in about 20 minutes.

Scarborough Fair B&B $$$

You can sample what living in Federal Hill is like at the Scarborough Fair Bed and Breakfast, located on one of the most historic (and beautiful) streets in the area. The original part of this solid brick home dates from 1801, but later additions have expanded the living and guest spaces tremendously. There are six guest rooms, some of which have private entrances, whirlpool tubs, gas fireplaces, and other high-end touches. There's free off-street parking (which is a *huge* bonus in this area), and guests can use the nearby Federal Hill Fitness center on Cross Street. It's also close enough to the Inner Harbor (about a five-minute stroll) that it's worth considering as your Baltimore base of operations.

MAP 4: 801 S. Charles St., 410/837-0010 or 877/954-2747, www.scarboroughfairbandb.com

Mount Vernon and Station North

Map 5

There are a couple of different types of lodging available in this gorgeous neighborhood, which is the city's most architecturally notable area. There are some cultural attractions within walking distance, and the Inner Harbor is a long, downhill walk to the south.

★ 4 East Madison Inn 💲💲

This massive 19th-century home (with a great little patio) is now host to nine guest rooms of varying sizes and opulence (there's an elevator at the rear of the house). Antiques and four-poster beds fill the house, and the wonderful main parlors soothe frazzled travelers with deep-blue walls and ornate fireplaces in brightly lit bays. Taking breakfast in the tree-canopied garden on the east side of the house is a great way to plan a day's adventures, perhaps starting at the Walters Art Museum, which is about two blocks away.

MAP 5: 4 E. Madison St., 410/332-0880, www.4eastmadisoninn.com

Hotel Brexton 💲💲

Built in 1891, this hotel housed a young Wallis Simpson, future Duchess of Windsor, in the early 20th century; three decades later, King Edward VIII was so in love with her that he abdicated his throne to marry Simpson when the British government did not approve of her two divorces. The newly renovated hotel pays tribute to its famous occupant by displaying an auction book that lists her former possessions in the small lobby. There's a great spiral staircase here, the 29 rooms have clean and minimal decor, and the theater and the symphony are a mere five-minute walk away. Note that the hotel has only 10 parking spaces (six are free; four cost $25/night), so guests may have to look for a parking garage or street parking.

MAP 5: 868 Park Ave., 443/478-2100 or 877/830-6708, www.brextonhotel.com

The Mount Vernon Hotel $$

Between the Inner Harbor and Mount Vernon's cultural attractions, this hotel has one especially great thing going for it: its prices. For about $120-140, you can get a perfectly fine if underwhelming hotel room or bi-level suite in a central location a couple of miles south from the Walters Art Museum. With the price comes somewhat limited amenities, but there are free hot breakfasts and free wireless Internet, and the hotel is less than a one-mile walk downhill to the Inner Harbor.

MAP 5: 24 W. Franklin St., 410/727-2000, www.mountvernonbaltimore.com

Peabody Court by Clarion $$

Request a corner room (they're some of the largest) with a view of Mount Vernon Place, and you'll have one of the finest views in town from this European-inspired Baltimore treasure. This historic 19th-century building has been a hotel since its construction and has changed names and brands over the years. The marble bathrooms and towel heaters are pleasant surprises, and the room furniture is of an understated colonial-era design. This hotel offers 104 rooms and a restaurant (George's on Mount Vernon Square), and most of all, a great location in the heart of Mount Vernon.

MAP 5: 612 Cathedral St., 410/727-7101 or 800/504-2405, www.peabodycourthotel.com

Hampden and Homewood   Map 6

While there's plenty to do (but nowhere to stay) in Hampden, the presence of the Johns Hopkins University in Homewood—a neighborhood whose only other notable attraction is the amazing Baltimore Museum of Art—is enough to support one nice hotel. Getting to the Inner Harbor by car from this part of town will take about 10 minutes, barring heavy traffic.

Inn at the Colonnade $$$

Across the street from the north end of the Johns Hopkins University campus, this sizable uptown hotel (run by DoubleTree) is a favorite of JHU parents and VIPs for its location and its amenities, like the in-house restaurant, spa, salon, beautiful lobby, and valet parking service. There are 125 guest rooms and suites, filled with modern, stylish beds and other furniture. Parking charges can really add up here, so be aware of the complex parking and valet policies. Some rooms can be on the small side, and occasional hiccups in service occur, but overall this hotel has a solid reputation.

MAP 6: 4 W. University Pkwy., 410/235-5400 or 800/222-8733, www.colonnadebaltimore.com

Excursions

Annapolis 244   Easton and St. Michaels 263
Frederick 255

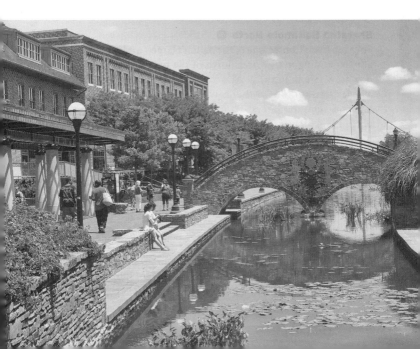

The state of Maryland encompasses some dramatically diverse terrain; to the west are mountains high enough (and snowy enough) to host ski resorts and winter sports. The central part of the state is somewhat hilly and full of suburbs, towns, and the city of Baltimore, but it's also home to farms, fields, and woods that eventually end on the waters of the spectacular Chesapeake Bay. On the other side of the bay, the eastern third of Maryland—the Eastern Shore—is an utterly different (and very flat) country, full of small towns, farms, rivers, marshes, and, eventually, the shores of the Atlantic Ocean and the beach towns that are swamped during the summer (and nearly abandoned over the winter). Though a winter ski trip is a bit much for a quick day trip out of Baltimore (it's three hours to the Wisp Resort in McHenry, Maryland, so it's not impossible), there are still plenty of different places to explore that are less than two hours from the concrete and cobblestones of Charm City.

Head west, and you'll be able to browse warehouses teeming with antiques, sample wines while listening to live music on a vineyard, and explore the single bloodiest day of America's Civil War past at Antietam battlefield—all in or near the historic town of Frederick. A short drive south leads to Maryland's stately and gorgeous waterfront capital, Annapolis, which is home to the U.S. Naval Academy, charming bed-and-breakfasts, and blocks of impressive colonial-era architecture. Past Annapolis, east across the majestic Chesapeake Bay Bridge, you can explore two distinctly different Eastern Shore towns. Shop for great gifts, dine on crab

HIGHLIGHTS

★ **Best Campus Tour:** If you think your college's alumni have racked up some impressive achievements, see how they stack up against the deeds of the men and women of the **U.S. Naval Academy.** This sprawling, monumental campus is unlike any other school (page 249).

★ **Best Civil War History Lesson:** It's a placid, quiet place today, full of dense woods, grassy rolling fields, and split-rail fencing, but **Antietam National Battlefield** was the site of the bloodiest day of battle during the U.S. Civil War; some 23,000 troops were killed or wounded (page 256).

★ **Best Wine Trail:** Take a drive through Frederick County to visit the three vineyards on the **Frederick Wine Trail.** In addition to sampling wine, you can hear live music, take guided tours, or just stroll the grounds and admire the grapes (page 258).

★ **Best Preserved Theaters:** If you're in Frederick, check the listings for the

Weinberg Center for the Arts, built in 1926. On the Eastern Shore, Easton's **Avalon Theatre** was built in 1921 and hosts bands, solo artists, and more (pages 259 and 264).

★ **Best Antiques Shopping:** Bargain and treasure hunters from Baltimore, Washington DC, and all over the region descend on the well-preserved and well-stocked old warehouses and **antique shops of Frederick** each weekend (page 260).

★ **Best Small-Town Museum:** Working boatbuilders, hands-on demonstrations, and living history can be found in the picturesque town of St. Michaels and its **Chesapeake Bay Maritime Museum** (page 269).

★ **Best Way to Experience Life as a Chesapeake Bay Waterman:** Climb aboard the H.M. *Krentz* or the *Rebecca T. Ruark,* two working Chesapeake Bay oyster boats that take passengers out on **Skipjack Tours** (page 269).

243

EXCURSIONS

cakes, and enjoy a concert at the historic Avalon Theatre in charming Easton. Just 15 minutes down the road, you can stay at a world-class resort hotel or tiny B&B, sample haute cuisine, and sail aboard one of two working skipjack sailboat fishing vessels from the waters around romantic, relaxing St. Michaels. Each destination is unique, and offers a completely different experience from the urban hum and buzz of Baltimore.

PLANNING YOUR TIME

If you're going to make any of these trips on the spur of the moment, Annapolis is probably the smartest bet—it's barely 30 minutes from Baltimore, and the road that leads there (I-97) is almost never congested on weekends. Annapolis is a great city because it's so compact; ditch the car near the visitors center, and you can be strolling the shops of Main Street in about 40 minutes after leaving Fell's Point or Federal Hill. There's plenty to do, see, and eat in Annapolis during a long afternoon, and leaving after dinner won't make you feel like you missed anything.

Traveling to Frederick is a bit more of a commitment, but it rewards those who plan their trip in advance. While there is lots of shopping and eating to be done, visiting the sights will take some forethought, especially if a side trip to Antietam National Battlefield is in order. Some of the other sights near Frederick are a car trip away, so think about what you want to do in town (or outside of it) before you get there.

Though it can be a breeze to get there, the route to Easton and St. Michaels is the most prone to traffic issues, thanks to the Chesapeake Bay Bridge and its propensity to clog up on warm-weather weekends. If you get to the bridge early enough, and there are no accidents, you can make it to Easton in 90 minutes from Baltimore, which is plenty of time to stroll the town's streets and still get in a quick visit to St. Michaels—but the charms of that small waterfront village are so great that many people wish they could spend the night there.

Annapolis

Back in 1649, a group of English Puritan colonial settlers—kicked out of Virginia for being too strident—formed a settlement where the Severn River empties into the Chesapeake Bay. They named their town Providence, and it prospered as a port for the inflow and export of goods, creating affluence and giving rise to stately homes and small estates along the hills surrounding the river—though the source of some of that wealth came from the loathsome trade in slaves. The town was later renamed to honor England's

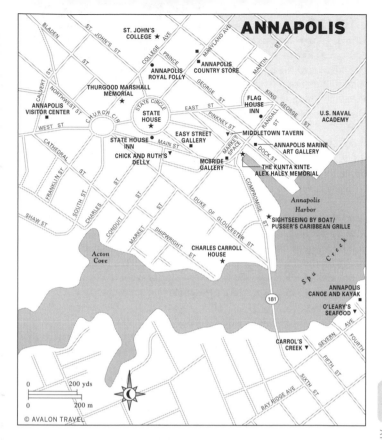

ANNAPOLIS

ST. JOHN'S COLLEGE ★
ANNAPOLIS ROYAL FOLLY
ANNAPOLIS COUNTRY STORE
THURGOOD MARSHALL MEMORIAL ★
ANNAPOLIS VISITOR CENTER
STATE HOUSE ★
FLAG HOUSE INN
U.S. NAVAL ACADEMY
STATE HOUSE INN
EASY STREET GALLERY
MIDDLETOWN TAVERN
ANNAPOLIS MARINE ART GALLERY
CHICK AND RUTH'S DELLY
McBRIDE GALLERY
THE KUNTA KINTE-ALEX HALEY MEMORIAL
Annapolis Harbor
SIGHTSEEING BY BOAT/ PUSSER'S CARIBBEAN GRILLE
Acton Cove
CHARLES CARROLL HOUSE ★
Spa Creek
ANNAPOLIS CANOE AND KAYAK
O'LEARY'S SEAFOOD
CARROL'S CREEK
181

0   200 yds
0   200 m
© AVALON TRAVEL

Princess Anne; when she became queen, she chartered Annapolis as a city, in 1708.

The town grew over the 18th century and managed, somehow, to avoid major modernization and the creep of 1970s urban renewal that wiped out so many historic areas. Today, downtown Annapolis is a strikingly well-preserved colonial-era waterfront enclave that serves as the state's capital. (Maryland's General Assembly is the longest-serving legislature in the United States; it first met way back in 1634.) The U.S. Naval Academy was built here, on the Severn River; watercraft are measures of wealth and competence for many people in this town, and Annapolis's boating and yachting obsession define this area's cultural landscape. The bustling, jumbled City Dock is home to expensive restaurants, expensive boats, and a see-and-be-seen crowd, but it's still a great place to simply hang out and watch Annapolitan life. The city's location midway between Baltimore and Washington DC makes it a popular day-trip destination for residents of both cities.

Charles Carroll House

If it seems like there are dozens of houses, roads, documents, and people named for Charles Carroll in Maryland, it's not a coincidence. But they're not necessarily named for the same Charles Carroll. There were at least three prominent Charles Carrolls throughout the state's early history; the **Charles Carroll House** (107 Duke of Gloucester St., 410/269-1737, www.charlescarrollhouse. com, Jun.-Sept. Sat.-Sun. noon-4pm, donation requested) on Spa Creek belonged to Charles Carroll the settler, whose father came to Maryland to escape persecution as a Catholic (Charles himself would be the only Catholic to sign the Declaration of Independence). The semi-preserved 1670 home now sits behind St. Mary's Church and is open for limited tours, as the home has been only partially restored. In a way, this makes it even more interesting, and you can see some of the interior structure and age of the house in ways more polished historic homes no longer reveal. Note the original front door, which is now sealed; it's on the second story since the land was regraded for the construction of the church.

The Kunta Kinte-Alex Haley Memorial

At the bottom of Annapolis's Main Street, along the City Dock lined with expensive yachts and strolling tourists, there's a collection of statues placed in the public walkway. A seated man is reading to three young children, who listen intently to him. The man is Alex Haley, the author of the groundbreaking 1976 book *Roots,* which (as both a book and a heavily watched 1977 TV series) did more to advance America's examination of the slavery era, and the repercussions of that time, than any other work in the past century. Kunta Kinte, Haley's direct ancestor, arrived on the continent as a slave on these very docks; this is the only memorial in the United States that acknowledges the name and place of arrival of an African slave. The memorial scene depicts Haley's explanation to the children of his past and ancestors, as well as the story of Annapolis's place as a center for slave trade in the 18th century.

Maryland State House

Construction on the original section of this historic building began in 1772, but wasn't finished until 1779, owing to a little interruption known as the Revolutionary War. Today, the **Maryland State House** (91 State Cir., 410/974-3400, www.msa.md.gov, Mon.-Fri. 9am-5pm, Sat.-Sun. 10am-4pm, free) is the oldest state capitol building still in use by a state legislature. The original section, built of wood and plaster, was joined by a more modern (and upgraded) section in the early 20th century, and features Tiffany skylights and Italian marble columns. The Old Senate Chamber filled with paintings of

Maryland politicians and period furniture is being re-created to look even more like it did when General George Washington resigned his commission to the Continental Congress; the Old House of Delegates and the State House Caucus Room were recently restored. Maryland's legislature is the longest continuously meeting legislative body in the United States; the first session was in 1634.

Sightseeing by Sailboat

When the weather is good and skies are clear but breezy, reserve a trip on one of the various watercraft that provide guided tours of Annapolis and the surrounding area. To keep things as authentic as possible, given Annapolis's colonial-era history, climb aboard a sailing vessel. The *Woodwind* (Pusser's Landing at the Marriott Waterfront, 80 Compromise St., 410/263-8994, www.schoonerwoodwind.com, two-hour weekend sail $42 adult, $27 child, $40 senior)—and her identical sister, the *Woodwind II*—is a two-masted 74-footer that can take 48 guests. There's also a special themed cruise every other Sunday; past events have focused on beer, wine, and local food.

St. John's College

In addition to the U.S. Naval Academy, the other unique bastion of higher education in Annapolis is this tiny school, founded in 1696, the curriculum of which is based solely on the so-called "Great Books" of history (and there's no religious affiliation, despite the name). There are no textbooks here (with the exception of language courses); instruction comes solely from the source material, no matter the subject. Freshmen start with the ancient Greeks; seniors study more contemporary works. It's not for everyone, obviously, but **St. John's College** (60 College Ave., 410/263-2371, www.sjca.edu, self-guided tours during daylight hours) has a reputation for turning out some very interesting young minds. The gorgeous campus doesn't hurt, either; lots of brick Georgian halls (McDowell Hall is the grandest) and dormitories, connected by tree-lined paths and grassy lawns. If you happen to be in Annapolis in April, see if you can catch the annual St. John's vs. the U.S. Naval Academy croquet tournament—this peculiar yearly matchup began in 1982 and is now a popular, quirky Annapolis tradition.

Thomas Point Shoal Lighthouse

If you're feeling frisky for a little summertime weekend adventure (and are relatively agile), you can take a boat ride out to a screw-pile-type lighthouse like the one that now resides in Baltimore's Inner Harbor. The **Thomas Point Shoal Lighthouse** (tours meet at the Annapolis Maritime Museum's Barge House, 723 Second St., Eastport, 415/362-7255, www.thomaspointlighthouse.org, $70) is

"The Most Beautiful Door in America"

Thomas Jefferson once said that the Hammond-Harwood House had the "prettiest door in America."

Annapolis has its share of renovated historical houses once lived in by the signers of the Declaration of Independence. But at the 18th-century mansion called **Hammond-Harwood House** (19 Maryland Ave., 410/263-4683, www.hammondharwoodhouse.org, Apr.-Oct. Tues.-Sun. noon-5pm, Nov.-Dec. noon-4pm, tours every hour, $7 adult, $4 child, $4 senior), its former residents and namesakes aren't famous at all. Wealthy tobacco planter Mathias Hammond commissioned architect William Buckland to build this "party house" for him in 1773 but never lived here; William Harwood's family were the last residents before it became a museum in 1940.

Still, there are two notable details worth admiring here. First is the white front door adorned with intricate carved woodwork; Thomas Jefferson once called it "the most beautiful door in America." (Tour guides have one of his old sketches of the house.) The second is the home's architecture, 95 percent of which is original—an unusual concept for structures of this age. The house itself has some beautiful

features, like the cool jib door in back that's easy to miss (the door blends in perfectly with its surroundings) and the two wings, or separate houses, originally intended to be rented out to businesses. Inside, the rooms are decorated as they would have been in the home's heyday with rich portraits, lavish furniture, and plenty of wood. If you have time, take the one-hour tour; although the chronology of past residents is sometimes hard to follow, it's fun to learn the history behind the house.

Afterward, walk across the street to the **Chase-Lloyd House** (22 Maryland Ave., 410/263-4683, Mon.-Sat. 2pm-4pm, closed Jan. and Feb.), which was originally built for Samuel Chase, one of the four Maryland signers of the Declaration of Independence. Chase never lived here, though; he sold the 18th-century mansion to Edward Lloyd before it was completed. Today, the first floor is open, as are the beautiful grounds out back. Note that about eight women live on the upper floors today, so the house has limited visiting hours.

about a half-hour boat ride from Annapolis's Eastport neighborhood in the center of the Chesapeake Bay; once you arrive, you'll disembark, ascend a ladder, and climb into the lighthouse through a small hatch. A docent takes guests around the lighthouse, explaining the role of these screwpile structures, and how the U.S. Coast Guard is restoring this particular lighthouse. This tour can be scratched if the weather or waves are foul; make reservations early, as only 18 passengers are allowed per boat trip.

Thurgood Marshall Memorial

The first African American to ascend to the Supreme Court of the United States, Baltimore native Thurgood Marshall was honored in 1994 (a year after his death) by the state of Maryland with this monument and statue, located outside the northwest side of the Maryland State House, on the **Lawyers' Mall** (College Ave. and Bladen St.). It's the spot where, in 1935, the Maryland Court of Appeals stood—and where Marshall (then a young lawyer) argued the *University v. Murray* case, which eventually helped end higher education segregation in Maryland state universities. Today, a life-size statue of Marshall stands before two pillars, one marked "Equal Justice," the other "Under Law." There are three other statues here: One is of Donald Murray, the plaintiff in that 1935 case; the other two are of children, symbolizing Marshall's work in 1954's *Brown v. Board of Education,* which desegregated public schools in the United States. There's also a timeline of important moments from Marshall's illustrious career.

★ U.S. Naval Academy

As you stroll along Annapolis's 250-year-old brick sidewalks, you may notice hundreds of immaculately attired and groomed young men and women in blindingly white uniforms. These are some of the U.S. Naval Academy's 4,400-strong brigade of midshipmen, all of whom will become ensigns in the U.S. Navy (or second lieutenants in the Marine Corps) upon graduation. The Naval Academy is basically the U.S. Navy's university, much like West Point is the U.S. Army's, and it's a leviathan (some 340 acres) of imposing marble buildings and monuments that looms to the northwest of the tidy streets and yacht-filled piers of Annapolis. Security at the Academy is rigorous; armed military guards are a noticeable and constant presence, and getting in for a tour requires a valid photo I.D. Begin your exploration at the **Armel-Leftwich Visitor Center** (52 King George St., 410/293-8687, www.usnabsd.com, daily 9am-5pm, reduced winter hours) where you'll learn about the exploits of Academy graduates past (like the legendary John Paul Jones) and contemporary (like astronaut Alan Shepard). The walking tour ($10 adult, $8 child, $9 senior), which takes 1.25 hours, takes visitors through the Academy's well-kept grounds and buildings, including massive Bancroft Hall, the world's largest dormitory—which has its own Memorial Hall where the names of all Academy graduates who have been killed in action are listed. Time your tour around noon to see the brigade march into formation and inspection; the precision and presence of the marchers is an amazing sight. And though it's not part of the main tour, stop by the **U.S. Naval Academy Museum** (118 Maryland Ave., 410/293-2108, www.usna.edu, Tues.-Sat. 9am-5pm, Sun. 11am-5pm, free), which has a great collection of artifacts, uniforms, fantastically detailed model ships, and maritime maps, prints, and paintings.

William Paca House

Of all the well-preserved 18th-century architecture in Annapolis, one of the most astounding buildings is the **William Paca House** (186 Prince George St., 410/267-7619, Mon.-Sat. 10am-5pm, Sun. noon-5pm, shorter winter hours, guided tours every hour on the half hour, admission $10 adult, $5 child, $9 senior), even though it's not as untouched as it first appears. Paca (pronounced "Pay-ka") designed and supervised construction of this house himself; completed in 1765, the home has a couple of odd architectural features, owing to Paca's training as a lawyer, not an architect. A Maryland legislator during the American Revolution, in 1776, he signed the Declaration of Independence; he later served as governor of Maryland. The abundance of Paca Blue (a sort of a dark robin's egg color) throughout the second floor of the house indicates the family's wealth. The rear gardens are impressive not only in their size and scale, but also because they have been returned to their colonial-era splendor; for most of the 20th century, they were covered by a hotel that had been built on the site. That building (which included the Paca home) was to be leveled in 1965, but instead, Annapolis's preservationists acquired the property, removed the hotel only, and restored the gardens and Paca's house.

RESTAURANTS

Annapolis is Maryland's capital city; as such, a steady stream of politicians, lobbyists, and powerful citizens from across the state and the nation (not to mention visiting boaters) frequently stroll its charming streets in search of outstanding wining and dining options. There are plenty of more accessible options as well, and the quality of eateries here is generally superb; lifelong residents and VIP visitors just don't abide second-rate.

For waterfront options, head across the Sixth Street drawbridge to Eastport, and the creekside dining at **Carrol's Creek Café** (410 Severn Ave., 410/263-8102, www.carrolscreek.com, Mon.-Sat. 11:30am-4pm and 5pm-10pm, Sun. 10am-1:30pm and 3pm-9pm) and **O'Leary's Seafood** (310 3rd St., 410/263-0884, www.olearys-seafood.com, Mon.-Sat. 5pm-10pm, Sun. 5pm-9pm), where you'll be able to indulge your seafood cravings. (O'Leary's is the more upscale of the two).

Not in the mood for anything fancy? The venerable **Chick & Ruth's Delly** (165 Main St., 410/269-6737, www.chickandruths.com, Sun.-Thurs. 6:30am-11:30pm, Fri.-Sat. 6:30am-12:30am) is a city institution, where everyone from the governor to the groundskeepers eat. The interior is a riot of color and classic diner furniture, all reds and yellows, with a variety of deli sandwiches (it's a kosher-style restaurant) named for famous local and international figures, heroes, and characters. You'll see midshipmen, yacht owners, state senators, senior citizens, landscapers, and tourists all happily jostling through this Annapolis stalwart.

Another venerable establishment is the upscale **Middleton Tavern** (2 Market Space, 410/263-3323, www.middletontavern.com, Mon.-Sat. 11:30am-1:30am, Sun. 10am-1:30am), located just off the City Dock. This bar and restaurant has hosted not only George Washington, but also Thomas Jefferson and Benjamin Franklin. The bar here is now best known for its oyster shooter: an oyster with cocktail sauce served in a shot glass, then chased with a beer. It's a tradition around these parts, but avoid it if you think you're not up to it—a reversal is not a pleasant experience.

For a great place to have a drink, head to the picturesque waterfront dock at **Pusser's Caribbean Grille** (80 Compromise St., 410/626-0004, www.pussersusa.com, breakfast Mon.-Fri. 6:30am-11am, Sat.-Sun. 7am-11am, lunch daily 11am-5pm, dinner Sun.-Thurs. 5pm-10pm, Fri.-Sat. 5pm-11pm) next to the Marriott Waterfront Hotel. You can also rent a kayak or canoe at **Annapolis Canoe and Kayak** (311 3rd St., 410/263-2303, www.ackannapolis.com, Mon.-Fri. 11am-7pm, Sat.-Sun. 11am-5pm spring and summer), paddle across Spa Creek to the restaurant, and call a server to place your order and literally have a drink on the water.

SHOPS

Annapolis is a popular tourist destination, so the shopping here is geared toward the weekend visitor; arts, crafts, jewelry, and souvenirs are big staples. If you want to just window-shop, take a slow stroll up Main Street or Maryland Avenue. For those who need a large haul of gifts, try the quaint **Annapolis Country Store** (53 Maryland Ave., 410/269-6773, www.annapoliscountrystore.com, Mon.-Sat. 10am-6pm, Sun. 11am-5pm) for toiletries and candles, children's toys and books, baskets, and a big stock of holiday items or **Annebeth's** (46 Maryland Ave., 410/990-9700, www.annebeths.com, Mon.-Thurs. 11am-10pm, Fri.-Sat. 11am-11pm, Sun. noon-8pm) for gourmet foods like the locally produced Fisher's popcorn and B More Nutz. A variety of handblown and handcrafted glass artworks from modern artists delight shoppers at **Easy Street Gallery** (8 Francis St., 410/263-5556, www.easystreetgallery.com, Mon.-Sat. 10am-6pm, Sun. 10am-5pm). Lovers of the water should head to **Annapolis Marine Art Gallery** (110 Dock St., 410/263-4100, www.annapolismarineart.com, Mon.-Sat. 10am-6pm, Sun. 11am-5pm) for prints and framed paintings and photographs of boating scenes in Annapolis and beyond. The largest art gallery in downtown Annapolis, featuring lots of nautically themed works by local artists, is the **McBride Gallery** (215 Main St., 410/267-7077, www.mcbridegallery.com, Mon.-Sat. 10am-5:30pm, Sun. noon-5:30pm, longer Thurs. hours).

HOTELS

The romantic character of Annapolis has long made it a favorite for Baltimoreans and Washingtonians looking for a nearby overnight getaway. There are many options for lodging, including enticing bed-and-breakfasts and small hotels found in well-preserved old buildings. The only downside to Annapolis's charm and popularity is that prices are rather high; expect to spend anywhere from $160 for a weekday night to $280 and beyond for a weekend night. On the plus side, competition is hot, so expect to get a very nice weekend breakfast included in your room rate and hosts who are really working to earn your business.

It's hard to beat the location of the **State House Inn** (25 State Cir., 410/990-0024, www.statehouseinn.com, $119-270), a large home built in 1786 that now has eight guest rooms furnished in period (or period-ish) furniture—some of which have whirlpool tubs. There's a nice big front porch on the State Circle side of this big yellow building, and while the hotel backs onto busy Main Street, inside it's quite quiet. Don't expect sparkling, immaculate conditions, but rather a lived-in, realistic inn that's more like a large B&B.

Just across the street from St. John's College is **Annapolis Royal Folly** (65 College Ave., 410/263-3999, www.royalfolly.com, $225-425). This large, slate blue 1870s-era home is adorned with extras like skylights, chandeliers, and a huge dining room. There are five guest rooms (out of 14 in the whole home), most of which offer serious extras (one occupies the entire third floor). The views of St. John's are so good that they should charge extra, though they don't; like most of the inns and B&Bs in Annapolis, you'll find your room is within a few blocks of the city's main attractions.

Three blocks from the Maryland State House, just outside of the pedestrian entrance to the U.S. Naval Academy, is the patriotic **Flag House Inn** (26 Randall St., 410/280-2721, www.flaghouseinn.com, $170-300). This house is host to five guest rooms, ranging from the two-room Fleet Suite (the only room on the second floor) to the cozy Sailing Capital room on the third floor; there's even a Far East room whose decor is inspired by the U.S. Navy's presence in Asia before WWII. Lots of nautical art fills the home and rooms, and the front porch makes for a great place to people-watch and relax.

If you'd like to get away from the (relative) bustle of downtown Annapolis, head across Spa Creek to Eastport and the picture-perfect **Inn at Horn Point** (100 Chesapeake Ave., Eastport, 410/268-1126, www.innathornpoint.com, $159-309). The Sequoia room offers the most amenities (like a gas fireplace and private balcony). The water taxi stops just three blocks from the inn, and conveys guests to Annapolis's City Dock; on foot, it's a 15-minute walk through the neighborhood and across the Spa Creek drawbridge.

INFORMATION
Visitors Center
The main Annapolis Visitors Center is near a large public parking garage; take a parking spot here and walk down into the main part of town, as parking and traffic downtown are immensely difficult, especially during spring and summer. This main visitors center is at 26 West Street; it's open daily 9am-5pm. There's a smaller visitors information booth right at City Dock that's open 9am-5pm daily from March to early October. The main center has lots of information, pamphlets, and brochures, as well as plenty of helpful guides and volunteers to assist you in planning your time in Annapolis. The information booth has the same resources, just on a much smaller scale.

Media
The *Capital* is Annapolis's sole daily newspaper and covers local issues and the various communities that surround the city. Annapolitans also read either the *Baltimore Sun* or the *Washington Post,* and sometimes both, depending on their needs and interests. The same split is true for television, as Annapolis can get stations from both Baltimore and DC. On the radio, Annapolis has only a few indigenous stations, including **WNAV 1430 AM** (talk) and **WRNR 103.1 FM** (modern rock).

GETTING THERE AND AROUND
Getting There
Annapolis is 30 miles south of Baltimore. By car, the best route to take is to get to I-97, a relatively new road built expressly to connect Baltimore and Annapolis; from there, it's easy to reach Route 50/Route 301 (head east), and then turn right on Rowe Boulevard; go straight for a little over a mile, then bear right as you enter Annapolis. It takes about 35 minutes by car or bus—and **Greyhound** (www.greyhound.com) does travel from downtown Baltimore (2110

clockwise from top left: quaint downtown area in St. Michael's; Chesapeake Bay Maritime Museum, St. Michael's; *Top Chef*'s Bryan Voltaggio's VOLT, Frederick

Haines St., 410/752-7682) to Annapolis, though the Annapolis bus
terminal is about two miles from the historic downtown, and you
will need to secure a taxi to get there. There is no rail service.

Getting Around
Once you're in Annapolis, everything is reachable by foot, which
is the best way to explore and enjoy this historic city. Most attractions are about a five-minute walk apart, though repeated trips up
Main Street—which is a bit of a hill—could prove tiring to some
people. For those who want to park at the Navy-Marine Corps
Memorial Stadium, the city operates an inexpensive (for downtown
use) **shuttle bus service** (410/263-7964, www.annapolis.gov); from
there, Annapolis Transit's Navy Blue line goes downtown Monday
through Friday and costs $2 each way. There's also a State line pri-
marily for commuters (but anyone can get on) that travels from the
stadium to the legislative buildings. You can catch a taxi pretty easily around City Dock. The walk from downtown Annapolis across
Spa Creek into Eastport takes about 10-15 minutes—longer if the
drawbridge is up.

Frederick

Founded as a major trading outpost in colonial North America in
1745, Frederick was first settled by German immigrants, who were
followed a century later by Irish men and women who'd come to
make their fortunes in the boom-time United States. The town—
which acts as a gateway to western Maryland and points beyond—
was built at the intersection of trading and transport routes that
headed to the fledgling nation's settlements and farms, and was
a strategic town during both the Revolution (Francis Scott Key,
who wrote the lyrics to "The Star-Spangled Banner" in Baltimore,
called Frederick home) and the Civil War. Today, it's a popular
small-town destination for residents of both Baltimore and nearby
Washington DC to visit, eat, and shop (and, sometimes, even relo-
cate). Frederick's charming downtown boutiques and abundance
of antiques shops, as well as nearby historic attractions like the
Civil War battlefield of Antietam, give visitors plenty of options.
Though the surrounding countryside is being developed into suburban housing, downtown Frederick has maintained its great historic buildings and small-town culture.

EXCURSIONS
FREDERICK

SIGHTS
Adventure Park USA
On the way to Frederick, heading west on I-70, you might notice a
modest roller coaster and a few wooden rooftops off to your left.

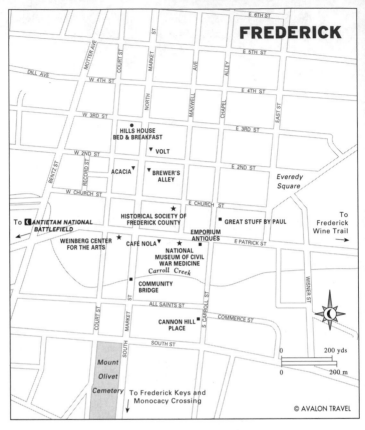

FREDERICK

E 6TH ST
E 5TH ST
DILL AVE
W 4TH ST
E 4TH ST
W 3RD ST
E 3RD ST

HILLS HOUSE
BED & BREAKFAST

▼ VOLT
W 2ND ST
E 2ND ST
ACACIA ▼   ▼ BREWER'S
              ALLEY   Everedy
                                       Square
W CHURCH ST   E CHURCH ST
                                              To
                ★   Frederick
To ◖ ANTIETAM NATIONAL   HISTORICAL SOCIETY OF   Wine Trail
     BATTLEFIELD   FREDERICK COUNTY   ■ GREAT STUFF BY PAUL →
                                  EMPORIUM
                                  ANTIQUES ■
WEINBERG CENTER ★   ★   E PATRICK ST
FOR THE ARTS   CAFE NOLA ▼   ★
                              NATIONAL
                            MUSEUM OF CIVIL
                              WAR MEDICINE
                          Carroll Creek
              ■ COMMUNITY
                BRIDGE

              ALL SAINTS ST
                                COMMERCE ST
              CANNON HILL
                PLACE
              SOUTH ST
                                   0   200 yds
Mount
Olivet   0   200 m
Cemetery   To Frederick Keys and
           Monocacy Crossing
                                    © AVALON TRAVEL

MOTTER AVE · COURT ST · MARKET ST · AVE · ALLEY · MAXWELL · CHAPEL · EAST ST · NORTH ST · BENTZ ST · RECORD ST · COURT ST · MARKET ST · SOUTH · S CARROLL ST · WISNER ST

This is **Adventure Park USA** (11113 W. Baldwin Rd, New Market, 301/865-6800, www.adventureparkusa.com, Sun.-Thurs. 11am-7:30pm, Fri. 11am-9:30pm, Sat. 10am-9:30pm, longer summer hours, admission $25.95 for a three-hour unlimited pass), a small but serviceable Wild West-themed amusement park that opened in 2005. Disneyland it's not, but it doesn't try to be—instead, it focuses on doing small well. There's the Wildcat Roller Coaster, the Horseless Carriage Go Karts, the West World Laser Tag...you get the idea. There's also miniature golf, a ropes course, a playground, a rock wall for climbing, and the usual array of eats and souvenirs. Crowds aren't a huge concern at this park, so consider taking a nighttime roller-coaster ride and getting some ice cream to liven up the short trip back to Baltimore.

★ Antietam National Battlefield

While most Americans have heard of Gettysburg—the Pennsylvania town that, in 1863, was the sight of the most costly battle of the U.S.

Civil War, and the turning point of the conflict—not everyone has
heard of **Antietam National Battlefield** (5831 Dunker Church Road,
Sharpsburg, 301/432-5124, www.nps.gov/anti, park open during
daylight hours, visitor center daily 8:30am-5pm, admission $4 per
person, $6 per family). Yet Antietam was just as important a bat-
tle, and one that changed the character of the war. Just west of
Frederick, near the town of Sharpsburg, the forces of Union General
George McClellan and Confederate General Robert E. Lee collided
as the Union troops attempted to keep Lee from further invading Union territory north of Washington DC. On the morning of
September 17, 1862, nearly 100,000 troops engaged in battle across
the rolling farmlands and woods of this part of the state. Twelve
hours later, the carnage ended, and some 23,000 Americans were
dead, wounded, or missing. It was the single bloodiest day of the
Civil War; a day later, Lee's troops withdrew to Virginia. Many of
the surrounding towns were turned into makeshift hospitals, aid
stations, and morgues; recent improvements in medicine and surgi-
cal procedures probably saved countless lives (details on this aspect
of the battle can be gleaned at the National Museum of Civil War
Medicine in Frederick).

Begin your tour at the visitors center, located roughly in the center of the battlefield (which is spread out over some four miles of
countryside). At the center you can watch a compelling film nar-
rated by James Earl Jones that sets the scene for the brutal combat
that took place here and view photos taken by some of the earliest
war photographers—some of which show dead soldiers splayed
across the same, now calm and green landscapes you'll be able to
traverse. The 8.5-mile, 11-stop tour is self-guided, and done via
automobile, bicycle, or on foot, but you can get a park volunteer to
ride along with you for a more in-depth explanation of the battle
and its repercussions. The tour is lined with picket fences of the
types built by the battle's soldiers, as well as cannon and numerous
monuments built to honor the soldiers of the various states who
sent their young men here to fight for their respective countries.

Frederick Keys

As befits a small, picturesque American town like Frederick, the
small, newly refurbished Harry Grove Stadium (capacity: 5,500)
that rises near I-70 is home to the minor league **Frederick Keys** (21
Stadium Dr., 301/662-0013, www.frederickkeys.com), a Class A af-
filiate of the major league Baltimore Orioles. This is the lowest level
of professional baseball, so the action on the field can be a little less
than stellar, but the atmosphere is very family-friendly, as are the
prices (tickets top out at $14). There's a Fun Zone for kids to run
around in and burn off steam, cheap hot dogs and beer, and post-
game fireworks events throughout the year. Spending a night—and

XCURSIONS FREDERICK

not a fortune—at a Keys game is a great way to cap off a day in historic Frederick.

★ Frederick Wine Trail

About a half hour outside of downtown Frederick is the **Frederick Wine Trail** (410/775-2513 or 800/999-3613, www.frederickwine-trail.com), a trio of vineyards in Mount Airy surrounded by rolling hills and the countryside that is still prominent in much of Maryland. Located next to horse and dairy farms, **Elk Run Vineyards** (15113 Liberty Rd., 410/775-2513, www.elkrun.com, Tues.-Thurs. 10am-5pm, Fri. 10am-9pm, Sat. 10am-6pm, Sun. noon-6pm) has won a slew of awards for its wines, the most recent being 2012 golds from the Atlantic Seaboard Wine Association and the International Tasters Guild for its cabernet franc; the winery also has live music on summer Friday evenings. Just two minutes away is **Lowe Vineyards** (14001 Liberty Rd., 301/831-5464, www.lowevineyards.net, Fri. and Sun. 1pm-5pm, Sat. 10am-5pm, Mon. holidays 1pm-5pm), a family-run business since the 1800s that makes about 17 varieties of dry, semisweet, and sweet wines; you can also take a walk through the grounds or enjoy a bottle and a cheese plate (or bring your own snacks) at one of the tables in the picnic area. Then, take about a 10-minute drive to the north to visit **Linganore Winecellars** (13601 Glissans Mill Rd., 410/795-6432, www.linganorewines.com, Mon.-Fri. 10am-5pm, Sat. 10am-6pm, Sun. noon-6pm), which offers daily tours and food and wine pairings and nearly 30 wines. This is a good place for visitors who enjoy sweet and fruit wines, which comprise nearly half of the list (there's also traditional chardonnay and cabernet sauvignon, too).

Historical Society of Frederick County

A grand 1820 home built by a local physician is now home to the **Historical Society of Frederick County** (24 E. Church St., 301/663-1188, www.hsfcinfo.org, guided tours Tues.-Sat. 10am-4pm, Sun. 1pm-4pm, admission $6 adults, $3 youth, children under 12 free), which can provide a good backdrop for the history of the people and culture of the area after its settlement by German immigrants in the mid-1700s. The home is set up to reflect the various purposes it served over the past 180 years, from private home to orphanage, and there's a fine collection of tall case clocks (a specialty of Frederick's craftspeople). A back room is designed for kids to learn about the town and its history, and there's also a historical archives in the basement. There's a medium-sized garden out back that's worth a stroll, and the well-stocked gift and bookstore has a plethora of local history tomes and maps.

What started as one man's personal collection of Civil War-era medical ephemera and artifacts is now the **National Museum of Civil War Medicine** (48 E. Patrick St., 301/695-1864, www.civilwarmed. org, Mon.-Sat. 10am-5pm, Sun. 11am-5pm, $7.50 adults, $5.50 child, $7 senior). The museum demonstrates how, despite archaic medical techniques and education, dedicated physicians and surgeons managed to save thousands of soldiers' lives—but often at the cost of a limb. Disease was the biggest killer, causing nearly two-thirds of the war's deaths. Though most of the museum is fine for visitors of all ages, there are a few disturbing images that could upset young kids. But the exhibits are often fascinating and provide an intriguing look into 19th-century medicine.

★ Weinberg Center for the Arts

The Tivoli theater—complete with crystal chandeliers, marble, and silk wall coverings—opened in downtown Frederick in 1926 to host films, plays, musicals, and other artistic endeavors. Though the building fell into serious disrepair by the 1960s (and that was before the flood of 1976), local businesspeople and activists restored the theater and reopened it in 1978 as the area's finest performance venue. That year, the building was renamed for Frederick residents Dan and Alyce Weinberg, who bought the place in 1959 and helped spur its renovation. The theater's pride and joy is the original 1926 Wurlitzer organ, which is still played today. Shows at the **Weinberg Center for the Arts** (20 W. Patrick St., 301/600-2828, www.weinbergcenter.org) now include small symphonic works, comedies, musicals, Shakespeare, Afro-Cuban artists, humorists, authors, and kids' stage shows. Check the Weinberg Center's schedule to see what's on stage during your visit.

RESTAURANTS

Downtown Frederick's popularity with urbanities from Baltimore and Washington DC has helped it support a broad range of good restaurants, some of which use local produce from the surrounding farms of Frederick County whenever possible. At the luxury end of the culinary world, **VOLT** (228 N. Market), *Top Chef* and *Top Chef Masters* contestant Bryan Voltaggio's restaurant housed in a beautiful 19th-century brownstone, thrills diners with contemporary food like rabbit with ham, mushrooms, and quinoa, softshell crab with celeriac, and tasting menus, including a vegetarian option. Also in downtown Frederick is **Acacia** (129 N. Market St., 301/694-3015, www.acacia129.com, Tues.-Thurs. and Sun. 11:30am-9:30pm, Fri.-Sat. 11:30am-10:30pm), a warm, unfussy bistro that offers Asian-inspired dishes and plenty of fish and poultry options. **Brewer's Alley** (124 N. Market St., 301/631-0089, www.brewers-alley.

Frederick's Top Chef

Several Maryland chefs were once competitors on popular TV cooking shows, but perhaps the most famous is Bryan Voltaggio, the *Top Chef* alumnus who lost the nail-biting final battle (and the chef's hat, so to speak) to his brother, Michael. But don't worry, he's doing fine: In 2013, Voltaggio moved up the TV ranks to *Top Chef Masters*. The two-time James Beard finalist also owns three restaurants in Frederick, his hometown, including **VOLT,** his flagship fine dining restaurant. Housed in a 19th-century brownstone, Volt is known for its creative dishes and tasting menus offered for dinner and brunch. There's even a table that is literally in the kitchen called Table 21; a seat here comes with a 21-course tasting menu, a hefty price tag, and a memorable experience.

Voltaggio's newer dining concepts are more relaxed affairs. **Lunchbox** (50 Carroll Creek Way, 301/360-0580, www.voltlunchbox.com) is a grab-and-go restaurant that whips up sandwiches, salads, and soups made with just a few fresh ingredients; it's a good place to stop for a quick bite to eat before shopping in downtown Frederick. Then about a mile outside of downtown in a former Nissan dealership is **Family Meal** (880 N. East St., 301/378-2895, www.voltfamilymeal.com), a diner-inspired concept that takes its name from the nightly family ritual, as well as the staff meal eaten at restaurants before service. Here, simple comfort food is served in a laid-back, minimally decorated space; try the fried chicken, which has been praised by critics. Families tend to flock here early in the evening with adults taking over at night, so plan accordingly for the crowd that suits you best.

com, Mon.-Tues. 11:30am-11:30pm, Wed.-Thurs. 11:30am-midnight, Fri.-Sat. 11:30am-12:30pm, Sun. noon-11:30pm) is a popular brewpub with an ambitious menu ideal for pairing with some of the establishment's year-round and seasonal beers. For a lighter meal, try **Café Nola** (4 E. Patrick St., 301/694-6652, www.cafe-nola.com, dinner Wed.-Sat. 5pm-10pm, brunch Mon.-Fri. 7am-3pm, Sat.-Sun. 9am-3pm), where fresh-made salads and sandwiches can help sustain weary tourists (and antiques hunters).

Just outside of town is **Monocacy Crossing** (4424 Urbana Pike, 301/846-4204, www.monocacycrossing.com, Tues.-Thurs. 11:30am-9:30pm, Fri. 11:30am-10pm, Sat. 3pm-10pm, Sun. noon-8pm), a hidden, homey local favorite with an emphasis on substantial dinners (such as beef medallions in bacon and lamb shank) and a small outdoor dining area.

★ ANTIQUE SHOPS

Frederick's history as a crossroads in early America means that the town was always awash in goods from across the region, so it's only natural that today, Frederick is one of the area's top stops for antiques shoppers. Stores range in size from small shops along the main drags to huge multi-dealer warehouses on the outskirts. **Emporium Antiques** (112 E. Patrick St., 301/662-7099, www.

emporiumantiques.com, Mon.-Sat. 11am-6pm, Sun. noon-5pm)
is the largest in downtown and combines the lots of more than
130 dealers in a 55,000-square-foot complex of buildings offering everything from grand French furniture to pop culture bric-
a-brac. About a ten-minute walk south is **Cannon Hill Place** (111 S.
Carroll St., 301/695-9304, www.frederick.com, Tues.-Sun. noon-
5pm); housed in a great building—a former stone granary built in
1790—it has two floors of vintage clothing, home furnishings, art,
books, and furniture from more than 40 dealers. **Great Stuff by Paul**
(www.greatstuffbypaul.com) has two locations, a sprawling old
warehouse downtown (10 N. Carroll St., 301/631-0004, Mon.-Sat.
10am-6pm, Sun. 11am-5pm) and a 52,000-square-foot behemoth
store just north of historic area (257 E. 6th St., 301/631-5340, Mon.-
Sat. 10am-6pm, Sun. 11am-5pm). And if Frederick can't satiate your
shopping needs, nearby New Market (east of Frederick) is known
as the "Antiques Capital of Maryland."

HOTELS

The historic charms of Frederick can be pretty alluring, so if you
decide to spend the night, there are two great options in town. If
you want to pass the weekend strolling the streets, your best bet is
Hill House Bed & Breakfast (12 W. 3rd St., 301/682-4111, www.hill-
housefrederick.com, $145-195), a three-story, four-room historic
Victorian town house. It's the closest lodging to downtown's shopping and dining, but it's just far enough from the main strip to offer
a little seclusion. Decorated with period furniture and antiques, two
of Hill House's rooms have private balconies, and the Steeple Suite
offers great views of the city's church spires.

Farther south, a short walk away from the relative bustle of
downtown Frederick, is **Hollerstown Hill Bed & Breakfast** (4 Clarke
Pl., 301/228-3630, www.hollerstownhill.com, $135-145), a large
Victorian-era home in a residential neighborhood that offers a
sweeping porch, garden and patio, and even a billiards table. The
second-floor Cottage Garden Room has a great sleigh bed and a
private porch that overlooks the gardens below, as well as the other
historic homes of the neighborhood.

Outside of downtown Frederick, there's a wide range of chain
motels available, as well as some other options. If you're not a fan of
Victorian decor, head west to Middleton and the **Inn at Stone Manor**
(5820 Carroll Boyer Rd., Middletown, 301/371-0099, www.stone-
manorcountryclub.com, $200-225), a long, sturdy 18th-century
home built of fieldstone. This inn is the most modernized of the
region's lodging options, though antiques still abound. The views
from all of the rooms of the estate's 100 acres of lawns, gardens,
ponds, and trees are exceptional. Most of the rooms have whirlpool tubs, and amenities include fireplaces and private porches.

And just a bit farther west is New Market, the "Antiques Capital of Maryland," and the small, three-room **Strawberry Inn Bed & Breakfast** (17 W. Main St., New Market, 301/865-3318, www.strawberryinnbnb.com, $125). Located on a pretty, tree-lined street, the inn is in the quaint downtown area close to antiques shops and a restaurant, and the Lincoln Room on the first floor is the best lodging option, as it has a private porch and a cool Victrola record player.

INFORMATION
Visitors Center

On your way into historic downtown Frederick, stop at the **Frederick Visitor Center** (151 S. East St., 301/600-4047, www.visitfrederick.org, daily 9am-5:30pm), which serves both the town and the county. There's generally at least two friendly staffers on the weekends to help you plan out your trip to the area, and there's a huge selection of brochures and pamphlets of the region's attractions. Before you leave, download on your phone the free *Official Frederick Visitor Guide,* produced by the tourism council, which has invaluable maps and guides to both the city and the outlying area. If you're not sure how to get your tour started, ask one of the staffers for recommendations.

Media

Frederick has one daily newspaper, the *Frederick News-Post,* that covers the city, county, and surrounding smaller municipalities. There's also the weekly *Frederick County Gazette,* one of a family of Maryland community newspapers. Frederick even has a monthly upscale lifestyle magazine, *Frederick,* which covers living in the area and offers information on events, dining, and shopping.

GETTING THERE AND AROUND
Getting There

Frederick lies nearly 50 miles west of Baltimore; the best means of travel is via car on I-70, a trip that should take about an hour. Be cautious about traveling this route during rush hour on Friday evenings, as traffic backups are common. **Greyhound** (www.greyhound.com) has a bus that runs from Baltimore (2110 Haines St., 410/752-7682) to Frederick's MARC train station (100 S. East St., 301/663-3311), about a half mile from the center of Frederick (note that the MARC train does not connect Baltimore and Frederick; it connects both cities to Washington DC but not to one another).

Antietam National Battlefield is about 30 miles west of Frederick (45 minutes by car) and best reached via I-70; take exit 29 onto Maryland Route 65 and head south to the town of Sharpsburg.

It's possible to spend your entire trip in historic Frederick on foot, wandering through the town's shops and sights, but brief car trips are necessary to see more of the area's attractions, particularly Antietam National Battlefield to the west. **TransIT** (301/600-9000, www.co.frederick.md.us), the local public transportation service, runs mostly during the week; service is curtailed on Saturday and does not operate on Sunday.

Easton and St. Michaels

Maryland's Eastern Shore is intriguing on many levels. First, it's (mostly) managed to retain its early American feel and character while the rest of the world has moved forward. This is still very agricultural land, occupied by fifth-generation farmers whose ancestors settled here in the 17th century. Even though several major cities are relatively nearby, the isolated geography of the Eastern Shore has kept out a lot of the modern world. Though millions of people pass through these parts on their way to the Atlantic Ocean resort towns of Ocean City, Maryland, and the Delaware beaches each year, very few people stop to do more than eat and fill up their gas tanks. After the construction of the Chesapeake Bay Bridge, some parts of the Eastern Shore gained residents and construction, but not too many people emigrated to this flat, undeveloped countryside.

These factors are probably why this area has become more popular in recent decades for wealthy professionals from Baltimore (and especially Washington DC) looking for a tranquil second home. There's waterfront property everywhere, and numerous creeks and rivers cut gently through the lush, flat lands here. Some of the old mid-shore towns, like Easton and St. Michaels in Talbot County, have become thriving social hubs for lifelong residents, tourists, and weekenders.

EASTON

Easton is the larger of the two towns and lies about 90 minutes from Baltimore. Founded back in 1711, Easton grew around the site of the first Talbot County courthouse; today, it's a full-fledged small town, with plazas and historic homes, lanes and alleys, and lots of bistros, restaurants, shopping, and taverns. It's also home to one of the Eastern Shore's gems, the restored Avalon Theatre, which really completes the small-town-America picture.

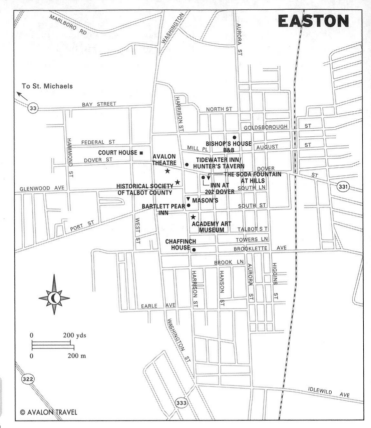

EASTON

To St. Michaels

Sights

Academy Art Museum

You wouldn't expect to find a museum like the **Academy Art Museum** (106 South St., 410/822-2787, www.academyartmuseum.org, Fri.-Mon. 10am-4pm, Tues.-Thurs. 10am-8pm, $3) in a small, off-the-highway town like Easton, but the collections here will impress any connoisseur. It's not the most regal building—it's an 1820s school-house—but the artworks inside are exceptional. Sculptures, paintings, and photographs from the likes of Ansel Adams, Baltimore's Grace Hartigan, Roy Lichtenstein, and Robert Rauschenberg fill out the galleries. There's also a very solid collection of American and European works on paper (drawings, prints, and etchings, for example).

★ Avalon Theatre

A small-town America masterpiece that (thanks to preservationists) escaped demolition, this 1920 theater opened to rave reviews for its

construction and design: glass doors, a soaring dome, a pipe organ, **265**
and other top-notch touches—which were subsequently removed
and replaced with art deco designs and fixtures in the 1930s. After
an expensive renovation in 1989, the **Avalon Theatre** (40 East Dover
St., 410/822-7299, www.avalontheatre.com) eventually found its
voice and role for the region, hosting performances from all sorts
of artists. Local bands, comedy troupes, duos and trios, classical
music, country, opera, soul, Broadway revivals and "hits" shows—
all manner of performers take the proscenium stage at this midsize
theater (about 400 seats).

Historical Society of Talbot County
Chronicling the changing ways of life of this part of the Eastern
Shore, the **Historical Society of Talbot County** (25 S. Washington St.,
410/822-0773, www.hstc.org, Tues.-Sat. 11am-3pm, reduced winter
hours, free) has a small collection of old photos, furniture, quilts,
and artifacts from the people who lived here, as well as items from
the industries that helped the region prosper, like canneries and
sawmills. Frederick Douglass was a Talbot County native, and artifacts from his time here, both before and after his escape, are on
display here. There's a $5 guided tour of historic Easton homes that
is offered April through November and can be given anytime during museum hours; call in advance to book.

Pickering Creek Audubon Center
The **Pickering Creek Audubon Center** (11450 Audubon Ln., 410/822-
4903, www.pickeringcreek.org, trails open daily dawn-dusk) lies
nine miles north of Easton (about 20 minutes by car). The 400-
acre nature preserve is home to a wide variety of animals, from
white-tailed deer to waterfowl, and covers marshes, fields, forests,
and waterfront. Pickering Creek is part of the National Audubon
Society, and membership in Audubon and/or Pickering Creek ($20
minimum, for one year) lets you use one of their canoes (available
Mon.-Fri. 9am-4pm); the hiking trails are open and free to use for
everyone. The two-mile Farm to Bay Trail winds through the deep
woods to the water, and it's the best way to see some of the abundant
fauna that calls this bucolic area home.

Restaurants
You'll find a wide array of dining options here, generally in a less-
than-stuffy atmosphere (most people here are on vacation, after
all). One of the town's most popular eateries morning, noon, and
night is **Mason's** (22 S. Harrison St., 410/822-3204, www.masons-
gourmet.com, lunch Mon.-Sat. 11:30am-2:30pm, dinner Tues.-Sat.
5:30pm-9:30pm). It started out as a candy shop but has evolved
substantially to serve popular lunches (get soup and a sandwich

The Chesapeake Bay Bridge

With the growth of Maryland in the 1930s, the need to move commerce from the agricultural Eastern Shore to the more populous parts of the state, and the growing desire of vacationers to travel to Maryland and Delaware's beach resorts, the five-hour drive from Baltimore to the Eastern Shore—which wound around the bay—became too much to bear. Some residents and businesspeople of the Eastern Shore and the rest of Maryland began to lobby for a bridge to connect this isolated section of the state with the mainland. Construction of a bridge crossing a narrow part of the Chesapeake Bay was approved in 1938, interrupted by World War II, and resumed in 1947. When the **Chesapeake Bay Bridge** (www.baybridge.maryland.gov) opened in 1952, it was—at a whopping 4.3 miles—the longest steel structure built over water in the world. It carries U.S. Routes 50 and 301 across the bay from Sandy Point, Anne Arundel County, into Kent Island, in Queen Anne's County; it was renamed the William Preston Lane Jr. Memorial Bridge in 1967 to honor the Maryland governor who had helped get approval for the bridge's construction.

Within about a decade, it was clear that the four-lane bridge was not big enough to handle increasing traffic. A second span of three lanes was approved and then completed in 1973; this is the northern bridge, which generally carries traffic westbound, though this can change during summer, when one of the lanes is turned over to eastbound drivers. This can be a bit confusing to newcomers to the bridge, but just follow the hundreds of orange traffic cones and barrels and marker lights, and it will all make sense. The view of the bay from the top of the bridge (about 190 feet up) is epic, especially when the waters are teeming with sailboats and massive cargo ships.

Ironically, even though the bridge was designed (and expanded) to allow for smooth travel between the Eastern and Western Shores, it often serves as a congestion point for traffic. This is because the multiple lanes of traffic (three or four lanes) on either side of the bridge must narrow to two or three, and on summer holiday weekends the backups can go on for miles. Inclement weather can also affect bridge traffic, and the winds can be quite strong at the bridge's summit. There is one toll plaza, located on the eastbound lanes of Route 50 on the Western Shore; the toll is $6.

Some drivers cannot deal with the height and openness of the bridge; the **Maryland Transportation Authority** (www.maryland.baybridge.gov) offers to connect these drivers with a private service to help them get across the span.

and head for the porch) and casual, continental dinners in the deep red dining room.

Just a couple of houses away is the lovely **Barlett Pear Inn** (28 S. Harrison St., 410/770-3300, www.bartlettpearinn.com, Wed.-Sun. 5:30pm-10pm), an inn that also happens to have a well-rated restaurant that serves tapas and entrées made with seafood and meat from local farms in a simply decorated room with a nice fireplace. There's live jazz and half-priced cocktails every other Thursday, and cooking classes every few weeks, too.

Those looking for a more relaxed dining experience for breakfast or lunch should head to **The Soda Foundation at Hills** (30 E. Dover St., 410/822-9751, www.hillssodafountain.com, Mon.-Fri. 8am-3pm, Sat. 9am-1pm), a 1950s-inspired diner in a great location: the very back of the Hill's Drug Store. Local reviewers have praised the side dishes from onion petals to french fries; there's are also fairly traditional frittatas, pancakes, burgers, and sandwiches. Try to grab a seat at the lunch counter and order a milk shake with your meal for the ultimate retro experience.

At the Tidewater Inn, the recently remodeled **Hunters' Tavern** (101 E. Dover St., 410/822-1300 or 800/237-8775, www.tidewater-inn.com, breakfast daily 7am-10:30am, lunch daily 11:30am-2pm, dinner daily 5pm-9pm, Sun. brunch 10am-2pm) features (not surprisingly) many dishes based on local seafood and produce; eating on their brick patio, near the outdoor fireplace, is strongly recommended.

Hotels

There are a variety of lodging options in Easton, but staying in the historic downtown area is ideal. In ascending order of size, here are three very different places to lay your head during your trip. First is the charming little **Bishop's House Bed & Breakfast** (214 Goldsborough St., 410/820-7290 or 800/223-7290, www.bishopshouse.com, $185-195), which is a well-restored and immaculate 1880s Victorian home just a couple of blocks from the center of town in a quiet residential neighborhood. There are five guest rooms, a full breakfast spread, and bicycles (and helmets) available for guests to borrow.

Just up the road is the much larger and more elegant **Inn at 202 Dover** (202 E. Dover St., 866/450-7600, www.innat202dover.com, $289-500), which also has five rooms, though four of these are suite-sized (and feature decor themes like Asia, England, and France). The inn is a former mansion, built in 1874, and has a sense of solidity and luxury, including a wonderful conservatory room. There's also a full gourmet restaurant in the home.

Last, and certainly not least, is the **Tidewater Inn** (101 E. Dover St., 410/822-1300 or 800/237-8775, www.tidewaterinn.com, $180-325). This full-service (and recently redone) hotel has 98 guest rooms and suites in a variety of configurations, as well as meeting facilities. The very good Hunters' Tavern, also newly remodeled, is here too.

Information
Visitors Center

Stop in at the **Talbot County Visitors Center** (11 S. Harrison St., 410/770-8000, www.tourtalbot.org, Mon.-Fri 8:30am-5pm, Sat. 9am-1pm) to get a map and some quick orientation to historic

Easton. You can also find out about an array of other towns and attractions in Talbot County here.

Media

Easton has one daily newspaper, the *Star-Democrat,* which covers much of the news of the mid-shore area and publishes a pretty substantial Sunday edition. The *Tidewater Times* is a small Shore-themed monthly magazine featuring essays and news of the community. There are two radio stations here: **WCEI 96.7 FM** (adult contemporary) and **WKHZ 1460 AM,** a Top 40 station.

Getting There and Around
Getting There

Traveling by car is your best bet to get to Easton, which is about 70 miles south and east of Baltimore (it's about a 1.5-hour drive). From Baltimore, leave town and drive south to I-97, toward Annapolis, and U.S. Routes 50 and 301. Cross the Chesapeake Bay Bridge, and continue on U.S. 50 south; turn right on Md. Route 331, which is Dover Road, and you'll soon end up right in the center of town (Easton has a good bit of sprawl around the highway; don't worry about the profusion of fast-food restaurants and gas stations you see on the way in). **Greyhound** (www.greyhound.com) busses run from Baltimore (2110 Haines St., 410/752-7682) to Easton as well; the drop-off in Easton (8359 Ocean Gateway/Rte. 50, 410/822-3333) is at a gas station and convenience store about two miles from historic downtown Easton. If you'd like to travel between Easton and St. Michaels, or all across this part of the Eastern Shore, there's the **MUST** (Maryland Upper Shore Transit, 866/330-MUST, www.mustbus.org) bus, but be aware that MUST has limited pickup and drop-off points and runs only during daylight hours.

Getting Around

Once you've made it to downtown Easton and parked your car, you can spend the day on foot exploring the historic buildings, shops, and eateries, and then maybe taking in a show that night at the Avalon. There are lots of other things to do outside of town (like the Pickering Creek Audubon Center) that will require a car, but it's easy to spend the whole trip just strolling through Easton.

ST. MICHAELS

Fifteen minutes west of Easton—and even farther from civilization—is St. Michaels, a much smaller town (it refers to itself as a village) right on the Miles River. St. Michaels avoided a nocturnal bombardment by the British during the War of 1812 through an ingenious trick; residents hung lanterns in trees and ship rigging, which led the English gunners to aim away from the darkened town. Having escaped that peril, the town has gone on to become a major destination for weekend getaways and upscale travelers; the Inn at Perry Cabin is an Orient Express hotel and the most exclusive resort hotel on the Eastern Shore. There are also lots of fine dining options, bed-and-breakfasts, and charming little shops and stores—leading St. Michaels to be dubbed "The Hamptons of the Chesapeake Bay," which has not thrilled all of the town's residents.

Sights

★ Chesapeake Bay Maritime Museum

This sprawling campus and working boatyard is one of the few heritage museums to live up to its mission: you'll be able to walk past (and maybe sail aboard) working boats, learn about life as a waterman, and chart the history of modern-day (and pre-European settler) civilization on the fertile bay. There are year-round demonstrations, classes, and lectures, which let guests get a real feel (and, sometimes, smell) of the fishing life. The sound of saws, planes, and hammers means that sailors, carpenters, and shipwrights are at work in the boatyard restoring classic old vessels or improving newer ones. Think of the **Chesapeake Bay Maritime Museum** (213 N. Talbot St., 410/745-2916, www.cbmm.org, Jun. 1-Aug. 31, daily 9am-6pm, reduced winter hours, $13 adult, $6 child, $10 senior) as a real-life Colonial Williamsburg without the phony costumes or accents; these are real people who make themselves available to talk about their lives and tools and boats. At the Waterman's Wharf, a re-creation of a typical crabbing shanty, visitors can see (and try) the tools used to capture crabs, eels, and other edible aquatic life. This museum complex is a living tribute to the traditions of the bay and the people who have made their homes here for centuries, and well worth a lengthy visit. (Kids will love it, too.)

★ Skipjack Tours

The lure of the water can be strong at places like St. Michaels, so if you want to experience firsthand what it's like to be a bay waterman, you're in luck. Skipjacks are sail-powered oyster-dredging boats, about 50 feet in length, that covered the waters of the bay in the 19th and 20th centuries. Today, there are only a few skipjacks that continue to harvest oysters from the bay. There are two working skipjacks that take out passengers: the **H.M.** *Krentz* (410/745-6080, www.oystercatcher.com, Apr.-Nov. two-hour sails 11am-1pm, 2pm-4pm, 5:30pm-7:30pm, $35 adult, $15 child) in St. Michaels and the *Rebecca T. Ruark* (410/829-3976, www.skipjack. org, two-hour sails Mon.-Fri. 11am-1pm and 6pm-8pm, Sat.-Sun. 11am-1pm, 2pm-4pm, and 6pm-8pm, $30 adult, $15 child) a brief drive south in Tilghman. Both are old vessels, but the *Ruark* is the more ancient mariner, as she was first built in 1886; the *Krentz* was launched in 1955. Both ships offer two-hour sails, where the captains regale visitors with tales of life on the water and the difficulty of making a living as an oysterman, and even let passengers do some manual labor, including dredging up oysters. These are working oyster boats, so don't plan on donning your dress whites and navy blazers for these excursions. The *Krentz* departs from the Chesapeake Bay Maritime Museum, located at 213 N. Talbot Street in St. Michaels. In tiny Tilghman, the *Rebecca T. Ruark* is docked at Dogwood Harbor (look for the skipjack with the "29" sign on the rigging).

Restaurants

The dining options at St. Michaels run the gamut from no-frills crab houses to award-winning gourmet meals, all within an easy walk from one another. On the waterfront, there are several large restaurants that cater to both locals and tourists; if you're looking for a big pile of steamed crabs, try the outdoor deck at the **St. Michaels Crab and Steak House** (305 Mulberry St., 410/745-3737, www.stmichaelscrabhouse.com, Thurs.-Tues. 11am-10pm). If you're not in the mood for cracking crabs, the seafood dishes at chef Michael Rork's waterfront **Town Dock Restaurant** (125 Mulberry St., 410/745-5577, www.towndockrestaurant.com, Mon.-Thurs. 11:30am-9pm, Fri.-Sat. 11:30am-10pm, Sun. 11am-9pm) are a big hit. The town's perennially top-rated (by residents, visitors, and regional media) restaurant is the romantic and rustic yet modern **208 Talbot** (208 N. Talbot St., 410/745-3838, www.208talbot.com, Wed.-Thurs. and Sun. 5pm-9pm, Fri.-Sat. 5pm-10pm), a very upscale gourmet restaurant that, while dedicated to superlative food (like fresh fish and steaks), is still a relatively laid-back operation.

Hotels

The gorgeous sunsets, the tranquil waters, the languid pace—all the things that make St. Michaels such a popular getaway—mean that there are a number of lodging options here, from over a dozen bed-and-breakfasts to world-class resorts. And there's one place to stay here that makes everything else seem like an old cot in a leaky tent: the **Inn at Perry Cabin** (308 Watkins Ln., 410/745-2200 or 800/722-2949, www.perrycabin.com, $375-770). This opulent retreat is centered around a sprawling, bright-white manor house right on the waters of the Miles River. There are more than 80 rooms, ranging from the merely wonderful to the unbelievably grand; there's also the Linden Spa here. Operated by the luxe Orient Express chain of exclusive hotels, the Inn at Perry Cabin is a lure for wealthy getaway couples, wedding parties, and anyone who wants to experience one of the best hotels in the United States.

Slightly smaller and less grand, but still wonderful, is the

20-room **Five Gables Inn & Spa** (209 N. Talbot St, 410/745-0100 or 877/466-0100, www.fivegables.com, $195-445). There are two kinds of standard rooms and two types of suites scattered throughout the four-house complex that makes up the Five Gables. There's also an Aveda spa on premises, plus a heated indoor pool.

There are lots of cozy little B&Bs throughout St. Michaels as well, usually in historic homes dating back to the late 18th century. One is **Dr. Dodson House** (200 Cherry St., 410/745-3691, www.drdodsonhouse.com, $250-275), a federal-style brick house with wide two-story porches and only three rooms (two with wood-burning fireplaces, one with an electric model) and a stellar reputation. It's just a single house away from the waterfront, and all of the shops and eateries of St. Michaels are an easy walk from here.

Information
Visitors Center
St. Michaels doesn't have a major visitors center, so stop at the **Talbot County Visitors Center** (11 S. Harrison St., 410/770-8000, www.tourtalbot.org, Mon.-Fri. 8:30am-5pm, Sat. 9am-1pm) in Easton to pick up some brochures and get any information you may need—though St. Michaels is so small, getting lost or confused is rather difficult. You could also visit the tiny **St. Michaels Museum at St. Mary's Square** (St. Mary's Square, 410/745-9561, May.-Oct. Fri. and Sun. 1pm-4pm, Sat. 10am-4pm) for a walking map of the town and answers to any questions you may have.

Media
St. Michaels gets most of its media from the surrounding larger cities; the Easton-published *Star-Democrat* covers the mid-shore area.

Getting There and Around
Getting There
You'll need a car to get to St. Michaels—or a boat. By car, it's an 80-mile trip (which will take about one hour and 50 minutes); leave Baltimore and take I-97 toward Annapolis, then U.S. Routes 50 and 301. Cross the Chesapeake Bay Bridge, and continue on U.S. 50 south; turn right on Md. Route 331, which is Dover Road, and you'll soon drive through Easton. Stop here to get information at the Talbot County Visitors Center before heading to St. Michaels. Take Bay Street (Route 33) west; it will turn into St. Michaels Road.

It's possible to take a **Greyhound** (www.greyhound.com) bus from Baltimore (2110 Haines St., 410/752-7682) to Easton (8359 Ocean Gateway/Rte. 50, 410/763-8090) and then catch a **MUST** (Maryland Upper Shore Transit, 866/330-6878, www.mustbus.org) bus to St. Michaels, but be aware that the MUST line has limited pickup and drop-off points and runs only during daylight hours.

You can pretty much abandon your car once you reach St. Michaels, as everything is a short walk from everything else. If you want to explore the region a bit more, you will need to drive or hire a boat. The skipjack *Rebecca T. Ruark* is southwest of St. Michaels in the even-smaller town of Tilghman, about a 12-mile, 25-minute drive west and south on Maryland Route 33.

Background

The Setting 274

History 276

Government and Economy 280

People and Culture 285

The Setting

The waters that lap gently against the seawalls of Baltimore's Inner Harbor are those of the Patapsco River; the city rose on three small towns built here, where the Patapsco joins with the Jones Falls, grows larger, and travels some 12 miles to the legendary Chesapeake Bay. The land rises quickly to the north, as you head away from the harbor. The bounty of the bay and ease of sea transport led to Baltimore's industrial boom, which defined the city's waterfront landscape until only recently. Much of the area outside Baltimore is still relatively underdeveloped, and north and northwest of the city are vast rolling hillsides and forests, as well as sprawling estates, horse and agricultural farms, and equestrian centers.

The neighborhoods of Baltimore are as varied as its citizens, ranging from 250-year-old waterfront communities to historic, European-inspired circles and parks to modern condos along the harbor. Much of Baltimore has benefited from the resurgence that began in the mid-1980s and recently enjoyed a second burst of construction, renovation, and popularity. But right next to many of the neighborhoods you'll visit are areas that haven't benefited from the city's good fortunes, and some of the city's greatest hidden treasures are located in areas best not visited after dark.

GEOGRAPHY AND CLIMATE

Baltimore is in roughly the north-central part of Maryland; it is some 130 miles from the eastern edge of the state (which lies on the Atlantic Ocean). The city curls around the broad Patapsco River, giving it the feel of being close to the ocean, rather than a riverfront metropolis. Much of downtown Baltimore is a mere 33 feet above sea level, yet despite being at the terminus of several small rivers, flooding is very rare here, unless a series of natural events manage to coincide (like, say, a hurricane arriving at high tide, which happened in 2003; it was the worst flooding in 70 years).

Baltimore covers about 91 square miles; 11 of those are water. (In contrast, Washington DC takes up only 68 square miles.) In the western and northwestern part of the city, you'll notice a sudden increase in elevation; that's where the taller Piedmont Plateau meets the lower Atlantic Coastal Plain. Several small streams (called "runs" and "falls" here) wind through parts of the city, ultimately ending at the Inner Harbor. Most of these are hidden by modern construction or rerouted by channels, including the Jones Falls, which runs parallel to President Street on the east side of downtown.

Downtown Baltimore's terrain is relatively flat, but if you head north on foot, you'll really notice the rapid rise. It's generally a very

walkable town (as ranked by some pedestrian advocacy groups), **275**
though the distances between attractions and destinations can be
a bit daunting, and occasionally will involve heading through economically depressed neighborhoods.

There are four distinct seasons in Baltimore, with each offering
the best (and worst) of its weather. Springs can be magnificent, as
can autumns. Be aware that summers can be fantastically hot and
humid (the average temperature is more than 88°F from June to
August, with July's average reaching 91°F). Winters start mild, but
can occasionally get very cold, and there's generally one major blizzard each year, usually in February. The city gets about 21 inches
of snow a year, but it often comes in one single storm. Rainstorms
are common—it rains about 40 inches a year in Baltimore—and
sometimes spring up unexpectedly, along with lots of lightning
and thunder, but generally do not last long.

ENVIRONMENTAL ISSUES

A visitor to 1930s Baltimore would have been treated to a pun-
gent smorgasbord of smokes, smudges, acrid odors, and toxic sub-
stances, not to mention the danger of a pre-OSHA world in which
industrial accidents were common and deadly. The very industries
that built the city in scope, scale, and wealth were also contributing
to the eventual health crises faced by its citizens, land, and water.
Steel mills, chromium plants, and chemical facilities—all of which
needed to be near the waters of the Inner Harbor, or needed the
water itself—lined Baltimore's shores for miles. Many of those factories are closed now, and much of what industry still operates near
the harbor is much less environmentally damaging. But the echoes
of those older days are still visible along the waterfront, and in the
poor health patterns suffered by the city's older residents, many of
whom spent decades working in those plants.

Ironically, the economic decline that hit the city starting in the
1960s did have one long-term benefit: It slowed down, and even
ceased, production at a lot of these factories. As cheaper overseas
facilities began to lure business away, Baltimore's once mighty operations shut down and laid off workers—terrible for the economic
health of the citizens and city, but a relief to the people's bodies, and
the surrounding water and air. Now, those industrial sites are being
removed and replaced with high-end hotels, condominiums, and
apartment towers, and the waterfront is being transformed once
again by new construction. Even with the reduction in local sources
of air and water pollution, summers in Baltimore can put a strain
on people prone to respiratory issues with high heat, humidity, and
ozone levels. Code Red Heat Alerts and Air Quality Action Days
are declared by state environmental officials; information can be
found at www.mde.state.md.us.

As far as the environmental impact of all the new construction, the best way to describe it would be "gradually improving." Many of the modern skyscrapers and projects around the city have a few environmental, energy-saving features, but there are only a handful of truly forward-thinking buildings in town. Construction projects by Johns Hopkins Hospital and the University of Maryland, Baltimore are meeting some LEED (Leadership in Energy and Environmental Design) standards, and a new hotel on President Street (Fairfield Inn & Suites) is the city's first LEED-certified hotel.

History

17TH AND 18TH CENTURIES

In 1608, when the English explorer Captain John Smith made his first voyage up the Chesapeake Bay to explore the largely unknown lands of what is now Maryland, he found that various Native American tribes had been living and working around the waters of the Patapsco River for tens of thousands of years, drawn by the area's fertile land and abundant animal and aquatic life. Smith met many Native Americans, sometimes with violent results as his party was attacked, but he also procured supplies and information from the more peaceful tribes he encountered. His reports back to England eventually led to European colonization and agricultural endeavors in the region, and helped lead to the founding of the Port of Baltimore, at Locust Point (which lies between Federal Hill and Fort McHenry) in 1706, in part to ship tobacco back to Europe.

Baltimore Town, the first proper European settlement in North America to bear the name Baltimore (a tribute to Cecilius Calvert, the second Baron Baltimore), was established in 1729. Baltimore is the name of a town in County Cork, Ireland; it means "town of the big house." This outpost would eventually merge with two other small settlements, Jones Town and Fell's Point, to create a much larger Baltimore Town. During the American Revolution, Baltimore's crucial role as a provider of soldiers, matériel, and ships made it a critical spoke in the burgeoning American industrial machine. On December 20, 1776, the Second Continental Congress met in Baltimore, as Philadelphia was endangered by approaching British troops. This made Baltimore the nation's capital for a three-month period. Following independence, Baltimore City continued to grow, and was incorporated on December 31, 1796; the burgeoning city was the nation's third largest at that point.

Though Baltimore escaped the Revolutionary War unscathed, the War of 1812 would prove far more perilous. Fresh from their successful destruction of the fledgling nation's capital in Washington DC in 1814, a flotilla of warships and troop carriers had sailed up the Chesapeake Bay and the Patapsco River, bound for Baltimore itself. The only thing that stood in their way was a series of sunken vessels, designed to block their entrance into the city's harbor, and a star-shaped defensive outpost called Fort McHenry. The fort's defenders held their ground despite a monstrous bombardment by the British, inspiring Francis Scott Key—held prisoner in a ship of that flotilla—to pen "The Star-Spangled Banner," which became the U.S. national anthem in 1931.

The Civil War affected the city's fortunes in different ways. The first shots fired of the war—even before the attack on Fort Sumter in South Carolina—were aimed by Baltimorean Confederate sympathizers at Union troops traveling by train through the city. Baltimore's anti-Union feelings ran deep, and slavery was still common in the city and outlying farms, estates, and plantations that made up much of rural Maryland. Those shots, fired by civilians, guaranteed the placement of a Union garrison in the city; the garrison's cannons still stand today atop Federal Hill, pointed at downtown just as they were in 1862. The war made many fortunes in the city, from those of railroad tycoons like John Work Garrett to merchants like Johns Hopkins, an abolitionist Quaker who would take the money he had made from supplying and supporting Union forces during the war and create a university and hospital that would bear his name and establish his legacy.

20TH CENTURY TO THE PRESENT

With the exception of the devastating February 1904 fire that destroyed 70 square blocks and more than 1,500 buildings, the first part of the 20th century was very good to Baltimore. Ships, steel, and goods that passed through the port—as well as other specialty products from furniture to crops—brought jobs and wealth to the city, which expanded into the surrounding countryside quickly, overtaking what had been country estates with blocks of row houses.

In 1948, Baltimore made a decision that would ultimately prove devastating, though at the time, it seemed shrewd. Baltimore City voted to stop annexing land from Baltimore County, which surrounds the city, and settle down to enjoy its growth, while the county remained rural and relatively less wealthy. When the new economy of the 1950s began to take hold, and people could move out to the suburbs with relative ease, that decision to remain separate from the county would result in the urban decay that is still

The Great Baltimore Fire

On a cold February morning in 1904, a small fire broke out in a downtown Baltimore warehouse. When it was finally extinguished nearly 30 hours later, much of the center of the city was gone; some 70 blocks were reduced to rubble, and more than 1,500 buildings were destroyed. Only one life was lost, but the city was in shock—some 35,000 people had no workplace to go to, it was the dead of winter, and hope was in short supply. But under Mayor Robert McLane, Baltimore quickly rebounded and used the destruction of the city's downtown as an opportunity to remake the town into a modern metropolis. Streets were widened, a new sewer system was installed, and fire-prevention measures were instituted in the new construction to help ensure that the city would never again burn so easily. One of the few downtown buildings to survive still stands today: head to the old Alex. Brown building (it's now a Chevy Chase Bank) at 135 East Baltimore Street. Touted as being "fire-proof" when it was completed in 1901, three years later it lived up to the builder's claims.

present today. In 1950, during the peak of the city's health and wealth, Baltimore's population was about 950,000; today, there are 621,000 people who call Baltimore City home; and vast parts of the city contain unoccupied row houses and dilapidated commercial and retail buildings. Unlike in many other metropolitan areas, Baltimore City is an independent jurisdiction from Baltimore County; when residents (and their taxes) left, the county grew prosperous (2007-2011 median household income: $65,411), while the city withered (2007-2011 median household income: $40,100).

The latter part of the 20th century marked grim times for Baltimore. Long-simmering resentment held by the city's large African American population toward institutional and cultural discrimination and segregation in Baltimore was brought to a head following the April 1968 assassination of Dr. Martin Luther King Jr. Rioting broke out and lasted for eight days; when it was finally over, some parts of the city were severely damaged (and remain so today), and race relations were permanently altered. The steady stream of middle-class residents (both Caucasian and African American) moving out to the county became a flood; parts of the city damaged by rioters were left in disrepair; and the power structure of Baltimore began to shift. This shift, along with economic depression, led to a population and capital drain that nearly mortally wounded the city. But in 1980, the opening of the new Inner Harbor and Harborplace—built on the former site of underused piers, empty lots, and shacks—signaled the "Baltimore Renaissance" and showed the United States that the city wasn't going to abide an ignominious death. Baltimore elected its first African American mayor, Kurt Schmoke, in 1987, and its first female mayor, Sheila

Dixon (also African American), in 2006. Despite a grim toll from drugs and poverty in many city neighborhoods, over the past two decades the city has made constant, if not always large, gains economically. Baltimore is now a majority African American city; that group makes up about 65 percent of the population, though African Americans also make up much of the ranks of the working poor and economically disadvantaged. That said, some prominent African Americans, both past and present—like late Supreme Court Justice Thurgood Marshall and recent Presidential Medal of Freedom winner Dr. Ben Carson, the prominent Johns Hopkins pediatric neurosurgeon—have called Baltimore home.

Baltimore has been in the headlines in the past decade for the achievements of hometown figures, like Little Italy native and California congresswoman Nancy D'Alesandro Pelosi, who became the first female Speaker of the U.S. House of Representatives. In the world of sports, the Baltimore Ravens of the NFL won the 2012 and 2000 Super Bowls, and local swimming phenom Michael Phelps became "the greatest Olympic athlete of all time" (his trophy's words) when he grabbed six medals at the 2012 London Olympics, bringing his grand total to 22, including the Olympic-record eight gold medals he earned at the 2008 Summer Games in Beijing. Another locally born sports star, NBA player Carmelo Anthony, has taken home his own gold medals at the London Games and the Beijing Games as part of the champion U.S. basketball team. The city has also gained a reputation as a popular, offbeat getaway destination.

Baltimore Today

The Baltimore you see today—abuzz with new office, hotel, and residential towers, and construction around the waterfront—is a concrete and steel monument to the work of the politicians and developers who managed to turn a wan, dirty, industrial harbor area into a place where exclusive developers like the Four Seasons and the Ritz-Carlton have erected luxury buildings. Constructed on the cornerstone formed by the wild success of Harborplace and the Inner Harbor, this second phase of Baltimore's rebirth has spread east, filling the land between the Inner Harbor and Fell's Point known as Harbor East, and to the south, wrapping around the water from Federal Hill to Locust Point.

On the real estate front, Baltimore has benefited from being close enough to other, larger, more expensive cities to be considered a real option for residence. During the real estate boom of the late 1990s and early 2000s, people priced out of nearby Washington DC began to discover and move to Baltimore. The charm and relative affordability of historic, lively neighborhoods brought young upscale residents into the city, sometimes pricing out the working-class folks who had helped maintain the neighborhood in sour economic times. New condominiums and luxury townhomes began to spring up all over town, a welcome sight after years of hemorrhaging population and boarded-up row houses. One peculiar aspect of old Baltimore that remains in action today is "The Block," a stretch of Baltimore Street east of downtown (and next to Baltimore City Police headquarters) that was once the scene of burlesque shows by legendary Baltimorean Blaze Starr. Today, most of the action is far seedier, and it's not a place to be at night. A few remnants of the old Block remain, but now it's mostly strip joints, adult bookstores, and a few greasy take-out restaurants.

Since the 2009 recession, Baltimore has had the expected higher unemployment rates, increased layoffs, and government furloughs. But the crisis has also led to a small but significant gain: While the surrounding and usually growing counties saw fewer new residents, the city's population grew by a few hundred people. This may not seem like much, but we're talking about a city that has faced 50-plus years of population decline. Bringing new families to Baltimore has been the cornerstone of Mayor Stephanie Rawlings-Blake's administration, and Latinos and Hispanics are the fastest-growing demographic, representing 4.2 percent of the population (25,960 people) in 2010—more than double its percentage in 2000. With this influx came several awful hate crimes in 2010, and, sadly, many immigrants who were afraid to go to the police for help. But an executive order signed by the mayor forbidding police from asking residents about their immigration status (in other words, leave that job to the federal agency that oversees illegal immigrants) appears to have quelled some of these fears, and the city has implemented several social programs to help ease tensions and make new Spanish-speaking residents feel more welcome.

Despite continuing issues with crime and drugs, the gains made by Baltimore in the past two decades have given residents a better and improved feeling about the future of this settlement on the shores of the Patapsco River.

Government and Economy

Even though the state capital lies a half-hour south in Annapolis, and much of the Washington DC-area suburbs are home to the state's wealthiest areas, Baltimore City's government (as well as that of Baltimore County) still carries an awful lot of clout around the state. This is due to the region's population, industry, and voting power; the area is also the recipient of much of the state's financial aid, owing to the tough conditions that still exist throughout the city.

Baltimore's economic landscape has undergone a series of tough changes this century. The once-mighty industry that helped drive the city—the port, the railroads, and the steel mills—has waned substantially, and now Baltimore's main employment sector is health care. Still, the city's unemployment rate hovers around 9-11 percent, about three percentage points higher than it was before the recession and a much higher rate than the surrounding suburbs.

GOVERNMENT

Baltimore City's current governmental structure consists of a mayor, who exerts a great deal of power, and a City Council, which is somewhat less able to wield its might. There are 14 council members from districts across the city and a council president. Both the mayor and the council members are elected for four-year terms, and the mayor has a three-term limit; council members have no term limits. Baltimore City's size means it also has plentiful representation in the state government's House of Delegates and Senate. The state legislature meets for only 90 days each year in Annapolis, beginning in January.

Mayor William Donald Schaefer (1971-1987) was cited as a big, plain-spoken reason for Baltimore's renaissance during his time period. Much of the credit for the more recent resurgence in the city went to (and was claimed by) Mayor Martin O'Malley, who took office in 1999. Becoming the Caucasian mayor of a majority African American city was no easy task; a confluence of political events and the split of the African American vote put O'Malley into City Hall. Though a lot of the construction that began during his term was envisioned and approved during Mayor Kurt Schmoke's administration, the city gained a renewed sense of pride, possibility, and hope during the O'Malley years. The homicide rate went down for the first time in years, though it remains depressingly high.

O'Malley became governor of Maryland in 2004, leaving City Hall to his successor, City Council President Sheila Dixon. In 2006, she was elected as the city's first female mayor, and the reviews during her first elected term were generally positive, though she did have a history of questionable dealings. That all came to a head in 2009, when Dixon was found guilty of embezzlement for using about $600 worth of gift cards intended for needy families. She later pled guilty to a subsequent perjury charge. The terms for her probation included resigning from office, performing 500 hours of community service, and giving about $45,000 to charity.

Following Dixon's 2010 resignation, City Council President Stephanie Rawlings-Blake succeeded her as mayor; she finished Dixon's term, then decisively won her own mayoral election in 2011. The cornerstone of her administration has been an initiative that would add 10,000 new families to Baltimore's residential base in the next decade, turning around the city's fifty-plus years of population decline. Her plans to entice families to move here include lowering the property tax and repairing dilapidated schools. Among Rawlings-Blake's other initiatives are "Vacants to Value," which would rehab the vacant homes that plague the city's less tourist-friendly neighborhoods.

Rawlings-Blake has been a big supporter of the Grand Prix of Baltimore, an IndyCar racing event that was supposed to showcase the city while giving it a much-needed economic boost. Unfortunately, the Grand Prix—already held for three of its planned five years—hasn't quite been a success: It's never reached its projected economic impact or found a consistent sponsor, and, residents and businesspeople who live and work downtown, where the race essentially shuts down streets for a week or so, have expressed mixed feelings about whether it should continue. In what seems to be a likely last straw, the race was officially canceled for 2014 and 2015 due to scheduling conflicts. Although the Grand Prix could restart in 2016, Rawlings-Blake has told the *Baltimore Sun* that there aren't any talks in the works yet.

ECONOMY

Baltimore's fortunes were first made on the waters of the Port of Baltimore, as tobacco and other goods from the New World were shipped back to Europe. Merchants, shipbuilders, and suppliers began to set up shop as a young United States grew, and as industrial advances were made, Baltimore was seemingly always ready to take up the next big going concern. Bethlehem Steel and Bethlehem Shipyards were two enormous sibling factories just outside the city that employed some 35,000 people during their heyday in the mid-20th century; the Port of Baltimore was one of the busiest in the nation for more than a century. But with the economic downturns that began in the 1970s, being a solely industrial city was a death sentence. Baltimore's factories, mills, and eventually its neighborhoods began to empty, sag, and close.

What saved Baltimore? Health care—and the Inner Harbor. The growth of health care as an industry in the United States gave Baltimore hope that it wouldn't slide into further ruin, as it had watched so many other "rust belt" cities do. And the presence of Johns Hopkins Hospital (and what is now Johns Hopkins Health System)—perhaps the planet's most famous and renowned medical center, and the 2013-14 #1-ranked "Honor Roll" hospital on the *U.S. News and World Report* Best Hospitals list, an honor that Hopkins has held for 22 of the publications 24 years—meant that Baltimore had an established, respected, and wealthy brand. Today, Johns Hopkins (through the health system, the university, and associated research and academic institutions) employs more than

53,350 people in Maryland; it's the largest private employer in the state, and claims to add about $9.98 billion to Maryland's economy. There's another major hospital in the area, too: the University of Maryland Medical System (UMMS), which employs about 15,000 across Maryland. And though many of the jobs Hopkins and UMMS provide are solid, high-salary positions, there hasn't been a direct replacement of the well-paying union jobs lost when the industrial sector collapsed.

In addition to Hopkins, Baltimore (and the surrounding area) has a few other major employers and well-capitalized companies, including mutual fund company T. Rowe Price, energy and power titan Constellation Energy, and spice-maker McCormick.

Health Care, Medical Research, and Biotechnology

Americans spend about $2.6 trillion on health care each year, and Baltimore's medical institutions have gained a large share of that by earning a national reputation as some of the best in the country. Leading the way is the behemoth Johns Hopkins University and Johns Hopkins Hospital, which have secured huge amounts of federal funding (about $1.88 billion in 2011, the most in the nation by about $930 million) in the past, in addition to generating income on their own. Both Hopkins and UMMS have completed large expansion and construction projects—Hopkins on the east side of town, and UMMS on the west. These projects have helped spur offshoot residential and commercial development or encouraged renovation of nearby neighborhoods. There are big challenges ahead, though, mainly because of the Congress-approved budget that requires the National Institutes of Health (NIH), one of Hopkins largest federal funders, to cut $1.55 billion from its budget. As a result, NIH is giving 640 fewer research grants, which could slow down research for cures and cause leading scientists to go abroad, according to those in the industry. As of 2013, despite the fact that Maryland's U.S. Senator Barbara Mikulski; Dr. Francis Collins, director of NIH; and Hopkins deans and executives came together at Hopkins' Charlotte R. Bloomberg Children's Center to protest the cuts, funds had not been restored.

A number of specialized research centers call Baltimore home; most notable of these are the city's National Institutes of Health facilities and the University of Maryland School of Medicine's Institute of Human Virology, which was founded and is directed by the famed AIDS researcher Dr. Robert Gallo. There are a number of other major hospitals and health systems in the region as well, including MedStar and LifeBridge, which each operate several hospitals, as well as Mercy Medical Center and the Greater Baltimore Medical Center.

Education

Baltimore City and the surrounding area are home to 15 colleges and universities of wildly different sizes, scopes, and missions. And just as in health care, Johns Hopkins is the big kahuna in town; the university (enrollment is about 5,150 undergraduates) is one of the nation's best, attracting students from across the country and the globe. The university's reach extends beyond its Homewood campus to other schools and facilities across the region, as well as overseeing the School of Medicine, one of America's best and most prestigious medical schools.

There are a total of about 120,000 full- and part-time college students across the greater Baltimore region. They attend a wide variety of schools, from small, private liberal arts colleges like Goucher and Loyola to state schools like Towson University and University of Maryland, Baltimore County. In between these ends of the enrollment scale, there are two historically African American colleges (Morgan State and Coppin State), the nationally ranked Maryland Institute College of Art and Peabody Institute, plus religious and other private colleges and universities.

Tourism

Baltimore wouldn't be the first place that would spring to mind if one were asked to name a city that depends on—and benefits greatly from—tourism. But ever since the opening of Harborplace, Baltimore has, for a variety of reasons, been a major draw to some of the more than two million people who live in the greater Baltimore metropolitan region. In 2010, Baltimore drew some 21 million visitors—one million more than the previous year, a significant jump given the recession-induced economic woes many people were facing at the time. (In comparison the Magic Kingdom Park at Walt Disney World drew 17 million visitors in 2011.) Those 21 million visitors to Baltimore dropped just over $4.4 billion during their trips, making tourism one of the city's most profitable sectors, though the jobs created by tourism are somewhat seasonal and generally not high-paying. In fact, a lack of hotel rooms downtown had been an issue for years; with the completion of the Hyatt and the Four Seasons and the renovations of several existing buildings, that has been largely addressed. It's a testament to smart urban rejuvenation, good planning, and canny marketing that a city like Baltimore can reap so many benefits from the tourist trade.

People and Culture

DEMOGRAPHICS

In 2007, for the first time since 1960, Baltimore managed to add more residents than it lost; this may not sound like the kind of stat that makes people jump for joy, but it's a moral and policy victory for the city's leaders—and often cited as a real indicator of Baltimore's resurgence.

There were 620,961 residents of Baltimore City in 2010 (the latest official federal stats); women made up 52.9 percent of the population. About 25 percent of the city is under 18 years of age, and 12 percent is over 65.

The city is majority African American (63.7 percent); Caucasians make up 29.6 percent; and the rest is predominantly Latino and Asian. The ratio of African American and Caucasian citizens in Baltimore City is reversed in Baltimore County, a result of the "white flight" from Baltimore City that occurred in the 1960s and 1970s.

The majority of Baltimore's first colonial residents were of English or Irish origin; later, they were joined by Europeans from across the continent. Baltimore's port was second only to New York City's Ellis Island as an intake center for European immigrants in the 19th century; more than two million people may have first set foot in North America by standing on the ground of Locust Point. Accordingly, Baltimore's neighborhoods took on the flavors and cultures of their residents' heritages; Little Italy, as well as Polish, German, Jewish, and Ukrainian enclaves formed around the harbor's neighborhoods.

Over the years, as Baltimore lost a huge chunk of its population, the city took on a slightly underpopulated feel. Even today, it's not a very dense city; you'll never feel like you're in Manhattan, or London, or Beijing as you walk the city's sidewalks and waterfront promenade. Lines form only for the most popular clubs and restaurants, and longtime residents will generally refuse to wait longer than five minutes for anything that doesn't involve a free meal, drink, or concert.

RELIGION

Maryland was founded in part to give persecuted Catholics from England and elsewhere a safe haven to practice their faith, and the nation's first Catholic cathedral and archdiocese were founded in Baltimore. The city's history as a point of immigration, transit, and commerce meant that people of all the major Christian faiths settled here and founded their respective houses of worship,

Deciphering Bawlmerese

Baltimorese (or "Bawlmerese," in Baltimorese) is the accent and manner of speech indigenous to Caucasian working-class Baltimore City residents, who came to the city from places like Poland, Ireland, and, during World War II, America's Deep South. The accent is a unique mix of a southern drawl, an almost Cockney-like pronunciation of certain vowels and mangling of consonants, and a specific canter to speech. Terms like "hon" are frequently used as terms of endearment to family and strangers alike. The accent has become both a point of pride and of contention with Baltimoreans, as newcomers and others will adopt the accent to sometimes mock blue-collar Baltimoreans. Yet there's an entire HonFest in Hampden in each year that draws huge crowds and has a "Best Hon" contest.

This guide may help you understand some of the folks you meet in Baltimore, but be cautious about trying any of it yourself, because a lot of the people who speak with the Baltimore accent don't think they have an accent. So, here's a primer: chop off as many consonants as you can; speak with a tightness in your throat; toss some superfluous "r"s into words that don't have them; and pronounce all "o"s fatly and at the front of the mouth, so they sound like "ouh." Thus, "Maryland" phonetically becomes "Merlin," "wash" becomes "warsh," and "tourist" becomes "terst." Check out more examples at www.baltimorehon.com.

from orthodox Ukrainians to German Lutherans to English Episcopalians. Jews also called Baltimore home, and grand old synagogues are scattered around town. Today, most of the city's residents are either Catholic or Protestant. Many of the city's best-attended churches are those serving the city's African American community, and most of these houses of worship are Baptist or African Methodist Episcopal (AME) churches.

ARTS AND CULTURE

Baltimore is best described as a bit of a cultural Madagascar. Because it was isolated from the truly innovative and exceptional arts scenes and pioneers, and it did not have the strong and well-endowed cultural institutions of major cities, Baltimore took what it could get and proceeded to evolve (or, in some cases, freeze) its own unique cultural scene, independent of much outside influence. That's proven to have been a good thing, in the long run, because with the "discovery" of Baltimore by artists and cultural mavens from New York City and Los Angeles in the past two decades, the city has gained credibility and respect for being a wonderland of offbeat, hidden talent.

But Baltimore also pays respect to venerated art traditions. The city is home to two nationally recognized arts colleges, the Maryland Institute College of Art (for visual artists) and the Peabody Institute (for musicians). There are also the Baltimore

School for the Arts, a special public high school for creative and talented teens that has educated artists and actors like Tupac Shakur, Jada Pinkett Smith, Traci Thoms, Josh Charles, and Lawrence Gilliard Jr. from *The Walking Dead* and *The Wire,* and the new Baltimore Design School, a middle/high school that welcomed its first class of students in 2013 to study mainly architecture, fashion design, and graphic design.

Classical art and music have long been treasured by Baltimore's citizens, be they blue bloods or blue-collar. The Baltimore Symphony Orchestra is well respected and well supported, and there are a variety of smaller companies and societies that perform classics from the Western musical and dance canons. But Baltimoreans like to rock out and dance and rap as well; Baltimore Club is a specific type of dance music with an insane number of beats per minute that will kick all the pretenders off the dance floor.

Culturally, Baltimoreans are an odd mix of North and South. You'll meet a lot of exceedingly polite and well-mannered people in Baltimore; you may also be told to do some things that are not physically possible by irate citizens.

Racial and economic divisions in the city are still prominent. African American Baltimore is a very different place from Caucasian Baltimore. The former exists in its own parts of town and goes to its own churches and social clubs and events, an extension of the paths segregation forced African Americans to go down in order to maintain and grow their own communities. There are a few places in town where people of all races mingle together, including the Inner Harbor.

Caucasian Baltimore is the Baltimore most often portrayed in films and on TV: think of John Waters's movies, rife with large women in tentlike housedresses and beehive hairdos (in 2009, mind you). There's a celebration of Baltimore's "hon" culture (short for "honey," as in, "Hey hon, pass me the crab mallet!"), organized by Hampden's Café Hon restaurant, which hosts HonFest each summer. Some festivalgoers compete in a "Best Hon" contest dressed up in cat's-eye glasses, big hair, and adopting the peculiar accent and dialect spoken by many working-class Baltimoreans of the mid-20th century. Many people who actually speak with a Baltimore accent (dubbed "Bawlmerese") aren't thrilled with their portrayal at these events, even though it is done out of adoration for a genuine city tradition and heritage.

Arts, Crafts, and Folk Traditions

The best place to start learning about Baltimore's cultural history is at the **Maryland Historical Society** (www.mdhs.org), which tracks the growth of the city and its traditions, particularly in crafts like furniture making, for which Baltimore became quite a hot spot in

A Cinematic Tour de Baltimore

Since Barry Levinson's 1982 film *Diner* (or, if you were cooler, John Waters's 1972 *Pink Flamingos*) introduced movie audiences to the peculiarities of Baltimore, the city has been the setting for films and TV shows—both playing itself and standing in for a variety of other cities. HBO's popular show *The Wire* was filmed and set in Baltimore, though local politicians were not thrilled with the show's image of Charm City.

Downtown

The **Hollywood Diner** was the set for Barry Levinson's classic buddy movie *Diner;* it's also been in *Sleepless in Seattle, Tin Men,* and TV's *Homicide: Life on the Street.* No longer an operating diner, the restaurant was moved from Fell's Point (where it was for *Diner*) to Saratoga Street, where it occupies a quiet corner near some parking lots north of City Hall.

Fell's Point

This is where you'll find the stately, if dilapidated, **City Pier** on Thames Street; this building played a police station in *Homicide: Life on the Street.* Doors on the east side of the building still have the words "Baltimore Police" painted on them, while on the right side is a plaque commemorating the show's cast and crew. *Sleepless in Seattle* was shot around the piers at the bottom of Broadway, where the Water Taxi docks, as was *Enemy of the State.* Near the corner of Fleet Street and South Broadway is the former **Copy Cat,** where *The Wire*'s Stringer Bell operated a real copy shop while helping to mastermind a drug cartel.

Mount Vernon

Much of Levinson's *Avalon* was filmed around Howard Street's **Antique Row,** a once-grand retail destination, and many of the antiques seen in *Guarding Tess* came from these shops.

Take a self-guided tour of the grand **Garrett-Jacobs Mansion,** a fantastic 19th-century urban palace; you might recognize its warm, rich interiors from a long list of films, including *Diner, 12 Monkeys,* and *He Said, She Said.*

If you're feeling particularly mondo, head to one of Baltimore's most storied gay bars, **The Drinkery.** It was just outside this venerable establishment that the actor Divine (Glenn Milstead) made cinematic history in *Pink Flamingos,* because this is where the fearless thespian did something far above and beyond the call of...um, "doody."

Hampden

The neighborhood of Hampden has featured prominently in many John Waters films, and "The Avenue" (36th St.) has seen plenty of action in his films: The titular character in 1998's *Pecker* hails from this part of town and the 1988 film *Hairspray* (which begat the musical) was filmed primarily here (the 2007 film version of the musical was shot in Toronto).

Head to the corner of 30th Street and Remington Avenue, just south of Hampden, to find **Charm City Cakes,** baker Duff Goldman's cake shop, featured on the Food Network's *Ace of Cakes.* While you can take pictures outside the imposing stone building, no visitors are allowed and the windows are covered with thick black plastic.

the early 19th century, exporting thousands of pieces of Baltimore **289**
Painted Furniture across the country.

Screen painting is a folk art peculiar to Baltimore; by painting pastoral or nautical scenes onto window screens or screen doors, locals realized they could both jazz up the fronts of their row houses and also keep folks outside from getting too clear a view of what was going on inside. With the proximity and density of row houses back in the early 20th century, these were both welcome discoveries.

To see what some of the city's most intriguing artists are doing, head to the **School 33 Art Center** (www.school33.org), a city-run arts facility in an old school in Federal Hill that exhibits art and provides studios. School 33 has lots of events, fundraisers, and tours throughout the year; the art here can vary from the very mainstream to the very experimental.

The Creative Alliance (www.creativealliance.org) is a popular organization that gets arts, artists, and citizens together to create and explore their respective worlds in new and interesting ways. The Creative Alliance works to preserve local traditions and arts and expose city kids to basic art principles, as well as teach them about Baltimore's art heritage. And it has the coolest reused building in town—the old Patterson movie theater in Highlandtown, just northeast of Canton.

Lately, a number of artist-run galleries and performance spaces have opened around the city, mainly in the Bromo Tower and Station North Arts and Entertainment Districts. Spearheaded by creative people who often hold down other jobs, most of these galleries do not keep regular hours, but they do host some fantastic and well-attended openings and events throughout the year.

Literature

The written word has long been a favorite way for Baltimoreans to express their desires, fears, appreciations, and opinions. The area seems to inspire people to write, perhaps because of the peculiarities of the town and its residents. Baltimore has played a central role in more than a few books; today, the city is the setting for the popular Tess Monaghan series of crime novels by former *Baltimore Sun* reporter Laura Lippman (who happens to be married to former *Baltimore Sun* reporter David Simon, creator of *The Wire*).

Baltimore is also a character in books, often woven into the novels of Pulitzer Prize-winner Anne Tyler, whose *The Accidental Tourist* was made into a film, some of which was shot in Baltimore. Johns Hopkins University's Writing Seminars count among the nation's premier writers' programs and have seen such authors and poets as John Barth, Russell Baker (who was raised in Baltimore), J. M. Coetzee, Howard Nemerov, Robert Stone, Mark Strand, and other luminaries lecture or teach. Novelist Madison Smartt Bell

BACKGROUND
PEOPLE AND CULTURE

teaches at Goucher, and Tom Clancy, whose best-selling novels centering on the derring-do of U.S. armed forces, was a Baltimore native.

As for nonfiction and criticism, there is no more studied or prolific scribe than the Sage of Baltimore, Henry Louis Mencken. During the early 20th century, H. L. Mencken—a writer for the *Sun*—authored innumerable essays and volumes of books opining on everything effecting the state, being, and mind of the American citizen. He enjoyed poking at commonly held "truths" and pointing out what he felt to be idiocy among his fellow Americans; Mencken played a large role in bringing about the 1925 Scopes Trial, which he dubbed the "Monkey Trial," as it made illegal (in Tennessee) the act of teaching evolution. Later examination of his works led to charges of bigotry, though many scholars have weighed his sometimes-cruel words against his always-honorable deeds. A large collection of Mencken's works and letters can be found in the **H. L. Mencken Room and Collection** at the Enoch Pratt Central Library; a trove of Menckenia, numbering nearly 6,000 items, was also acquired in 2007 by Johns Hopkins University for its Sheridan Libraries.

Another famed chronicler is Pulitzer Prize-winner and historian Taylor Branch, who has called Baltimore home for decades. His three-part series, *America in the King Years,* examined civil rights era U.S. history from 1954 to 1965. Branch has won several other prominent awards for his work, including a MacArthur Foundation Fellowship (commonly known as the "genius award").

Baltimore area poets are a small but impressive band. Ogden Nash was a native of Rye, New York, who spent 37 years in Baltimore. Former U.S. poet laureate Lucille Clifton lives just outside Baltimore in nearby Columbia. Fellow poet Elizabeth Spires (a Hopkins alum) teaches at Goucher College north of the city; her husband is Madison Smartt Bell.

Though he died and is buried here, Edgar Allan Poe did not write any of his classic tales of the macabre during the roughly three years he lived in Baltimore; still, the town claims him as one of its own, and the city's NFL team, the Baltimore Ravens, are even named in honor of his most famous work. The team's mascots? Three cartoonish ravens, named Edgar, Allan, and Poe. Yes, really.

Many other authors of note were either born here and moved elsewhere, or spent some formative years here. Pulitzer Prize-winner Upton Sinclair, whose *The Jungle* exposed the realities of the slaughterhouse, is a Baltimore native. Frederick Douglass, born a slave on Maryland's Eastern Shore, escaped from Baltimore to become a free man, abolitionist, and writer; his 1845 autobiography, *Narrative of the Life of Frederick Douglass, An American Slave* is now a classic of American letters. Hard-boiled detective novel scribe Dashiell Hammett was a Maryland native and grew up in

Baltimore, where he later worked as a private dick. Gertrude Stein **291** was a student at Johns Hopkins School of Medicine, but dropped out in 1901 to pursue other, more literary interests. And Leon Uris, best known for the novel *Exodus,* was born and raised in Baltimore.

Music

Perhaps the most famous song in America (after "Happy Birthday") was composed off the shores of Fort McHenry back in 1814, when Francis Scott Key penned "The Star-Spangled Banner." But many other great songs, songwriters, and musicians have gotten their start here or used Baltimore to springboard to bigger and brighter stages, most notably jazz legends Cab Calloway and Billie Holiday. A statue to Holiday was erected some years ago in the city, but because of construction at the installation site, the statue is currently difficult to find and even more difficult to enjoy.

African Americans with Baltimore roots or connections have made a lasting and meaningful impression on American music, beginning with legends like Calloway, Holiday, Eubie Blake (there's a small **Eubie Blake National Jazz Institute and Cultural Center** in midtown that hosts photo exhibitions and jazz performances), Cyrus Chestnut, Bill Frisell, The Orioles, and Chick Webb. Baltimore's Pennsylvania Avenue used to be home to several renowned clubs and venues for African American performers, as segregation prevented them from taking the stage in Caucasian neighborhoods. The Royal Theater was the crown jewel of these venues and known nationwide, though today it's just an empty lot and the rest of Pennsylvania Avenue's once-grand cultural sites are all gone or in massive disrepair. Some contemporary African American artists who've gone on to stardom from the small stage of Baltimore include Toni Braxton, Dru Hill and their former member SisQó, and Mario; local hip-hop artists and DJs who aren't household names but still pack houses around town (and in other parts of the world) include Rod Lee, Blaqstarr, and Ultra Naté. These artists provide a pretty good cross section of what kind of music gets played here; the ubiquitous Baltimore House dance music, with its high-tempo beats, is also easy to find and hear (and feel, with a good bass system).

Baltimore's Southern tinges are revealed in the prevalence of country and bluegrass shows that are a regular occurrence around town. The city's large Irish American population means there are several traditional Irish pubs in town, many of which bring first-class musicians to Baltimore for regular weekend shows. Baltimore has long been a steadfast, head-banging, hard rock town, but has appreciated quirkiness in its musicians as well. One look at the list of rock musicians who hail from Baltimore proves that fact: Tori Amos, David Byrne, John Doe (of the seminal L.A. band X), Greg

Kihn, Gina Schock (drummer of The Go-Go's), and Frank Zappa were all born here, and a more diverse and inspired group would be hard to find. Counting Crows singer Adam Duritz is a Baltimore native, as are the members of the critically acclaimed band Animal Collective.

The independent music scene in Baltimore has drawn some national attention, including coverage from *Rolling Stone* and MTV, in the last five years. The biggest acts (relatively speaking) of this new indie world include the mellow duo Beach House; the folk rock twosome Wye Oak; the groups Dope Body, Loving the Lie, and Roomrunner; rapper Cex; rapper Spank Rock; and Wham City, a musical collective fronted by a talented singer/songwriter/sound-maker named Dan Deacon.

Television and Film

Many Americans first got to know Baltimore through Barry Levinson's 1982 film *Diner,* which told the tale of a group of young men growing up in 1959 Baltimore. The film explored the city's dedication to friendships, class distinctions, football, and the culture of the diner, and is now considered a classic American movie. Then there were those who first learned about Baltimore from John Waters's 1972 *Pink Flamingos,* which chronicled the odd antics and exploits of a massive transvestite named Divine trying to keep her title as "The Filthiest Person Alive." That film showed another side of Baltimore, one that was much stranger, more bizarre, and more unrestrained by the mores of Baltimore society. Both films were honest chronicles of the experiences of Baltimore's residents, though the two couldn't be less alike in subject matter.

More recently, another realistic portrayal of Baltimore drew national and international praise and a devoted (if not vast) following: HBO's *The Wire,* which ran for five seasons and ended in 2008. Created by David Simon, a former *Baltimore Sun* reporter, the show took viewers into the bleak, desperate, and often hopeless world of Baltimore's drug economy, exposing the angels and devils on all sides. The show made local politicians a bit apoplectic, but critics called it the best show on television in the past decade, if not ever. Shot almost entirely in Baltimore, *The Wire* was a regular and beloved presence around town, and the stars of the series were embraced and adored by both upstanding citizens and those whose lives too-closely mirrored those of the criminals on screen. The most well-known local actress may be Felicia "Snoop" Pearson, the young woman with a troubled past who beat a murder conviction and joined *The Wire* in 2004; Pearson was arrested in a Baltimore drug raid and pleaded guilty to conspiracy to sell heroin in 2011. A statement from Simon after the arrest said, "we believe the war on drugs has devolved into a war on the underclass, that in places like

West and East Baltimore, where the drug economy is now the only factory still hiring and where the educational system is so crippled that the vast majority of children are trained only for the corners, a legal campaign to imprison our most vulnerable and damaged citizens is little more than amoral." Following her guilty verdict, Pearson was sentenced to three years of probation.

Though Baltimore was the site, in 1954, of the original *Romper Room,* one of the country's first television programs for children, the city's modern television career began with another David Simon project, *Homicide: Life on the Street.* Filmed frequently around Fell's Point, this show about Baltimore homicide detectives ran on NBC for seven years, from 1993 to 1999, and starred several notable actors, including Ned Beatty, Andre Braugher, Melissa Leo, and Yaphet Kotto. *Roc,* a Fox show set in Baltimore (though filmed in Los Angeles) and starring Baltimore native Charles S. "Roc" Dutton, aired from 1991 to 1994. Baltimore has also been the set for the Food Network's *Ace of Cakes,* a reality show that tracked the trials, tribulations, and fondant disasters of baker Duff Goldman's Charm City Cakes, located near the Hampden neighborhood, from 2006 to 2011. Most recently, the Netflix's series *House of Cards* and the HBO vice presidential drama *Veep*—both set in Washington DC—have filmed in locations around Baltimore like the Four Seasons Baltimore, the George Peabody Library, and the Maryland Institute College of Art.

Baltimore has played itself in a long list of films; a brief run-down of the better movies includes three other "Baltimore" films by Barry Levinson: *Avalon, Liberty Heights,* and *Tin Men.* Also check out *The Accidental Tourist, Twelve Monkeys, Home for the Holidays, Ladder 49, Sleepless in Seattle,* and anything by John Waters. His most accessible films are *Hairspray, Cry Baby, Serial Mom* (starring Kathleen Turner, who studied drama at the nearby University of Maryland Baltimore County), and *Pecker.* Baltimore has also served as a celluloid stand-in for many towns, as its varied architecture can substitute for other, more expensive cities: check out *Enemy of the State, Live Free or Die Hard,* and *Washington Square.*

FESTIVALS AND EVENTS

Baltimore's parks and streets are host to a surprising array of beloved annual events, from tiny neighborhood block parties to enormous three-day extravaganzas like Mount Vernon and Station North's Artscape. Many of the various ethnic groups who moved to Baltimore in the 19th century and set up their own little enclaves—like Lithuanians, Greeks, Ukrainians, and Italians—host festivals featuring the traditional foods, music, and dances of their home countries. These sorts of neighborhood events occur all spring and summer long, and are held on the neighborhoods' streets or at nearby parks. Stop by any of them to get some great food and hear some obscure music and learn a little bit about Baltimore's treasured ethnic neighborhoods.

At the other end of the spectrum are the city's blockbuster festivals, which attract hundreds of thousands of visitors to see national musical acts, enjoy the arts, or just hang out. The biggest of these is July's Artscape, but the Preakness Stakes also brings huge crowds to town each May. Watch out for the collateral effects of some special goings-on, like the Kinetic Sculpture Race, which also shuts down part of some city streets.

There are lots of intriguing, weird, peculiar, and captivating festivals, gatherings, and events across the city all year long. There's Otakon, a national convention of Asian anime fans; the Night of 100 Elvises, which actually takes place over two nights, each packed with Elvis tribute artists; and the High Zero Festival of experimental music, where the concepts of songs and melodies are totally rewritten (or just destroyed). These are the kinds of only-in-Baltimore events that make the city so fascinating, not only for visitors, but for the people who call Charm City home.

Winter
The Mayor's Christmas Parade
During **The Mayor's Christmas Parade** (Hampden, www.mayorschristmasparade.com), which happens every first Sunday of December most years, the streets of Hampden are filled with a peculiar collection of high school cheerleaders and marching bands, floats, motorcycles, a steam calliope, classic cars, Santa Claus, a woman dressed like Underdog, and maybe even some brightly costumed Bolivian marchers. Oh, and the mayor of Baltimore will be there, too, waving from the backseat of a convertible. It's a fitting event for quirky Hampden, and during the medium-sized parade, the streets are lined with families, hipsters, and assorted other local characters.

Miracle on 34th Street
Taking its name from the classic holiday film, **Miracle on 34th Street** (Hampden, 34th St. between Keswick Ave. and Chestnut Ave., www.christmasstreet.com)—a Hampden tradition in which every resident on one block of 34th Street takes holiday light decoration to an unreal level—begins around Thanksgiving, and the lights don't go out until after New Year's Day. Tens of thousands of people drive countless miles to either cruise slowly through the street or stop and enjoy it on foot. The sidewalks are packed with bundled-up visitors drinking hot chocolate and gawking at the snowmen built from hubcaps, gigantic glowing Santa Clauses, and rivers of colored lights that flow over the houses and even across the street itself.

The Night of 100 Elvises

The Night of 100 Elvises (410/494-9558 or 888/494-9558, www.nightof100elvises.com), an annual event that raises money for the Johns Hopkins Children's Center and Guardian Angels, is actually held on two nights, owing to its popularity (inevitably on the first Friday and Saturday in December). This massive homage to everything Elvis features a massive array of Elvis tribute artists (don't call them impersonators), bands playing Elvis songs, fried peanut butter and banana sandwiches, dancing—as well as a lounge, a bar, and a building packed with happy guests mingling with Elvises and Santa Claus and Vegas-style showgirls. It's been covered by the Discovery Channel and Japanese television, and there's nothing else like it in the United States.

St. Patrick's Day Parade

Baltimore's proud Irish American citizens have helped make the **St. Patrick's Day Parade** (downtown, www.irishparade.net) one of the city's biggest events (held on the Saturday closest to St. Patrick's Day, not the actual day). The spectacle features bagpipe-brandishing marching bands, St. Patrick-honoring floats, and a popular 5K race that has thousands of runners hurtling through downtown streets packed with pleasantly inebriated parade-goers. Irish bars across town have all-day music and Irish dancing, along with Guinness and corned beef. Downtown is basically closed off to car traffic for this daylong celebration of the patron saint of Ireland; plan any trips accordingly.

Washington Monument Lighting

During the **Washington Monument Lighting** (Mount Vernon Place, 410/244-1030), held on a chilly Thursday night in early December each year, Mount Vernon Place overflows with more than 5,000 onlookers as the city's mayor and assembled VIPs flip the switch that turns on the colored strings of lights that adorn the Washington Monument. There's also a small but impressive fireworks display, as well as vendors selling seasonally appropriate hot cider and roasted chestnuts. Dubbed "A Monumental Occasion," it's a popular event with families, and an adored city tradition that really marks the beginning of the holiday season in Baltimore.

Spring
Flower Mart

Perhaps the most civilized city festival, the family-friendly **Flower Mart** (600 N. Charles St., 410/274-5353, www.flowermart.org) takes place around the Washington Monument in Mount Vernon; regular attendees arrive in a riot of colorful attire that blends in with the elaborate floral displays. Enormous, gaudy hats are de rigueur at this early-May floral festival (there's a contest for the most impressive), and vendors sell all manner of live and cut plants and flowers, along with food and drinks. The traditional treat to get at this event is the lemon stick: a lemon cut in half with a peppermint stick stuck into it. Suck on the peppermint stick to get the de-soured lemon juice. It's another "only in Baltimore" tradition, one that lasts for two days (Friday and Saturday).

HonFest

Back in 1994, the owner of Hampden's Café Hon decided to put on **HonFest** (Hampden, 36th St., www.honfest.net), a tribute festival to the colorful local residents—like the strong working-class Caucasian women who wore beehive hairdos and greeted everyone as "hon"—who were thought to be fading away as times changed. Now a two-day-long weekend event in mid-June that takes up Hampden's main drag (36th Street, or "The Avenue"), there are lots of activities for kids, as well as bands and food and beer—plus the crowning of Best Hon, where faux-hons don their biggest wigs, cat's-eye glasses, and best "Bawlmer" accent to vie for the title.

High Zero Festival

Held at the end of spring, **High Zero Festival** (Theatre Project, 45 W. Preston St., 410/752-8558, www.highzero.org) is not for everyone, unless everyone likes experimental and improvisational music, often made using nontraditional instruments...like rocks, metal, and furniture. Plenty of traditional instruments are employed as well, but in very untraditional ways, creating atonal, oddly structured music that can be very difficult to understand or comprehend. Still, that doesn't mean it's not worth going to a performance or two, as this peerless festival has drawn international attention from people looking to push the boundaries of conventional sound and music.

Johns Hopkins University Spring Fair

An annual spring (late April) event for nearly 45 years, **JHU's Spring Fair** (3400 N. Charles St., 410/516-7692, www.jhuspringfair.com) opens up the campus to the public for a weekend mix of music, food, crafts, and art, as well as a healthy contingent of nonprofit and socially active booths and displays. There's a big section for kids, but in addition to the usual rides and activities, the college kids sneak in some fun motivational education projects for children to encourage reading and learning. The big draw comes on Friday night, when a major alternative performer (maybe hip-hop, maybe rock, maybe something weirder) takes the stage.

Kinetic Sculpture Race

If it's early May and Saturday, and you see a giant pink poodle about the size of a U-Haul rolling down the streets of downtown Baltimore, you've stumbled upon the **Kinetic Sculpture Race** (starts at the American Visionary Art Museum, 800 Key Hwy., 410/244-1900, www.kineticbaltimore.com), a smile-inducing and whimsical combination of mechanical engineering, artistic creativity, pedal power, and buoyancy. Teams build people-powered sculptures of varying sizes and structural integrity levels, then pedal them all over the city, braving a series of muddy, off-road challenges as well as a water obstacle course in Canton. Winners and losers—that's not the point of this preposterous carnival. The point is just being a part of it.

LatinoFest

With the surge in Baltimore's Latino population in recent years, the area of north Fell's Point has gone from being somewhat under-populated and sparsely occupied to thriving with new immigrants who have brought their own cultural outlets to the city. **LatinoFest** (Patterson Park, www.latinofest.org), once a smaller city festival, is now one of the larger ones. Held at Patterson Park on a weekend in June, there are plenty of art, food, and drink vendors, and some great performances from Latino musicians both local and international.

Maryland Film Festival

For a city with such a stellar cinematic history, it took a while for Baltimore to host a film festival; the **Maryland Film Festival** (the Charles Theatre, the MICA Brown Center, and The Windup Space, 410/752-8083, www.md-filmfest.com) didn't start until 1998. Still, it's been worth the wait, as the festival now attracts a great mix of local, national, and international films, speakers, and even a super-secret sneak preview every year, the content of which audiences are sworn to not reveal. Shorts, animation, documentaries, and a couple mondo oddballs—and a total of about 50 feature films and 75 short films—make up the bulk of the schedule for this four-day event held in early May.

Maryland Hunt Cup

First run back in 1894, the **Maryland Hunt Cup** (Worthington Valley, Baltimore County, www.marylandsteeplechasing.com) is the grandfather of the state's steeplechase racing series, as well as the oldest steeplechase race in the United States. Though most people (rightly) think of Kentucky as the nation's premier horse racing state, horses have played a big part in northern Baltimore County's history, both as farm animals and as racers. This race celebrates the latter role in an all-day event held at Worthington Valley in Hunt Valley, where the country squires and dames assemble in their finery to drink, dine, and hobnob. There are plenty of regular folks here, too, as the excitement of this four-mile, 22-gate steeplechase draws crowds from all walks of life to the valley on a Saturday in late April.

The Preakness Stakes

On the third Saturday in May, Baltimore's Pimlico Race Course is host to **The Preakness Stakes** (Pimlico Race Course, 5201 Park Heights Ave., 410/542-9400, www.preakness.com), the middle jewel in horse racing's Triple Crown (the first is the Kentucky Derby; the last is the Belmont Stakes). For the week before the race, Baltimore hosts all sorts of parties, events, festivals, and other activities for the tens of thousands of visitors who descend on the city for pre-race fun. Hot-air balloons fill the skies, and it seems like there's a hospitality tent on every patch of ground around the Inner Harbor. Race day itself brings traffic on I-83 to a halt as the throngs head for Pimlico (the infield alone groans under the beer-sodden feet of some 104,000 people), and the evenings usually see bars and restaurants filled with tired, sunburned folks.

Summer

African American Festival

The two-day **African American Festival** (1101 Russell St., 410/244-8861, www.africanamericanfestival.net), which takes place in early July, lures crowds and big-name musical acts like Patti Labelle and Fantasia to Baltimore to celebrate African American culture and also take part in a great event. Food, crafts, vendors, health screenings, and children's activities are the other attractions at the festival, held in the sprawling parking lots between Oriole Park and M&T Bank Stadium in Camden Yards.

Artscape

Described as "America's largest free public arts festival," **Artscape** (Mt. Royal Ave. and Charles St., www.artscape.org) is a pretty amazing thing for several reasons. First, it's a festival that literally everyone in the city—no matter what economic, social, or cultural background—goes to, making it a rare place for residents to interact with one another. Second, it's an art festival, which makes its popularity even more astonishing. And third, it's always really hot on the July Artscape weekend, but the crowds—estimated at about 500,000 over Friday, Saturday, and Sunday—keep coming, and everyone manages to stay cool. Held on both Charles Street and Mount Royal Avenue in the Station North and Bolton Hill neighborhoods, this huge event draws more than 150 vendors, as well as some top-notch musical acts that perform all week-end long.

Baltimore Pride

Baltimore Pride (Mount Vernon and Druid Hill Park, 410/777-8145, www.baltimorepride.org) is the city's annual gay pride fes-tival, held since 1975; spanning a weekend in June each year, the event draws an estimated 30,000 attendees, performers, and vendors. There's a block party and parade in Mount Vernon, a festival in Druid Hill Park, a pre-event cocktail party, a high heel race up hilly Charles Street, and DJs and musicians performing throughout the day. In 2013, this event was also billed as host-ing the state's first mass same-sex wedding ceremony. About 20 couples participated, thanks to Maryland's 2012 approval of same-sex marriages.

Otakon

An *otaku* (it's a Japanese word) is a person who is a devoted fol-lower of Asian pop culture, including (but not limited to) anime, video games, comics, and movies. **Otakon** (Baltimore Convention Center, 1 W. Pratt St., 610/577-6136, www.otakon.com), then, is a convention of *otaku,* and it's fitting that a slightly off-center city like Baltimore would get a slightly off-center convention like this. It's one of the largest in the nation (more than 32,000 people came in 2012) for people whose devotion to anime involves creating elabo-rate homemade costumes and props—which leads to some strange sights around the convention center, as suited businesspeople wait to cross the street with people in enormous white PVC helmets, boots, and plastic swords. It's held for three days, beginning on a Friday, in early August.

Ports America Chesapeake Fourth of July Celebration

Join a crowd of several hundred thousand as people flock from all over the Baltimore region for the huge **Ports America Chesapeake Fourth of July Celebration** (Inner Harbor, events start at 4pm) fire-works show, launched from barges in the center of the harbor. There are plenty of vendors, bands, and things to do starting in the after-noon, and the fireworks display itself is a big-budget spectacular that looks great reflected on the windows of the waterfront office towers. In places like Harbor East, Fell's Point, and Federal Hill, folks start staking out spaces well before sundown, so plan accord-ingly if you're trying to get in or out of the Inner Harbor area that night—parking can be nonexistent, and the traffic jams out of the area can be frustrating.

BACKGROUND
PEOPLE AND CULTURE

Scapescape

A relatively new music festival, **Scapescape** (Station North, 410/962-7075, www.stationnorth.org) is still finding its footing, but seems to have found a home in Station North about two miles north of the Inner Harbor. The most recent event was a four-day extravaganza at the end of August with more than 100 local bands and musical acts performing on seven stages at venues and bars across the neighborhood. Organizers have said that their goal is to expose attendees to as many acts as possible, and the event certainly is a great way for those curious about the local music scene to listen to the rock, rap, pop, indie, experimental, and club musicians who live in Charm City. There are also theater performances and gallery shows. A new Scapescape Facebook page is started every year, and it's the best way to get details about venues, ticket prices, and lineups.

St. Anthony Italian Festival

When the Baltimore Fire of 1904 destroyed much of downtown, the residents of Little Italy gathered at the St. Leo the Great Catholic church and prayed to St. Anthony for the salvation of their neighborhood. The fire never made it across the Jones Falls and Little Italy was spared; to thank St. Anthony, a festival was held that year, and every year since. Now, for a weekend in early June, there's lots of great Italian food, dancing, music, and a Sunday bocce tournament at the **St. Anthony Italian Festival** (Exeter and Stiles Sts., Little Italy, 410/675-7275).

Fall

Baltimore Book Festival

The **Baltimore Book Festival** (Mount Vernon Place, 600 N. Charles St., 410/752-8632, www.baltimorebookfestival.com), a two-and-a-half day celebration in late September of Baltimore's literary history, from authors to books and libraries, is a bibliophile's dream. The fun includes lots of book vendors hawking interesting reads, from expensive rarities to cheap bulk books, and a variety of panels, speakers, readings, and discussions featuring local and national writers, as well as a stage with a full schedule of cooking demonstrations (and samples!). There's also the usual assortment of food and music, all found around the Washington Monument in Mount Vernon.

The Baltimore Running Festival & Marathon

Many cities have had successful marathons for years; though **The Baltimore Running Festival & Marathon** (begins and ends at Camden Yards, 410/605-9381, www.thebaltimoremarathon.com), held in early October, was started only in 2001, it's quickly become a big hit with prominent runners, especially with the addition of larger purses and route improvement that removed some seriously unpleasant hills (though there are still plenty of uphill inclines for those who like a challenge). More than 25,000 people ran in 2012. The course winds all over the central part of the city, making travel impossible in those areas during race morning and early afternoon.

Free Fall Baltimore

Thanks to **Free Fall Baltimore** (citywide, 410/752-8632, www.freefallbaltimore.com), a simple and brilliant promotion sponsored by the city and some corporate partners, many of Baltimore's best attractions, museums, and venues are free throughout the month of October. In addition, unique events ranging from music performances to festivals are held, all free of charge. To get passes to specific events, and to find out about all the available gratis entertainment, go to the Free Fall Baltimore website.

The Great Halloween Lantern Parade

The beauty of **The Great Halloween Lantern Parade** (Patterson Park, Pulaski Monument, Eastern and Linwood Aves.), a community-based art project, is hard to capture in words, but picture some 1,000 children and adults walking through the chilly autumn air, trekking across the winding and dark paths of Patterson Park's fields and woods, carrying candlelit lanterns, and wearing costumes ranging from simple capes to enormous papier-mâché skeletons and fantastic beasts. Some parade-goers play instruments, some clang bells, some walk in spooky silence. It all adds up to an amazing experience for spectators and participants alike.

Tour du Port

Organized by Maryland's largest pedestrian and bicycling advocacy group, the popular bike event **Tour du Port** (starts at the Canton Waterfront Park at the Korean War Memorial, 410/960-6493, www.onelesscar.org) lets riders take one of several long rides through the city and parts of the Port of Baltimore, from a long 63-mile ride to a brisk 14-mile jaunt. On a Sunday in late September, some 2,000 riders begin their morning at this annual event, which covers territory from the Inner Harbor all the way out to North Point State Park in Baltimore County. Proceeds go to help make the state safer and easier for people looking to ditch their driving habits.

Essentials

Getting There 303

Tips for Travelers 309

Getting Around 305

Information and Services 314

Getting There

What's the best way to get to Baltimore, located about midway down the Eastern Seaboard of the United States? It really depends on your point of origin. Baltimore is right on I-95, making it a cinch to reach from points north and south. If you live in a city like Philly, New York, or DC, you might consider hopping on one of the many private buses that now run up and down the I-95 corridor, sometimes for ludicrously low fares. There's also rail travel, and Baltimore's Penn Station is right in the middle of the city (though not near any hotels).

Air travel is another option; Baltimore/Washington International Thurgood Marshall Airport is serviced by some low-cost carriers, and since it's not a hot destination city like Miami, airfares to Baltimore can dip if airlines want to entice folks to travel to Charm City.

You can even enter Baltimore by boat; from the Chesapeake Bay, just follow the Patapsco River up and into the docks and piers of Fell's Point.

BY AIR

Ten miles south and just a 15-minute drive from downtown Baltimore, **Baltimore/Washington International Thurgood Marshall Airport** (410/859-7111, www.bwiairport.com) is one of the busier regional airports in the nation. About 22.68 million people moved through BWI in 2012, partly due to its somewhat recent expansions and its completion of an entire new gate for low-cost **Southwest Airlines** (www.southwest.com), which is responsible for more than half of the airport's passenger load. Unlike at some modern airports, BWI's nonflying amenities—like full-scale malls and entertainment—are limited to a good variety of bars and restaurants, as well as some solid if uninspired shopping in the airport's Airmall, which is spread across the entire facility.

In addition to Southwest, nine major national carriers fly into and out of BWI. There are also a few international airlines, such as Air Canada, British Airways, and Condor. One interesting note: because of BWI's proximity to Washington DC not only do lots of Washingtonians come to BWI looking for cheaper fares than at Reagan National Airport, but the Transportation Security Administration road tests new equipment and tactics at BWI quite often, so don't be startled to see some new gizmo or when asked some new questions during your screening here. For domestic flights, arrive at least one hour early; backups at the security checkpoints can be quite long during peak travel times. International flights require passengers to arrive at least two hours early.

BY TRAIN

Baltimore's central train station is **Pennsylvania Station** (1500 N. Charles St., 800/872-7245, www.amtrak.com), a massive old building that was renovated several years ago and is now a gleaming gem of a rail station. Amtrak service runs up and down the East Coast and to points west from this station seven days a week, and the high-speed *Acela Express* trains greatly reduce the traveling time to five other major East Coast cities. During the week, a commuter rail line called MARC (Maryland Area Regional Commuter) runs from Washington DC to Baltimore and a few small stops north of the city; it's another reasonably priced option. Amtrak times and rates run roughly as follows: from New York City, 2 hours 45 minutes, $129; from Philadelphia, 1 hour 15 minutes, $79; and from Richmond, Virginia, 4 hours, $46.

Pennsylvania Station—you'll know it by the large, modern, metal Male/Female statue out front—is very near the center of the city geographically and within walking distance of Mount Vernon and Station North. The Charm City Circulator, the city's free shuttle bus system, also stops here on its purple line route, but taking a cab is always a good option, too.

BY BUS

The city's main **Greyhound** station (2110 Haines St., 410/752-7682, www.greyhound.com) is a few blocks south of downtown in a rough-and-tumble industrial section of south Baltimore. Service runs seven days a week, multiple times a day. Wandering around the neighborhood after dark is not a sound idea, but the station itself is generally secure and safe. Travel by taxi to downtown from the station; the walk is very long and not recommended for safety reasons, though it's possible to do during daylight.

A more cost-effective option may be to take one of the more homespun bus operators that have sprung up in recent years. Running from New York City to Washington DC, with stops in Baltimore, these small bus lines offer incredibly cheap rates (around $30 round-trip to New York City) and are a viable alternative to traditional bus transportation. One service that conveniently picks up passengers next to Pennsylvania Station is **Bolt Bus** (1610 St. Paul St., 877/265-8287, www.boltbus.com). There is also service by **MegaBus** (877/462-6342, www.megabus.com) that travels from Baltimore to several East Coast locations, but this line drops off and picks up far out in the suburbs (at the White Marsh Mall MTA Park & Ride), and travelers won't be able to secure a way to the city proper without taking a long MTA bus ride (Route 35), or making a phone call to a cab company.

Baltimore can be accessed by three interstate highways: I-95, which runs north and south along the Eastern Seaboard; I-83, which begins in Baltimore and runs north up to Harrisburg, Pennsylvania; and I-70, which runs west to Frederick and into the heart of the United States.

Since Baltimore is right on I-95, it's easy to reach from points to the north (like Philadelphia, which is about two hours away by car, and New York City, just under three and a half hours) and south (Washington DC is less than an hour away; Richmond, Virginia, is under three).

Getting Around

It's possible to traverse Baltimore by foot, depending on your itinerary, but having a car makes life a lot easier here. Either way, here's a handy guide to quickly figuring out where something is by its street address: If it's a street with a "north" designation (like North Highland Street), it's above Baltimore Street, which runs east to west; South Highland Street is below that. For east and west boundaries, the border is Charles Street, which runs one-way northbound right through the center of town (it is, however, a two-way street in Federal Hill and south Baltimore).

The best public transportation system is the new (and free!) Charm City Circulator bus system; it travels by most major attractions consistently throughout the day. Biking is also a good possibility for getting around, though the long climb northward from downtown will test your fitness (and calves); new bike paths and lanes make this option less perilous than in years past.

AIRPORT

Getting to and from the airport is a breeze (if you're driving, it's right off MD 295, the Baltimore-Washington Parkway), and there are several easy ways to make the journey. First is the **Light Rail** (mta.maryland.gov/light-rail), which runs from downtown Baltimore to a shuttle bus stop near the terminal. At $1.60, it's the unbeatable low-cost champ—but it doesn't run all the time (generally operates 5am-11pm Mon.-Fri., and starting at 6am on Sat. with Sun. hours being severely reduced). When the trains aren't running, you'll need to take the 17 bus instead; the fare is still $1.60, but there are a lot more stops. The **MARC commuter rail** (mta.maryland.gov), which runs between Baltimore's northern exurbs and Washington DC, also makes a stop at BWI; it's a cheap (around $4) alternative if it fits your arrangements.

The second option is to take one of the many shuttle vans, like the **SuperShuttle** (800/258-3826, www.supershuttle.com), that operate between Baltimore and either the major hotels or a pick-up point of your choosing. These run about $15, but offer a good bargain compared to a private taxi.

Grabbing a cab to or from BWI can be a costly, if convenient, travel solution. If you're heading right downtown, it will cost about $35; heading farther into the city will increase the price. There are several cab services that serve BWI and Baltimore.

There is the usual armada of rental car agencies at BWI, offering varying rates depending on the type of vehicle you rent. Given Baltimore's often sparse parking space selection, a small, compact vehicle will suit you just fine around town. If you're planning on taking a day trip, a larger car might make the trip a little more enjoyable. The airport's centralized car rental facility is about a 10-minute drive from the airport itself.

PUBLIC TRANSPORTATION

Operated by Veolia Transportation in partnership with the Baltimore City Department of Transportation, the new **Charm City Circulator** (410/350-0456, www.charmcitycirculator.com, Mon.-Thurs. 6:30am-9pm, Fri. 6:30am-midnight, Sat. 9am-midnight, Sun. 9am-9pm, reduced winter hours) is Baltimore's best and most convenient public transportation system. Its fleet of 21 shuttle buses travel four routes in the city. The orange line will get you to many of Baltimore's downtown and Little Italy museums, the purple line goes north to Mount Vernon and Station North's cultural attractions, and the banner route travels through Federal Hill to Fort McHenry. The shuttles are scheduled to arrive every 15 minutes, making this a convenient service for those who don't mind the buses' frequent stops.

Baltimore also has a couple of other public transportation options that are operated by the **Maryland Transit Administration** (410/539-5000, mta.maryland.gov). Bus service runs throughout the city, though it is primarily used for weekday transportation to and from work; weekend schedules are less comprehensive and cover less of the city. There are a few central bus routes (like the 1, 3, 7, 11, and 17) that span the city well on the main north-south and east-west axes, but if you're trying to get somewhere away from the main attractions on a weekend, a bus is not the best option.

There are two public rail options as well, though both have only one line. The first is the **Light Rail** (mta.maryland.gov/light-rail), which runs from Cromwell Station in Glen Burnie in the south all the way north to Hunt Valley Mall, in northern Baltimore County. This is a good option for traveling between certain areas, such as from Camden Yards to Mount Vernon or Station North, but the line does not provide any east-west coverage. The second rail option is the **Metro Subway** (mta.maryland.gov/metro-subway); designed primarily for commuters from the northwestern suburbs heading into downtown and to Johns Hopkins Medicine's facilities on the east side of the city, this is an option for certain trips, but is not particularly useful for getting across town to sightsee. If you plan on heavy use of the system and want to purchase an **MTA Transit Link Card,** you can do so online (mta.commuterdirect.com).

DRIVING

While you can get around Baltimore by cab, bus, and on foot, having a vehicle will make travel a lot faster and let you get out into the countryside and take a day trip or two. If you decide to rent a car after your arrival, there are numerous outlets for all the major rental agencies in town; your best bet is to check the companies' websites for specials and convenient locations.

Parking can be tricky downtown during the week; the city has long suffered from a shortage of spaces, so if you're not at a major hotel (which will almost assuredly charge you extra to park in its garage), you'll probably be parking at a nearby surface lot, or you can take your chances with on-street parking.

Figuring out where and when you can and cannot park in certain places is a bit of a challenge if you're not used to city regulations. Many of the popular neighborhoods have time-based and resident-only parking restrictions, so read carefully any signs near where you've chosen to park; many major downtown thoroughfares prohibit parking on certain sides of the street during rush hours (southbound in the mornings, northbound in the afternoons). Electronic parking machines are common in Baltimore, but study the information on the machine nearest your parking space to determine the length of time you can stay and the hours of required pay parking (Sundays are free in most areas).

Driving while in Baltimore should be relatively painless if you have driven in a major city before; things move fast and with a purpose here, and lollygagging is not appreciated. If you're a cautious, slow driver who likes to sightsee through your windshield and stop in the middle of downtown to ask directions, be prepared for some colorful (and profane) suggestions on how to improve your driving.

If you're driving in Baltimore during an ice or snow event, be forewarned that the city's drivers are generally less than skilled when it comes to negotiating a vehicle through inclement weather.

TAXIS

There are several major (and several minor) cab companies in Baltimore: **Yellow Cab of Baltimore** (410/685-1212) is the largest, but **Diamond** (410/233-6000) is another major provider. Even though the city has more than 1,100 registered taxicabs, hailing (or finding) one in certain parts of town at certain times of night can be nigh on impossible, so either have a cab company's phone number with you and call from your cell phone, or have the restaurant or bar call you a cab (they're generally more than happy to do so, and getting a call from a business seems to improve response time). It costs $1.80 to get in a cab in the city, and about $2 a mile after that. The limit to the number of passengers in a cab is four, more or less; a ride from Homewood to downtown should cost about $6. Taking a cab from BWI to a downtown hotel (or the reverse) can cost about $35.

Somewhat surprisingly, the Yellow Cab of Baltimore has several Toyota Prius hybrid cars, which you can try to request when you call.

WATER TAXI

If you're planning on staying mostly around the Inner Harbor area, consider using the **Water Taxi** (410/563-3900, www.baltimorewatertaxi.com) to get around. This regular shuttle service (look for the boats with blue awnings) makes 17 stops all across the harbor, going as far east as Fort McHenry (during the warm months), and covering all the major waterfront destinations from Locust Point clockwise to Fell's Point and Canton all year long. It's a beautiful way to see the city, and the captains are generally up for a chat, which can reveal some amazing salty tales of the city and the harbor.

The Water Taxi and the City of Baltimore also have a new free commuter service called the Harbor Connector that takes passengers to Locust Point from either the Frederick Douglass-Isaac Myers Maritime Park in Fell's Point or the Canton Waterfront Park in Canton. Though the boats are primarily for commuters, anyone is welcome to ride. Note, though, that the service is only offered on weekdays 7am-7pm.

BICYCLING

With the addition of many new bicycle lanes throughout the city, visitors to Baltimore will see more and more two-wheeled conveyances on the streets than in years past. A Bicycle Master Plan for the city was created in 2006, and the results today are more (and more clearly marked) lanes, places to lock up bikes at popular destinations, and a friendlier environment. There are several local groups dedicated to riding in the city and getting people on bikes, like **Baltimore Spokes** (www.baltimorespokes.org) and **Velocipede** (www.velocipedebikeproject.org). That being said, riding a bike in Baltimore can still be a risky proposition, particularly on the busy thoroughfares that barely have room for two lanes of cars. Baltimore has several very good bike trails that run through it, including the Gwynns Falls Trail and the Jones Falls Trail.

DISABLED ACCESS

Almost all of Baltimore has been modified to comply with the Americans with Disabilities Act, meaning that ramps or lifts are in place to allow all visitors to access businesses and sites. Note that in some parts of historic older neighborhoods, the terrain may preclude travel by wheelchair. Both the **MTA transit system** (410/539-5000, mta.maryland.gov) and private cab companies can provide specialized vehicles on request.

Tips for Travelers

TRAVELING WITH CHILDREN

For those heading to Baltimore with children, a few basic commonsense rules should apply. It's a real city, with real traffic, so kids need to be watched around downtown intersections, which can be confusing and often filled with cars and buses moving at very high speeds. There is also a light-rail along Howard Street, which glides right along the sidewalks and can sneak up on unsuspecting pedestrians. Crowds at the Inner Harbor can be pretty thick during the warmer months, and lines to attractions can be long, so pack distractions and snacks accordingly. The best public restrooms are at the **Baltimore Visitor Center** (401 Light St.), which is between the National Aquarium in Baltimore and the Maryland Science Center in the Inner Harbor, and the **Fell's Point Visitor Center** (1724 Thames St.).

Parents looking for a good resource for things to do with the kids should check out *Baltimore's Child,* a monthly publication that covers mostly education and parenting but also has a good list of events and special happenings for kids (there's an online version at www.baltimoreschild.com).

WOMEN TRAVELERS

Baltimore is a great city for women traveling alone as long as they keep in mind the usual rules and avoid areas of potential issues, such as areas where overly intoxicated people congregate and cause mayhem. Most of the people you'll meet in Baltimore are friendly and willing to suggest great (and safe) places to visit on your own at various times of the evening. Bustling neighborhoods like Fell's Point and Federal Hill are safe at night because of the crowds, though deserted side streets (and much of downtown) can be dicier for those traveling alone at night. Night is really the only time to be concerned about safety, as daytime incidents are very, very rare here, especially in busy areas. Police officers are not always easy to find in many areas, as they are off in the high-crime regions of town, but the Inner Harbor is very heavily patrolled at all times by officers on foot, on bicycle, and in small vehicles.

SENIOR TRAVELERS

Getting around the Inner Harbor is a cinch, and there isn't much rowdiness there during the day to ruin your trip; the same is true with other neighborhoods, but those with lots of bars can be a bit much for those looking for a peaceful night out. Much of the waterfront area is very flat and good for walking, and while there are a good deal of stairs around, access ramps are plentiful. There's a good mix of both new and more traditional attractions, all of which are equipped to meet with any particular needs. Most of the big attractions and hotels will offer special rates for seniors, as well as additional discounts (and seniors can ride public transportation for about one-third of the normal cost); these aren't as popular at restaurants, so ask at individual eateries. Safety isn't an issue in the popular neighborhoods, though traveling alone at night in less-populated sections of town might court trouble. Baltimore's role as a health care hub for the region means there is a panoply of world-class hospitals in the downtown region, if needed.

GAY AND LESBIAN TRAVELERS

Baltimore is a popular city for gays and lesbians to both visit and live in; a generally well-informed and tolerant population makes for a refreshing lack of unpleasant experiences for LGBT residents and tourists. The grand homes and cultural sights that populate the Mount Vernon neighborhood have led many people to call the area home, and Mount Vernon is acknowledged to be the heart of the city's gay community, in terms of residents, events, and attractions.

Resources worth checking out include *Gay Life* (www.baltimoregaylife.com), the state's biggest gay, lesbian, bisexual, and transgendered monthly newspaper, and the **Gay, Lesbian, Bisexual, and Transgender Community Center of Baltimore and Central Maryland** (www.glccb.org), which has some basic info and events listings.

TRAVELERS WITH DISABILITIES

Almost all of Baltimore's most popular sights and attractions are easily accessible for all visitors, and citywide compliance with the Americans with Disabilities Act (ADA) is relatively high, particularly in the downtown area. Neighborhoods like Fell's Point (lots of paving stones) and Mount Vernon (lots of hills and steps) might challenge visitors with disabilities, though even in those areas there are ways to get nearly everywhere. Most of the waterborne attractions in town can accommodate all tourist needs, given advance warning; the Water Taxi has ramps at all docks.

The **Maryland Transit Administration** (410/539-5000, mta.maryland.gov) has expanded its ability to service customers with disabilities with more chair-lift local buses, while other transportation methods (like rail options, including light-rail, the Baltimore subway, and MARC) can accommodate wheelchairs via elevators at the stations. The MTA offers reduced rates for people with disabilities which work out to be about one-third the regular cost of travel.

WEATHER

Baltimore's location near the coast, but not on it, and near the South, but not really in it, and near the Appalachian Mountains, but to the east of them, means that the city gets the best of, but not the worst of, the region's climates. The mountains fend off the brutal "lake effect" snowstorms that blanket cities to the west; the inland location means that tropical storms wear down by the time they hit the city; and while the heat and humidity can be dreadful, the scorching temperatures don't last as long as down south. Baltimore gets about 40 inches of precipitation each year, with 21 of that being from snow in January and February, mostly.

July is consistently the hottest month in Baltimore, with an average high of around 91°F. Note that temperatures in the center of Baltimore City will be significantly higher than in the less-dense regions, as the swaths of concrete and blacktop serve as a heat sink, absorbing more of the summer's relentless sun. The coldest month is January, with an average high of 25°F, though an occasional arctic blast will sweep through, dropping temperatures into the teens at night.

Ozone and air quality are big problems during long, hot stretches of the summer, when the air stagnates and becomes unhealthy. Warnings are on the web (www.cleanairpartners.net), broadcast on radio and TV, and published in newspapers.

WHAT TO TAKE

The best guide for selecting clothing for Baltimore should be the weather forecast for your visit. If you're going to be walking around during the heat of summer, you should favor light clothes, as there is a lot of sun-exposed pavement to cover. Thunderstorms can spring up suddenly during spring and summer, so bringing an umbrella or raincoat for a multiday visit is a wise idea. Nights can be cool in spring and autumn, and serious cold spells don't usually begin until January, which means you won't need your parka unless you're visiting during the few frigid months. A few of the city's large natural areas, like the Maryland Zoo, Fort McHenry, and Patterson Park, can get pretty buggy during the warmer months, so if you're planning on spending a long afternoon at any of them, some insect repellent is a wise accoutrement. If you're a runner, the flat areas around the Inner Harbor are great for a medium waterfront circuit (Fell's Point to Fort McHenry and back is about 10 miles), so consider packing your running shoes and workout clothes.

Once a notoriously dress-down town, Baltimore has recently decided to spruce up its appearance a bit. Still, if your regular outfit is a golf shirt, loafers, and khakis, or a simple print dress or plain pants and flats, you'll fit in just fine. Note that most locations around the Inner Harbor are used to welcoming tourists in all manner of attire and should have no issues with shorts and sneakers for dinner.

Some of the newer, trendier restaurants and lounges do have (and enforce) dress codes, however, so you may want to do a little research before heading out for the evening. And a few of the city's more landmark restaurants require coats for men; venues like the symphony and the opera also pride themselves on looking dapper. Consider bringing at least one more dressy outfit, like a coat and slacks or a nice dress, to make the most of your visit.

CONDUCT AND CUSTOMS
Smoking

In February 2008, smoking was banned in bars and restaurants (along with almost all other public indoor spaces) in Baltimore City and across the state. This has led to many notoriously smoke-filled places applying new coats of paint and changing their upholstery to get out the years of nicotine and smoke stench; thus, you'll never encounter so many Baltimore bars looking (or smelling) as good as they do now. A couple of cigar-centric bars and lounges have obtained permission to offer smoking areas, but they're not the kinds of places you would accidentally walk into and be surprised to smell smoke. One by-product of the smoking ban is that the streets of Baltimore are now filled with people stepping outside of taverns and restaurants for a cigarette; sidewalks can be jammed with smokers and clouds of smoke, particularly in nightlife-rich areas like Fell's Point and Federal Hill.

Hours

Baltimore is a 2am town—except when it's a 1am town. Not every liquor license is created equal in Baltimore (there are both 1am and 2am licenses), so you may want to ask your barkeep when closing time is if you're about to order another round of martinis at 12:45am, Two neighborhoods where getting caught in the late-night "drunk o'clock" rush hour can be a bit challenging are Fell's Point and Federal Hill; young males full of alcohol can be occasionally aggressive, though it's generally toward each other. Many taverns and clubs operate on "bar time," 10-20 minutes ahead of actual time. Restaurants begin closing their kitchens around 10pm, although on weekends you may be able to eat later. There are a multitude of great all-night dining options, if you enjoy basic meals that contain lots of grease and eggs. And downtown Baltimore can get pretty quiet after 6pm, especially on weeknights in the winter, though the Inner Harbor area is still alive with activity throughout the year, especially on the weekends.

Tipping

Many service workers in Baltimore are thrilled to get a good tip because, frankly, some Baltimoreans can be lousy tippers. Maybe it's the city's thrifty, blue-collar past. At any rate, here's an opportunity to make an impression. Tip 15-20 percent on all food and beverage service, and you'll make a friend who could come in handy on a return visit. This tip range applies to other services like cabs and concierges, though it's on a sliding scale depending on the degree of difficulty of the job.

Tipping in hotels varies from place to place, but here's who should get something for their efforts, in order of appearance: the door attendant who gets your bags, the concierge who maybe gets you some tickets to a ballgame or show, the person who brings room service, the housekeeping staff, and once again, the door attendant who gets you a cab and gives you a tip on a restaurant. From $2-20 should cover all of these people, and will probably enhance the quality of your stay. If you stiff everyone, expect to get a similar level of assistance and information.

HEALTH AND SAFETY
Hospitals and Pharmacies

There are several major hospitals in the downtown area, with a few others farther from the Inner Harbor. In the city's center are **Mercy Medical Center** (www.mdmercy.com) and the huge **University of Maryland Medical Center** (www.umm.edu); south of Federal Hill is **MedStar Harbor Hospital** (www.medstarharbor.org); and east of Homewood is **MedStar Union Memorial Hospital** (www.medstarunionmemorial.org). The famed **Johns Hopkins Hospital** (www.hopkinsmedicine.org) and its various world-class specialty centers are roughly a mile north of Fell's Point on North Wolfe Street, though Hopkins has other hospitals across the city and region.

Emergency Services

Call 911 if you have a serious medical or safety emergency (alternately, dial 311 if you have a noncritical situation that may still require law enforcement, fire, or medical personnel). If the power goes out, call **Baltimore Gas and Electric** (BGE, 877/778-2222). If you see a power line in a hazardous situation or smell natural gas, call BGE at 800/685-0123. Water and sewer problems are handled by the Baltimore City Department of Public Works; call 311. Baltimore City's Poison Control Center can be reached at 800/222-1222.

Safety

Much of the Baltimore discussed in this book is found within safe, healthy neighborhoods, where trouble is generally rare and crimes are minor. If a neighborhood is clean and you see people of all ages sitting out on their front steps, it's a safe place to be. Yet Baltimore has a serious reputation as a dangerous city, one it has earned through years of violence by young men against each other, generally as a result of the illegal drug trade. But much of this violence occurs in parts of town that 99 percent of tourists and visitors will never go (unless they are looking for locations used in the television show *The Wire*). In the words of a former Baltimore City health commissioner, "Baltimore is actually a very safe city if you are not involved in the drug trade. If you are involved, it is one of the most dangerous in the United States." This is a grim reality, but it is a true statement in all respects. However, it should not preclude you from taking advantage of the chance to explore and experience this great American city.

It is only after dark that extra care should be used, and generally only in areas lying outside those discussed in this book—though even the safest neighborhoods may have unlit, secluded spots that are best left unexplored at night. The region north of Fell's Point and Little Italy can be unsafe at night, as can the area north of Canton, south of Federal Hill, and east and south of Homewood and Hampden. In Mount Vernon, there are generally lots of people and activity on certain blocks, surrounded by empty zones where crimes are more common. Also note that there has been a recent wave of stolen cell phones, but those who stay aware of their surroundings while talking or using the Internet generally are fine.

Information and Services

MAPS AND TOURIST INFORMATION

The best central location for any maps, brochures, guides, and general information about sightseeing and exploring Baltimore can be found at the Inner Harbor's **Baltimore Visitor Center** (401 Light St., 877/225-8466, www.baltimore.org/visitor-center), the low glass building with the gray roof on the west side of the waterfront. Not only is this place filled with printed materials and helpful staffers, there are lots of kiosks and terminals where you can find out more info and even purchase tickets to events and attractions.

The only neighborhood with its own full-time visitors center is

Fell's Point (1724 Thames St., 410/675-6751, www.preservationsociety.com); it's worth stopping by for information, maps, and a look around at the artifacts, as well as for recommendations from the staff. Many of the major downtown hotels also offer large selections of brochures and information, and the concierges there should be able to help with most basic inquiries and can recommend sights, restaurants, and other attractions.

MEDIA AND COMMUNICATION
Phones and Area Codes

There are two area codes in the Baltimore region: 410 and 443. The 410 area code has two zones; in the north and west, it covers the central part of Maryland, including the city and the counties of Baltimore, Carroll, and Howard, among others; the southernmost area covers the Annapolis area (Anne Arundel County) and the Eastern Shore's many counties, and is considered a long-distance call. The 443 area code was added in 1997 and often is used for cellular telephones, though some city restaurants use it as well; it covers the same region as 410. You must include the area code, whether it is 410 or 443, when dialing a phone number.

Internet Services

The **Enoch Pratt Free Library** (410/396-5430, www.prattlibrary.org), Baltimore City's public library system, offers Internet access to all library patrons; a library card is not required for use. There are 22 branches of the library, including the **central library** (400 Cathedral St.), which is the largest and best option for high-speed wireless connectivity. Other free access spots include many of the city's coffee shops and even a couple of taverns. Most hotels and BWI Airport also have wireless Internet, though it's not always free.

Mail and Messenger Services

There are many **United States Postal Service** post offices in Baltimore; check www.usps.gov or 800/275-8777 for locations. The central Baltimore post office is at 900 East Fayette Street downtown, at the foot of I-83 and just across the street from the Phoenix Shot Tower; this sprawling building has extended hours and services. There are also several **FedEx** (www.fedex.com/us) locations in the city, as well as four **UPS** stores (www.theupsstore.com).

Messenger services are also available; good bets include **Maryland Messenger** (www.marylandmessenger.com) and **Metro Express of Baltimore, Inc.** (www.metroexpressbaltimore.com).

Magazines and Newspapers

The *Baltimore Sun* is the city's major newspaper and only daily paper, and has won numerous Pulitzer Prizes in its past. The *Sun*'s

Relocating to Baltimore

Baltimore has done a surprisingly good job of marketing itself to out-of-towners, particularly from Washington DC, in the past decade—the city's relative affordability, great neighborhoods, and fun, quirky ethos and spirit are all selling points. The quasi-public agency that handles this is **Live Baltimore** (343 N. Charles St., 410/637-3750, www.livebaltimore. com), which has all sorts of materials and knowledgeable staffers to help those considering making Charm City their home. Their detailed neighborhood maps and information are second to none and are frequently used by residents for research. They can also provide cost-of-living info, as well as information on taxes and fees and lots of other incredibly useful data.

Finding a Job

The city's Department of Human Resources lists jobs online at human-resources.baltimorecity.gov. Johns Hopkins University and Hospital, as well as the University of Maryland Medical System (UMMS), are major employers in Baltimore and good places to look for work. Find their job postings online at www.hrnt.jhu.edu/ jhujobs (for Johns Hopkins) and www. ummscareers.com (for UMMS).

More online resources worth looking at include the usual career sites especially **Indeed** (www.indeed. com), more community-based operations like **Craigslist** (baltimore.craigslist.org), and those of the major city newspapers.

Housing

Live Baltimore is the preeminent source for information about finding a neighborhood that's right for you. It also has tips on finding a home or apartment to purchase (or rent) in Baltimore, though much of the information the agency provides is geared toward those purchasing a home. If you are looking to buy real estate, Baltimore City has several financial incentive programs that can result in some decent savings; Live Baltimore has a good webpage (www. livebaltimore.com/financial-incentives) to help you search through the options. A listing of condo and rental properties by neighborhood can be found on the **Downtown Partnership of Baltimore**'s website (www.godowntownbaltimore. com), and homes for sale, as well as more properties for rent, are advertised on community web listings, like Craigslist, or on the real estate pages (both printed and online) of the city's major local newspapers, particularly the *Baltimore Sun* and the *City Paper*. Unlike in some other major cities, if you're looking to rent, you don't need to acquire the services of a real estate agent. If you are looking to buy, however, there are several major real estate companies that will be happy to help you find a place to purchase (Long and Foster and Coldwell Banker are the region's largest). There are also an increasing number of web options for direct buyer and seller transactions.

parent company also publishes the free *b,* geared toward a younger readership and published weekly. *City Paper* is the city's alternative weekly free paper, and is a good resource for finding bands, concerts, and other event listings.

Other publications include the *Baltimore Business Journal,* which covers regional business; the *Daily Record,* which covers law and business; the *Catholic Review;* and the *Baltimore Jewish Times.* The historic *Afro-American Newspaper* (called "The Afro") is one of the

nation's oldest African American-owned and operated papers. *Gay*
Life is the state's primary monthly paper for the gay, lesbian, bisexual, and transgendered communities.

Baltimore magazine is the city's glossy lifestyle publication, and the oldest city magazine in the nation. Its regular "Best Restaurants" and "Best of Baltimore" features are handy guides to the city's top destinations. Baltimore *Style* is another great lifestyle magazine that covers the region.

Radio and TV
There are seven television stations in Baltimore, covering all of the major networks and PBS, seen locally on **Maryland Public Television** (www.mpt.org).

A good listing of Baltimore stations can be found at www.ontheradio.net. The most useful stations to know are **WERQ 92.3 FM** (urban contemporary and hip-hop), **WPOC 93.1 FM** (country), **WEAA 88.9 FM** (jazz), **WBJC 91.5 FM** (classical), **WIYY 97.9 FM** (rock), and **WBAL 1090 AM** (news and talk). Baltimore's public radio station is **WYPR 88.1 FM,** which plays NPR shows and local interest broadcasts.

PUBLIC LIBRARIES
Baltimore's public library system, the **Enoch Pratt Free Library** (www.prattlibrary.org), is one of the first in the nation, and remains one of the better city libraries in America today. First begun in 1882, with a gift of more than $1 million from Enoch Pratt, the library he envisioned "shall be for all, rich and poor without distinction of race or color, who, when properly accredited, can take out the books if they will handle them carefully and return them." That was a big deal back in 1882, as Baltimore was still a very segregated city. The central library first opened in 1886 (then on Mulberry Street) followed by several branches soon thereafter; a large donation from Andrew Carnegie in the early 20th century allowed for even more branches to open. Despite some budget cuts and branch closures in the 1990s, the library has recently begun to add new branches and update buildings and services to better serve Baltimore's citizens.

The current **central library** at 400 Cathedral Street (410/396-5430) was built in 1931, and today houses more than 3,500,000 books, periodicals, tapes, and other publications. An addition was added a few years ago, which included a new and expanded African American collection and a new home for the Maryland Room—a collection of Baltimore and Maryland-specific publications and tomes, and an intriguing place to browse.

PLACES OF WORSHIP
Baltimore (just as the rest of Maryland) was founded in part by Catholics who were unwelcome in England; fittingly, Baltimore

is home to the nation's first cathedral and first archdiocese. But many other religions also found a home in Baltimore, and their houses of worship can be found all across the city. Protestant and Catholic churches abound throughout Baltimore; some are grand and historic, while others are more humble places to commune with a higher power. Jewish communities also flourished here, though many city Jews moved to the county in the mid- and late 20th century and set up new synagogues there.

The *Catholic Review* newspaper provides lots of good information on Catholic services and community events; the **Archdiocese of Baltimore** has a useful website at www.archbalt.org. The **Basilica of the Assumption** (409 Cathedral St., 410/727-3565, www.baltimore-basilica.org) is the city's grandest Catholic cathedral and the first in the United States.

The *Baltimore Jewish Times* is a good resource for finding out about the variety of Jewish congregations in Baltimore City and the surrounding suburbs; **The Associated: Jewish Community Federation of Baltimore** has a comprehensive list as well at www.associated.org.

Baltimore's traditionally African American churches are some of the most popular in the region and serve as both anchors of the community's spiritual health and advocates for the community's physical needs and concerns. The largest and most established congregations include **Bethel AME Church** (1300 Druid Hill Ave., 410/523-4273, www.bethel1.org) and **Leadenhall Baptist Church** (1021 Leadenhall St., 410/752-5191, www.leadenhallbc.org).

Buddhists should explore the website of the **Buddhist Network of Greater Baltimore** (www.bngb.org) to find a nearby group or center; Muslims can contact the **Islamic Society of Baltimore** (www.isb.org) for a list of places to attend prayers.

MAJOR BANKS

Once home to several major local banking concerns, Baltimore is now just another branch city, albeit one served by a wide variety of national financial corporations. **Bank of America, M&T Bank,** and **PNC** have many branches and ATMs across the city. A few local banks remain, including **1st Mariner Bank** and **Harbor Bank.** Expect to pay from $2-3 per ATM transaction if the machine is not operated by your bank.

Resources

Suggested Reading

HISTORY, NONFICTION, AND GENERAL INFORMATION

Bell, Madison Smartt. *Charm City: A Walk Through Baltimore.* Crown Publishing Group, 2007. Bell, an award-winning novelist, took a variety of strolls through some of Baltimore's best-known and least-traveled neighborhoods, using the slow pace of a walk to unfurl the history and character of each area. This is a great book to familiarize yourself with the city, its past, and its residents.

Hayward, Mary Ellen, and Frank R. Shivers Jr. *The Architecture of Baltimore.* Johns Hopkins University Press, 2004. A beautiful book that's an update of a classic tome that chronicled the creation of the city. This new version, a hefty 416 pages, uses photos, maps, and narrative to tell the tale of Baltimore's buildings.

Hirschland, Ellen B., and Nancy Hirschland Ramage. *The Cone Sisters of Baltimore: Collecting at Full Tilt.* Northwestern University Press, 2008. A fascinating look at the lives and pursuits of the modern-art-collecting Cone sisters (Claribel and Etta), written by the great-niece and great-great-niece of the Cones. A great companion book to a tour of the Cone Collection at the Baltimore Museum of Art.

Kasper, Rob. *Baltimore Beer: A Satisfying History of Charm City Brewing.* The History Press, 2012. Kasper, a former *Baltimore Sun* reporter, traces Baltimore beer-drinking and brewing history, from the 19th-century breweries built by German immigrants to the current rebirth of craft ale brewing that's sweeping the city.

Lisicky, Michael J. *Baltimore's Bygone Department Stores: Many Happy Returns.* The History Press, 2012. An exploration of Baltimore's shopping heyday when four big department stores graced the streets, this book also discusses the effects of major historical events on the city, like the riots that broke out after Dr. Martin Luther King Jr.'s assassination.

Sandler, Gilbert. *Jewish Baltimore: A Family Album*. Johns Hopkins University Press, 2000. Sandler is the city's most prominent social historian, first as a journalist, and then as a civic resource, hired on by foundations and museums for his knowledge. This book traces the growth of, and life within, the Jewish communities of Baltimore, and their gradual migration to the suburbs.

Simon, David, and Edward Burns. *The Corner*. Broadway Books, 1998. Few books manage to explain the nation's (and Baltimore's) ruin due to illegal drugs, as well as show the immediate and long-term human toll, as this book, by the creator of *The Wire*.

LITERATURE AND FICTION

Lippman, Laura. *Baltimore Blues*. Avon, 2007. The first of the former *Sun* reporter's Tess Monaghan crime novel series, this quick read has Tess tailing a loathed defense attorney through Baltimore's streets—and then investigating his murder.

Lippman, Laura. *Baltimore Noir*. Akashic Books, 2006. Lippman serves as editor of this collection of crime fiction featuring Charm City and its less-savory inhabitants: 16 tales of malfeasance and murder, set all over town, rich in local lore and color.

Mencken, H. L. *Happy Days: Mencken's Autobiography: 1880-1892*. Vintage Books, 1982. The first of Mencken's three-volume "Days" autobiography, this book tracks the days and thoughts of a young Mencken in the bustling Baltimore of the late 19th century.

Tyler, Anne. *The Accidental Tourist*. Ballantine Books, 2002. Almost all of Tyler's rich, character-driven books are set in Baltimore, but this tale of a heartbroken couple is the one with the most fans. Tyler's 1989 novel *Breathing Lessons* won the Pulitzer Prize.

Suggested Viewing

Diner. Directed by Baltimore native Barry Levinson, this 1982 film re-creates his experiences growing up in Charm City during 1959. A great film, and a great primer on Baltimore life.

Global Harbors: A Waterfront Renaissance. This revealing 2008 documentary traces the development of Baltimore's revolutionary Inner Harbor, interviews the main players in the project and its creation, and reveals how its success drew international attention and copycats.

Hairspray. John Waters's 1988 breakthrough (to a wider audience, that is) film traces the trials and tribulations of Tracy Turnblad in 1962 Baltimore, confronting prejudices and bigotry while also learning to dance—and love. This film, which is filled with music but not a true musical, begat the hit Broadway production, which begat a 2007 film version of that musical. Stick with this, the original, which was shot in Baltimore.

The Wire. No other television show has so defined or revealed a city as former newspaper writer David Simon's unrelenting look at the effect of the war on drugs on the citizens of Baltimore—from regular people, to addicts, to cops, to crime kingpins, to schoolkids, to the media. The series first aired on HBO in 2002, and lasted for five seasons.

Internet Resources

GENERAL INFORMATION

Baltimore Collegetown Network
www.baltimorecollegetown.org
This collaboration between 15 Baltimore-area colleges and universities provides tips on how to navigate the city; places to eat, drink, and hang out; and cultural suggestions. Useful for college kids and people traveling with teens looking for something to do that won't bore them to death.

Bawlmerese
www.baltimorehon.com
This good-natured listing of examples of the local dialect ("Baltimorese," which in that dialect is said as "Bawlmerese") is a pretty thorough listing of the ways some Caucasian working-class Baltimoreans speak; the dialect itself is beginning to vanish due to urban gentrification.

City of Baltimore
www.baltimorecity.gov
The city's official website provides links to the mayor's office, city council, and the numerous city agencies that keep Baltimore moving and working. There's a surprising amount of info here, as well as great ways to contact city officials or answer civic questions.

Downtown Parternship of Baltimore
www.godowntownbaltimore.com
A nonprofit formed to encourage residents, businesses, and visitors

to come to Baltimore, the Downtown Partnership of Baltimore lists the contact information for rental and condo buildings by neighborhood and has contact information for attractions all over the city.

Enoch Pratt Free Library
www.prattlibrary.org

In addition to providing the library catalog online, this site has plenty of historic and cultural information and suggestions. There are also links to the numerous ways to contact a librarian to ask a question, from getting an important date in Baltimore history to more scholarly queries.

Live Baltimore
www.livebaltimore.com

Created as part of Baltimore's efforts to lure residents and show off the city's charms, this website is also a great place to learn about the town's varied neighborhoods, and there are dozens of useful links and informative pages to be found here.

Visit Baltimore
www.baltimore.org

Operated by Visit Baltimore, this is a very comprehensive and user-friendly site, offering listings and information on the city, attractions, and events. A great single-site resource to answer many basic (and even some obscure) questions about Baltimore. Visitors can also find special deals and bargain packages for tourists here.

EVENT LISTINGS

Baltimore Fun Guide
www.baltimorefunguide.com

A colorful, easy-to-use collection of events, exhibits, and more, searchable by lots of different criteria, and there are special offers and package deals to be found here, too.

City Paper
www.citypaper.com

The city's independent, alternative weekly's website has the best guide to the less-traditional events, activities, and happenings that are going on in Baltimore.

Baltimore Sun
www.baltimoresun.com/events

The website for the city's daily paper offers information on an enormous amount of events, restaurants, clubs, and more of Baltimore's social goings-on, though the details can be a little scant.

Bmore Art

www.bmoreart.com

Dedicated to the city's growing and vibrant independent arts scene, Bmore Art is a broad and comprehensive guide to what's happening at galleries, worthwhile upcoming shows, crafts, and general news about Baltimore arts and artists.

Dining Dish

www.diningdish.net

Focused on all things culinary, Dining Dish posts about restaurant promotions and deals, chef tournaments and other events, and cooking classes throughout the city.

The Mobtown Shank

www.sugarfreak.typepad.com

A mix of politics, music, art, and Baltimore events, all presented with a vociferously liberal bent and (generally) a knowing wink. Run by the co-owner of Hampden's Atomic Books.

Index

A

Academy Art Museum: 264
Adventure Park USA: 255
African American Festival: 298
air travel: 303, 305
Amaranthine Museum: 59
American Visionary Art Museum: 50
Annapolis: 244-255
Antietam National Battlefield: 256
area codes: 315
Art Gallery of Fells Point: 151
arts: 143-162, 286, 287
Artscape: 298
Avalon Theatre: 264

B

Babe Ruth Birthplace and Museum: 32
B&O Railroad Museum: 62
background: 273-301
Baltimore-Annapolis Trail: 184
Baltimore Arena: 147
Baltimore Blast: 174
Baltimore Book Festival: 300
Baltimore Civil War Museum: 43
Baltimore Ghost Tours: 175
Baltimore Museum of Art: 59
Baltimore Museum of Industry: 51
Baltimore National Heritage Area
    Walking Tours: 168
Baltimore Orioles: 169
Baltimore Pride: 299
Baltimore Ravens: 172
Baltimore Running Festival &
    Marathon, The: 300
Baltimore Rowing Club: 187
Baltimore Streetcar Museum: 52
Baltimore Waterfront Promenade: 181
banks: 318
baseball: 169
Basilica of the Assumption: 52
bicycle rentals and resources: 180,
    182, 183
bicycle trails: 180, 184
bicycling: 308
Bikram Yoga: 183
biotechnology: 283
boating: 178, 185
Bromo Seltzer Arts Tower: 33
Brown Memorial Park Avenue
    Presbyterian Church: 53
bus transportation: 304

C

Canton: 21; map 3
Capt. Don's Fishing Charter: 174
Carroll Park: 185
Center Stage: 158
C. Grimaldis Gallery: 154
Charles Carroll House: 246
Charles Theater, The: 153
Charm City Food Tours: 176
Charm City Roller Girls: 179
Charm City Skate Park: 179
Charm City Yoga: 178
Chesapeake Bay Maritime Museum:
    269
Chessie Paddleboats: 169
children, traveling with: 309
cinema: 147, 149, 153, 160, 161
Clifton Park: 186
climate: 274
communication: 315
concert venues: 147, 149, 154
conduct: 312
crafts: 287
Creative Alliance at the Patterson: 152
cruises: 174
Crystal Moll Gallery: 153
culture: 143-162, 285-301
Current Gallery: 156
customs: 312
Cylburn Arboretum: 187

D

demographics: 285
disabilities, travelers with: 310
disabled access: 309
Dominic "Mimi" DiPietro Family Ice
    Skating Center: 179
Domino Sugars Sign, The: 51
Downtown and Inner Harbor: 20;
    map 1
Downtown Sailing Center: 182
driving: 305, 307
Dr. Samuel D. Harris National Museum
    of Dentistry: 33
Druid Hill Park: 183
Duckpin Bowling: 175, 185

E

Easton 263-272
economy: 282
Edgar Allan Poe House & Museum: 63

education: 284
emergency services: 313
environmental issues: 275
essentials: 302-318
events: 293
Evergreen: 63
Everyman Theatre: 148
excursions: 240-272

F

Federal Hill: 21; map 4
Federal Hill Park: 51
Fell's Point: 20; map 2
Fell's Point Visitor Center: 46
festivals: 293
film: 292, 320
Flower Mart: 295
folk traditions: 287
football: 172
Forest Park: 186
Fort McHenry National Monument and
    Historic Shrine: 64, 187
14Karat Cabaret, The: 158
Frederick: 255-263
Frederick Douglass-Isaac Myers
    Maritime Park: 47
Frederick Keys: 257
Frederick Wine Trail: 258
Free Fall Baltimore: 301

G

galleries: 151, 153, 154, 160, 161
Gallery Four: 156
Garrett-Jacobs Mansion: 55
gay and lesbian: 310
geography 274
George Peabody Library: 55
Geppi's Entertainment Museum: 34
golf: 185
government: 281
Goya Contemporary: 160
greater Baltimore: 22; map 7
Great Halloween Lantern Parade, The:
    301
Gwynns Falls Trail: 184
gyms: 174, 178, 180, 182, 186

H

Hampden and Homewood: 22; map 6
Harbor East and Little Italy: 20; map 2
Harborplace: 35
health: 313
health care: 283
health clubs: 174, 178, 180, 182, 186
High Zero Festival: 296

Hippodrome Theatre, The: 148
Historical Society of Frederick County:
    258
Historical Society of Talbot County: 265
Historic Ships in Baltimore: 35
history: 276-280
Homewood: see Hampden and
    Homewood
Homewood Museum: 60
HonFest: 296
Horse Racing: 188
hospitals: 313
hotels: 222-239; see Hotels Index
hours: 312
Howard Peters Rawlings Conservatory
    & Botanic Gardens: 60

IJ

Ice Skating: 179
IMAX Theater at Maryland Science
    Center: 147
indoor soccer: 174
information and services: 314-318
Inner Harbor: see Downtown and Inner
    Harbor
internet resources: 321
internet services: 315
itineraries: 24-28
Jewish Museum of Maryland: 44
Johns Hopkins University Spring Fair:
    296
Joseph Meyerhoff Symphony Hall: 154

KL

kayaking: 169, 187
Kinetic Sculpture Race: 297
Kunta Kinte-Alex Haley Memorial,
    The: 246
Lacrosse Museum & National Hall of
    Fame: 61
Lake Montebello: 184
Landmark Theatres: 149
LatinoFest: 297
lesbian and gay: 310
LGBT: 310
libraries: 317
Light Street Cycles: 180
literature: 289
Little Italy: see Harbor East and Little
    Italy

M

MAC Harbor East: 174
magazines: 315
mail: 315

maps: 314
Maryland Art Place: 36
Maryland Film Festival: 297
Maryland Historical Society: 55
Maryland Hunt Cup: 297
Maryland Institute College of Art
    Galleries: 156
Maryland Science Center: 36
Maryland State House: 246
Maryland Zoo in Baltimore: 61
Mayor's Christmas Parade, The: 294
Meadowbrook Aquatic Center: 186
media: 315
medical research: 283
Merritt Athletic Clubs Canton: 178
Merritt Fort Avenue: 180
Merritt's Downtown Athletic Club: 182
messenger services: 315
Miracle on 34th Street: 294
Mount Clare Mansion: 65
Mount Pleasant: 186
Mount Vernon and Station North: 21;
    map 5
music: 291

NOP

National Aquarium in Baltimore: 37
National Great Blacks In Wax Museum:
    66
National Museum of Civil War
    Medicine: 259
neighborhoods: 20-22
newspapers: 315
nightlife: 121-142; see Nightlife Index
Night of 100 Elvises, The: 295
Northern Central Railroad Trail: 185
Otakon: 299
parks: 169, 183, 187
Patricia and Arthur Modell Performing
    Arts Center at The Lyric: 154
Patterson Bowling Center: 175
Patterson Park: 49
people: 285-301
pharmacies: 313
Phoenix (Old Baltimore) Shot Tower:
    44
phones: 315
Pickering Creek Audubon Center: 265
Pierce's Park: 169
Pier Six Pavilion: 149
Pimlico Race Course: 188
planning tips: 20
Port Discovery Children's Museum: 39
Ports America Chesapeake Fourth of
    July Celebration: 299
Preakness Stakes, The: 298

Princeton Sports: 183
public transportation: 306

R

radio: 317
reading, suggested: 319
recreation: 163-189
Reginald F. Lewis Museum of Maryland
    African American History & Culture:
    45
religion: 285
resources: 319-323
restaurants: 67-120; see Restaurants
    Index
Ripley's Believe It or Not!: 40
Riverside Park: 180
Robert E. Lee Park: 187
Robert Long House: 47
Robert McClintock Studio & Gallery:
    151
roller derby: 179
Rotunda Cinematheque, The: 160
running: 181

S

safety: 313, 314
sailing: 182
Scapescape: 300
School 33 Art Center: 153
Secrets of the Seaport Walking Tour:
    176
Segs in the City: 176
Senator Theatre, The: 161
senior travelers: 310
shops: 190-221; see Shops Index
sights: 29-66
Silber Art Gallery: 161
Single Carrot Theatre: 161
skateboarding: 179
Skipjack Tours: 269
smoking: 312
spectator sports: 169, 179, 188
sports and activities: 163-189
Sports Legends Museum at Camden
    Yards: 40
S.S. John Brown: 49
St. Anthony Italian Festival: 300
Star-Spangled Banner Flag House: 46
Station North: see Mount Vernon and
    Station North
Steven Scott Gallery: 151
St. John's College: 247
St. Michaels: 263-272
Stoneleigh Lanes Duckpin Bowling
    Center: 185
St. Patrick's Day Parade: 295

Strand Theater Company: 158

T

taxis: 307
television: 292, 317
Theatre Project: 160
theaters: 148, 152, 158, 161
Thomas Point Shoal Lighthouse: 247
Thurgood Marshall Memorial: 249
Tidewater Yacht Service: 185
tipping: 313
tips for travelers: 309-314
Top of the World Observation Deck: 42
Tour du Port: 301
tourism: 284
tourist information: 314
tours, guided and walking: 168, 175, 188
trains: 304
transportation: 303-309

UVWXYZ

Urban Pirates: 175
U.S. Naval Academy: 249
Vagabond Theater: 152
Velocipede Bike Project: 182
Walters Art Museum: 56
Washington Monument, The: 58
Washington Monument Lighting: 295
water taxis: 308
Wayne Schaumburg: 188
weather: 311
Weinberg Center for the Arts: 259
West Marine: 178
Westminster Hall and Burying Ground: 42
William Paca House: 250
women travelers: 309
Woodwind (sailboat): 247
worship, places of: 317
yoga: 178, 183
Zippy Tours with Zippy Larson: 189

Restaurants Index

Abbey Burger Bistro: 97
A Common Ground: 114
Afters Café: 102
Akbar: 110
Alchemy: 114
Aldo's: 79
Ambassador Dining Room, The: 118
Amicci's: 76
Angelo's Pizza: 112
Annabel Lee Tavern: 92
Artifact Coffee: 113
Attman's: 80
Atwater's: 119
b: 106
Bagby Pizza Co.: 82
B&O American Brasserie: 71
Ban Thai: 71
Bertha's: 90
Black Olive, The: 92
Blue Agave: 102
Bluegrass Tavern: 99
Blue Hill Tavern: 93
Blue Moon Café: 85
Bo Brooks: 95
Bonaparte Breads: 86
Bond Street Social: 86
Brewer's Art, The: 106
Brick Oven Pizza: 90
Café Hon: 113
Captain James Landing: 85

Cazbar: 73
Charleston: 77
Charmery, The: 117
Chazz: A Bronx Original: 79
Chesapeake, The: 107
Cinghiale: 79
City Café: 107
Claddagh Pub: 93
Daily Grind: 86
Da Mimmo: 76
Dangerously Delicious Pies: 95
Ding How: 85
Donna's: 114
Dukem: 109
Faidley Seafood: 72
Firehouse Coffee Company: 93
Fleet Street Kitchen: 77
Food Market, The: 114
Fork & Wrench: 94
Germano's PIATTINI: 78
Gertrude's: 115
Golden West Café: 118
Gordon Biersch Brewery Restaurant: 75
Heavy Seas Alehouse: 75
Helmand, The: 103
Henninger's Tavern: 87
Hull Street Blues: 97
Iggie's: 108
Jack's Bistro: 94
Jimmy's Restaurant: 89

Joe Squared: 107
Kali's Court: 92
Kumari: 110
LAMILL Coffee: 76
Langermann's: 94
La Scala: 80
La Tavola: 80
Lebanese Taverna: 82
Louisiana: 88
L.P. Steamers: 101
Mama's on the Half Shell: 96
Marie Louise Bistro: 109
Matsuri: 98
Matthew's Pizzeria: 95
Minato: 104
Miss Shirley's Café: 70
Mr. Rain's Fun House: 99
My Thai: 83
Nacho Mama's: 96
Nick's Fish House & Grill: 120
Nick's Oyster Bar: 102
Ouzo Bay: 81
Pabu: 75
Papermoon Diner: 117
Pazo: 83
Peter's Inn: 87
Petit Louis Bistro: 119
Phillips Seafood: 72
Piedigrotta: 81
Pierpoint: 87
Pitango: 89
Pratt Street Ale House: 71
Prime Rib, The: 104

Regi's: 100
Rocket to Venus: 115
Roy's: 82
Rusty Scupper: 103
Ryleigh's Oyster: 103
Sabatino's: 77
Salt: 88
Sascha's 527 Café: 108
Sip & Bite Restaurant: 89
SoBo Café: 100
Sotto Sopra: 109
Spoons: 97
Station North Arts Café: 106
Sushi Hana: 119
Suzie's Soba: 113
Talara: 83
Tapas Teatro: 112
Ten Ten: 78
Thai Arroy: 99
Thai Landing: 105
Thairish: 105
Tio Pepe: 110
Tutti Gusti: 96
Vaccaro's: 81
Waterfront Kitchen: 88
Watertable: 72
Werner's Restaurant: 70
Wine Market, The: 100
Wit & Wisdom: 78
Woman's Industrial Kitchen: 104
Woodberry Kitchen: 115
XS: 108
Ze Mean Bean Café: 90

Nightlife Index

after hours: 124, 136
An die Musik LIVE!: 140
Bad Decisions: 127
bars: 124, 127, 132, 133, 136, 141
Bartender's: 132
Brewer's Art, The: 136
Captain Larry's: 133
Cat's Eye Pub, The: 128
Charm City Art Space: 140
Chesapeake Wine Company: 132
Club Bunns: 125
Club Charles: 136
Club Hippo: 138
Club 1722: 136
Club Orpheus: 127
dance clubs: 127, 131, 138
Depot, The: 138
Drinkery, The: 139

Duda's Tavern: 128
8x10: 135
Explorer's Lounge: 124
gay and lesbian: 125, 138
Get Down, The: 131
Grand Central: 139
Havana Club: 126
Horse You Came In On Saloon, The: 128
James Joyce Irish Pub & Restaurant: 127
John Steven: 129
Liam Flynn's Ale House: 137
Little Havana: 133
live music: 125, 135, 140, 141
lounges: 126, 135, 140
Mahaffey's: 132
Max's Taphouse: 129
Metro Gallery: 140
Mosaic: 126

Mount Royal Tavern: 137
Mum's: 133
One-Eyed Mike's: 129
Ottobar, The: 141
Owl Bar, The: 137
Paradox: 124
PBR Baltimore: 125
Power Plant Live!: 125
Pub Dog Pizza & Drafthouse: 135
Ram's Head Live: 125

Red Maple: 140
Rye: 129
13.5% Wine Bar: 141
13th Floor, The: 137
V-NO: 131
WC Harlan: 141
Wharf Rat, The: 130
Windup Space, The: 138
wine bars: 131, 132, 141
Zeeba Lounge: 135

Shops Index

About Faces: 203
A Good Yarn: 197
Alliance Comics: 203
aMuse: 197
An die Musik: 208
Antique Center at Federal Hill: 207
Antique Row Stalls: 209
A People United: 208
arts and crafts: 197, 210, 217
Arundel Mills Mall: 219
Atomic Books: 210
Avenue Antiques: 217
Babe: 198
Baltimore Clayworks: 217
Belvedere Square: 220
Best of Luck Candy & Gifts, The: 193
Book Escape, The: 204
books: 203, 207, 210, 218
Breathe Bookstore Café: 211
Brightside Boutique & Art Studio: 204
Charlotte Elliott and The Bookstore
    Next Door: 217
children's stores: 197, 213
clothing and accessories: 193, 195, 198,
    201, 204, 208, 213, 218
Cloud 9: 201
Corduroy Button: 197
Corradetti Glassblowing Studio &
    Gallery: 210
Cupcake: 198
Dimensions in Music: 208
Doggie Style: 205
Dogma: 203
Doubledutch Boutique: 213
Downtown and Inner Harbor: 194
Dubey's Art and Antiques: 209
El Suprimo: 200
Federal Hill: 205
Fell's Point: 201
Fells Point Surf Co.: 199
Form: 213

furniture and home decor: 199, 204,
    214, 218
Gallery, The: 194
gift and specialty: 193, 199, 201, 204,
    214
Hampden: 215
Handbags in the City: 195
Harbor East: 196
Hats in the Belfry: 199
Housewerks: 218
Howl: 215
Imperial Half Bushel, The: 209
In Watermelon Sugar: 214
Ivy Bookshop, The: 218
Jos. A. Bank: 193
Kelmscott Bookshop, The: 211
Kiss N Make Up: 216
Lovelyarns: 210
Ma Petite Shoe: 215
Maja: 199
Matava Too: 219
McCormick World of Flavors: 194
Milagro: 213
M Salon: 206
Mud and Metal: 215
music: 200, 208
Normal's Books and Records: 218
Nouveau: 219
Pandora's Box Boutique: 204
pet supplies and grooming: 203, 205,
    215
Poppy and Stella: 200
Read Street Books: 207
Samuel Parker Clothier: 218
Sassanova: 196
Second Chance: 221
Seeds: 216
shoes: 196, 200, 215, 219
Shofer's: 204
shopping centers and districts: 194,
    196, 201, 205, 215, 219

Sideshow at the American Visionary
    Art Museum: 205
Sixteen Tons: 214
Soft and Cozy Baby: 213
Sound Garden, The: 200
South Moon Under: 195
Spa at the Four Seasons Hotel
    Baltimore, The: 196
spa, bath, and beauty: 196, 203, 206, 216
Sprout: 216

Studio 921 Salon & Day Spa: 207
Su Casa: 199
Towson Town Center: 220
Trohv: 214
True Vine, The: 211
2910 on the Square: 201
Under Armour Brand House: 195
Urban Chic: 196
Village of Cross Keys: 220
vintage and antiques: 207, 209, 217, 221

Hotels Index

Admiral Fell Inn, The: 233
Baltimore Marriott Waterfront: 231
Blue Door on Baltimore: 234
Brookshire Suites: 226
Celie's Waterfront Inn: 234
Courtyard by Marriott : 231
Days Inn Inner Harbor: 226
1840s Carrollton Inn: 231
Embassy Suites Baltimore: 227
Fairfield Inn & Suites : 232
4 East Madison Inn: 236
Four Seasons Hotel Baltimore: 232
Hampton Inn and Suites Inner Harbor:
    227
HI-Baltimore Hostel: 227
Hilton Baltimore: 228
Homewood Suites by Hilton Baltimore:
    233
Hotel Brexton: 236

Hotel Monaco Baltimore: 228
Hyatt Regency Baltimore: 228
Inn at Henderson's Wharf, The: 234
Inn at the Colonnade: 237
Inn at 2920: 235
Mount Vernon Hotel, The: 237
Peabody Court by Clarion: 237
Pier 5 Hotel : 233
Rachael's Dowry Bed and Breakfast:
    229
Radisson Hotel at Cross Keys : 239
Renaissance Baltimore Harborplace
    Hotel: 229
Royal Sonesta Harbor Court Baltimore:
    230
Scarborough Fair B&B: 235
Sheraton Baltimore North: 239
Springhill Suites by Marriott: 230

Photo Credits